Discipline and discord
in the Labour Party

D1234775

WITHDRAWN

To my mother, Paulette
and in memory of my father, Ben Shaw

Discipline and discord in the Labour Party

The politics of managerial control in the Labour Party, 1951–87

Eric Shaw

Manchester University Press
Manchester and New York

Distributed exclusively in North America and Canada
by St. Martin's Press Inc.,
175 Fifth Avenue, New York, NY10010, USA

Copyright © Eric Shaw 1988

Published by Manchester University Press
Oxford Road, Manchester M13 9PL, UK

Distributed exclusively in the USA and Canada
by St. Martin's Press Inc.
Room 400, 175 Fifth Avenue, New York , NY 10010, USA

British Library cataloguing in publication data
Shaw, Eric
    Discipline and discord in the Labour Party : the politics of
    managerial control in the Labour Party
    1951–87.
    1. Great Britain. Political parties
    I. Title
    324.24107'09

Library of Congress cataloging in publication data
Shaw, Eric
        Discipline and discord in the Labour Party : the politics of
    managerial control in the Labour Party, 1951–87 / Eric Shaw.
        p. cm.
        Bibliography: p. 371.
        Includes index.
        ISBN 0–7190–2482–X : $35.00 (U.S. : est.). ISBN 0–7190–2483–8
    (pbk.) : $10.00 (U.S. : est.)
        1. Labour Party (Great Britain)—History. 2. Great Britain–
    –Politics and government—1945–   I. Title.
    JN1129.L32S455 1988
    324.24107'09—dc19   87–35042

ISBN 0 7190 2482 X *hardback*

Typeset in Great Britain
by Northern Phototypesetting Co, Bolton

Printed in Great Britain
by Biddles Ltd, Guildford and King's Lynn

Contents

Introduction

Studies of the internal politics of the Labour Party have generally concentrated on a familiar range of problems concerning power and ideology with the prime focus upon the policy-making process.[1] But a prerequisite for any party is the ability to sustain itself organisationally; this entails the establishment of, firstly, a framework of rules apportioning rights and duties amongst the various tiers of organisation and, secondly, a minimal level of internal cohesion. These two, interlinked requirements – safeguarding the rules (and, hence, the integrity of party institutions) and maintaining cohesion – constitute the field of party management. This is a vital segment of a party's inner life since its success in achieving its goals (whether defined in terms of electoral success or realising its values or both) depends upon its capacity to harness the commitment and loyalty of its members and to regulate conflict in such a way as to prevent energy-consuming and electorally damaging disputes. For a confederal democratic organisation like the Labour Party, which seeks election to government to accomplish social change, party management is both vital and particularly difficult. It is this subject – the politics of party management – to which the present study is devoted.

Management implies authority, since a party can only be managed by a central body endowed with appropriate powers and responsibilities. But the way in which the managerial function is performed – that is a party's managerial regime – may differ considerably. The key variable is control, that is the capacity of managerial authorities to regulate or direct the activities of the membership. Managerial control varies along two main dimensions, centralisation and discipline. Centralisation refers to the distribution of rights and duties between higher and lower level units, discipline to the use or threat of sanctions as instruments of party management.[2]

The first half of this work examines in some detail Labour's managerial regime in the 1950s and early 1960s – the era of (what we shall call) social-democratic centralism. The social-democratic centralist regime was characterised both by a high degree of centralisation and strict discipline. Alan Watkins has colourfully recalled this period: 'a hint of heresy, a whiff of recalcitrance, and Sara's[3] tanks would emerge at dead of night from the concrete garages deep under Transport House [the Party's then headquarters] and move unstoppably towards the offending part of the country.'[4] Not everybody within the Party would accept this picture; indeed, as we shall see, perceptions of the regime of the 1950s and early 1960s have themselves had a substantial impact upon the course of Labour's politics. Right-wingers like Denis Healey have looked back upon these years as a time when 'the tradition of tolerance' was established.[5] In complete contrast the same years have entered the folklore of the Party's left as the age of witch hunts, bans and explusions. 'Transport House controlled the Party's internal regime with a rod of iron. Any signs of dissent among the Party's rank and file were crushed through stringent disciplinary procedures.'[6] However, there has never been a systematic empirical analysis of the social-democratic centralist regime. One of the prime purposes of this study is to remedy this omission. How did the regime operate? What were its objectives and rationale? How comprehensive was this managerial control of Party life?

To many commentators of the time, Labour's strict managerial regime of the 1950s and early 1960s attested to the power of the Party machine. Yet within the span of a decade or so the social-democratic centralist regime had been replaced by a far more lenient one. If the stringent managerial regime did not derive from any inherent features of mass political organisation (or any exigency of the wider political system) upon what was it based? We suggest some answers to this question.

From the second half of the 1960s, as we shall see, Labour's internal regime underwent a cumulative process of change. The process commenced with a policy of 'liberalisation from above', a deliberate attempt by more liberal Party managers and an NEC[7] slowly shifting to the left to ease discipline and enlarge the sphere of discretion of local Party organisations. This study both charts and seeks to account for this liberalisation process. By the late 1970s the NEC, presided over by a left-wing majority, had instituted a much more permissive managerial regime; we discuss in some detail its character and consequences and argue that the decisive step was not, as is widely believed, the abolition of the Proscribed List.

However, this alteration in Labour's managerial regime was not simply the product of decisions taken at the top. This becomes evident after 1982 when, with the left ousted from control, a centre-right majority, perturbed in particular by the rise of the Militant Tendency, strove to re-assert managerial control. The results were meagre and the first drive against Militant petered out. In the social-democratic centralist era Trotskyist activity had been curtailed by the erection of ideological boundaries which excluded revolutionary organisations. Why did it not prove possible to rebuild them? More fundamentally, why did the effort to revive central control encounter such resistance? One reason was the vigorous opposition of the left, but we also identify broader changes in the Party which militated against central control: a transformation in the social composition and orientation to political activity of the membership and a collapse of the procedural consensus which had sustained and legitimated stricter forms of discipline. We also draw attention to another crucial development: the growth of judicial intervention in Labour's internal affairs, commencing with the important Pembroke judgement in 1969, whose profound implications for the definition and exercise of central power have been almost entirely neglected.

The growth of Militant, however, posed key managerial problems that could not be evaded, not least because forces outside the Party constantly drew them to the attention of the electorate. These problems were dramatised by the multiple crises surrounding the largely Militant-controlled Liverpool City Council in the mid 1980s. In 1986 the Party launched its second offensive against Militant, but this time with more success. Why the difference of outcome? As we will illustrate a key factor was the decision of a substantial section of the left (the 'soft left') to back disciplinary action. We examine the reasons which prompted this crucial revision of traditional left opposition to explusions.

The problems dealt with in this study have deep roots and in the first chapter we trace the evolution of Labour's managerial regime since the constitutional settlement of 1918. But 1951 has been chosen as the main point of departure for two reasons. Firstly the outburst in that year of fierce intra-party dissension after a period of relative harmony during the post-war Labour Government, raised acute problems of Party management. Secondly, an analysis of the leadership's response to the Bevanite challenge from 1951 to 1955 affords both illuminating insights into the character of social-democratic centralism and provides a benchmark from which to compare the development of Labour's managerial regime in later years.

This work combines a narrative and an analytical method. It is structured as follows. Chapters two to six examine the workings of the

social-democratic centralist regime in key areas of Labour's internal life
– the handling of organised dissent (Chapter two), the balance between
central power and local autonomy (Chapter three), the role of the
national Party in adjudicating local disputes (Chapter four), and in
overseeing the selection of parliamentary candidates (Chapter five) and
the reaction of the centre to Trotskyist penetration (Chapter six), concluding with an analysis of the conditions which sustained that regime
(Chapter seven). Chapter eight discusses the period of liberalisation
from the late 1960s to the early 1970s. Chapters nine to eleven survey
the left NEC's managerial regime from the mid 1970s to the turn of the
decade in the fields of parliamentary selection (Chapter nine), adjudication (Chapter ten) and Trotskyist activity (the first part of Chapter
eleven). The bulk of Chapter eleven examines the crisis of Party management in the early 1980s; and the final chapter focuses on Labour's
renewed battle against the Militant Tendency in the context of a shift
back towards a firmer managerial regime. In the course of the analysis,
at various points, we explore Labour's fundamental managerial problem: the endeavour to reconcile cohesion and organisational
effectiveness with diversity and dissent.

Acknowledgements

I have incurred many debts in the preparation of this study. I would like
to acknowledge the aid of the Nuffield Foundation and the Research
Committee of Manchester Polytechnic's Faculty of Humanities, Law
and Social Science in meeting travel and other expenses. The library
staff at Manchester Polytechnic has been of unfailing assistance. I
would also like to thank the Labour Party and the London Labour Party
for access to their archives; Stephen Bird, the Labour Party archivist, has
been of great help over the years.
    I am grateful to the considerable number of people who kindly
allowed me to interview them. With one or two exceptions (where
anonymity was preferred) I list their names in the note on sources at the
end of the book. I am particularly grateful to Lord (Reg) Underhill, Ian
Mikardo and Jim Mortimer for reading and providing very valuable
observations on large sections of the manuscript. I would also like to
thank David Howell and Patrick Seyd, who examined the doctoral
thesis upon which this book is based, for their useful comments, and
Manchester University Press's anonymous referee for his perceptive
eye.
    Steve Kelly and Ian Williams generously allowed me to read their
unpublished manuscript on the 'Rise and Fall of Militant Merseyside';
Brian Ripley kindly allowed me to inspect the Jimmy Deane Collection;
Liz Atkins, Will Bradshaw, Tony Duckworth and Brian Morron helped

me in a variety of ways. Thanks are due to my typist, Jeanette Mahon, who battled courageously with my handwriting.

Special debts of gratitude are due to the following: Lewis Minkin, as supervisor of my doctoral thesis, patiently read successive drafts with meticulous care and provided much invaluable advice both in written comments and in the course of many conversations. I benefitted greatly from his unrivalled knowledge and analytical grasp of the Labour Party. My parents-in-law, Pat and Ern Hoare stepped in at critical times to help look after the children. I am deeply grateful to my wife Susan for the many calls I made upon her patience and understanding, and to my children, Laurie, David and Oliver (whose births punctuated the preparation of this work) for making sure I avoided the mistake of believing that writing is the first priority in life. My greatest debts are to my mother for her encouragement and to my father who incessantly prodded and cajoled me into writing this book but sadly did not live to see it completed.

Notes on usage

I use 'Party' to refer to the national organisation of the Labour Party; 'party' to refer to local Labour Party units. NEC Minutes (in notes) are Minutes of the NEC or other committee; NEC in citation refers to papers submitted to the NEC.

Chapter one

The evolution of managerial control

1.1 Party management and the structure of control: the 1918 constitution

The Labour Party's internal life, as well as its external role, has been profoundly influenced by the circumstances of its birth. It arose, as is well-known, from a desire amongst trade unions to protect their interests through improved political representation. At the same time – the end of the nineteenth century – the main Socialist organisations, the Independent Labour Party, the Fabian Society and (to a lesser extent) the Marxist Social Democratic Federation had reached rather gloomy conclusions about the potential of a socialist party on the German model. Hence, they sought to engender a shift by trade unions to independent political action. The outcome was the establishment, in 1900, of the Labour Representation Committee, renamed later the Labour Party.

The Labour Party differed from most continental socialist parties: it was neither socialist nor was it (in terms they would have understood) a party. It was, essentially, an alliance of autonomous organisations – trade unions and socialist societies. This imparted to it a distinctive constitutional quality: it was a confederation, whose constituent units were sovereign in the management of their own affairs. The Party's own directive organs – primarily its executive committee – exercised only such powers as affiliated organisations chose to relinquish. The Party had no constituency membership and no branches. Its organisation in the country – as Ross McKibbin has shown – relied upon existing trade union branches and trades councils, over which Labour's Executive exercised some influence but little direct authority.[1]

The First World War convinced Labour's leaders, firstly, that the prospects for rapid growth were encouraging and, secondly, that the existing organisational machinery was defective. Opinion gradually shifted in favour of the construction of an organisationally more integrated party. The result was the 1918 constitution. In a memorandum to the Executive in September 1917, Party Secretary Arthur Henderson had proposed 'the reorganisation of the Party with a view to a wider extension of the membership, the strengthening and development of local parties in the constituencies, together with the promotion of a larger number of candidates, and the . . . [adoption] of a Party programme.'[2]

Labour's task was in effect to establish an effective vote-getting machine which could contest elections on the basis of a distinctive programme and with a supporting organisation in the country. The 1918 Constitution attempted to meet this, firstly by committing the Party (loosely) to a socialist objective and, secondly, by altering its organisational structure. The majority of unions remained resistant to a continental-style socialist party. They were willing to accept a socialist commitment and the strengthening of party organisation, but only on condition that the revised constitution afforded them a large measure of control. The result was the replacement of the confederal structure by a hybrid: the newly formed branches in the country were to be under the direction of the National Executive Committee (NEC) whilst the trade unions remained wholly autonomous, retaining the bulk of votes at Conference and controlling virtually all seats on the Executive.

The impact of the 1918 constitution upon Labour's programme and objectives has been extensively discussed. Much less attention has been paid to its implications for the structure of management and control within the Party. Responsibility for party management was vested primarily in the NEC.[3] But one is struck, when examining the 1918 document, by the paucity and ill-defined character of the managerial powers conferred upon the NEC.

One can distinguish here between the Executive's formal managerial authority and its specific managerial or regulatory powers. The former refers to its generalised right, as prescribed by the constitution, to issue directives binding upon all Party organisations and members, the latter to specific powers given to the NEC enabling it to regulate the manner in which subordinate units exercised their rights and duties.

In the first category, the NEC was given responsibility 'for the conduct of the general work of the party', for ensuring that, as far as practicable, 'properly constituted organisations' were set up in the constituencies; for implementing Conference decisions and, subject to an appeal in Conference, for interpreting the Constitution and rules in cases of disputes.[4]

In the second category, the only specific managerial powers conferred on the NEC were over the selection of parliamentary candidates. CLPs were required to co-operate with the NEC in the nomination of Labour candidates; Executive approval was required before a candidate was formally adopted; and the NEC was empowered to decide which themes from the Party's programme should be featured prominently in candidates' election addresses.[5]

Managerial control in the Party was limited by three factors, two constitutional and one organisational. Firstly, the NEC was equipped with few sanctions which it could use without securing prior Conference authorisation. Secondly, its capacity to exert control over the rank and file was restricted by its inability to regulate the flow of members into the Party. All members of affiliated organisations (trade unions and socialist societies) were entitled to join the Party, together with any individuals who subscribed to its constitution and programme[6] (the latter being defined as comprising any proposal which obtained a two-thirds majority at Conference). Notable by its absence (in comparison to continental socialist parties) was any requirement to adhere to a set of principles or beliefs, aside from those specified in the section on Party objects.

The framework of rules is only one element determining the scale of managerial control. A Party also requires an apparatus of control, that is organisational means to monitor or scrutinise the activities of constituent units and ensure compliance with rules or authorised directives. Throughout most of the 1920s, Labour's organisational apparatus was rudimentary. The organisational staff was small in number and poorly equipped (in terms of office accommodation, secretarial assistance etc.)[7] The Party was almost entirely dependent upon trade unions for funds, both nationally and locally. Although local parties were in theory subject to central direction, in practice they enjoyed considerable autonomy. This is particularly evident in the crucial sphere of parlimentary selection. Whilst, constitutionally, a candidate had to be 'sanctioned'[8] by the NEC, the large measure of control this implied was largely vitiated by organisational and financial aspects of local parties; organisationally, many (until well into the 1920s) were either trades councils writ large or heavily reliant upon affiliated trade union branches; financially, their capacity to contest elections was almost entirely dependent upon trade union munificence.[9] Here – as we shall see later – Labour's organisational origins bequeathed a lasting legacy. Central control over parliamentary selection was restricted less by the constitutional rights of local parties than by their financial and organisational dependence on trade unions.

In many key respects the 1918 constitution was a landmark, shaping future developments. But – and this has not been appreciated – in the crucial area of management and control the Party was still in a molten state. Central power remained weakly defined, and local parties and individual members retained considerable latitude in the pursuit of their political activities. In the sphere of party management, the formative period was the decade *after 1918* not the years preceding it. The weakness of the centre is illustrated by Labour's long and difficult struggle to combat Communist activity within its ranks. But, as we shall seek to establish, it is precisely out of the exigencies of that struggle that a far more centralised managerial structure was to emerge.

1.2 Managerial control and the communist connection, 1920–1929

In 1921, the Third Congress of the Communist International instructed its recently formed British branch to seek affiliation into the Labour Party. The object of the exercise, it candidly announced, was to facilitate the weaning of the masses from the Labour Party by providing 'a higher platform' to 'denounce their opportunist leaders'. Two characteristics of the Labour Party, the Comintern claimed, afforded opportunities for Communist penetration. The first was organisational: the freedom allowed all constituent organisations 'of propaganda and organisational activity in favour of the dictatorship of the proletariat'; the second was political: 'its principle of uniting all the industrial organisations of the working class'.[10]

The Comintern had seized upon two traits of the Labour Party which did, indeed, distinguish it from most of its sister parties. Organisationally, despite the changes introduced in 1918, Labour continued to exhibit pronounced confederal features. The bulk of the Party's members consisted of the membership of affiliated organisations, that is trade unions and socialist societies (which, in 1918, included the ILP, and the British Socialist Party). Since members of these organisations were automatically enrolled into the Labour Party, the Party itself, as we have seen, possessed very limited entry controls. Thus, at the time of its foundation in 1920, probably the bulk of Communist Party adherents were members of the older Party, in their status either as trade unionists or as members of the BSP (the largest of the groups which combined to form the CPGB). Further, affiliated trade unions were free to choose whom they liked to represent them in Labour Party organisations – as delegates to Annual Conference, constituency parties and so forth. This provided the Communist Party with a valuable additional channel for inserting its adherents into Labour's decision-making forums.

Politically, many within the Labour Party still subscribed to a conception of its original function as a *party of interest* – the political vehicle of the organised working class – rather than (as with most continental socialist parties) *a party of principle* committed to an established doctrine. The only principle (aside from the anodyne) to which Party members were under any sort of obligation to conform was 'the common ownership of the means of production' – a principle which (as the CPGB frequently noted) more keenly espoused by Communist than by most of Labour's leaders.

The Communist challenge was not, of course, confined to Britain. Throughout the continent, social democratic and Communist parties were locked in (often far more venomous, sometimes, violent) combat. Indeed, the threat to the ascendancy of reformism was far more formidable in Germany, France or Italy. But only in Britain did Communism pose an acute *internal managerial problem*; in none of the other major Socialist International parties was it possible, as in the Labour Party, for leading Communists to denounce their social-democratic adversaries from the podiums of the latter's own party conferences.

We shall argue that the major factor responsible for the tightening of managerial control in the Labour Party in the 1920s was the organisational needs bred by the struggle to eradicate Communist influence. Finding itself poorly equipped, the NEC progressively sought enhanced powers, culminating in the revised constitution of 1929, which formalised and solidified a major extension of central authority.

1.2.1   *Resisting Communist affiliation*

The NEC's initial task was a defensive one: to resist a series of bids by the Communist Party for affiliation. Since, as one Communist Party leader proudly proclaimed, the purpose of affiliation was to 'take by the hand so as to better seize the throat',[11] it was, predictably, consistently and overwhelmingly rejected by Labour's Annual Conference.[12]

The prospect of the CP securing affiliation was always a remote one. The NEC and the bulk of the unions were adamantly opposed – hardly surprising since the CP rarely bothered to camouflage or restrain its expressions of hostility and contempt for 'reformists of every shape and colour.'[13] Further, the Executive was convinced that the CP's promise to abide by the Party's constitution was worthless for two reasons. Firstly, under its own rules the CP was not an independent party but the national branch of the Communist International; and, secondly, it adhered to the precepts of democratic centralism which meant, inter alia, that it was bound by the decisions of the Communist movement's supreme authority, the Comintern, which, in practice, meant the Kremlin. In Ramsay MacDonald's words, the CP was 'signed, sealed and delivered, mind, body and soul to whatever instructions they got from Moscow'.[14] Yet the leadership was aware that rejection of Communist affiliation on these grounds alone might not be sufficient to convince those unaware of the intricacies of Communist politics, and prepared to grant the benefit of the doubt to their erring comrades. Labour's leaders became increasingly persuaded that the surest way of blocking the CPGB's persistent efforts to smuggle itself into the affairs of the larger party was to highlight the *ideological* gulf separating them.

This was most clearly exhibited in an interesting exchange between the two parties in 1922. In a rather unusual procedure, it was agreed that the NEC submit a questionnaire to the CPGB and then reconsider its application for affiliation on the light of its response. The Executive forwarded four questions; one simply queried the sincerity of the application, but the others were designed to demonstrate the unfitness of the Communist Party, on doctrinal grounds, to affiliate to the Labour Party. This, of course, could only be done by endowing Labour with an explicit ideological character. Hence the NEC enumerated two key principles, sharply demarcating Labour from its left-wing antagonist. Firstly, it defined its objective (ostensibly quoting Labour's constitution) as the achievement of 'the political, social and economic emancipation of the people by means of Parliamentary democracy'. Secondly, it declared that it was 'a fundamental principle of the Labour Party to confine its operations to lawful means'.[15]

This attempt to construct an ideological boundary on Labour's left lacked – as the CP was quick to observe – an explicit constitutional grounding since a commitment to Parliamentary means did not figure in Labour's Constitution. The NEC later rather lamely (and inaccurately) explained that the fabricated quotation was merely 'a summary of various clauses' in the Constitution.[16] Similarly the second 'basic principle' was equally extra-constitutional, and was by no means embraced by all in the Party, as George Lansbury was soon to show in his defiance of the law in Poplar.[17]

These constitutional niceties cut little ice with the NEC at the time, though the failure to incorporate adherence to Parliamentary institutions into the Party rules was to store up trouble in the future. Labour's leadership, always averse to doctrinal debate, approached the question in a pragmatic spirit – how best to build a cast-iron case against the CPGB's affiliation. In this it was largely successful. Adherence to Parliamentary democracy soon came to acquire the status of a fundamental Party principle, an unwritten accretion to the constitution. There were, of course, a variety of factors pushing Labour to adopt an explicitly articulated social-democratic (or democratic socialist – the two terms were interchangeable at the time) basis: to knit together the disparate elements within the Party, to convert a pressure group into a competitor for governmental power armed with a coherent programme and so forth. All this has been recognised. Two other exigencies impelling Labour in the same direction have, however, been neglected.

The first was electoral. The potential for Labour's electoral growth in the early 1920s was obviously massive. But, to realise this potential, it was essential, its leaders held, to combat 'red menace' propaganda by reassuring the voters of the impassable gulf of principle dividing Labour from 'Bolshevism'. This was not purely electoral calculation – men like MacDonald, Henderson and Snowden were staunchly, fiercely even, anti-Communist. But, at the time, (the early 1920s) this sentiment was not shared with equal fervour by many of Labour's industrial leaders and (*a fortiori*) activists. Indeed a large minority within several trade unions (most notably in the Miners' Federation) actually favoured CP affiliation although, because of the block vote system, this was masked in actual Conference votes. Many others were only (initially at least) tepid in their opposition. Hence – and this was the second exigency – to mobilise resistance to Communist applications it was important to affirm vigorously the major differences of principle between Labour and its revolutionary rival.

The outcome, then, of the debates over Communist affiliation was to bestow upon Labour a sharper ideological profile transforming it from a party of labour into a social-democratic party committed to the achievement of socialism (however defined) by Parliamentary means.[18] As a corollary of this the protection of the Party's ideological borders became a key managerial objective. This implied enhanced managerial control since only the NEC was qualified (constitutionally and organisationally) to accomplish this task.

1.2.2 *The drive to eradicate Communism*
But the Communist question had by no means been resolved. The CPGB was barred from affiliation to the Party on grounds of ideological incompatibility; but what, then of the position of individual Communists? Under the existing rules, as members of affiliated organisations, they were entitled to participate fully in Labour's affairs. Henderson, the Party's Secretary, expressed the frustration of many senior figures when he warned Conference in 1922 of 'the "enemy" right in the midst of them, listening to all the private and confidential discussions and . . . taking the information to (rival) parties'.[19] Yet the NEC was powerless to prevent this. As the Executive acknowledged in a statement to Conference in 1924, many Communists 'technically' fulfilled membership conditions by accepting the constitution and programme of the party[20] (there was, at the time, no requirement to accept its principles or policies.)

A comparison with the SPD is illuminating here. The centralisation of power which Robert Michels so brilliantly analysed prior to 1914[21] was taken even further after the end of the War. By 1924 its Executive was empowered to expel any member held to work against the interests of the party and possessed powers 'of almost dictatorial proportions'.[22] In the very same year, Labour's NEC confessed its helplessness to combat Communist efforts to disrupt it from within: 'neither affiliated trade unions nor local Labour Parties are in a position to debar their [i.e. Communists] association with their Party or curtail their activities to undermine the whole purpose of our movement from within'.[23]

Thus, under the existing constitution, the NEC could not prevent individual Communists joining the Party, forming factions directed from outside, being appointed as officers or delegates to Annual Conference or, indeed, standing as Parliamentary candidates. Henderson signalled as much when, on being faced by a disgruntled delegate from a constituency (Leith) whose candidate (a Communist) had been refused endorsement whilst Saklatvala (a better known Communist) had obtained it, he confessed that the latter had met all constitutional requirements.[24] The NEC lacked the powers to combat what it regarded as a serious threat to Labour's organisational integrity; throughout the rest of the decade it strove incessantly to remedy this weakness.

How serious a threat did the CPGB pose to Labour's integrity? The best measure of this is the scale of Communist participation within it; this was not massive, but neither was it insignificant. Harry Pollitt (a prominent Communist later to be appointed leader) calmly informed his fellow delegates to the 1923 Labour Conference that the previous year there had been seven Communists amongst their number, and currently there were 38.[25] In the 1922 General Election three Communists stood as Labour candidates (one, Saklatvala, was elected); the following year this had risen to seven.[26] In 1924 this fell to four, with Saklatvala once more being returned.[27] Although no reliable information exists, it seems likely that Communists exercised influence in a considerable number of local parties.[28]

The NEC, nevertheless, moved slowly. The first step in a process which was to steadily augment its stock of managerial powers was taken in 1922. On the recommendation of the NEC, Conference adopted constitutional amendments designed to lay down conditions of eligibility for delegates. In future 'every person nominated to serve as a delegate (at any level) shall individually accept the Constitution and Principles of the Labour Party'. Further 'no person shall be eligible as a delegate who is a member of any organisation having for one of its objectives the return to Parliament or to any Local Governing Authority, of a candidate or candidates other than such as have been endorsed by the Labour Party, or have been approved as running in association with the Labour Party'. (This latter designed to cater for the Co-operative Party.)[29]

The following year, however, the NEC was forced to retreat, and dropped the second clause. There were two reasons for this: firstly, it could be invoked to disqualify not only Communists but members of associations like the National Union of Teachers, which promoted candidates from all parties; secondly, and more significantly, it stumbled against the confederal character of the Party – there was nothing the Party, under its existing powers, could do to prevent trade unions nominating whom they pleased as delegates.[30]

Despite prodding from some of its members, like Herbert Morrison, the rapidly rising star of the London Labour Party, the NEC continued to proceed cautiously. Thus in October 1923, its Organisation sub-committee reaffirmed the right of Communists to be accepted as candidates, as delegates, as affiliated members and as individual members'.[31] How do we account for this circumspection? There were two main factors, firstly the considerable support, amongst Labour's rank and file, for the right of individual Communists – as fellow socialists and fellow combatants in the class struggle – to remain in the Party. As we have seen many, particularly on the left, adhered to the original conception of the Party as primarily a vehicle of working class political action. For those who espoused a class-conflict perspective, the CP was 'an integral part of the working class movement'.[32] George Lansbury, a leading spokesman of the left, whilst repudiating Communist 'methods' nevertheless refused to regard them as enemies since they stood four-square in the contest with capital.[33] This view was (and continued for many years to be) fairly representative of left-wing opinion: it was not prepared to elevate the questions of 'method' (i.e. the Parliamentary route to socialism) to the status of fundamental Party principle requiring the exclusion of all revolutionaries from its ranks.[34] The prevalence of these views amongst Labour's activists undoubtedly inhibited the NEC from taking a tougher line against Communists since, deprived of their co-operation, the task of implementing such a line would have been made significantly harder.

Left-wing objections alone, however, would not have deterred the NEC from swifter action against the Communists. The second factor was far more decisive: the Executive was unwilling to instigate any action unless it was assured of the endorsement of most of the affiliated trade unions. This point is central to understanding the internal politics of the Labour Party and merits lengthier consideration.

The unions restricted the scope and exercise of managerial control in the Party in two ways. Firstly, because they commanded the bulk of Conference votes, no measure could pass without their approval. Further, the NEC's ability to influence the way they cast their votes was severely curtailed by their consitutional autonomy. A comparison with the contemporary SPD illustrates this point. Its leadership was able to reduce the Party's Congress – ostensibly the sovereign body – to a virtual rubber-stamp primarily because of its control over most of the organisations which elected delegates to it.[35] Because of the unions' constitutional independence this option was not available to Labour's NEC.

Secondly, in the years of Labour's adolescence, the balance between the confederal and unitary elements in its make-up lay very much with the former. This was reflected in the limited authority the Party exerted over its affiliated organisations. Its internal structure resembled a feudal system. The writ of the monarch (i.e. the NEC) extended to his personal estates (the CLPs etc.) but not much further. The feudal lords (the trade unions) offered a general fealty but insisted upon determining for themselves the nature and extent of the dues they owed the monarch. They were not prepared to admit his direct intervention in the way they managed their own estates, even if this affected the quality of their feudal dues.

Thus, affiliated unions acknowledged the general authority of the Party's senior organs (the NEC and Conference) over matters which fell within their jurisdiction. But in practice they were wholly independent in the conduct of their own internal activities, including the nature of their input into the Labour Party: they were solely responsible for selecting delegates to the various tiers of Labour's organisation – constituency, borough, regional and national – and retained full rights to nominate whomsoever they pleased as Parliamentary candidates. The NEC, composed almost entirely of people elected by trade union votes and mainly of trade union officers, fully respected this 'feudal system'. It was reluctant to take any steps which might be perceived as abridging trade union rights, without their consent.

This 'feudal system' was very much the product of Labour's confederal origins; but, by the mid 1920s, its defects were increasingly evident. To continue the analogy, the flaw at the heart of Labour's 'feudalism' was (as in the original) insufficiently developed central authority. Any community, or organisation, if it is to prosper, must be able to repel hostile incursions across its frontiers, to protect what we call its *organisational integrity* against external threats. In the first half of the 1920s this requirement was not being adequately met. Labour's leadership (primarily, in this context, the NEC) could not prevent the adoption of candidates whose prime loyalty was to an unfriendly outside agency. And its ability to repel the danger, posed by Communist penetration, to both internal cohesion and organisational integrity was impaired by its lack of influence over affiliated organisations. Hence the exigency of organisational effectiveness provided a powerful impulse towards centralisation. Nevertheless, the 'feudal' aspect of the system ensured that the impulse could only be realised to the extent that the 'feudatories' themselves voluntarily suspended or surrendered their privileges. This they were only prepared to do if convinced that circumstances and self-interest both warranted such altruistic acts. As a result the tempo of centralisation, propelled forward by the drive against Communist infiltration, was very much set by the unions themselves.

The situation was rendered more urgent by Labour's very success. By the middle of the decade it had firmly established itself as the Conservative Party's main competitor and in 1924 for the first time in its history, formed a (minority) government. Throughout the Labour Government's short and precarious life its opponents sought to discredit it by tarring it with the Bolshevik brush, culminating in the famous (and forged) Zinoviev letter. The charge was positively surrealistic, but none the less potent for that. Labour's earnest rebuttals could be mocked by the ability of its enemies to 'name names' – avowed Communists within the ranks of its MPs and Parliamentary candidates. Hence it was not surprising that the NEC responded by seeking greater powers over the selection procedure. At the 1924 Annual Conference it proposed that no member of the CPGB should in future 'be eligible for endorsement as a Labour candidate for Parliament or any Local Authority'.[36]

Significantly, the NEC's main anxiety was to counter charges that this step represented 'an unwarrantable interference with the rights of affiliated organisations'.[37] Probably for that reason, Frank Hodges MP, a senior figure within the Miners' Federation, was deputed by the NEC to propose the motion. He made two main points: firstly, he decried as anomalous rules which required the Party to endorse Parliamentary candidates who denied its 'fundamental' commitment to the democractic method. As the body entrusted 'with the guardianship of Party principles'[38] the NEC should be entitled to reject individuals who repudiated them; secondly, Hodges – traversing more difficult terrain – reasoned that, in the act of accepting its constitution, affiliated unions 'had delegated the function of sanctioning candidates . . . to the Labour Party'.[39] Most unions were persuaded by the case and the motion passed by 2,450,000 votes to 654,000.[40]

The passage of this motion enhanced central control over the flow of Parliamentary candidates but left untouched the wider question of Communist involvement in Labour Party affairs. This reflected the NEC's cautious tactics. Other elements within the Party, however, were dissatisfied with the Executive's approach. Most unusually, the initiative was seized by a constituency party:[41] Sutton proposed a motion calling for the outright exclusion of all Communists from the Party. This move presented the rare spectacle of representatives from Labour's rank and file leading the drive for tougher discipline.

The NEC was clearly caught off balance and shied away from committing itself, aware that such an across-the-board ban would be highly controversial. No mention was made of the Sutton resolution by either Hodges in his opening speech or Morrison in his summing up. Nevertheless, it was carried – narrowly – by 1,804,000 votes to 1,540,000.[42]

The passage of the resolution opened up – as the NEC was doubtless aware it would – a constitutional hornets' nest. A left-wing delegate immediately rose demanding to know whether this meant that, in future, no Communist was eligible to attend Conference as a trade union delegate. The chairman refused to give a ruling, simply stating that it was for the NEC to interpret it.[43]

This was a sensitive matter, since it directly impinged upon the right of trade unions to appoint whomever amongst their political-levy-paying members they wished as a delegate to Labour Party Conferences.[44] The NEC hesitated – doubtless reflecting anxiety amongst its membership, composed mainly of trade union officials, about taking any action which curtailed the rights of affiliated unions. It appointed a sub-committee to consider the matter. This reported that the 'logical interpretation' of the Sutton resolution would be to exclude CP members from 'participating' in any shape or form in Labour Party activities. The NEC considered the report in February 1925, and, again procrastinating, decided to collect more information. Hardline anti-Communists, like Morrison, were furious. 'Far better would it be' he exclaimed 'to let the Communist Party affiliate and allow their people in with full rights, bag and baggage, than to continue to present policy of wobble, wobble, wobble.'[45]

By the 1925 conference, the NEC shifted somewhat to Morrison's position, but was still restrained by fear of offending trade union susceptibilities. The outcome was a differential handling of (to return to our analogy) its 'personal estate' and its 'feudatories'. It recommended that Communists should be banned from membership of local Labour Parties. But its approach to Communist participation via affiliated organisations was much more guarded. It 'desired to intimate to the Conference that *in its opinion* affiliated trade unions can only act consistently with the decisions of the Annual Conference in its relation to the Communists *by appealing* to their members when electing delegates to national or local Labour Party Conferences or meetings, to refrain from nominating or electing known members of non-affiliated political parties, including the Communists'.[46]

The laboured and deferential wording of the resolution reflected the NEC's anxiety about appearing to encroach upon trade union territory and prerogatives. And, indeed, apart from the Communists (and those left-wingers, who regarded the former as comrades in a common cause) the main resistance to the resolution came from speakers worried by the threat to trade union autonomy. The reference back of the relevant item in the NEC report was moved and seconded by Manny Shinwell and W. J. Brown (of the Civil Service Clerical Association), both of whom had been forceful opponents of CP affiliation. Brown argued that the Labour Party rested upon 'two separate and distinct bases'. Politically, the Party was composed of a group of people who shared the same political outlook – hence it was quite appropriate to exclude Communists from their ranks. But, industrially, Labour retained its status as 'an expression of working class opinion'; as a legitimate strand of working class opinion, the Communists had a right to participate, as trade unionists, in the Labour Party.[47] In reply, Henderson was eager to reassure the unions. The resolution was not an attempt to dictate to them it was simply an 'appeal' to them to comply with conference decisions.[48]

Labour's handling of the Communist question in the next two years reflected this differential approach to local party and affiliated organisations. The NEC pursued a strict interpretation of the Liverpool (1925) Conference resolutions as they pertained to those bodies directly subordinated to its authority. It ruled that Communists were ineligible for appointment as officers, delegates or members of the Executive Committee of any local party. A number of party organisations refused to comply and, for the first time, the NEC intervened ruthlessly to enforce discipline. In 1925–6 thirteen organisations were disaffiliated for defiance of the Liverpool decisions; ten more followed them into the wilderness in 1926–7.[49]

The NEC displayed no comparable enthusiasm for exerting its authority over affiliated unions. Prominent Communists continued to be appointed as delegates to Party Conferences by their unions. This gave rise to oddities – absurdities even – amusingly illustrated by one episode at the 1925 Annual Conference. In the course of a speech moving the reference back of the NEC report, the delegate of St Paul's Borough Labour Party and Trades Council, F. J. Jackson, admitted to being a Communist. The chairman interrupted, and ruled that Jackson, as a Communist, was ineligible to act as a delegate – and promptly asked Harry Pollitt to move the reference back! He denied charges of inconsistency, arguing that Pollitt was a duly accredited delegate of his union. He then confirmed that, in so far as they were appointed by their unions, Communists still had a right to act as delegates.[50] The situation bordered on the ridiculous and obviously could not have been tolerated for long.

1.2.3 *The assertion of managerial control*

Within a couple of years, the NEC felt emboldened enough to grasp the nettle. The decisive change was the rising anti-Communist temper of most senior trade unionists. This reflected three developments. Firstly, the collapse of the General Strike in 1926 after the ignominious retreat of the trade union establishment provoked fierce and much resented attacks upon 'treacherous' union leaders by the Communist Party. Secondly, the mounting hostility of union leaders to the CPGB was reinforced by their anxiety about its swelling influence within their organisations, primarily via the medium of the 'national Minority Movement'.[51] By the mid 1920s the NMM had gained many adherents through the trade union movement and featured in a number of industrial disputes. It was unsparing in its denunciation of 'right-wing bureaucrats'. Taking advantage of the increasing evidence of the factional activities of NMM caucuses, a number of powerful union leaders persuaded their conferences to discipline Minority Movement activists for 'disruption'.

The third development stemmed from a shift in Comintern thinking in the late 1920s. The International began to retreat from its earlier strategy of working within the established structures of the Labour movement; on its instructions the CPGB struggled to set up parallel union organisations outside the official framework.

Such behaviour, predictably, further infuriated the trade union establishment. Inevitably, this mounting hostility towards Communism spread to trade union behaviour on political issues. Union leaders, previously 'lukewarm in backing up the Labour Party Executive's resistance to "infiltration" ' now became much more receptive to firm measures.[52] The NEC judged that the time was now ripe for sterner action.

It made two main recommendations to the 1928 Party Conference. The first pronounced any persons acting as candidates in opposition to Labour candidates or who were 'members of political parties declared by the Annual Conference or by the NEC in pursuance of Conference decisions to be ineligible for affiliation to the Labour Party' to be henceforth ineligible as delegates to any Party Conference or meeting 'no matter by whom they are appointed'. The second tightened the meaning and enlarged the obligations of affiliation: in future it would be held to imply 'general loyalty to the decisions of the Party Conference' and would debar 'affiliated organisations and their branches from promoting or associating in the promotion of candidates for Public Authorities in opposition to those of the Labour Party'.[53]

These recommendations finally banned Communists from involvement in the Labour Party. But they had a more general repercussion; they involved a significant extension of central authority over affiliated organisations. As we have noted, the NEC had, until this point, been chary about making any claims which appeared to challenge the sovereignty of affiliated trade unions. It was prepared to deliver 'opinions' and launch 'appeals' to the unions, but not to instruct them on how to conduct their affairs, even if these directly impinged upon Labour Party organisation. This not only suggested a degree of deference towards the trade unions' jealously guarded prerogatives; it also reflected a belief that the Executive lacked the authority to intrude in any way upon the internal processes of trade unions.

The 1928 rule-changes had two effects. Firstly, they established the general principle that affiliation to the Labour Party entailed an obligation to abide by the decisions of *its* sovereign body. Secondly, the Party now asserted the right to regulate the way in which affiliated organisations exercised the rights and responsibilities of affiliation, laying down criteria to which such organisations were expected to conform.

The Comintern responded to the ever more inhospitable climate the Labour Party was offering to its adherents by devising new tactics. After the holding of Conferences attended by delegates from a substantial number of Labour Party organisations in London and Manchester the National Left-Wing Movement was formed in 1926.[54]

The NLWM was ostensibly an independent alliance of radical socialists drawn from a variety of political and industrial organisations. In reality, it was directed by the Communist Party via the 'fractions' which Communists were instructed to form in all left-wing Groups.[55] The NLWM was designated as the main instrument by which a revolutionary socialist opposition was to be built in the Labour Party and its existing leadership deposed.[56] It had an immediate and considerable impact. Within a short time, and primarily through its efforts, Communist influence in the Labour Party was 'spreading as never before',[57] causing even the doughty and capable anti-Communist, Herbert Morrison, serious problems in London.[58]

However, by this time, the NEC was no longer prepared to countenance any threat to the integrity of the Party, or any defiance of its authority. It denounced 'the organised and financed conspiracy to honeycomb our Labour Party organisation[59] and displayed an unprecedented willingness to employ disciplinary measures in carrying out its managerial role. It launched a sustained drive to eliminate Communists and their allies from the Party, brooking no disobedience from local organisations. Between 1926 and 1929, 27 local party organisations were disaffiliated.[60] By 1929 the NEC could report with some satisfaction that 'practically all difficulties experienced in constituencies in recent years owing to Communist activities have now been overcome'[61] – although, it needs to be added, this consummation was only achieved with the collusion of the CPGB itself.[62]

1.3   The consolidation of managerial control, 1929–1931

1.3.1   *Revision of the constitution*
The incremental growth of mangerial control which occurred in the 1920s, primarily in response to the contest with the Communists, was completed and codified in the extensive revision of the constitution in 1929. In simple quantitative terms, the constitution was doubled in length; matters which had been only vaguely alluded to or omitted altogether were spelt out more clearly. Lines of authority were clarified and rights and duties more precisely delineated. All this redounded to the benefit of the National Executive, as the Party's senior directive body. As a result, the most notable feature of the 1929 constitution, compared to the 1918 version, was the strengthening of central control.

This strengthening took three forms: the NEC's formal managerial authority was boosted, its regulatory powers were augmented and it was equipped with more potent disciplinary sanctions. We shall examine each of these in turn.

Firstly, the 1929 rule revisions amplified and confirmed the formal (rule-governed) subordination of members and lower level units to the NEC and entrenched its function as the custodian and arbiter of Party rules. Thus the Executive was invested with the responsibility to enforce the constitution and rules and to make final decisions (subject to modification by Conference) as to 'the meaning and effect of any rule or any part of this Constitution and Standing Orders'. It was also given the right to propose to Conference such constitutional amendments as it deemed appropriate.[63] Further, it was charged with ensuring the establishment of Party organisations in constituencies and boroughs 'in accordance with the rules'. Constituency and central (borough) parties were in turn required to 'submit [their] Political Rules to the NEC'[64] and 'adopt the Rules laid down by the Party Conference'. These clauses were more significant than they appeared. The NEC's responsibility for both overseeing the establishment and vetting the rules of all local parties could be construed as evidence of their constitutional inferiority to the Executive, conferring upon the latter all such rights and duties as were not explicitly granted to the former. In short, they could be – and indeed were – interpreted as broad enabling powers validating a centralised interpretation of the constitution.

The NEC's managerial authority was given a sharper cutting edge by increasing its stock of disciplinary powers. In pursuance of its duty of enforcing the constitution and rules it was empowered 'to take any action it deems necessary for such a purpose, whether by way of disaffiliation of an organisation, or explusion of an individual, or otherwise'. Any such action was to be reported to the next Annual Conference.[65]

Some of these powers figured, or may have been considered to be implicit, in the original constitution. But, as codified and extended in the 1929 version, they broadened the areas in which the NEC was authorised to act without having to obtain prior grants of authority from Conference. In most cases, Conference approval was still required – but *a posteriori*; inevitably, where the standing of the NEC was in question, Conference rubber-stamped its decisions. No longer was the Executive compelled to seek prior Conference authority for making a wide range of managerial decisions: this afforded it greater latitude to act unilaterally, with greater speed and decisiveness, thereby boosting Labour's managerial capability. The basis of central authority was strengthened and, as we shall see below, the broad enabling powers given to the NEC furnished a solid constitutional foundation for the more energetic and rigorous exercise of its powers.[66]

The 1929 Constitution also augmented the NEC's specific managerial powers. Five areas of Party activity were subjected to greater central regulation. Firstly, in the realm of political beliefs a new section on 'conditions of membership' was added. Henceforth both affiliated organisations and individual members were required to 'accept and conform to the Constitution, Programme, Principles and Policy of the Party'.[67] Since the 'Programme, Principles and Policy' were either only vaguely or not at all defined, this provided the NEC with considerable leeway in deciding criteria of eligibility for Party membership. (Until well into the 1960s the term 'Principles' retained the meaning it had acquired in the 1920s – a commitment to change by Parliamentary and legal means, though, as noted, this was never formally incorporated into the constitution.) This enabled the Executive to define and guard more rigorously the frontiers of the Party by means of (what we shall call) ideological regulation, or controls over belief.

A second major change had a two-fold effect of enhancing the NEC's ability to defend the organisational integrity of the Party and extending its control over the behaviour of its members. A new clause debarred from the Party 'members of political parties or organisations ancillary or subsidiary thereto declared by the Annual Conference . . . or by the NEC in pursuance of Conference decisions to be ineligible for affiliation to the party.[68] This right to declare organisations ineligible for affiliation soon came to be known as proscription and, over the next thirty years or so, featured as one of the NEC's key control mechanisms. The following year the NEC decided to compile a List of Proscribed Organisations, 'organisations ineligible for affiliation to the Labour Party', which was circulated to all constituency parties.[69] These two steps should not be confused: the first (the rule-change) endowed the Executive with the right to proscribe; the second (the List) was a method of putting this right into operation. In other words – and this was to become a contentious matter half a century later – a decision to dispense with the latter would in no way curtail the former.[70]

For our immediate purposes, however, the two can be taken together (as was intended). Proscription figured so prominently in Labour's disciplinary armoury for a generation that it deserves more extended exploration.

From the mid 1920s onwards the Comintern encouraged its affiliates to forge links with non-party 'progressives'. This — in Britain as elsewhere – initially took the form of the creation (on Communist initiative) of ostensibly broad-based organisations (of British branches of international organisations) usually geared to campaigning on specific issues, or mobilising support for a particular policy stance (e.g. 'The Workers International Relief', to help victims of imperialist or fascist oppression; 'The Friends of Soviet Russia' etc.) Those organisations, whilst often successful in recruiting prominent non-Communists were, the NEC claimed (usually on solid evidence) 'ancillary or subsidiary to the Communist International'.[71]

The NEC reacted by issuing a circular in February 1930 listing seven such bodies and declaring them ineligible for affiliation to the Labour Party. The effect of this (the establishment of a Proscribed List) was two-fold. Firstly, it rendered members of these bodies ineligible as individual members of the Party, delegates to the Party, locally or nationally (i.e. they were excluded from acting as delegates of affiliated organisations to Annual Conference and central and Constituency GMCs) and as Labour candidates for Parliament or local government.

Secondly, under their own rules, constituency organisations were precluded from entering 'into affiliation with' or giving finance or other support to proscribed bodies;[72] this was held to apply to individual members as well as local parties acting in their corporate capacity.[73] Thus proscription, as a control mechanism, had two aspects: firstly as a weapon to resist Communist penetration and, secondly (and more diffusely) as a device to limit the freedom of Party members to associate with whomsoever they pleased in the conduct of their political activities. The significance of this will become evident when we consider the politics of the 1930s.

The third area can be treated briefly. In a new clause, the NEC was given the power 'to adjudicate in disputes that may arise between affiliated and other Party organisations', its decisions to 'be binding on all organisations concerned'.[74] This should be seen in context with the production in 1930 of model Standing Orders to govern relations between Labour Groups on local authorities and local Labour Parties, which were increasingly troubled by political strains and jurisdictional conflicts. The new clause, coupled with the formalisation of relations between local parties and Labour Groups, transformed the NEC into the ultimate arbiter in local disputes.[75]

The fourth area, Parliamentary Selection, is a key internal process in any Party committed to achieving its goals by electoral means. This was the only area in which NEC powers were presented with any specificity in the 1918 Constitution. The major effect of the 1929 changes was to strengthen central control over all phases of the selection process.

The original (1918) rules had stipulated that the NEC 'shall co-operate with the Local Labour Party in any constituency with a view to nominating a Labour candidate', and required that its approval must be secured before a candidate was finally adopted.[76] The 1929 amendment extended central control in a number of ways. Firstly, the whole procedure of selection was explicitly subjected to NEC direction since (in a new clause) it was affirmed that it must take place 'in accordance with the procedure laid down by the Annual Party Conference on the rules which apply to Constituency and Central Labour Party'. Secondly, the Executive's capacity to influence the choice of candidates was enlarged by a new clause laying down conditions an individual must fulfil to be selected or endorsed. In future any individual had to be an individual member of the Party and be a member of a union affiliated to the TUC or recognised by the TUC as a bone fide union. Further, no member of an organisation declared by Conference or the NEC to be ineligible for affiliation could be selected. Finally, all candidates had to accept and conform to the Constitution, Programme, Principles and Policy of the Party.[77]

The intent of the clause was obviously to prevent the adoption of Communists, or others of dubious loyalty, as Labour candidates. But it also reinforced the NEC's control over candidate selection in general because of its discretion in determining whether an individual's views were comparable with the '3 P's', placing at its disposal an instrument which could be used to penalise the dissident or nonconformist as well as the disloyal.

1.3.2 *The exit of the ILP and the tightening of Parliamentary discipline*

The fifth area is appropriately treated last as it concerns a segment of internal Party life which fell within the joint jurisdiction of the NEC and the PLP (and its senior organs) – the rights and duties of individual Labour MPs. The relevant section of the Constitution was not, in fact, revised in 1929 but two years later, and in response to a specific set of circumstances – severe dissension within the PLP during the lifetime of the second Labour Government (1929–31), most acutely between the Parliamentary leadership and the ILP.

The status of the ILP, under the 1918 constitution, was something of an anomaly, bequeathed by the circumstances of the Party's birth. We noted that Labour's constitution was a hybrid, part unitary, part confederal. To a large extent, this coincided with the division of the Party into political and industrial sections. However, included in the confederal section were 'the socialist societies'.[78] No problems were raised by the Fabian Society, which was solely a research propaganda body. But the same could not be said of the ILP – a fully fledged political party in its own right, with the whole machinery of a party, including a Conference, Executive, branches in the country, and its own programme, principles and policy.

Relations between the Party and the unions were relatively harmonious in the 1920s with a broad agreement on policy reinforced by an agreed division of functions. But what of the ILP? To what extent was it (and its members) subject to the final authority of Labour Party institutions? Initially the obvious potential for conflict was muted by the considerable overlap in leading personnel and the broad similarity in outlook between the two (although the ILP was always on the left of the Labour Party). Both of these conditions ceased to obtain in the late 1920s as the ILP, under a new radical leadership shifted further to the left. But it was during the 1929–31 Labour Government that stresses became unmanageable, as ILP MPs bridled at the suffocating orthodoxy of the second MacDonald administration.[79]

This brought to a head the question of Parliamentary discipline. The PLP was primarily responsible for maintaining discipline and cohesion in its own ranks. The obligations imposed upon it in its infancy were not particularly onerous, nor did they become more so under the new constitution of 1918. It asserted it to be 'the duty of every Parliamentary representative of the Party to be guided by the decision of the meeting of such Parliamentary representatives, with a view to giving effect to the decisions of the Party Conference as to the General Programme of the Party'. Candidates, if elected, were required to 'act in harmony with the Constitution and Standing Orders of the Party in seeking to discharge the responsibilities established by Parlimentary practice'.[80] The 1929 revision merely added the duty of successful candidates to accept and conform to the Constitution, Programme, Principles and Policy of the Party. In addition, in the same year a set of PLP Standing Orders were adopted, although no immediate attempt was made to enforce them.[81]

The framework of rules governing the behaviour of PLP members was thus relatively insubstantial when Labour assumed office, for the first time as the largest party, in 1929. It was unable to cope with the strains as ILP stalwarts responded with anger and rebellion at the tepid and conservative policies pursued by the Government. The two parties then moved in opposite directions. The ILP National Administrative Council emphasised, in 1930, the organisation's 'distinctive function' and denied the right of Labour's leadership to restrict its 'liberty of action' or trammel the behaviour of its MPs when 'fundamental socialist issues are involved'.[82] The NAC pursued the dual policy of seeking to impose tighter control over ILP MPs and asserting its own autonomy from the Labour Party.[83] Inevitably this intensified the conflict between the two organisations. The PLP report to the 1931 Conference bemoaned the growing indiscipline within its ranks. In particular, it took exception to the fact 'that a section of the Party has been organised to carry out its own policy which at many points has been in conflict with the decisions of Party meetings'.[84] The NEC accordingly recommended constitutional amendments to stiffen PLP discipline. In future, all Labour candidates had to 'undertake to act in harmony with the Standing Orders of the Parliamentary Party'. Any successful candidate who failed to do so would in addition be 'considered to have violated the terms of this constitution'.[85] This empowered the NEC to expel from the Party any persistent Parliamentary rebel – a power more deadly than simple withdrawal of the whip (expulsion from the PLP).

The Parliamentary leadership was determined to assert its authority and enforce Party discipline as embodied in the Standing Orders; the ILP leadership was equally determined to resist. The collapse of the Government, the defection of MacDonald and others and the formation of the 'National Government' transformed the political situation, but the momentum driving the two parties apart was too strong. Negotiations broke down on the issue of Standing Orders and the ILP decided to disaffiliate.[86]

The significance of this episode was two-fold. Firstly, it inaugurated a period of stricter PLP discipline. Labour MPs were henceforth constitutionally bound, on pain of explusion, to conform to PLP Standing Orders. This reflected the general trend, apparent in the wider Party, towards a more centralised managerial system. Secondly, the behaviour of the ILP Group and the circumstances of its departure left an enduring suspicion and hostility towards any attempt to form 'a party within a party'.

We need here to distinguish between the literal and metaphorical meanings of this phrase. The ILP was literally 'a party within a party'. As a component unit within a confederal organisation, it possessed most of the accoutremenets of an independent political organisation. With its disaffiliation the line between the unitary and confederal segments of the Party coincided much more closely to that between its political and industrial wings. After 1931 the Party was never prepared to countenance a dual system of authority within the political wing.

In the metaphorical sense, the episode bred a lasting antipathy to organised factions within the Party. The rights of the ILP to formulate its own policies and propagate its own principles (in so far as they fell within the domain of non-revolutionary socialism) and seek to mobilise support for them was never seriously disputed: the final bone of contention was the refusal of the ILP to submit itself to the authority of the larger Party. But, within a few years, these rights, when exercised by others, were challenged and the bounds of legitimate dissent were substantially tightened.

1.4 The evolution of the managerial regime, 1931–1939

1.4.1 The drive against organised dissent

In the 1920s, the NEC faced the formidable task of pulling together and injecting some order and discipline into a new political formation containing many disparate elements. Finding itself poorly provisioned with managerial powers, it set about accumulating these, a process complete by the end of the decade. A centralised authority structure, vesting extensive powers in the Executive had been constructed.

Further, a number of key managerial objectives had emerged: the defence of Labour's ideological frontiers, the maintenance of its organisational integrity and, more latterly, a drive to assert the authority of the Party over its constituent units. This had evolved in an ad-hoc fashion and could not be said to constitute a *managerial regime* that is a coherent, consciously elaborated approach to party management. This is precisely what was to develop in the 1930s – a formative decade for Labour in this as in other respects.

The character of this regime, as it took shape, can best be understood by situating it in the context of the managerial problems the Party leadership confronted in that turbulent decade. Three major problems can be identified. The first is familiar: the protection of Labour's ideological and organisational integrity against what the leadership saw as persistent Communist efforts to infiltrate or sow confusion within it. The problem was magnified (in the leadership's eyes) by the growing willingness, eagerness even, of the Party's left to co-operate with the CPGB in various forms of united or popular fronts.

Any political organisation which aspires to be both open and effective must strike some balance between internal cohesion and the accommodation of diverse viewpoints. The second problem was deciding precisely where that balance should lie. It can be illuminated by a comparison with the left in France in the period. The Communist Party demanded monolithic conformity and would brook no dissent, effectively extinguishing the rights of its rank and file. The socialists (SF10), in contrast, tolerated and, indeed, officially sanctioned organised rival currents – but, by the end of the decade, virtually disintegrated as a coherent political formation.[87] Neither example inspired the Labour Party as it sought its own resolution to the dilemma.

The third problem was directly related. What was the most suitable method for settling internal party differences? As a democratic party, Labour's answer was: through an institutionalised system of majority decision-making, in which the rule of the majority is binding on all. But to what extent? How much constraint upon the rights and activities of minorities does majority rule in practice entail? The matter remained, as Labour entered its fourth decade, still largely unresolved.

These problems have, for analytical purposes, been separated. In reality, they all were threaded into a complex tapestry, into which were also woven ideological disputes and factional rivalries. But if the leadership's response was shaped by an array of motives and considerations, it was evident, as the decade wore on, that it followed a consistent pattern.

Relations with the Communist Party continued to dominate Labour's managerial agenda. After the Nazi seizure of power in 1933, the Soviet Union jettisoned its sectarian stance and instructed all Communist

Parties to seek alliances with other political forces. Initially, in Britain, this took the form of enlisting the participation of non-Communists in issue-oriented bodies like the revived National Unemployed Workers' Movement.

A number of (mainly left-wing) Labour Party members, impatient with (as they saw it) the feebleness and inertia of Party leaders, were eager to take part in the hunger marches and demonstrations organised by the NUWM, and to participate in the work of a number of other allegedly front organisations.[88] This incurred the wrath of the NEC, convinced that any joint action between Labour and Communist Party members could only be to the former's detriment. The CPGB, Morrison warned, was 'by carefully planned underground organisation, deliberately trying to make the maximum of trouble for the Labour Party'.[89] He admonished those Party members who allowed themselves to become accomplices in this project. This the Executive was not prepared to tolerate and in 1934 at its urging Conference extended the ban on membership of proscribed organisations to association with them[90] – though, it should be noted, the extension was not formally incorporated into Party rules.

The NEC justfied this step on the grounds that 'loose association with the Communist Party is just as dangerous to the interests of the Labour Party as is Communist membership itself'.[91] But – as left-wingers were quick to protest – 'association' was a protean concept and the new rule substantially widened the range of membership activities subject to central regulation. The young and eloquent MP for Ebbw Vale, Aneurin Bevan, denounced the move as an attempt 'to bring about in the Party itself a goose-step to prevent us from engaging in any form of activity which has not first of all received the blessing of the Executive Committee'.[92]

This was Conference hyperbole and the new rule was not in fact strictly enforced. Nevertheless, it did signify a narrowing of the sphere of discretion allowed Party members. The NEC's defence was to emphasise the importance to Labour, operating in a hostile and threatening environment, of maximum unity and discipline – even at the cost of restraining those who (in Ernest Bevin's words) 'claim a liberty in their own conduct almost amounting to licence'.[93]

In 1936 the deteriorating international climate and the outbreak of civil war in Spain stimulated enthusiasm for a United Front between Labour, the CPGB and ILP. The campaign in the Labour Party was spearheaded by the Socialist League[94] which occupied the role vacated by the ILP as the organised focus of left-wing activity within Labour's ranks.

The 1936 Annual Conference pronounced against any form of joint activity with the Communists. Undeterred, the League's leaders continued to champion the cause. At its Annual Conference in January 1937 the League – narrowly – voted to endorse a 'Unity Manifesto' to be signed jointly with the CP and ILP, notwithstanding a warning salvo from the NEC condemning any organised promotion of united or popular fronts.

The Executive responded quickly and ruthlessly. Its first step was to disaffiliate the League. Whilst this severed the formal ties binding it to the Party, it left the group (as a non-affiliated organisation) free to continue the campaign for unity. The NEC did not find this congenial and in March took the more drastic step of proscribing the League, rendering its members ineligible for continued membership of the Labour Party. The League felt it had no option but to disband. However, leading supporters of the Unity Campaign (including Cripps and Bevan) elected as individuals to continue working with Communists and ILPers for 'working class unity'. The NEC promptly instructed all members to refrain from participating in any way in United Front activities.[95]

These measures – which succeeded in extinguishing the Unity Campaign – signalled the installation of a much tighter disciplinary regime. The disaffiliation and proscription of the Socialist League marked a major break with the more pluralist spirit of the 1920s. This spirit had survived – somewhat muted – the departure of the ILP. Although (unlike the ILP) the League never challenged the authority of the Labour Party, it was a fully-fledged organised faction, with its own decision-making structure, branches in the country, membership, propaganda outlets and policy. It operated as an organised centre for left-wing dissent, promoting and mobilising support for its own policies and challenging the leadership on many points.[96]

By the mid 1930s, party pluralism was out of favour. The general drift to a more centralised authority structure, together with the ILP's rebellious behaviour between 1929 and 1931, and MacDonald's traumatic defection combined to reduce sharply Labour's tolerance of factional activity. Further, the trade unions, with their traditions of solidarity and disciplined collective action, had become a more potent force throughout the Party. Their antipathy to factionalism had, in turn, been deepened by a decade or more of sustained Communist effort to expand their influence in the unions by constructing cells and caucuses.

As a result, the balance between cohesion and diversity was altered. In this climate, the banning of the Socialist League was probably inevitable. It reflected not only a stronger impulse towards unity but also a growing propensity, on the party of the NEC, to use discipline as an instrument of party management. Previously only (alleged) Communist front organisations had been proscribed. Whatever its sins, the League did not fall into this camp. It was proscribed for allegedly transgressing Conference decisions and imperilling the unity and integrity of the

Party.[97]

The suppression of the League demonstrated the NEC's determination to impose its authority. Conference decisions were to be rigidly enforced at the expense, if necessary, of local party autonomy. In 1938 a new campaign was launched in favour of a Popular Front (embracing both Socialist and other progressives). The NEC moved swiftly to crush it. It instructed all members to withhold support from 'other political bodies that don't share the Party's policy or . . . demoractic socialist objectives.'[98] The Executive, in effect, claimed the right to penalise any Party unit or member which consorted with groups of which it did not approve – without even the pretence that this promoted Communist infiltration. Nor was it an idle threat. Several CLPs ignored the directive and helped form local popular fronts. As the NEC somberly reported, they were 'either prevailed upon to liquidate the new organisations or, where occasion warranted . . . were disaffiliated'.[99]

It was in the following year, however, that the new, stringent regime manifested itself most dramatically. In January 1939, in a last bid to mobilise opposition to appeasement and reverse the drift to war, Stafford Cripps produced a memorandum urging the NEC to organise a Popular Front, embracing all opponents of the Government. A special NEC rejected the memorandum by 17 votes to 3. Having anticipated this, Cripps had already arranged for its immediate circulation throughout the Party. The NEC was furious; it demanded that he withdraw the memorandum and sign a pledge reaffirming his loyalty to the Party. He refused and was accordingly expelled. Nevertheless, a 'National Petition Campaign' in support of the Cripps project was launched, attracting the support of leading left-wingers (including Bevan), trade unionists (Lawther and Watson from the MFGB) and luminaries from outside the Party (e.g. Keynes). A number (including the two miners' leaders) relented under NEC pressure; those who did not – Bevan, Strauss, Sir Charles Trevelyan and others – were expelled from the Party: a decision reaffirmed by Conference in May (four months before the outbreak of war). With the left within the Party decapitated, Cripps's campaign collapsed.[100]

The expulsion of Cripps, Bevan and other left-wingers was the most drastic disciplinary step ever taken by Labour against dissidents within its ranks. At issue were two opposed conceptions of how the Party ought to operate. To the NEC, Cripps' campaign for a Popular Front, and his provocative decision to circulate his memorandum immediately were acts of complete irresponsibility: they fomented dissension within the Party, undermined its integrity and exhibited a blithe disregard for Conference decisions. Cripps, and his supporters, disagreed. Not only was a new initiative to dislodge the National Government fully merited by desperate international circumstances, it was also quite proper for any member of a democratic party to do his utmost to alter its policy if he believed it misplaced. He defended his decision to circulate his memorandum – the basis for his eviction – on grounds of principle: that a minority could only hope to change established policy by disseminating its views, without hindrance, to the rank and file. This was 'cardinal to the survival of any democracy'.[101]

Such arguments were unpalatable to the new managerial orthodoxy of the 1930s. If firm action had not been taken, Hugh Dalton averred on behalf of the Executive, 'disintegration and demoralisation would have spread throughout the Labour movement'. This appeal to unity and loyalty was coupled with an attack on minorities who refused to submit to the will of the majority.[102] All members were fully entitled to express their views within the machinery of the Party. But dissent had its limits. Here lies the deeper significance of the episode: it was a boundary-setting exercise establishing 'the limits beyond which the Party cannot tolerate the generation of internal controversy'.[103] What were these?

In effect, the line was drawn at persistent and organised propagation of 'programmes and policies diametrically opposed to those of the Labour Party', or any activity which undermined 'the integrity of the Party and the authority of ... Conference'.[104] Cripps, Bevan and others had stepped outside the line; they were expelled less for their action in 1939 than for their behaviour throughout the decade.[105] Their fate symbolised the managerial transformation of the Labour Party.

1.4.2 Social-democratic centralism

Managerial decision-making in the 1930s exhibited a coherence absent in the previous decade. Our brief review indicates that Party authorities were influenced by three main considerations. The first was the maintenance of party democracy; Labour's leaders in this period adhered to a distinct doctrine of party democracy, the centrepiece of which was the concept of majority rule. The second consideration was the upholding of party unity, even at the expense of the curtailing of minority rights. The third was the protection of the Party's organisational and ideological integrity, particularly in face of the Communist challenge. The three considerations combined to form a *managerial doctrine*, an internally consistent set of principles which shaped the NEC's understanding of Labour's managerial needs and its own responsibilities; hence, we can speak of the emergence of a *managerial regime*. I shall use the same term, social-democratic centralism, to refer both to the doctrine and the regime it spawned. I have chosen the term became of its broad connotations – a combination of intra-party democracy, a centralised power structure and a distinctive ideological profile.

A central contention of this study is that Labour's approach to party management from the start of the period covered in detail (1951) until the mid- 1960s was to a considerable degree shaped by its leaders' adherence to social-democratic centralist doctrine. It furnished guidelines as to how the Party should handle its managerial problems and established a set of procedural norms defining the rights and duties of its members. Further, as a series of beliefs commanding a wide measure of support, it constituted a procedural consensus which legitimated the Party's structure of power and authority. For this reason we shall now examine in more detail its three main components: majority rule, party cohesion and integrity.

Majority rule Unlike its major rival, the Labour Party has always laid claim to the proud boast that it is a democratic political organisation: that decisions reflect the will of the majority and that the leadership is fully accountable to the membership. By the 1930s an explicitly articulated doctrine of majority rule was the cornerstone of the newly consolidated managerial regime.

The NEC's claim to exercise managerial control flowed from its dual status as custodian of the constitution and of Conference decisions. Conference sovereignty was the linchpin. As Lewis Minkin has written 'Conference acted as the sovereign court of appeal where the issues were finally settled not only on major policy, but also over important acts of individual and group dissent.'[106] Thus, whilst all members had the right freely to express and promote their views within the machinery of the Party, final authority resided with Conference and its decisions were binding upon all.

To what extent did this entail restraint on the rights of minorities to propagate their views? By its very nature, intra-party democracy implies some limits upon membership rights – else the majority's voice could not prevail. But opinion differed within the Labour Party about how much. The left vigorously opposed any constraint on the articulation of dissent. 'No pressure of control should be imposed to limit the expression of rival views', Cripps insisted. 'It is the vigour and struggle of contending views that preserves the warmth of life within a democracy.'[107] Social-democratic centralists disagreed. They regarded persistent, vocal and uninhibited attacks on basic Party policies as inconsistent with loyalty to majority decisions, and hence an affront to Party democracy. Their accent upon the binding quality of majority decisions reflected a conception of democracy (not shared by left-wing critics) which envisaged it both as a set of institutional arrangements for decision-making and as a mechanism through which a distinct general will emerged. 'Let us have free and frank discussions', Hugh Dalton argued in the debate over Cripps's expulsion, 'followed by majority decisions loyally accepted by all. Without some measure of healthy discipline and the submission of the individual to the collective will, there can be no democracy, but only egotism and anarchy.'[108]

This notion of a 'collective will' reflected a unitary conception of the Party as a body characterised by common interests, goals and values; it was an organ of collective class representation geared to the realisation of values shared by all its members. Majority decision-making was the method through which the general will was constructed. It was but a short step from this to treat persistent dissident behaviour as open defiance of Party democracy.

Few leaders can resist the temptation to identify the general will and the good of the Party they head with their own perpetuation in office. Yet Dalton's formulation was by no means entirely self-serving. There was, in this period, a widespread respect for the virtues of strong leadership – a cultural trait which the Labour movement imbibed from society at large. Within the Labour Party, vigorous leadership was legitimated by the democratic principle. Popularly elected and with the full support of Conference, power-holders had the right to expect loyalty from the rank and file.[109] But this, it was averred, was power exercised in the common cause; by maximising the Party's collective ability to impose its will on the environment the energetic assertion of leadership benefitted all.

Majority rule was also vigorously defended because it provided a settled method for resolving differences and, hence, a vital factor in sustaining party cohesion.

Party cohesion   All mass political organisations need to reconcile competing pressures for unity and diversity. The second component of social-democratic centralism was its inclination to tilt the balance in favour of unity, to be buttressed, if need be, by sanctions. By the 1930's, the maintenance of maximum cohesion had emerged as a managerial imperative.[110]

There were three main reasons for this. Firstly, the Party, entering the political fray, must present an image of unity: signs of disarray within its ranks would estrange potential supporters and reduce its credibility. This view helps account for the vigour with which many leadership stalwarts embraced the principle of majority rule. It was as much a means as an end. It provided a method for reaching authoritative and binding decisions on the basis of which Labour could present a united front to the outside world. Secondly, a reforming party, with a mission to accomplish, must be capable of harnessing its full energies, in a concerted fashion, if its efforts were not to be dissipated.

The third reason for the heavy accent on cohesion was perhaps the most important. After the debacle of 1931, the power and prestige of trade union leaders expanded very considerably. This further tightened the already substantial hold of the trade union ethos on the Party's collective consciousness. At the heart of this ethos lay the values of solidarity, unity and loyalty. These values were communicated by tradition and confirmed by experience – the awareness that success, even survival, depends upon standing together, uniting behind the organisation and its leadership, upon collective action rooted in a willingness to subordinate one's personal views and interests to those of the organisation as a whole. Solidarity and institutional loyalty, being functional requisites for successful action, take on a moral hue: loyalty becomes instinctual, a moral imperative.

It is not surprising that the toughest exponents of social-democratic centralism were drawn from the ranks of the unions. To men like Bevin, the betrayal of the intellectuals in 1931 – as he, somewhat whimsically, saw it – underlined the superiority of the trade union approach: and he pursued relentlessly and, at times, with venom, those like Cripps and Bevan who were 'splitting the movement'.

What effect did this accent on party unity have on the role of dissent? It may be useful to distinguish between the articulation and the organisation of dissent. In both cases social-democratic centralism argued that the maintenance of cohesion required and justified some measure or regulation of membership activity. But the intensity of regulation varied considerably.

Laski bemoaned the Party's attempts to enforce 'a mechanical unity of outlook'.[111] But this was unfair. Social-democratic centralism did not envisage rigid ideological control on the Communist model. Members were free to hold and promote a wide range of views. But certain, albeit loose, parameters were laid down. The NEC claimed the right to expel members from the Party 'where differences are fundamental or where they constitute a wide divergence from the principles, programme and policy of the party'.[112] And, indeed, these were amongst the grounds for the disciplining of Popular Front supporters in 1938, and Cripps and his lieutenants in 1939.

But it was rare for dissidents to be punished on these grounds alone. The organisation of dissent represented, from the social-democratic centralist standpoint, a much greater danger to cohesion. Concerted attempts by dissenters to alter Party policy smacked of 'factionalism'. This was not, in itself, a punishable offence. Bodies like the Constituency Parties Movement of the 1930s,[113] campaigning for what were deemed to be legitimate objectives were unwelcome (there being an instinctive dislike for 'unauthorised activity') often reproved but not banned. But tolerance had its limits. Here the two principles of majority rule and cohesion combined to foster a hostile view of 'factions'. Groups which possessed both a formal organisation and policy objectives which clashed with major planks of Labour's authorised programme were perceived both as divisive and – because they sought to overturn majority decisions – undemocratic. The Socialist League fell into this category. Its continued operation was so flagrantly at odds with social-democratic centralism that its eventual suppression was inevitable.

Integrity   The third managerial principle was the defence of Labour's organisational and ideological integrity. We have already discussed its genesis and manner of operation in some detail, so we can confine ourselves here to a brief summary. The emergence of the protection of the Party's integrity as a key managerial imperative arose largely from the threat of Communist penetration. The NEC's response was to render explicit Labour's social-democratic identity and, upon this basis, to construct ideological frontiers to keep out alient elements who sought to manipulate the Party's machinery for their own purposes.

Labour was to be troubled during the years of the wartime coalition (1940 to 1945) by a certain amount of internal dissension. But the chief cause of this – the handling of the war effort – was a factor which gave this period a character of its own and the Party's wartime managerial experiences left no significant legacy. As we note below, the years of the post-war Labour Government were, until the resignation of Bevan in 1951, relatively strife-free. For this reason we take 1951 – the year Labour returned to opposition – as our main point of departure.

The following six Chapters will examine the way in which the social-democratic centralist regime operated in the period 1951 to the late 1960s. Chapter two explores the response to the challenge of organised left dissent, in the form of Bevanism, in the early 1950s; Chapters three, four and five turn to the degree and character of central control over local parties; Chapter six investigates Labour's response to Trotskyism; Chapter seven examines the factors sustaining the centralised control structure in this period.

Social democratic centralism and the Bevanite revolt 1951–55

2.1 Introduction

Party management in the 1950s has entered the mythology of the
Labour Party. For many, on the right, these were years of sane and
balanced leadership, of moderation triumphing against its foes: for the
left, in complete contrast, they were a time of ruthless discipline, of
'right-wing intolerance, hatred and spite'.[1] The prime purpose of this
chapter is to elucidate the nature of Labour's managerial regime – its
goals, methods and effects – by exploring in detail the decade's
dominating episode: the leadership's response to the Bevanite challenge
of 1951–55.

The pattern of managerial decision-making had been set by the close
of the 1930s. The texture of Labour's internal regime – social-
democratic centralism – had been fashioned in that decade and much of
the Party's behaviour in the 1950s can be seen as the application of
established norms and principles.

The post-war Labour Government was (from the viewpoint of party
management) an interregnum. Although a number of pro-Communist
MPs were drummed out of the Party, discipline was relatively relaxed
(e.g. the PLP's Standing Orders were suspended in 1946). This was
primarily because opposition to Government policy (mainly in
international issues) never congealed into fixed factional alignments.[2]

This began to alter in the final months of Labour's tenure when
Aneurin Bevan (together with Harold Wilson and John Freeman)
dramatically resigned from the Government over the pace and funding
of the rearmament programme. The existing 'Keep Left' ginger group
was joined by the three ex-Ministers and promptly rechristened 'the
Bevanites'. With an election imminent, differences were patched up and
Labour's defeat was followed by a few months of uneasy calm.

2.2   The Bevanite revolt: (1) The tightening of Parliamentary discipline

The period of calm came to an abrupt halt with a major backbench revolt over rearmament in March 1952. From that point, until the very eve of the next general election in 1955, Labour was rent by fierce internal strife.

The revolt was precipitated by the Conservative Government's first Defence White Paper, which largely regurgitated proposals worked out during the previous administration. Labour's shadow cabinet recommended the tabling of an amendment approving the proposals but expressing a lack of confidence in the Conservatives' capacity to carry them out. This was approved by a handsome majority in the PLP, against Bevanite resistance, and a three-line whip was issued. It was anticipated that not all MPs would comply but the scale of the revolt shook the leadership. Amidst 'a scene of passion',[3] 57 Labour MPs defied the whip and voted against the white paper.

The remarkable feature of the episode – from the vantage-point of a later generation – is less that the revolt occurred than the response to it. PLP loyalists were furious. Senior figures within the Party hierarchy demanded the harshest penalties. Chief Whip Willie Whiteley urged the expulsion of the ringleaders, including Bevan.[4] Hugh Gaitskell contemplated with equanimity 'the prospect of Bevan and some others having to go out of the Party altogether. Indeed there would have been some advantage for it would have left us much freer to attack him.'[5]

The reaction seems quite disproportionate. Later, Labour governments survived numerous revolts – here there was not even a government to sustain. Further, turning to the specific issue, Bevan could hardly have been expected to endorse a rearmament programme presented by a Conservative government when his objections to essentially the same programme had precipitated his resignation from the Labour cabinet the previous year. Finally, given the suspension of Standing Orders in 1946 it was not at all clear that any serious disciplinary offence had been committed.

How, then, can we account for the response? Firstly, the atmosphere of the time was not conducive to calm deliberation. The Korean War was still being waged and frenetic Cold War emotions did not invite fine distinctions between critics of the scale of the rearmament effort and pro-Soviet elements. Secondly, the PLP had been untroubled by rebellions on this scale since the departure of the ILP; hence it struck many as a rupture with established traditions of parliamentary discipline. Thirdly, the rebellion was widely perceived as an affront to cherished, if as yet unwritten, conventions and norms of behaviour. Unbending social-democratic centralists, like Deakin and Whitely,

demanded 'self-discipline based on full democratic discussion and unswerving obedience to majority decisions once they had been taken'.[6]
For many in the Party the revolt presaged a concerted left-wing assault
on the leadership, dangerous not only in its object, but in the cavalier
disregard of the basic principles of Party democracy it exhibited.

However, for the time being, cooler counsel prevailed. The PLP, at
the prompting of the middle-of-the-road 'keep calm' group rejected the
Shadow Cabinet's call for sanctions against the rebels.[7] Nevertheless,
by agreeing to the reimposition of Standing Orders, a first step was
taken towards a tighter disciplinary regime. The new Standing Orders
formally banned voting against a three-line whip and restricted the
right to abstain to 'matters of known, deeply held personal conscientious scruple' (the so-called conscience clause). In 'cases of serious or
persistent breaches of Party discipline' the PLP was empowered to
withdraw the whip and, if it chose, recommend to the NEC expulsion
from the Party.[8]

The reimposition of a formal disciplinary code failed in its objective
of stemming the Bevanite tide. The Bevanite Parliamentary group was
now better organised, with a membership, regular meetings, officers
and advisers. It concerted tactics, framed alternative policies and via
the *New Statesman* and (especially) *Tribune* with its popular 'Brains
Trust', sought to muster support in the constituencies. Lines of cleavage were crystalising and the atmosphere within the Party rapidly
soured.

The leadership were aware of the radical mood in the Party and probably anticipated a difficult conference in the Autumn. But at the 1952
Morecambe Conference, Party and Union leaders were stunned by the
spirit of virtual insurgency amongst the constituency delegates.
Debates were fiery and acrimonious with insults flying freely through
the conference hall: 'Shut your gob' barked Will Lawther, President of
the NUM, at seething constituency delegates.[9] Whether by chance or
design, a disproportionate number of Trotskyist and pro-Communist
delegates were called to the rostrum to move resolutions.[10] 'This Conference is going rapidly mad', groaned George Brown.[11]

As it happens, the leadership suffered no major reverses on policy.
This was partly because the NEC chose to conciliate radical sentiment,
which had spread to a number of major unions, by accepting some left-
wing demands, most notably a substantial programme of nationalisation. Largely as a result, a number of resolutions on controversial
issues passed with large majorities. The real climax of the Conference
came when the results of the ballot for the constituency section of the
NEC were announced. 'For once', the *New Statesman* exclaimed, 'the
sensationalists are right'.[12] Morrison and Dalton, two of Labour's most
senior and respected figures had been ousted by prominent Bevanites,

Harold Wilson and Richard Crossman. All but one of the seven constituency seats were now held by left-wingers (the seventh by the conciliatory James Griffiths). All gained an absolute majority of the votes cast,
with Bevan getting nearly all the one million available. 'The Bevanites'
successes (and, even more, Mr. Morrison's defeat) have produced something akin to frenzy among the managers of the Party, who had never
before faced an unmanageable challenge.'[13]

The shocked indignation of Labour's establishment was most forcefully articulated by Hugh Gaitskell in a well reported speech at Stalybridge – which he himself called 'for me an unusually violent speech . . .
a call to battle'.[14] He thundered at the constituencies' temerity at
removing Morrison: an act of 'gross political ingratitude . . . a piece of
blind stupidity'. Most provocatively of all, he drew attention to allegations that one-sixth of all constituency delegates at Morecambe were
Communists.[15]

From this reaction, one might have inferred that the left was on the
point of sweeping the Party. In fact, the Bevanites were hopelessly
outnumbered on the NEC and stood no prospect of dislodging their
opponents. The right remained solidly in control, with the massive
artillery pieces of the big unions committed and available to crush the
left-wing insurgents. Placed in context, the establishment's response
seemed to verge on panic.[16] That response only become intelligible
when one appreciates the manner in which the leadership apprehended
the situation.

Morecambe was unprecedented; it violated ingrained expectations.
Major political figures of the stature of Morrison and Dalton had never
before been deposed from the NEC. The Labour Party had always prided
itself as a democratic organisation – but this was coupled with a due
regard for its leaders and a presumption that they be treated with proper
consideration. But most fundamentally of all, the events at Morecambe
– and the conviction these had been masterminded – offended social-
democratic centralist principles. 'The thing that affonts union leaders
more than anything' *The Times* recorded 'is the way in which the
Bevanite group acts, or at least the way in which they believe it acts, as
an organised faction within the Party.'[17] This, indeed, was the burden of
Deakin's charge in his address to Conference, when he demanded that
'this dissident element in our midst' disband its organisation.[18] The
significance of Morecambe, the *New Statesman* commented, lay in the
fact that the ordinary membership of the Party had succeeded 'in forging
itself into a coherent group, gained a majority and used the constitutional machinery to register an effective protest and shift policy noticeably leftward'.[19] From the viewpoint of the leadership, the events of
Morecambe had been orchestrated by an organised faction, which had
been responsible both for the defeat of Morrison and Dalton and for

fomenting a spirit of insubordination.

Even prior to Conference there had been denunciations from middle-ranking leaders of a 'party within a party'. After Morecambe, demands for disciplinary action against the Bevanites mounted in intensity and vehemence, eventually sweeping an initially reluctant Attlee along. 'What is intolerable' he pronounced, 'is the existence of a party within a party with a separate leadership, separate meetings, supported by its own Press. It is inimical to effective action in the House. It breeds suspicion and uneasiness throughout the movement.'[20]

Wilting before a massive and concerted onslaught, the Bevanites (after some heated debate) decided to throw their loosely-knit group open to all who chose to attend its meetings. But the leadership was unimpressed. The shadow cabinet recommended to a PLP meeting an ultimatum demanding the immediate dissolution of the Bevanite group.[21]

The debate that then took place was a highly significant one. To what extent did MPs have the right to organise themselves and seek, in a concerted manner, to contest the views of the majority? Attlee – under considerable pressure – took a hard line: 'Groups' he argued, 'are alright [sic] for a special purpose, but what I disapprove of is an omincompetent Group like the ILP used to be.'[22] After a long and acrimonious debate, the PLP passed by 188 votes to 51 the shadow cabinet resolution calling for the 'immediate abandonment of all group organisations within the Party other than those officially recognised; it further calls all members to refrain from making attacks on one another, either in the House, the press or the platform'.[23] The Bevanite group very reluctantly decided to comply and disbanded. To *The Economist*, the ban on groups, coupled with the reimposition of Standing Orders, installed 'a far more rigid discipline than ever before experienced in British politics'.[24] For over a decade, no organised group activity within the PLP was permitted and, on a number of occasions, persistent dissidents (including, in 1961, Michael Foot) were deprived of the whip.

What was the effect of this ban on factions? It did not, in practice, preclude all organised opposition, but it did inhibit it. Left-wingers henceforth always had to anticipate a possible heavy-handed response from the leadership and tailor their plans accordingly. One incident illustrates this. An informal Bevanite lunch debated a suggestion to re-form a loose group, with meetings disguised as social occasions. Crossman commented: it sounded 'fantastically elaborate but the fact is that the ban on group activities really does make it difficult to formulate any serious policy or to behave in a reasonable way. Yet, on the other hand, the ban has got to be accepted and acted on else we shall be in trouble'.[25]

With its capacity to organise as a Parliamentary-based faction curtailed, the effectiveness of Bevanism, as a political current, was curbed.

But it weathered the storm, largely because it possessed an influential extra-Parliamentary arm.

2.3 The Bevanite revolt: (2) squeeze on extra-Parliamentary dissent

In his controversial Stalybridge speech, Gaitskell released the pent-up fury of many on Labour's right when he angrily denounced the leading left weekly, Tribune: 'Indeed, its very existence, so long as its pages are devoted to so much vitriolic abuse of party leaders is an invitation to disloyalty and disunity. It is time to end the attempt of mob rule by a group of frustrated journalists'.[26] Whilst (unlike the Trotskyist *Socialist Outlook* (which was proscribed in 1954)[27] no direct attempt was ever made to imperil 'its very existence', it was for two years subjected to intense pressure designed to transform it into a more 'responsible' organ of opinion. This was not a planned campaign, in the sense that it was rationally considered and drawn up in advance. Rather it consisted of a collection of more or less unco-ordinated (and sometimes impulsive) steps. Yet, at a deeper level (as we shall see) a definite pattern is discernible.

The offensive against the extra-Parliamentary dimension of Bevanism was precipitated by a seemingly minor episode. In January 1953 an article appeared in *Tribune* noting Government efforts to woo the trade unions by capitalising on signs of strain between some powerful union leaders (Deakin, Lawther, Williamson and Lincoln Evans of the steel union) and the Party over the Morecambe commitment to a substantial programme of public ownership. A further report rebuked Lincoln Evans for accepting a knighthood at a time when the Government was denationalising steel.[28]

At an NEC meeting shortly afterwards, Morgan Phillips, the Party Secretary, announced the receipt of a message from the General Council of the TUC (also meeting at Transport House) protesting against the Tribune articles and calling upon the Executive to prevent any repetition. After a 'bad-tempered debate'[29] the NEC passed a resolution deploring the articles and urging all Party members to refrain from 'personal attacks'.[30]

'At this point', Crossman recalled 'Harry Douglas said, "the next logical thing to do is to examine the Tribune Brains Trust and see if they are a party within a party"'. Attlee appeared surprised but did not object, whereupon Edith Summerskill, a waspish right-winger, demanded stronger measures. 'I mean expelling those who are suspected of fellow travelling.' 'This was said' Crossman recounted 'with her eyes fixed on Ian [Mikardo] who I think is the most hated of the Bevanites.'[31] The Executive then carried by nine votes to six a motion that the Organisation Sub-Committee 'enquire into, and report on the machinery and organisation of the Tribune Brains Trust, and whether or not such an organisation constituted a party within a party'.[32]

The 'Brains Trust' as one of their organisers later recalled were the 'core of the (Bevanite) campaign' in the country. Consisting of teams of Bevanites, they toured the constituency parties, presenting the left-wing case, a 'massive apparatus' for which the demand was 'insatiable'.[33] They were regarded with particular suspicion by Labour right-wingers who saw behind them the devious hand of the Bevanite master-organiser, Ian Mikardo.

The National Agent's Department produced a report criticising the Brains Trust but failing to find any evidence of breaches of the Party's rules.[34] Notwithstanding, the trade unionists on the Organisation Committee were 'determined to ban' them. Left-wing NEC members denied that they were used to promote Bevanism, to which a trade unionist, Bill Webber, riposted, 'It was not what's said there that matters. It is the fact that they are organised.'[35]

After 'three and a quarter hours of the most appallingly dreary atmosphere of subdued bickering',[36] the Sub-Committee resolved 'That this committee is of the view that the organisation of the Brains Trusts through Tribune is contrary to the spirit and intention of recent decisions of the PLP', adding that 'propaganda of this kind should be conducted through the formal machinery at the disposal of the PLP'[37]

This was interpreted as constituting a ban on the Brains Trust. But it was an impetuous decision, taken in the heat of the moment and with no proper consideration of its purpose and effects. To many – and not just Bevanites – it was a gross abuse of the rights of members. 'Utterly intolerable', the centrist John Strachey protested: 'What country is this anyway – the birthplace of political liberty or some totalitarian state?'[38] At the February NEC both the Party leader and the conciliatory-minded James Griffiths queried the Sub-Committee's recommendation. Nevertheless, the NEC ratified it – but then Morgan Phillips promptly emptied it of meaning by denying that it prohibited the Trusts.[39]

The offensive against the Trusts failed[40] – though only, according to Bevan – because it had been botched. Harry Douglas's impulsive move had pre-empted (and discredited in advance) a more wide-ranging campaign against the Bevanites being prepared by Deakin.[41] But the failure was not complete; pressure from the disciplinarians contributed to a growing rift between 'moderate' and hardline' Bevanites – the former, like Crossman and Wilson, urging more circumspection, the latter refusing to give any ground.[42]

And the pressure upon *Tribune* and the Bevanites did not relent. J. P. W. Mallallieu MP, a member of the weekly's editorial board, came under fire from irate colleagues in the PLP for writing that some of his fellow MPs who sported Bevanite sympathies before their constituency parties then proceeded to back right-wing candidates in the shadow cabinet elections.[43] This less than shattering observation was interpreted as casting a slur upon the integrity of MPs and Mallallieu was arraigned before the PLP. Only by dint of Attlee's effort did the errant MP escape punishment.[44]

But the determination of hardline right-wingers to restrain *Tribune* was mounting. Crossman concluded a diary entry on a special – and tempestuous – NEC meeting on 'party unity' by observing that 'the burden of [the hardliners] charge is now directed against the periodicals. It is the journalists they really fear.'[45]

Events soon bore this out. In 1954 the small National Association of Stevedores and Dockers called a strike over compulsory overtime; many TGWU members joined in. The Transport Union's leader, Arthur Deakin, denounced the strike, claiming that it had been engineered by Communists. *Tribune* tartly commented that such claims merely revealed Deakin's ignorance and indifference.[46]

Deakin was furious. He did not take easily to criticism and doubtless genuinely regarded *Tribune's* reporting as irresponsible and inflamatory. But he had for long abhorred the weekly[47] and the incident may well have confirmed his belief in the Bevanites' dangerous softness towards the far left. It seemed to him – and like-minded trade unionists – an ideal opportunity to strike, and a letter from the General Council was despatched to the NEC calling for action.

There followed a long and heated discussion. Driberg and Crossman pleaded for 'the independence of socialist papers', but were brushed aside. By 20 votes to 5, the Executive passed a remarkable resolution denouncing the offending article as an 'unwarranted, irresponsible and scurillous attack on the leadership of the TGWU ... calculated to impede an honourable and orderly settlement of the dispute and as a breach of the injunction that members of the labour movement should not indulge in personal attacks on one another'.

Further, it was agreed (with two dissentients) to write to the three members of Tribune's editorial board (Michael Foot, Jennie Lee and J. P. W. Mallallieu) asking them 'how they can reconcile their attack on the leadership with their membership of the Party' – clearly hinting at expulsions.[48]

Such, without doubt, was the intention of Deakin and his allies.[49] The Bevanites feared the worse. Bevan told Attlee that, if the three were expelled, he would resign.[50] The six Bevanite members of the NEC also agreed – Wilson and Crossman reluctantly – that they too would quit.[51]

But once more the hardliners had blundered. The issue was a singularly ill-chosen one and – in a powerful and eloquent broadside – *Tribune* counter-attacked, charging the NEC with an attempt to suppress freedom and democracy in the Party.[52] If criticism, it argued, became personal simply by attacking a named person in his public capacity then the frontiers of free debate were seriously narrowed. The leadership would degenerate into oligarchy if not exposed to 'the strictures of the awkward, unorthodox, challenging minority'.

Morgan Phillips, on behalf of the NEC, responded in a social-democratic centralist vein: 'It is a fundamental principle of democracy', he insisted, 'that policy decisions should be based on the majority view'. The party, he added, was entitled to expect that minorities 'will accept and observe majority decisions'.[53]

But the ham-handedness of the Executive's tactics boomeranged. Liberal-minded opinion (inside and outside the Party) was not impressed by the proposition that attacks on trade union leaders was in some way inconsistent with Party membership. Further, finding constitutional grounds for expulsions would have strained the resourcefulness of Transport House. Finding its position unsustainable (politically and intellectually) the NEC was forced to retreat.[54]

Tribune continued to irritate – sometimes infuriate – the leadership, but this most serious effort to subdue the paper proved to be the last.[55] However, Arthur Deakin, the prime mover, was not unduly distressed. He commented pithily 'We've thrown the sprats back in the water. There's no point in keeping them while the mackerel's still swimming about.'[56]

2.4 Catching the mackerel: The bid to expel Aneurin Bevan

The most extraordinary episode in the internal politics of the Labour Party during this period was the bid to expel Aneurin Bevan. Bevan has long since entered Labour's pantheon of saints; his memory is consecrated, his thoughts reverentially quoted: and two successive Labour Party leaders have counted themselves amongst his devoted admirers. From the vantage-point of the 1980s it seems inconceivable that, at the height of his fame, he came within one vote of expulsion.

Very full (though not entirely consistent) accounts of the sequence of events are now available.[57] We shall restrict our description to the minimum necessary to render the episode intelligible.

A starting point is the position of Bevan himself in the Party. He had been, by 1955, active in the Labour movement for more than three decades; an MP since 1929; an influential, if controversial, figure since the 1930s; the architect of the Party's proudest and (to date) most enduring achievement, the NHS; a brilliant orator and highly-skilled Parliamentarian; wildly popular amongst activists – though a difficult, impetuous, mercurial colleague for many of his fellow members of the PLP. He was a man who, if circumstances had been more propitious, might have led the Party – but on 23rd March 1955 found himself on the brink of expulsion.

Bevan only narrowly escaped – and the main significance of the episode lies precisely in the narrowness: both that a politician as notable and (in the constituencies) popular as he could *almost* be expelled – and that an inveterate nonconformist, a goad to his critics, could not be *quite* expelled. In effect, we are addressing two issues: firstly, the astringency of the central regime which sanctioned such a drastic move and, secondly, the counter-forces operating within the Party which (just) prevented it.

Why was the attempt made to eject the tempestuous Welshman? We should distinguish between two types of reasons: the ostensible ones, that is the charges made against Bevan for which he was arraigned before the PLP and the NEC; and the underlying ones, that is the motives of those who were awaiting an opportunity to pitch him into the outer darkness.

The underlying causes were the more important and merit consideration at the outset. By 1955 a number of powerful figures within the Party (including Gaitskell, Deakin and probably Morrison and Williamson) had become convinced that Bevan would have to go.[58]

Why? Undoubtedly they were influenced by a variety of considerations: personal animosity; the belief that the Welshman was an incorrigible trouble-maker, an egotist driven by a relentless appetite for power; that he alienated floating voters vital for the future success of the Party; that he was congenitally incapable of abiding by the rules and accepting majority decisions and hence would always be a disruptive force.

The impact of Bevan's explusion, if carried through, would have been very considerable. The boundaries of permissible dissent would have contracted and future critics would have been more inhibited about carrying their opposition too far. But, above all, it would have had a profoundly demoralising effect upon left-wing dissidents, many of whom may have quit in dismay or adjusted their aspirations to what now seemed feasible. This would have facilitated the emergence of a more rigorously managed and conformist party on the SPD model. According to Attlee, this was precisely what his two senior lieutenants, Gaitskell and Morrison, sought. 'Each of them thought that one day he might succeed me as leader, and he wanted to inherit a disciplined party. Both wanted Bevan brought to heel well in advance.'[59]

What were the ostensible reasons? In a document he wrote for consideration by Attlee[60], Gaitskell noted that the case against the South Wales MP was largely based on his conduct in the House of Commons on three quite separate occasions.

In April 1954 Attlee – keen to maintain a bipartisan approach to foreign policy – had signalled his approval of the Government's backing for a new anti-Communist alliance in South East Asia (SEATO). A disgruntled Bevan then rose and interrogated Attlee in a way which implied in a most brazen manner a lack of confidence in his leader.[61] At a meeting of the shadow cabinet the next day Bevan was rebuked for his behaviour, though not formally censured. Bevan responded by announcing his resignation from the shadow cabinet.[62]

The second offence occurred almost a year later. In January 1955 Bevan proposed that Labour should table a motion calling for talks with the Soviet Union pending ratification of the treaty permitting German rearmament. The PLP rejected the proposal but, notwithstanding, the Bevanites placed it upon the order paper and collected over 100 signatories. This was a traditional method of publicising backbench opinion, but, in the climate of the times, the majority of Labour MPs regarded it as a deliberate affront. 'Although technically there had been no breach of the Standing Orders', Gaitskell acknowledged, he hastened to add that 'it was certainly contrary to their spirit'.[63] A special meeting of the PLP was called to consider the matter and Bevan and his supporters were condemned for transgressing majority decisions.[64]

Shortly after, the PLP decided – with few objections – to back Government plans to build an H Bomb. In the debate in the House of Commons, however, Bevan challenged the decision and then appeared to snub, quite ostentatiously, his own leadership by declaiming that the Bevanites would lead the opposition to the Government, in default of more effective action by those entrusted with the task.[65]

Within a few hours Bevan had compounded the offence when, again, he interrogated Attlee, on the floor of the House, over whether the Opposition front-bench agreed to a nuclear response to a conventional attack. Further, when the division was called, along with 61 others, he abstained on Labour's official motion.[66]

For many MPs, furious at Bevan's behaviour, this was the final straw. George Brown, a fervent loyalist at the time, denounced the Welshman for publicly repudiating his leader 'in the most humiliating and damaging way', and persistently spurning majority decisions.[67] A special meeting of the shadow cabinet was called and several senior members, including Morrison and Gaitskell (and the more junior Jim Callaghan) pushed for the withdrawal of the whip. Attlee demurred but in a characteristically tepid and laconic fashion and was overuled. The majority was clearly intent on a showdown since, most unusually, it opted to make the issue a matter of confidence to pressurise waverers – the whole shadow cabinet would resign if the PLP rejected its recommendation.[68]

The PLP met on March 16. Bevan was unrepentant[69], but opinion was evenly balanced. A compromise motion proposed by Fred Lee calling for a censure in place of withdrawal of the whip was narrowly defeated by 138 to 124 and the shadow cabinet motion was carried by

141 to 112.

The question was what to do next. The Standing Orders stipulated that the matter be referred to the NEC. The majority of the shadow cabinet wanted to utilise this to procure Bevan's explusion. They argued that withdrawal of the whip merely divested Bevan of his responsibilities to comply with the whip, but imposed no real penalties, since he was bound to be re-admitted to the PLP before a general election. The only real punishment was expulsion from the Party.

Since the battlefield had shifted from the PLP to the NEC, the trade unions were now, for the first time, directly involved. A great deal of lobbying took place. Gaitskell, Deakin and Williamson sought to exert their considerable weight in order to muster a majority for expulsion. It was hinted that the unions would be less forthcoming in filling the Party's coffers for the imminent elections if there was any vacillation.[70]

The resolution to expel Bevan debated at the NEC called to discuss the matter was framed in terms of his refusal to comply with majority decisions (and not his personal affronts to the leader). The decision rested on a knife edge. 'When it began to look highly probable that Bevan would be expelled, Attlee broke off his doodling'[71] and proposed that a special Sub-Committee be set up to interview him over his conduct. This was narrowly agreed by 14 votes to 13 – and the ebbulient left-winger was effectively off the hook.[72]

The thrust of the charges levelled against Bevan at the Special Sub-Committee was his sustained violation of the social-democratic centralist principles upon which the Party was run. He was accused of persistent attacks on Party and union leaders, repeated refusals to accept majority decisions and forming an organised group with its own press.[73] Bevan's opponents were unimpressed by his defence; but, despite Jim Haworth's change of heart (which meant that a majority now favoured expulsion) the psychological moment had passed. The reconvened NEC accepted Bevan's apology and assurances (cleared in advance with Attlee) though it warned that it would take 'drastic action against any future violation of Party discipline.'[74] Shortly after, with an election imminent, the whip was restored and Bevan was back in the fold.

Why did Bevan escape expulsion? It is worth addressing the question, not only because Bevan's escape was a significant political fact in itself, but for what it tells us of the pattern of discipline and control in the Labour Party.

Firstly, there was a concaternation of fortuitous circumstances: Jean Mann, a vitriolic opponent who wanted him expelled, chose not to vote for the key motion for rather idiosyncratic tactical reasons; Jim Haworth decided he wanted Bevan out of the Party – but only after the moment had passed; Edith Summerskill, the most ferocious of all of Bevan's critics, was chairman of the Party and, to her anguish, deprived of the use of her casting vote by the alertness of Ian Mikardo's daughter, settled in Israel, who at the last moment altered the date of her marriage so that her father would be able to return to cast his decisive vote.[75] Thus, if the roulette wheel had not spun in his favour, Bevan would have been expelled.[76]

Chance also assisted Ebbw Vale's MP in two other respects: the proximity of a general election and the coincidence of boundary reorganisation. If, however, fortuitous in one sense, in another they were not: they only assume their full importance if they are placed in a wider context. It is to this we shall now turn.

The response in the wider Labour movement to the threat to Bevan was electric. Two unions (ACAT and the AEU) and 151 CLPs protested to Transport House against the withdrawal of the whip from Bevan.[77] There were other rumblings of discontent. The NUR executive opposed expulsion. So too did the South Wales NUM, which called for a national conference to consider the matter. Margate CLP decided to convene a conference of CLPs to protest against any disciplinary moves against Bevan. Unambiguous evidence of the turmoil which would be provoked by drastic disciplinary action came from meetings of the Scottish and North-West Regional Councils, when refusals by the chairmen to permit resolutions denouncing the threat to Bevan provoked uproar.[78] Inevitably, there would have been a furious row at Conference if the sword had fallen.

For the waverers, awareness of massive opposition to the expulsion weighed heavily for two reasons – both linked to the impending election. Firstly, the spectacle of a party collapsing into a state of tumult and recrimination was highly unlikely to commend itself to the voter. Secondly, it was feared that thousands of Party workers would refuse to participate in the election campaign if Bevan was thrown out, debilitating the Party machine[79] – this at a time when most believed that elections were won and lost on the doorstep.

Apprehension over rank and file sentiment was aggravated by boundary reorganisation. As Gaitskell noted in his diary, MPs usually virtually immovable were suddenly exposed to constituency pressures.[80] This may have accounted for the smallness of the majority to deprive Bevan of the whip[81] – which robbed the vote of some of its moral force and undermined the case for outright expulsion.

Another decisive factor – which, alone, probably turned the table – was Attlee's opposition to expulsion. Several trade union leaders, otherwise keen to exclude the fiery Welshman, were inhibited by loyalty to the leader. Despite all the pressure that Deakin and Williamson could muster they were reluctant to oppose his will.[82]

It was always improbable that Attlee would have backed efforts to drive Ebbw Vale's MP out of the Party. It grated with his whole style of leadership as evolved over twenty years. He saw himself as a conciliator, with a responsibility to accomodate divergent viewpoints as far as possible. In some ways his leadership was a paradox. He presided over the Party during the high noon of social-democratic centralism – yet was always sceptical of the value of forcing decisions through by mechanical majorities. It was during his years that the leadership was buttressed by the 'Praetorian Guard' of trade union leaders – especially the Deakin–Williamson–Lawther triumvirate – yet he was never close to them, nor did he share their disciplinarian attitudes and autocratic style.

Perhaps this was not a paradox: social-democratic centralism was able to permeate the internal life of the Party precisely because it had as a leader a man who urged restraint and was able to mitigate its operation, hence rendering it more acceptable to the membership. This – aside from personal factors – helps explain his resolve to stay in harness long enough to dash Morrison's hopes of replacing him. He was convinced that the Londoner would have adopted a much tougher attitude towards the left and, hence, fomented rather than assuaged divisions.[83]

As Phillips Williams has shown,[84] Gaitskell, as Attlee's successor, strove in his early years as leader to placate rather than eliminate his (less resolute) opponents. When he did – in the 1959–61 period – revert to his earlier disciplinarian posture he stirred the embers of revolt so vigorously that the flames virtually engulfed the Party – hence paying a post-facto compliment to his predecessor's very different approach to leadership.

Attlee's restraining hand tipped the balance. But the fact that the expulsion move nearly succeeded, against his expressed desire, indicates (aside from his own faltering grip) the strength of forces within the Party willing to resolve divisions by coercive means – prepared, at the cost of a massive internal upheaval, to crush left-wing dissent by decapitation. So two conclusions can be drawn from the episode: there were factors operating powerfully to inhibit recourse to disciplinary action. Yet – since the outcome was knife-edged – the impulses towards a stricter discipline and a tighter regulation of dissent were sufficiently strong to require a formidable conjunction of circumstances to override them.

In retrospect, the disciplinarians may well have achieved their aims. Although this is speculative, it may well be that the harrowing pressure to which he had been subjected and his hair's-breadth escape had taken its toll on Bevan and dulled his rebellious instincts. The bid to expel Bevan, paradoxically, brought the period of Bevanite controversy to an end. Bevan did achieve a measure of success in that, after two failed attempts, he succeeded in 1956 in defeating the right-wing block vote and obtaining the Treasurership.[85] This strengthened his power base and his bargaining power with the new leader, Hugh Gaitskell. But it may also be that perhaps psychologically prepared by his testing experience Bevan was, by 1956, ready for a reconciliation with the leadership and for the dramatic and irreparable break in the following year (caused, ironically, by his repudiation of unilateralism) with the left-wing forces which for so long he had inspired, mobilised and, indeed, epitomised.

In fact, the left-wing tide was already receding. The Bevanites had not been crushed, but the strain of surviving a harsh and unrelenting regime was heavy and they were unable to sustain their momentum. In this context, Bevan's defection in 1957 was a devastating blow to the left. He 'no longer provided a cover for its weaknesses. Deprived of his leadership, it was revealed as an army without much leadership or political coherence.'[86]

2.5 Party discipline and the Bevanite challenge

Writing at the close of the Bevanite controversy, in 1955, Robert MacKenzie noted that Labour 'appears to lean towards a dangerously rigorous conception of party discipline which sometimes appears to resemble the Communist conception of democratic centralism.'[87] And, indeed, the thread running through our account of the leadership's response to Bevanism was its disposition to resort to discipline as its main instrument of management. Why was this?

Labour's managerial regime of the 1950s was the summation of its collective experience of the inter-war years. Social-democratic centralism was now established doctrine. It provided a frame of reference which shaped the way in which Bevanism was perceived; and it supplied a set of managerial principles which guided the leadership's response. Thus, the Bevanites were charges with a persistent disregard of majority decisions and a feckless disdain for party unity; in the words of Arthur Deakin, a stern, unbending social-democratic centralist, they flouted 'those principles and loyalties to which our movement has held so strongly throughout the whole course of its existence'.[88]

This furnished the scaffolding upon which the structure of hostility to Bevanism was built. The masonry was formed from the Party's managerial requirements in the early 1950s, as understood by the leadership. First and foremost was the need for unity – the disciplined unity of mass movement competing against a formidable rival in a tight two-party system. 'The fact is' Attlee commented 'that in political, as in other forms of warfare, the leadership must be able to rely on his troops when he is fighting his opponent. The more that discipline is self-imposed the better, but discipline there must be unless one is prepared to lose the battle.'[89]

The military analogy was significant: it was a device for exhorting the rank and file to greater effort against the common foe. But it was also a technique of control. It justified strict discipline whilst discrediting the 'carping critics' (Deakin's phrase), the egotists and power seekers who gave aid and comfort to the enemy. And it displaced the argument, from the terrain of policy (where the leadership might feel vulnerable) to that of management, where critics could be outmanoeuvred and isolated by appeals to loyalty and solidarity.

There is a natural impulse, amongst all power-holders, to enlarge their area of discretion and minimise the constraints to which they are subjected. This, we have suggested, was strengthened and lent justification by social-democratic centralism: the more ready the members were to conform to majority decisions – the less resistance they offered – the more effectively the leadership could promote the Party's collective goals.

But there were other, more specific reasons, arising out of the immediate political context, why Labour's establishment sought to free itself of constraints. Firstly, leading strategists – pre-eminently Morrison – were convinced that, in an intensely competitive two-party system, Labour's strategy must be geared to enlising middle-class floating voters. This had two corollaries. Firstly, the Party must project an image of moderation and responsibility, avoiding doctrinal pronouncements and controversial policy commitments. Secondly, to enable Labour to respond swiftly to shifts in the popular mood a fair margin of manoeuvre was required for the leadership. Mainstream thinking on policy ran parallel to this. Activist enthusiasm for further nationalisation was shared by neither the political nor industrial hierarchy. Morrison called for a period of consolidation; Gaitskell and other revisionist intellectuals wished to discard public ownership as a key Party objective; and right-wing trade union leaders signalled their satisfaction with the existing balance of the mixed economy.[90]

Thus electoral and policy goals reinforced the social-democratic centralist bias towards firm and unfettered leadership. It was precisely this that the rise of Bevanism imperilled. The Morecambe conference was a dramatic demonstration that Labour's establishment would not be given the free hand it desired. It was encumbered by commitments to extended public ownership which it greatly resented. And the deposition of senior Party statesmen, Morrison and Dalton, in favour of young and ambitious left-wingers was a disagreeable revelation of radical fervour igniting the constituencies.

The leadership was shaken and disturbed by the heady developments of Morecambe – and the impetus it afforded the left. Many right-wingers were convinced that the revolt of the constituencies – as manifested particularly in the NEC elections – had been orchestrated by an elaborate Bevanite organisation. The sense of being beleaguered steadily mounted. In 1953, Roy Jenkins, a close ally of Gaitskell, complained that CLPs 'are now opposition-minded, the Bevanites have it their own way'.[91] A year or so later Crossman recorded his 'impression that the right-wing is really getting desperate at the feeling that their support in the constituencies is slipping even further and further away and that more and more MPs are being accused by their constituency parties of betraying socialism'. They pinned the blame for this, Crossman added, on 'some terrible Mikardo organisation and [on] the New Statesman and Tribune'.[92]

We have described the NEC's efforts to tame *Tribune*. But these were not simply the product of political and personal animus. They also reflected a realistic assessment of the role *Tribune*, its Brains Trust and other left-wing papers played.

In 1954 Gaitskell had sought to persuade Cecil King, the powerful chairman of the Mirror Group, to establish a new right-wing Labour weekly, complaining 'how handicapped we were vis a vis the Bevanites because of the New Statesman and Tribune and Reynolds [News]'[93] On the face of it, this view was an extraordinary one. The circulation of the left papers was minute compared to the rest of Fleet Street which was (including Labour's own Daily Herald) unremmittingly, in some cases, ferociously hostile to the Bevanites. When directly challenged by Crossman on this point, Gaitskell riposted: 'It [i.e. *Tribune*] is read everywhere in the constituencies. It is the single most important factor which our people on the right complain of.'[94]

The future Party leader and his colleagues were not being paranoid: they had sensed that the left press, and the Brains Trust, threatened a major source of leadership control – command over internal channels of communication. Where this prevails, as Neumann has written, holders of power in a political party can stifle 'the voice of counter-propaganda and alternative solutions and the rise of a substitute elite'.[95] In this situation, rank and file discontent, however widespread, would be atomised, diffused and easily contained.

The left-wing press, with its large audience in the constituencies, and its close links with the Bevanite leadership[96] denied the Party leadership this potent source of control – to the great chagrin of Gaitskell at least.[97] They provided an alternative view of events, and propagated and focused opposition behind a clear set of rival policies. All this had the effect of rendering more taxing the leadership's efforts to assert control over the Party.

At least as important in the Bevanite drive to contest the right's supremacy were the Brains Trust, the Parliamentary group (and its more informal and discreet successor) and the so-called Bevanite 'Second Eleven'.[98]

The existence of this organisation (always more rudimentary than the right supposed) reflected a realisation that a scattered and fragmented opposition could never prevail against the Party machine. In the words of Stephen Swingler, a Bevanite MP, 'Because a mere aggregation of individual dissentients makes no impact upon the highly organised and expertly advised leadership of a modern party . . . minorities must focus their endeavours and seek expert guidance for themselves.'[99]

Ramshackle though it was, there is little doubt that Bevanite 'organisation' did much to mobilise constituency opinion and give shape and direction to rank and file dissatisfaction. *Tribune*, for example, *did* assiduously promote a left 'slate' for the NEC's constituency section.[100] Together with the *New Statesman* – both widely read by Party activists – it ensured that the leadership never dominated Labour's internal agenda.

It was understandable then, that Gaitskell should perceive the left papers as a serious 'handicap'. Together with the other elements of the Bevanite 'organisation' they *did* narrow the leadership's margin of freedom and complicate its task of impressing its will upon the Party. This added urgency to the Party establishment's determination to stamp out 'factionalism'. Pluralism within Labour's ranks may have been lively, but it was fragile. From the 1930s onwards, as we have seen, concerted resistence to the leadership was regarded with opprobrium; it might be tolerated for a while but never accepted as wholly legitimate. Crossman sought to persuade Morrison that 'if a minority isn't allowed to organise, then what you get is the dictatorship of the Executive or, respectively the Parliamentary Committee [i.e. Shadow Cabinet]. Opposition' he reasoned 'is the life-blood of democracy'. The deputy leader was unmoved: the proper place for opposition was in parliament, within the Party it could not for long be counternanced[101]

From the social-democratic centralist standpoint, organised opposition traduced established norms, injuring the sense of what was right and proper. In conversation with Crossman, Gaitskell, soon to be elected leader, exclaimed: 'Bevanism is, and only is, a conspiracy to seize the leadership for Aneurin Bevan. It is a conspiracy because it has three essentials of conspiracy, a leader in Bevan, an organisation run by Mikardo and a newspaper run by Foot . . . it's got to be cleaned up.'[102]

This perception of Bevanism as illegitimate, coupled with the common impulse of leadership to resist challenges to its position, paved the way for ruthless measures. The diffusion of social-democratic centralist principles throughout the Party rendered the recourse to sanctions more feasible. Leading Bevanites were not unaware of this. Immediately after his diary entry recording his conversation with Morrison (recounted above) Crossman reflected that 'in the long run no party can tolerate rival organised factions fighting for power . . . On no account must we suggest that we approve in principle of the [Bevanite]

Group, as part of the Constitution of the Party or as a good thing in itself.'[103]

Given the hold of social-democratic centralism upon Party opinion, the leadership could rely upon the backing or, at least, acquiescence of many who did not identify politically with it.[104]. However, commitment to these principles was not distributed evenly throughout the Party; it was most pronounced amongst trade union officials. Much of the energy and many of the initiatives behind the drive against the Bevanites emanated from such officials. Many union leaders insisted upon unflinching respect for majority decisions: this both lay at the heart of their understanding of Party democracy and (in their view) was the bond that held it together. Factionalism, Tom Williamson insisted, 'can have no place in our democratic organisation',[105]

Those sentiments were deeply ingrained in the traditions of British trade unionism: they imparted to social-democratic centralism its moral force and its broad appeal within the Party. The aversion to factionalism was part of a syndrome of values and norms which cherished loyalty, solidarity and disciplined unity in action. Confronted by the awesome power of capital, labour could only survive and advance its interests if it mobilised the dedicated loyalty of its members. 'Men who are compelled to wage class war', Crossman later reflected 'cannot worry unduly about minority rights'. Not surprisingly, seasoned veterans of the class war 'have made a dogma of majority decisions and developed a habit of obtaining these decisions without too much regard for minority opinion'.[106]

This tells only part of the story. Right-wing union leaders, like Deakin, Lawther and Williamson (and their counterparts in the Engineering Union) were as much seasoned veterans of the struggle against Communism as of the 'class war'. Factionalism, in their view, was the characteristic Communist technique to subvert properly-constituted leadership. Whilst Bevanism was the driving force of the left in the Party, within the unions the left was predominantly Communist. To some union leaders the distinction may well have been too fine to register; to others the advantages of tarring the Bevanites with the Community brush were too obvious to be missed; whilst yet others – in both wings of the movement – were convinced (in the scornful words of Jean Mann, MP) that the Bevanites were 'infiltrated and dominated by Communists'[107]: either the willing accomplices or unwitting dupes.

In fact, all the leading Bevanites (if not all their adherents in the constituencies) were resolute critics of Communism and the Soviet Union. But in the icy temperatures of the early Cold War a virulent anti-Communism featured prominently in the ideology of Labour's right (both in the Party and the unions) and nuances were easily – and conveniently – overlooked.[108] The fact that the Bevanites' main support in the unions was in those where the Communist presence was strongest was used to mobilise opinion against them. Fear of Communist penetration – partly genuine but, perhaps, partly fabricated – heightened the exasperation already felt towards organised opposition and increased the propensity to use discipline to curb it.

'By 1955' David Howell had written 'nothing seemed more secure than the control of the Party by a coalition of trade union and parliamentary loyalists'.[109] The social-democratic centralism regime had demonstrated its muscularity and effectiveness. The leadership had tightened its control over the Party, repulsed a formidable challenge and, free of restraint, was able to complete its task of converting the Party into a vehicle of moderate and modest social reform. A disheartened and demoralised left might easily have relapsed into a state of torpor and impotence – the fate of its counterpart in the SPD – if it had not been rescued by a *deus ex machina* in the shape of Frank Cousins.[110]

But the indirect consequences of these years of rigid control were somewhat different from its immediate impact. The Bevanites, politically, had survived, but the experience had been a searing one. The imposition of a harsh parliamentary discipline, the constraints, threats of explusion, the harassment of *Tribune* and the Brains Trusts, all culminating in the bid to drive Bevan from the Party – this etched itself indelibly upon the left's collective memory. The legacy was a lasting mistrust of all forms of Party discipline. In the following decades former Bevanites (in particular Crossman and Mikardo) were to make major contributions to the relaxation of Labour's managerial regime. Later still, the enduring hostility to disciplinary methods, now deeply inlaid into the left's psyche, was to powerfully shape the Party's response to a quite different phenomenon – the Trotskyist Militant Tendency.

Chapter Three

Central control and local autonomy, 1951 to the mid 1960s

3.1 Introduction

Political parties differ radically in the rigour with which leaders seek to direct and control the activities of their members. At the one extreme stands the highly regimented democratic centralist model; at the other the loosely organised and permissive American parties which make virtually no demands upon their adherents.

Labour has never tried to impose Communist-style discipline upon its members. Nevertheless – in contrast to both earlier and later decades – in the social-democratic centralist period (from the 1930s to the 1960s) the political conduct of the Party rank and file was subject to a high degree of regulation. The stringent managerial regime described in the previous chapter governed the wider pattern of relations between the centre and the membership. This chapter examines the degree of control exercised over the general political activities of local parties and individual members.

Prime responsibility for party management lay with the NEC, serviced by the Party's Head Office (known in this period by its location, Transport House). Any potential for conflict with the Parliamentary leadership this may have bred was removed by their close working relationship. An agreed division of labour gave rise to a system of integrated organisational control; in effect the NEC (and Transport House) defined its managerial role in a way that served the interests and buttressed the authority of the PLP leadership.[1] Thus, in this period, one can speak unproblematically of a Party 'centre'.

3.2 Disciplinary procedures

Until 1955, the NEC's managerial duties were discharged mainly by the Organisation Sub-Committee (although, in common with other sub-committees, its decisions had to be ratified by a full executive meeting). In October of that year[2] it was agreed to devolve disciplinary matters to a newly created Chairmen's Committee (consisting of the chairs of all sub-committes and of the Party).[3] But evidently there was some dissatisfaction with this arrangement. Three years later responsibility was returned to the Organisation Committee.[4] But the old problem of overload soon recurred and finally in 1961 it was decided to set up a three man sub-committee (comprising two senior members of the Organisation Committee, George Brown and Ray Gunter, plus the National Agent, Len Williams) which was charged with the detailed review of disciplinary cases.[5] These Sub-Committees were serviced by the National Agent's Department (NAD), whose responsibilities covered disputes and disciplinary cases, the selection of Parliamentary candidates and a very wide range of organisational matters.[6]

The majority of NEC members rarely participated in disciplinary issues, content usually to rubber-stamp the recommendations placed before them. The key decisions were taken by senior Party officials, especially the head of the NAD, the National Agent and Assistant National Agent, and the Chairman of the appropriate Committee. In addition, Hugh Gaitskell, as Party Leader, displayed a keen interest in managerial questions[7] – a practice which was deliberately not followed by his successor, Harold Wilson. Particularly influential through the period were the NAD's two senior officials, Len Williams (National Agent until 1962 when he succeeded Morgan Phillips as General Secretary) and Sara Barker (Assistant National Agent until 1962 when she replaced Williams).

3.3 Associational controls

Central regulation over the general political activities of members (either as individuals or as assembled in local parties[8]) took two main forms in this period: internal associational controls regulating the right to organise or co-ordinate opposition to the official policy and leadership of the Party; and external association controls (via the device of the Proscribed List) restricting involvement with outside political organisations.

Through this period, the NEC insisted that Labour's formal machinery catered fully for those who wished to participate in the Party's policy-making process; and, as we have seen, it always regarded with suspicion those who sought – outside the proper channels – to mobilise resistance to majority decisions (as embodied in the pronouncements of Conference and the NEC). Hence, it consistently strove to forestall all 'unauthorised' conferences – invariably defined as either unconstitutional, or disruptive of Party unity (or both).

A number of examples illustrate this. In 1952, Ealing South CLP decided to call a delegate conference of constituency parties and affiliated unions to stimulate a critical discussion of the NEC's recently published statement on foreign policy. However, the organisers were told by regional Party officials that 'it was not part of the function of a CLP to call regional conferences' and warned that if they persisted in acting unconstitutionally, the NEC would ban the meeting.[9]

A decade later two other parties earned reprimands for similar misdemeanours. In January 1962 Aberdare CLP circulated South Wales parties proposing to convene a conference on unilateralism; the following year Oxford City party invited MPs, CLPs and trade unions to a meeting on the problems of the motor industry. Both were told that they were exceeding their powers and instructed to cancel their arrangements.[10] Similarly, Margate CLP attracted a rap on the knuckles for calling a conference to rally opposition to Bevan's proposed explusion, again on the grounds that it was behaving unconstitutionally.[11]

The NEC viewed attempts by constituency parties to muster support for their resolutions to Annual Conference with no less of a jaundiced eye. This was significant since many left-wingers suspected – correctly[12] – that their efforts to influence Conference decisions were being circumvented by adroit management of the Conference agenda and compositing procedure. On at least three occasions, the Executive tried to stifle such initiatives.[13]

There was an element of bluff in this. The organisers of one of the initiatives, *Victory for Socialism* (then a small left-wing ginger group) simply ignored the NEC's warnings and held its conference – well attended by constituency and affiliated organisations.[14] The NEC chose to overlook this act of defiance, probably calculating that any benefits that might accrue from a show of strength would be more than outweighed by the ructions it might cause. Hence safety may well have lain in numbers.

The instances so far covered all concern ad-hoc initiatives for limited purposes. For two decades after the banning of the Socialist League no serious effort was made to establish a nation-wide left pressure group with a formal membership and organisation. Bevanism was primarily a Parliament-based phenomenon, albeit with an extra-Parliamentary arm in the form of the Brains Trusts and the Second Eleven. But it never evolved into a fully fledged organisation on the model of the League.[15]

The decision, in 1958, to set up such a body was mainly a reflection of the weakness and demoralisation of the left, after Bevan's defection (preceded by that of Wilson and Crossman) the previous year. The surviving 'Bevanites' (Foot, Mikardo etc.) effectively took over VFS, revamping and substantially enlarging it; for a few years it was to be the major focus of organised left-wing activity. Unlike the Bevanites, it sought to enrol left-wingers in the constituencies and unions as well as in the PLP. Plans were laid to recruit thousands of members and establish an elaborate organisational structure with local branches, a policy-making conference and an elected executive – very much along the lines of the Socialist League.[16]

The NEC reacted angrily. Once the true scale and goals of the new organisation became evident 'the fat was in the fire', as Crossman recorded in his diary. 'All at once the trade unionists there clicked back into the intolerance which had marked their behaviour throughout the whole Bevanite crisis.'[17] It was decided to despatch a monitory letter to VFS and all CLPs, and to invite the former to meet the Chairmen's Sub-Committee to reconsider their plans.[18]

Morgan Phillips accordingly wrote to Swingler expressing 'consternation' at the decision to relaunch VFS, referred to the 1946 constitutional amendment banning from affiliation to the Party any organisation 'with its own programme, principles and policy for distinctive and separate propaganda or which possessed its own branches in the constituences'[19] and hinted that VFS might be proscribed and its organisers expelled.[20]

At the subsequent meeting between the Chairmen's Sub-Committee and VFS representatives the latter were pressed on two points: the issuing of policy statements and the establishment of a national organisation with branches in the constituencies – grounds upon which (it was supposed) VFS could be proscribed. Swingler disclaimed any intention of adopting a 'separate programme' and emphasised that the group would be loosely organised with no central direction. The meeting was inconclusive: the organisers continued with their preparations, though with some modifications, whilst the NEC took no further action.[21]

The Times claimed a victory for Gaitskell in the 'battle for discipline . . . with just one heavy broadside';[22] the leader's biographer agreed that 'the threat' receded after VFS abandoned its plans to set up local branches.[23] Jo Richardson, VFS's Secretary, demurred; whilst acknowledging that the organisation backtracked somewhat, she denied that it was unduly impaired.[24] VFS did, indeed, survive and campaigned energetically for a number of years, though it is possible that it operated in a looser and less centralised manner than originally envisaged. Significantly, when a successor organisation aspiring to establish a more centralised left-wing faction, the Unity Group, was set up it operated in a semi-secretive fashion out of fear of provoking sanctions.[25]

Whatever the impact of its 'one heavy broadside', it does appear that the NEC retreated somewhat from its initial very tough stance. There were a number of reasons for this. Firstly Gaitskell, initially a proponent of a harsh line, may well have been in two minds, not wishing to imperil his new *rapprochement* with Bevan, already considerably annoyed by the leader's intransigence on the issue.[26] Secondly, the General Secretary was in fact uncertain whether it lay within the NEC's powers to proscribe VFS, and was anxious about possible legal difficulties.[27] Thirdly, the left itself was at a low ebb and, unlike the Bevanite period, posed no real threat to the established order. This diminished the case for discipline, whilst the onset of a pre-election period urged against the resumption of intra-party hostilities. Finally, VFS's concessions may well have helped tip the balance.

In 1961 the National Agent drew up a paper seeking to establish a boundary between acceptable and unacceptable types of group activity. A national organisation with branches throughout the country which advocated an opposition line over the whole range of Party policy would be 'getting near the border of what is permissible' – in others words a group like VFS was just about tolerable. But, he added, 'an organisation which also set out to secure control of the Party's machinery locally and nationally by its members acting as organised factions would be well over the line'.[28]

Williams' formulation established two criteria of acceptability: the purposes of a group and its mode of organisation. A group crossed the line of the permissible where it *both* challenged the broad thrust of Party policy *and* formed a centrally-directed body geared to gaining control over Party organisations. This view seems to have shaped the NEC's definition of the situation in 1958. Thus Gaitskell's main fear was the emergence of a disciplined, centralised faction operating throughout the constituencies.[29] The leader was giving expression here to a long-standing sentiment, nurtured in the battles against Communism and, as the fate of the Socialist League demonstrated, finding maturity in the 1930s. VFS's willingness to offer concessions on this point, however, helped assuage the NEC's greatest anxiety.[30]

3.4   The NEC and the constitution

A comparison of the 1950s and early 1960s with later decades testifies to a rigorous degree of central direction; activities like convening conferences, sustained and systematic lobbying for Conference resolutions and forming and operating well-organised pressure groups, accepted as a matter of course in the 1970s, were all subjected to varying degrees of restraint. Why?

Much of the explanation lies in the leadership's aversion to 'factional activity', already discussed.[31] Thus, time and again, the NEC objected to behaviour as 'calculated to impair the unity of the Party', seeking to overturn majority decisions or to undermine properly constituted authority. All of this, knitted together and legitimated by social-democratic centralist percepts, nourished a restrictive view of membership rights.

Yet the NEC could only exert such control over the rank and file as it was constitutionally empowered to do. It was fully aware of this – one of the Party's inheritances from its trade-union progenitors being a deep respect for the rules. Indeed, it was precisely on the grounds of constitutionality that the Executive justified its limitation of membership rights.

However, many of the activities of which it disapproved were not, in fact, expressly disallowed by the constitution. Labour's constitution, like other such texts, was often vague and ambiguous; a notable feature of the social-democratic centralist regime was its propensity – evident from the mid-1930s – to define it in a centralist manner.

We have distinguished between two types of constitutional prerogatives granted to the NEC in the field of management: formal managerial authority, as embodied in broad enabling powers, and specific regulatory rights. The former empowered the NEC to enforce the constitution and rules, to decide the 'meaning and effect of any rule or any part of this Constitution' and required it to establish, maintain and approve the rules of party organisations in every electoral unit.[32] Such enabling powers can be construed in either an extensive or restrictive manner. The NEC, in the social-democratic centralist period, preferred the extensive option.[33] This derived from the view that the constitution contained certain 'implied norms', or, in the Executive's favoured formulation 'a spirit and purpose'. As custodian of the Party rules it devolved upon the NEC to elucidate this 'spirit and purpose', hence enhancing its discretion in deciding standards of conduct appropriate for Party members. Not surprisingly, its conception of the constitutionally and politically objectionable tended from time to time to coincide.[34] The doctrine of implied norms combined with the NEC's reliance upon its broad enabling power to extend the scope of central regulation of membership activities significantly beyond that explicitly established by the constitution.

The obverse of the NEC's permissive definition of its own powers was a strict construction of those of local parties (and individual members). They were presumed not to possess rights unless these were expressly ceded to them. Thus, such activities as we have discussed above were judged to be unconstitutional, less because they breached any specific article than because they were *ultra vires* – they constituted (again in a phrase frequently used) 'usurpations of the authority' of the NEC and Conference.[35]

Not only were the rules themselves interpreted in such a way as to extend central jurisdiction over rank and file behaviour; it was also expected that they be strictly enforced. This facet of constitutional centralism was given added impetus by the bureaucratic conception of their roles held by senior officials entrusted with the task of implementing managerial decisions and, in practice, often responsible for formulating them. In this period the two key figures were Len Williams and Sara Barker. Both, at the time and subsequently, were denounced as authoritarian, and intolerant of dissent.[36] Though they were undeniably sympathetic to the dominant right-wing block, such accusations were misconceived. They were first and foremost loyal and dedicated servants of the Party, executing their tasks in what they considered to be an impartial fashion. The mainspring of their conduct was less political bias than a bureaucratic understanding of the requirements of party management. They were convinced that the imperatives of bureaucratic effectiveness – tightly rule-governed behaviour, loyal and prompt compliance with official directives – were also prime virtues in party management.

Yet – despite its avowal of impartiality – this bureaucratic ethos reinforced rather than balanced an instinctive suspicion of the left. Because its practitioners were professionally engaged in two major activities, administering the Party and organising its electoral effort, anything which detracted from these were seen as damaging. Bureaucratic apoliticism fed antipathy to the left, because left-wing mobilisation against the official policy and leadership of the Party was regarded as disruptive, impairing the smooth running of Labour's electoral machine and diverting the energies of members from their proper (organisational and administrative) tasks.

The stress of Party officials like Williams and Barker upon the rigid observance of the rules and tight regulation of conduct was fortified by other characteristically bureaucratic traits: an assumption that a hierarchical ordering of an organisation's affairs and a proper deference to duly-constituted authority maximised its capacity to achieve its goals; a distrust for any form of 'unauthorised activity' or rank and file initiatives; and a conviction that the organisation would only cohere (and, hence, operate effectively) to the extent that its rules were fully and faithfully followed. Thus it was not so much hostility to left-wingers as the logic of their own role-definitions that led senior Party officials to adopt stances which could be construed as rigid and intolerant.

3.5 The Proscribed List

As we have seen, the NEC was equipped with the power to proscribe organisations in 1929; the following year, it was decided to compile and regularly up-date a list of such organisations.[37] Since then, only one constitutional change had occurred. This was in 1946 when, in response to renewed Communist Party applications seeking affiliation, the NEC recommended a constitutional amendment. This read:

'political organisations not affiliated to or associated under a National Agreement with the Party on 1st January, 1946, having their own Programme, Principles and Policy for distinctive and separate propaganda, or possessing Branches in the Constituencies or engaged in the promotion of Parliamentary or Local Government candidates, or owing allegiance to any political organisation abroad shall be ineligible for affiliation to the party'.[38]

The intention of this new clause was to finally bolt the door on Communist attempts to gain affiliation; but it also had the effect of, for the first time, establishing specific criteria on the basis of which organisations could be proscribed and their members excluded.

By 1957 some seventy organisations had at one time or another figured on the Proscribed List; of these some thirty had either altered their names or disappeared, leaving forty listed bodies, three-quarters of which were regarded as Communist 'front' organisations.[39]

Proscription had been introduced in 1929 to protect the organisational and ideological integrity of the Party against infiltration and subversion by the CPGB. In the post-war era, whilst this threat diminished, it remained primarily an instrument to combat (perceived) Communist influence (though its secondary purpose of eradicating Trotskyist 'entryism' gained steadily in importance[40]). Hence the main grounds for the inclusion of an organisation in the List was its alleged status as a Communist 'front'.

No central unit for collecting information or monitoring the activities of Communist-inspired or pro-Soviet groups was ever established, nor was any one official ever assigned specific responsibility for these tasks.[41] Transport House leaned heavily on other organisations to supply information. The main sources were as follows:

(a) The publications of proscribed organisations themselves. These were perused for useful information (e.g. composition of their Executive Committees); records were kept of Labour Party members associated with them;
(b) Regional organisers' reports. These occasionally contained details of the political leanings and associations of constituency office-holders and other prominent members;
(c) Foreign Office material (some of which was assumed to be supplied by Special Branch);
(d) Common Cause, a right-wing body which monitored the activities of far left groups.

Organisations were added to (and, from time to time, deleted from) the list according to circumstances (e.g. a Soviet peace offensive which might spawn new groups) or in response to recommendations from Party bodies (e.g. Regional Councils) or officials. For example, in 1952 the NEC proscribed the National Committee for the Celebration of International Women's Day and the British Youth Festival on the grounds that both were connected with existing proscribed front organisations.[42]

Responsibility for compiling the list lay with the National Agent's Department and the Organisation Committee and, generally, few additions were made, and in a somewhat random fashion. A major exception occurred in 1953 when the size of the list was substantially enlarged with eighteen fresh proscriptions. They fell into two categories – the so-called 'friendship societies' (e.g. the British–Chinese Friendship Association) and 'peace groups' (e.g. the World Peace Council, Teachers of Peace).[43] What happened was rather unusual. Without consulting the NAD the International Department had submitted a report to the Overseas Sub-Committee on 'peace' and 'friendship' soieieties. In response the Sub-Committee recommended they all be proscribed. NAD officials were never told the source of the International Department's information, though they assumed it to be the Foreign Office and Special Branch.[44] There were also doubts about the value of this major expansion of the list. Whilst a large number of Party members fell under the scrutiny of Transport House, the NEC, as the years passed, became increasingly reluctant to take action against the more prominent amongst them; this had the effect of undermining the list's credibility.

What was the purpose of the list? Though the Communist Party by the 1950s was no longer interested in infiltrating its Labour rival (most of its efforts were now expended on strengthening its industrial base), with the onset of the Cold War in the late 1940's hostility towards the Soviet Union and Communism had become a *leitmotif* of the social-democratic creed.[45] So it was with the utmost mistrust that Labour reacted to Moscow's various peace campaigns in the early 1950s, in particular its efforts to woo non-Communists by encouraging the formation of 'peace' and 'friendship' societies. The NEC denounced them as 'front' organisations 'set up for the purpose of enticing non-Communists to support policies and activities in harmony with the Communist Party line'.[46] Within the context of the social-democratic centralist regime this provided adequate justification for the proscription of such groups and the expulsion of those who persisted in participating in them.

How did the list operate in practice? It is difficult to paint a full picture. Constituency parties were authorised to expel any member who belonged to a proscribed organisation. But such expulsions would only be brought to the attention of the NEC and, hence, appear in the records if the expelled appealed. Many might have acquiesced.[47]

However, it seems unlikely that really large-scale expulsions occurred, since these would have been reported in the left-wing press.

A few examples illustrate the impact of the list upon local parties. In 1952 a York Peace Group was set up, chaired by a veteran Labour Party member (Frank Smithson) and including Methodist and Anglican Ministers, Quakers, other Labour Party members and a solitary Communist. It affiliated to the West Yorkshire Federation of Peace Groups. In 1953 the Federation decided to send delegates to the Soviet-sponsored Vienna Peace Congress, whose UK organiser was the proscribed British Peace Committee. Shortly after, Smithson spoke at a conference convened by the West Yorkshire Federation and promptly received a missive from Labour's Yorkshire Regional Organiser (John Anson) instructing him to sever his connection with the York group. He refused and was expelled by his CLP.[48]

According to *Tribune*, a total of 221 people were expelled in Yorkshire because of their membership of peace groups. These groups were often affiliated to the West Yorkshire Federation but not to the (proscribed) British Peace Committee.[49] The 1953 NEC Report noted that the Federation 'supported' the British Peace Committee but was not itself proscribed. At the request of Labour's Yorkshire Regional Council, the Executive decided to remedy the omission by placing the Federation on the list.[50]

The episode is revealing for the light it sheds on the NEC's managerial practices. As the NEC's account obliquely conceded, the expulsions were based on doubtful constitutionality: in effect, members were disciplined for belonging to (non-proscribed) local groups, affiliated to a (non-proscribed) federal body which was alleged to 'support' a proscribed organisation. The actual constitutional grounds for expulsion are *membership* of a proscribed organisation. Nor was the episode an isolated one. In February 1953 the National Agent reported that several constituencies had excluded members who had *attended* the Vienna Peace Congress – measures which the Executive thereupon endorsed.[51] The following year a councillor (who had attended a conference in the USSR as part of a delegation arranged by the proscribed National Assembly of Women) was expelled by her local party (Bolsover) for refusing to undertake not to *speak at meetings* organised by banned groups.[52]

These managerial practices were justified by the NEC's doctrine of constitutional centralism. The latitude this afforded for central regulation could also be used to sort out troublesome parties. In 1951 Hull Labour Party established contact with (the non-proscribed) Hull Peace Council. John Anson, the Yorkshire Regional Organiser (incorrectly) advised that association with the Peace Council was incompatible with Labour Party membership. The NEC endorsed Anson's action and (probably at his instigation) decided to mount an enquiry into the Hull party.[53]

The enquiry report, submitted by the National Agent, drew attention to pronounced 'fellow-travelling' influence in the affairs of Hull Labour Party. The NEC used the opportunity provided by the investigation to institute measures designed to combat this influence and to impose a (post-facto) ban on Hull Peace Council.[54]

The NEC's capacity to restrict the propagation of views to which it took exception was undoubtedly enhanced by this expansive interpretation of its disciplinary powers.[55] But the incidence of proscriptions and expulsions was very uneven. A quite disproportionate number occurred in one region – Yorkshire. This may well have reflected the priorities, energy and influence of the Regional Organiser, John Anson.[56] This uneven incidence suggests that Labour Party members who engaged in what was considered the dubious activity of consorting with bodies promoted by or associated with the Communist Party stood a differential risk of incurring penalties for it. Further, whilst the NEC was generally prepared to sanction disciplinary action, it rarely initiated it; this was left to local parties, perhaps encouraged by regional officials (who certainly would have been involved at an early stage).

Reliance upon local initiative reflected the absence of an efficient and properly resourced national control and monitoring system.[57] This inevitably diminished the value of the list. This weakness was coupled with others. Firstly, it was difficult to keep track of pro-Soviet organisations given their propensity to dissolve and reappear in a slightly different guise. More seriously – as our examples indicate – only relatively obscure individuals were caught in the net: the Party was rather more reluctant to expel members who achieved a certain prominence in either the industrial or political wings of the movement.

Some Party leaders and officials chafed at this, and felt that the law should bear equally upon the famous and the obscure alike. They were soon to be given their opportunity.

3.6 Three peers and a canon: the decline of the Proscribed List

Whatever the defects of the Proscribed List, the NEC – perhaps through institutional inertia – made no effort throughout the 1950s to overhaul its workings. But a re-appraisal did take place early in the next decade. After the relative tranquillity of the late 1950s, the Party was plunged into the turbulent controversy over nuclear weapons policy. Fresh from his victory over the unilateralists at the 1961 Conference, Gaitskell resolved to impose tighter discipline over the Party.[58] The energetic George Brown was elected to the key post of Chairman of the Organisation Committee, eager to exploit more fully its managerial powers.[59]

In 1962 the World Council of Peace convened a World Disarmament Congress to be held in Moscow in July. Arrangements in Britain were handled by the British Peace Council, like the World Council a proscribed body. Amongst the sponsors were Earl (Bertrand) Russell, the eminent philosopher; Canon Collins, like Russell a leading force in CND; Lord Chorley, and the distinguished social scientist Baroness Wootton. All were veteran Labour Party members.

George Brown, the new Chairman of the Organisation Committee, strongly supported by Sara Barker,[60] leapt at the opportunity to enforce the Proscribed List more strictly. Under their prompting the Organisation Committee resolved to take a tough line – to demonstrate that even the eminent would not be spared the rigours of Party discipline. At the Committee's behest, the General Secretary wrote to the sponsors (except Baroness Wootton who was originally overlooked) reminding them that Party rules forbade them from being a member of 'or taking part in the work of' proscribed organisations and warning them – on pain of expulsion – to terminate their sponsorship by the next NEC Meeting (i.e. the following week).[61]

Replies were received from Chorley and Russell.[62] The former wrote that he was not a sponsor of the Congress, though he supported its aims, and was unaware that any of the organisations concerned were proscribed. Russell's letter, in contrast, was terse and defiant: 'I am a speaker at the meeting in Moscow to which you allude and I intend to remain so. You are, no doubt, within your rights in objecting to a member of the Labour Party speaking at this Conference and you will, of course, take whatever action you think fit.'[63]

But Brown and his supporters had over-reached themselves. At the May NEC, in a 'powerful and moving' speech, Richard Crossman queried whether an ultimatum threatening expulsion was the most sensitive way of treating 'the world's most eminent social-democratic philosopher' during his 90th birthday celebrations'.[64] Most Executive members acknowledged the crassness of its Sub-Committee's behaviour and it was agreed, at Crossman's suggestion, to interview the four individuals before taking further action.[65] Interviews were held the following month with Lord Chorley and Canon Collins, conducted by several senior Party officers. Chorley explained that he had never intended to sponsor the Congress so the issue in his case was speedily resolved. The case of Canon Collins was more difficult but eventually a face-saving compromise was agreed.[66] Russell, however, was in no mood to compromise. He wrote laconically that since he did not intend to withdraw his sponsorship he saw no point in attending an interview.[67]

At this point, the National Agent discovered a way of extricating the Party from its mounting embarrassment. Enquiries had disclosed that

Russell's constituency party had not issued him a 1962 membership card. This neatly resolved the problem. As 'Earl Russell was not currently a member of the Labour Party', the Organisation Committee reported 'no action is necessary'.[68]

But the Sub-Committee's solution was too transparently a pretext for ridding the Party of Russell without incurring the public odium of expelling him. As was well known, it was not at all unusual for members not to renew their subscription until well into the year.[69] Nevertheless, opinion on whether to exclude Britain's most renowned living philosopher – for forty years a staunch critic of the Soviet Union – was evenly balanced. It was finally agreed, by twelve votes to ten, to exonerate him because his transgression was 'an isolated case'.[70]

There can be little doubt that the main reason for the NEC's retreat was the storm of opposition it aroused; its astonishing clumsiness in threatening highly-respected and long-serving Party members with expulsion offended liberal opinion. The fact that two were also prominent CND supporters also infuriated many constituency activists. But there was another reason which caused the Executive to hesitate.

Here we must turn to the case of Lady Wootton. She had declined her invitation to attend an interview pleading a family illness. But a letter to Hugh Gaitskell – circulated to the Organisation Committee – conveyed her real reason. It effectively threw a grenade into the proceedings. After defending a policy of encouraging a dialogue between Communists and non-Communists she added that she could 'find nothing in the Labour Party constitution' which precluded co-operating with, as against membership of, proscribed organisations; hence the NEC had no constitutional warrant for expelling her.[71]

The NEC backtracked and decided to drop the case against her.[72] But her intervention raised a much wider issue, for (as we have seen) the Executive had been routinely expelling[73] individuals for *associating* with rather than being *members of* proscribed groups. The constitutionality (and, hence, lawfulness) of this procedure was now in question.

Evidently, the lesson the NEC drew from the fiasco over Russell and his co-sponsors was that its own powers were inadequate. It decided to seek a tightening of the rules and proposed a constitutional amendment which would incorporate into the constitution the established practice of banning not only membership of but 'association with' proscribed organisations.[74]

The overtones of the McCarthyism from which the USA had only recently escaped were so strong that the left (and middle-of-the-road opinion) responded furiously. *Tribune* exhorted Conference to 'overturn the leadership's vicious new doctrine'.[75] Left-wing NEC members (Castle, Driberg, Jennie Lee and Mikardo) denounced the attempt to further stifle the rights of dissidents, whilst Crossman – now occupying a centrist position – launched a scathing attack in his regular column in *The Guardian*.[76]

The debate at Conference was stormy. Speaking on behalf of the NEC, Brown defended the amendment as necessary to resist Communist and Trotskyist infiltration and to help the Party protect naive and gullible people from being led astray by subversive elements.[77] The speech was punctuated by hostile interruptions. Most critical speakers were left-wing trade unionists, including Frank Cousins, the powerful and forceful leader of the transport workers. But the most damaging intervention came from a right-wing MP and QC, Elwyn Jones. He pointedly noted that only three countries had included 'guilt by association' clauses in their legal codes – Nazi Germany, the Soviet Union and South Africa. He recalled that, as a judge at the Nuremberg trials (of Nazi war criminals) he and his colleagues had rejected the doctrine. He concluded, damningly, by condemning the amendment as 'a terrible affront to liberty'. The reference back was then moved – and carried by 3,497,00 votes to 2,793,000. The words of the Party Chairman (Harold Wilson) announcing the result were 'lost in a tremendous ovation'.[78]

A remarkable episode had ended with an astonishing result. Never before had the NEC been snubbed by Conference on a major constitutional and disciplinary issue. Why did it happen this time?

Probably the hamfisted way in which the NEC (and, in particular, George Brown) had handled the Russell affair had already alienated many who were normally leadership supporters. It now seemed to be compounding its errors by seeking to arrogate yet more powers to itself. Secondly, this was undoubtedly one of the rare occasions when the debate at Conference had a profound effect on the outcome. Elwyn Jones' persuasive speech had been matched by aggressive and unconvincing performances from Brown and Charles Pannell MP. At least one union, USDAW, switched sides after the debate and the voting figures suggest that other traditionally loyalist unions must have followed suit.[79] Finally, there was an element of bad timing. After two bitterly divisive conferences, the 1962 Conference aimed at raprochement as a more conciliatory Hugh Gaitskell tried to mend fences with his left-wing critics; in such a climate the constitutional amendment must have struck some delegates as reeking too much of one final bid to settle old scores.

3.7 Appraisal

What was the overall impact of the NEC attempts to constrain rank and file activity? Associational controls did undoubtedly restrict the mobilisation of dissent. This is seen most notably in the case of VFS which was inhibited in its choice of organisational methods to promote the left-wing cause. It is, however, doubtful whether this had a major effect on the balance of forces within the Party; after the decline of Bevanism the position of the left was so weak that the leadership had no real need to resort to disciplinary measures to thwart any challenge to its rule.

The most potent single weapon in the NEC's disciplinary armoury was the Proscribed List. Yet its utility in achieving its professed goals was questionable. Undoubtedly, a small number of individuals – enthusiasts for the Soviet Union, pacifists and others – who had the temerity to challenge Cold War orthodoxies were punished. But these were the lesser fry. However, it did have a certain value in entrenching right-wing control of the party. The philosophy underpinning it – that co-operation with Communists was an illicit activity – encouraged those (including, at times, Hugh Gaitskell) who blurred the boundary between 'fellow-travelling' and genuine dissent over foreign policy in order to discredit left-wing critics. More specifically, involvement with a proscribed organisation always figured in the dossiers the NAD maintained of suspect left-wingers and influenced office recommendations when such individuals applied for membership of the 'B List' of available parliamentary candidates or were seeking NEC endorsement for their candidates.[80]

Proscription came to epitomise for the left the regime of intolerance within the Party in this period, and one of the left's key managerial priorities was to secure its abolition. This was finally achieved in 1973.[81] The importance of this step has, however, been exaggerated by both its supporters and opponents[82] for the major legacy of the Russell *imbroglio* was to greatly diminish its effectiveness.

The episode is redolent with irony. What began as a bid by George Brown and Sara Barker in particular, to tighten Labour's managerial reins had the effect of loosening them. If the attempt to expel Russell and Collins had succeeded (and if the constitutional amendment had been approved) then one besetting weakness of the list – that it ensnared only small game – might have been remedied. A precedent would have been set, and the crime of 'association with Communists' may have become an affective instrument (as happened in the SPD) for suppression left-wing dissent.[83] Instead the double rebuff to the NEC helped discredit the principle of proscription. Any NEC member who henceforth urged disciplinary measures for participating in the work of banned organisations was mocked by left-wingers for risking 'another Bertie Russell'.[84] Indeed there were no further proscriptions for two decades after 1962.[85] The lessening of tension between West and East, and between Social Democracy and Communism, also reduced the incentive to pursue Party members involved in proscribed organisations. As the 1960s wore on, increasing numbers of prominent left-wingers filled posts in proscribed organisations; no steps were taken against them.[86] Several years before it was abolished, the Proscribed List had ceased to be effective as an instrument of control.

Chapter Four

Adjudication, 1951 to the late 1960s

4.1 The NEC as adjudicator: The constitutional position

In any political party, disputes are bound to occur over the meaning and application of the rules; these may take the form of jurisdictional conflicts between party units or of disagreements over the propriety and appropriateness of disciplinary action. As in the state at large, parties require an organ to investigate and deliver binding judgments on such matters. Most socialist parties have established a separate body to perform this quasi-judicial function. However, the Labour Party had chosen to assign it to its chief executive organ, the NEC.

One can distinguish between two judicial tasks: adjudication in disputes and acting as an appeals court. In both cases, the NEC played the pre-eminent role. It is empowered by the constitution to adjudicate in disputes between Party organisations.[1] The more important task, however, is the second. General Committees of CLPs were required by their rules 'to take all necessary steps to safeguard the Constitution, programme, principles and policy of the Labour Party'. Where this involved the punishment or expulsion of individuals or organisations the latter had the right to appeal to the NEC, which was empowered 'to confirm, vary or reverse' any decision taken by the constituency party.[2] Similarly any member of a Labour group (i.e. Labour representatives on local councils) deprived of the whip for violation of Standing Orders had the right to appeal to the NEC 'whose decision shall be final'.[3] For simplicity of exposition we shall use the term 'adjudication' to refer to both these quasi judicial tasks.

To relieve the load upon the NEC, Regional Organisers were expected to keep in regular contact with local parties and Labour groups and to be fully appraised of any developments which might cause difficulties: a major part of their work was to placate and reconcile aggrieved parties, hence lessening the use of discipline as a method of resolving disputes.[4]

Where an appeal was lodged with the NEC, or where a local settlement of a dispute was not possible, then some national response was required. This could take a variety of forms: enquiries might be conducted by the Regional Organiser, by a panel drawn from the Regional Executive Committee (REC), by the National or Assistant National Agent or by a team of NEC Members.[5] In all cases reports were submitted to the appropriate committee of the NEC (Organisation or Chairmen's) though additional documentation might be appended by the Regional Organiser to the National Agent for his or her eyes alone.[6] Reports always contained a judgment upon the merits of the case and recommendations. These had to be approved by the sub-committee and ultimately the NEC; in this period it was rare for them to be amended in any significant way.

The form of an enquiry took depended upon the seriousness of the case and upon prior involvement by Regional Organisers.[7] Enquiry teams were almost invariably serviced by a regional or national official. He (or she) would draft the report and then submit it to other members of the team for their comments; if drafted by a regional official it would (prior to being placed before the appropriate NEC sub-committee) be perused by the National Agent who might contact the Regional Organiser for clarificiation.[8]

Disputes precipitating disciplinary measures and appeals to the Executive were caused by a wide range of factors: personality clashes, the behaviour of troublesome or idiosyncratic individuals, parochial disagreements as well as more serious differences over policy or jurisdictions. Many of them were of a type that could occur in any organisation; a substantial majority lacked any significant political dimension.[9] Far from enquiry teams scouring the countryside for left-wing rebels – as some critics alleged – the bulk of their work was prosaic and politically uncontentious.[10]

In the rest of this chapter we shall focus upon the minority of disciplinary cases which raised significant political issues. These fall into three categories: discord between local parties and Labour groups, discipline within local parties and discipline within Labour groups – categories which, as we shall see, are analytically distinct but which often, in practice, overlapped. We shall review each of these in turn and then explore in detail two major disputes (in Liverpool and Nottingham Labour Parties).

4.2 Disputes between Labour groups and local parties

Labour membership on local councils expanded rapidly after 1918, but no immediate attempt was made to establish a framework of rules governing relations between local parties and their elected representatives. However, throughout the 1920s, there were a series of disputes between the two as Labour groups resisted efforts to subject them to outside Party control. 'Party headquarters were besieged with requests for help to resolve such difficulties.'[11] In 1930, in response to a particularly bitter clash in Liverpool (a harbinger of the future) the NEC, at Morrison's urging, set up a sub-committee to devise Model Standing Orders to regulate the relationship between Party and group. These were drafted largely by Herbert Morrison and approved at the 1930 Annual Conference.[12] They were subsequently amplified by a 'Memorandum on Labour Groups in Local Authorities'.[13] Together they set up a structure of rules defining the roles, rights and responsibilities of Party units operating in the sphere of municipal government.

The local party[14] was given the right to determine 'election policy' but responsibility for taking decisions on 'matters coming before the Council' was assigned to the group, which, furthermore, had the right to decide its own policy.[15] What was the relationship between election and group policy? According to the Memorandum, 'Group policy is determined with the general framework of the election policy'; and it adds that 'questions of practical application continually arise, and not infrequently decisions have to be taken on matters not specifically covered by the election policy. On all such matters it is the definite responsibility of the Labour group to take decisions'.[16]

These loosely worded rules were wide open to differing interpretations. The parallel with the long-running controversy over the powers and jurisdiction of the Party's Conference and its Parliamentary representatives is self-evident. Precisely how much latitude did the group have in interpreting and implementing election policy? What sanctions, if any, were available to the party if it felt that election policy was being spurned?

Where relations between party and group were generally harmonious, differences could easily be smoothed over. Where they were not, where the two were separated by political divergences, then the potential for a double clash – over both policy and jurisdiction – was obvious.

Little research has been done in this area, but the available evidence suggests that major disagreements between a party and its elected municipal representatives were much rarer in the 1950s and 1960s than in the last decade.[17] Nevertheless, given the sheer number of Labour groups, incidents of conflict were inevitable from time to time. Where the conflicts were serious, or where the use of sanctions gave rise to appeals, the NEC would become involved.

In this period, Executive adjudication followed a consistent pattern. The Memorandum on Local Groups contained (for the benefit of over-enthusiastic local parties) the minatory reminder that 'attempts to control local administration from outside and to undermine the public

responsibilities of Councillors have proved disastrous'.[18] This was inte-
preted to mean that any attempt by local parties to enforce their policy
preferences (whether or not these had been formally incorporated into
the election manifesto) was improper. For example, in 1956 the Slough
Borough Labour Group and Eton and Slough CLP clashed over housing
policy. The latter passed a resolution denouncing the (ruling) Labour
group for violating election policy and demanding that it alter course.
The NEC enquiry report (written by Len Williams, the National Agent)
was unambiguous: the resolution was 'an attempt to dictate to the
Labour Group and completely out of order'.[19] The following decade the
Birmingham Borough Labour Party complained that the Labour council
had reversed accepted housing policy, without any consultation. The
NEC riposted that, whilst the borough party had the right to draw up
election policy, it was for the group to decide its policy in council.[20]
This came close to saying that it was for a Labour council to judge what
items in the election manifesto could be implemented and which could
not.

Local parties lacked any direct means to compel groups to carry out
election policy. But they were by no means impotent; indeed they were
rather better placed than the national Party to exert pressure on elected
representatives. This was due to two significant differences in the
procedure for the selection of candidates. Firstly – in contrast with the
Parliamentary procedure – sitting councillors enjoyed no automatic
right of reselection; they had to be selected anew before each electoral
contest. Secondly, only members of the official list or panel of local
government candidates were eligible for selection. The party was responsible for the composition of the panel. The General Committee of
the appropriate Party unit (Borough, Central, Constituency, etc.) was
empowered 'to refuse endorsement of any nomination [to the panel] if it
thinks fit'; further it was given the right to make a 'final decision' if a
selection dispute occurred.[21] In other words, sitting councillors could
be removed if they lost the confidence of either their ward parties (by
deselection) or the borough party (via exclusion from the panel).

Where a councillor was deselected by his ward, there was (if the proper
procedures had been followed) little he could do.[22] Much more contentious was the use by the local party of membership of the panel as a lever
to influence the composition or behaviour of the group. This the NEC
was not prepared to tolerate. Thus in 1956 Eton and Slough CLP
resolved to incorporate opposition to a differential rent scheme into the
next statement of election policy and to exclude from the panel anyone
who refused to accept it. The Slough Labour Group appealed to the NEC,
which pronounced the CLP's resolutions unconstitutional 'as they were
an attempt to influence Group policy by an implied threat against
members . . . seeking re-election'.[23]

The dropping of councillors from the panel for political reasons was a very rare occurrence until the mid 1950s when bitter differences over the introduction of differential rent schemes prompted a number of local parties to use membership of the panel as an instrument to influence council policy. In 1957 Jack Cooper (a senior GMWU official) formally complained to the NEC that councillors were being evicted for political reasons rather than for performance and urged that this practice be stopped. The NEC responded by passing a resolution 'recommending to local Labour Parties that retiring Councillors should not be omitted from the panel of candidates without their consent or without very good reason'.[24] ('Recommendations' of the NEC were in practice treated as binding directives.)

This resolution was wholly consistent with custom and practice. The use of the panel to strengthen the party's hand vis-a-vis the group, would, the Executive held, upset the 'constitutional relationship' between the two bodies[25]. In Morrison's words, any attempt to subject councillors to outside direction would demean them to the level of 'automata, robots, instruments of a body which is not elected by the people' and reduce local democracy to 'a farce'.[26]

For this reason the NEC insisted upon reinstating councillors to the panel removed for 'political' reasons.[27] Yet it is not at all evident that it was within its powers to do so. As the NAD itself acknowledged, councillors could not, under the rules, be afforded the same protection as MPs.[28] Indeed the rules stipulated that the local party was empowered to refuse endorsement of a nominee to the panel if it so chose; no facility (at the time) existed for an appeal to a higher body. Rather than formally modifying the rules, the NEC – in line with its commitment to constitutional centralism – chose to invoke 'the spirit and intention of the Rules' when 'advising' local parties not to disregard the claims of councillors seeking re-election.[29]

4.3 Constituency discipline

By the 1950s steady electoral advance in local government over two decades had converted many urban councils into Labour bastions. The leadership of ruling Labour groups acquired considerable power and prestige, not only within the Council Chamber but also in the local party. Often councillors occupied key positions in the local party organisation, which effectively fell under the sway of the group leadership. This gave rise to group-based local establishments which became an increasingly marked feature of Labour politics in its urban heartlands.[30]

Mastery over the local party machine helped these establishments repel any challenge to their ascendency by placing the disciplinary powers of constituency organisations at their service. The Party nationally only became involved when the disciplined appealed to the NEC. Such cases were uncommon but, when they occurred, the Executive consistently interceded (except where serious procedural irregularities had occurred) on behalf of the local establishment.[31]

In this period, the Labour Party in Islington precipitated more NEC enquiries than in any other area. The local establishment operated a particularly rigorous disciplinary regime which ensured a steady flow of appeals to the Executive. The Islington party was, then, not typical; but an examination of NEC adjudication affords a valuable insight into the national Party's attitude to the use of discipline as an instrument of control in local Labour politics.

Labour control of Islington in this period was complete, holding virtually all council seats. The party, in turn, was dominated by a small clique – bound together by ties of family and friendship as well as ideological affinity – based upon the group leadership.[32] By the late 1950s a pattern of decay which was to plague many other Labour strongholds in the following decade was already well advanced in Islington – low, and steadily dwindling membership, political inertia and the ossification of party structures.[33]

This rendered local establishments vulnerable to 'take-overs' by eager new recruits. As a barrier against this, the Islington parties (especially Islington East) operated a system of membership screening. The beliefs, affiliations and past activities of applicants (which included those who were simply transferring their membership from other CLPs) were carefully scrutinised to check upon any political waywardness or unreliability. Thus, in 1958, eight applicants (two already members in other constituencies) were refused admission largely, it would appear, because of their involvement with CND, and appealed to the NEC.

East Islington was well known – notorious, its critics would aver – for its lack of enthusiasm for new members. Those who were sufficiently keen to actually seek out membership – often a time-consuming enterprise in the Labour Party – were, in particular, regarded with suspicion, and 'subjected to intensive investigation and even interrogation by Party officers'.[34] This was ostensibly because the CLP had, in the past, only with difficulty averted a Trotskyist take-over.[35] In fact, it was not from this quarter that the party feared infiltration; the main danger appeared to be a group of CND stalwarts[36] – a dubious ground for denying entry since CND was a proscribed organisation. So what was the NEC's response?

After some hesitation – and under the prodding of the East Islington party and its MP, Eric Fletcher – the NEC confirmed the exclusion of four members and deferred the entry of another two for six months.[37] Two of the four were pacifists – both were practising Christians and hostile to the far left.[38] They were excluded on the grounds that their admittance would precipitate 'a recurrence of trouble and dissension' within the CLP.[39] Precisely what this meant was never specified but both the local party and the NEC seemed primarily disturbed by their enthusiasm for CND.[40] The two others were (in addition to their CND activities) supporters of the Trotskyist journal *Socialist Review*. Their exclusion was upheld on the grounds of association with a journal which organised activities designed to promote 'a policy which differs from that of the Labour Party'[41] – though it should be noted *Socialist Review* had never been proscribed.

Two points are worth making here. Firstly, the grounds upon which the exclusions were upheld were very broad indeed. East Islington's main objections to the applications were, it seems likely, primarily motivated by the threat they posed to the ruling establishment. The NEC exercised its discretion in interpreting the constitution to the full in finding suitable grounds for approving the CLP's action. Secondly, the four were never informed of the charges levelled against them, or given the right to defend themselves. As Kingsley Martin remarked 'it is almost impossible for the accused to find out what is wrong, or to get a proper hearing. Isn't it time for Labour to adopt rules which British justice accepts for the protection of personal liberties?'[42]

4.4 Discipline in Labour groups

Every Labour group is expected to operate in accordance with the Model Standing Orders drawn up in 1930 (and hardly changed until the 1980s), though amendments are permitted if approved by the NEC. Just as strains between the extra-Parliamentary Party and the PLP have their equivalent locally in friction between Party and group, so too do the disciplinary problems of the PLP have their echo in council groups.

Standing Orders for Labour groups were in fact rather more stringent than those for the PLP. Thus members were 'expected not to *speak* or vote at meetings of the Council in opposition to the decisions of the Labour Group, unless the Group had decided to leave the matter to a free vote'.[43] A conscience clause allowed councillors to abstain but, as in the PLP, this was confined to a narrow range of issues (religion, temperance etc.').[44] In other matters, group members were subject to tighter restrictions than their Parliamentary counterparts: they were only allowed to table resolutions or amendments at council meetings if they had secured authorisation from the group or its officers.[45]

Acceptance of Standing Orders was required of all group members. The group was empowered to withdraw the whip (i.e. expel) any member who violated the Standing Orders, although only after consultation with the executive of the appropriate Party organisation (and subject to an appeal to the NEC).[46]

If construed rigidly, the Standing Orders were a recipe for a very exacting disciplinary regime. The NEC was itself aware of this and recommended a measure of 'elasticity' to take account of local circumstances.[47] This reflected the Party's unwillingness to impose a uniform pattern of discipline: Groups were given a considerable degree of autonomy in deciding how (within the framework of Standing Orders) to organise themselves.

In practice, variations in group discipline went far beyond differences in 'elasticity'. Thus, some groups opted for a lenient interpretation of Standing Orders: no item before council was subject to a whip unless the Group specifically decided.[48] Others adhered to a stricter interpretation: every group decision was whipped unless it was decided to the contrary (although here there were significant variations in the propensity to penalise members for breaking the whip).[49] Given the limited literature on the subject it is impossible to generalise about the overall pattern of discipline. It was never as rigid as Labour's opponents claimed at the time; nevertheless, the sheer number of appeals considered by the NEC suggests that a considerable number of groups did operate a fairly stringent regime.

It is important to distinguish between the pattern of local conflicts in this period and in more recent years. Protracted disputes between rival left-right factions over a range of key policy issues (such have occurred since the late 1970s in Manchester, Bristol, Coventry, Newcastle and many London boroughs)[50] were very unusual; the ascendency of the existing group leadership was very rarely challenged or endangered.[51] Most 'rebellions' involved only a handful of councillors (or an isolated individual), were conducted over a single or a narrow range of issues, were episodic and did not reflect entrenched political or factional cleavages. Many acts of indiscipline – as recorded by enquiry reports – sprang from personal grievances and antagonisms. Where the cause *was* difference over issues, the issue was often of a highly parochial, sometimes trivial nature which yet generated bitter animosities. Often the disputes were over matters which would plague any voluntary organisation which sought to instill a measure of order and harmony within a highly diverse membership – amongst whom the truculent, the obstinate and the eccentric were always present.[52]

Nevertheless, a significant minority of cases did reflect disagreement over policy and raised important issues of group discipline. NEC adjudication in such cases were shaped by four major principles, largely derived from social-democratic centralism.

The core principle was majority rule. 'It would be a failure of a Group, Sara Barker wrote 'if after discussion and decision individual members of the Group failed to accept majority decisions.'[53] Binding group decisions were commended as the most democratic way of formulating policy. Coupled with this accent on majority decision-making was an emphasis upon the collective character of representation. Labour councillors were elected primarily because they fought under the Party's colours and were, as a body, collectively responsible to the electorate for their actions.

This principle was (in this period) widely accepted in the Party. The question of how far it should extend – that is the degree to which the behaviour of councillors should be subject to group decisions – was more contentious. The NEC view was that members should be bound by group decision only on matters of policy, not of administrative detail. In practice the distinction between the two was blurred, leaving much room for interpretation. The NEC's preference – here we reach its second principle of adjudication – was for a restrictive interpretation. In Sara Barker's words: 'There are limits to the use of the free vote. Even matters which superficially do not affect Party policy may have policy implications.'[54] Thus, on a range of issues which did not automatically fall under the rubric of 'policy' the NEC agreed that members should be bound by group decisions.[55]

The third principle was respect for the rules and for the authority of the group and its officers. This reflected two social-democratic centralist motifs: firstly, a stress on the importance of formal rules in maintaining the effectiveness of its decision-making procedures and, secondly, a faith in the virtues of firm leadership.[56] The viability of the group as a force for change was maximised by strict adherence to its rules and loyalty to its leadership. Thus, whilst the NEC often felt that disciplinary penalties were unduly harsh, it was loath to appear to endorse any infringement of the rules (however minor), or any defiance of the authority of the group. Misdemeanours such as speaking in council against a group decision and tabling a motion in council without consulting the group were deemed to be serious breaches of Standing Orders.[57] Whilst the NEC frequently lessened the *severity* of disciplinary action taken in such cases, it almost invariably affirmed its *validity* as a means of ensuring compliance with group rules and decisions.[58]

This brings us to the fourth of the NEC's adjudicating principles: its emphasis upon discipline as a mechanism for settling internal disagreements and maintaining group cohesion. As we have already observed, all parties must seek a reconciliation between the need for unity and effective decision-making on the one hand, and the rights of minorities on the other. Consistent with its social-democratic centralist outlook, the NEC, in its adjudicating role, swung the balance in favour of the former. This is reflected in its judgement in two areas.

The first concerned the circumstances in which the use of discipline was regarded as an appropriate method of resolving disputes. The NEC

adduced two main criteria: the importance of the issue and the defend-
ant's past record. Where the issue was a major item of policy (most
frequently housing) and the appellant was a persistent offender then the
NEC would approve the loss of the whip and (in some cases) expulsion
from the Party.[59] Other criteria were regarded as of little or no relevance.
For example, the Executive was prepared to endorse disciplinary actions
without regard to the size of a Labour group's majority: it sanctioned
withdrawals of the whip in situations where Labour held virtually all
seats on the council, hence where its rule was not at all endangered and
where its own 'backbenchers' might constitute the only source of
criticism.[60]

Similarly, the NEC was not impressed by the defence that rebel
councillors, in defying the group, were adhering to the election policy,
or that they enjoyed the support of the local party. This was to be a
frequent and painful source of contention in later years, but relatively
rare in this period. One notable exception was in Birmingham in 1963.
Eleven councillors defied the whip and voted against a rent increase.
They were backed by the Borough Labour Party who noted that they
(and not the group) were following election policy. Nevertheless, eight
who refused to sign an unqualified apology were deprived of the whip.[61]
The subsequent enquiry – conducted at a rather higher level than usual
by Ray Gunter, Chairman of the Organisation Committee, and Sara
Barker, the National Agent – dismissed the appellants' defence, on the
grounds that the group was wholly within its rights to decide its own
policy and recommended the restoration of the whip only if they signed
a rather abject apology.[62]

The second area concerned the range of actions considered to be
sanctionable. Restrictions upon minorities, or dissident individuals,
went beyond the way they cast their vote in council. Councillors were
also expected to desist from publicly criticising a Labour council in the
media or elsewhere.[63] Islington, as usual, offers an interesting – though
not necessarily typical – instance. The Executive agreed to re-admit to
the Party a councillor expelled for vociferous public attacks on the
council's housing policy (which the enquiry report conceded was 'not a
good one') but only if he specifically undertook to refrain from criticising 'either the Group or the Party in public through the medium of the
press, TV, public platform statements or any other medium'.[64]

Sara Barker spelt out the ultimate justification for this accent on strict
group discipline. 'Labour Groups on local authorities are the instruments used to express and achieve Labour's policy on local Government
issues. Labour Councillors having been elected to carry out a declared
policy should work as a team and not as individuals.'[65] From this
perspective unity and discipline were indispensable ingredients for a
reforming party which sought to utilise the resources of local

government to promote its goals.

But, as a left-wing council leader argued, 'the rigid enforcement of Standing Orders can have the effect of stultifying discussion, silencing opposition and inhibiting a member from questioning those entrusted with special responsibility'.[66] Indeed an analysis of NEC adjudicating decisions discloses a tendency to view persistent dissent as irresponsibility or a congenital incapacity to conform to majority opinion. Definitions of sound and reasonable behaviour sometimes appeared to place not only the truculent and egotistical beyond the pale, but also the younger and more radical spirits who bewailed the circumspection and lack of enterprise of many Labour-controlled councils.

The enthusiasm for discipline is understandable where a political party is embarking upon an ambitious programme of reform and encountering stiff resistance from its opponents. The reality was often different. Bulpitt's analysis of local politics in this period shows that the parties were rarely divided over major issues, and that Labour groups did not envisage themselves primarily as vehicles for wide-ranging social reforms; indeed policy formulation was generally given a low priority.[67] He concluded that 'parties appear to want to practise political restraint, to avoid really divisive issues'.[68]

The reality, certainly by the 1960s, was that many Labour councils, particularly in the Party's strongholds where Conservative representation was minimal, had themselves become transmuted into the establishment. Perhaps savouring a status and perquisites which their manual occupations could never offer, Labour councillors in those areas were sometimes tempted to employ the disciplinary weapon to curb more troublesome and restless colleagues who threatened to disturb the tranquil flow of their lives. Where this happened – as classically in Islington[69] – NEC intervention provided a further prop to sustain ruling right-wing establishments.[70] Hugh Gaitskell himself at one point conceded that discipline in Labour Groups was too often 'arbitrary and intolerant'[71] and shortly after an official party statement urged a liberalisation in the application of Standing Orders.[72] But this appeared to have little effect either on group behaviour or NEC adjudication.

Another key adjudicating principle, an insistence upon protecting the autonomy of the groups against pressure from the local party, worked in the same direction. In theory both party and group had their own sphere of responsibility, the former to frame the election manifesto, the latter to put it into effect and manage council business. In practice, as the NEC would not have been unaware, the group more often than not monopolised policy-making rights and the party was reduced to the status of an onlooker.[73] Nevertheless, as we shall see in the cases of Liverpool and Nottingham, the national Party was quick to intercede on behalf of a beleaguered group leadership whenever a local party strove to rectify the imbalance in its favour – partly, it may be, because of an instinctive sympathy for those who shared its ideological orientation but also because of a general conviction that Labour's elected representatives should not be subject to Party control.

4.5 Dissension and NEC adjudication in Liverpool Labour Party, 1951–1963

Neither of the two disputes which we shall now examine in detail – in Liverpool and Nottingham – were typical, in the sense that they were representative of the NEC's adjudicating cases. Nevertheless, they merit closer investigation for a number of reasons. Firstly, in both cases central intervention had a substantial impact upon the local balance of political forces and, hence, upon their eventual outcome. Secondly, both disputes raised important issues: the jurisdictional struggle between party and group, the clash between an entrenched, right-wing establishment and more radical competitors for power and (in Liverpool) the nature of group discipline. Thirdly, as each of the issues were to prove highly troublesome in the internal politics of local Labour parties from the mid 1970s onwards, these earlier disputes provide a useful basis of comparison and, hence, helps illuminate the evolving pattern of NEC adjudication.[74]

Local disputes, we have suggested, rarely (in this period) took the form of entrenched factional rivalries. Liverpool was an exception. Since at least the 1920s the party had been divided into competing factions. This factional struggle, which entered into an acute phase in the 1950s was multidimensional in character. Left-right divisions played a part but, as Baxter has shown, these were overlain by other fissures: personal and geographically-based antagonism, religious friction and, above all, the pressure from younger and ambitious politicians to displace the existing establishment and gain access to power and position.[75]

In the 1930s opposition to the ruling establishment of Alderman Hogan was led by the energetic left-winger John Braddock. In the following decade, Braddock succeeded to the leadership inheriting both much of Hogan's power base and his more conservative beliefs. Until Braddock's death in 1963 he, and his ebulient wife Bessie Braddock, the MP for Liverpool Exchange (and, for a time NEC member), dominated the city's Labour politics.

Until the early 1950s the Braddock-led establishment held a tight grip upon the Liverpool party. Oppositional elements had existed throughout the preceding decade, ranging from Trotskyists like Jimmy Deane (later to be a founder of the Revolutionary Socialist League and its progeny, the Militant Tendency) to mainstream left-wingers, Bevanite in outlook, like Bill Sefton. Under the leadership of the Sefton group, these elements coalesced and – profiting from the nation-wide upsurge of Bevanism – succeeded in ousting the establishment from the control of the Trades Council and Labour Party (TCLP) in 1952.[76]

The following year the local elections (all-out elections because of major boundary re-organisation) brought a considerable acretion to the strength of the Labour group, and in particular, of the anti-establishment forces. Whereas previously they had numbered no more than a handful, henceforth they comprised about one-third of all Labour councillors.[77] The confluence of these two events inaugurated a decade of factional strife, which only closed with the assumption to the leadership of Bill Sefton.

The establishment's loss of control over the TCLP immediately altered the pattern of internal political rivalries. Henceforth the competition between the two factions took the form primarily of a power struggle between group and Party. The NEC first became involved in 1953 as a result of a decision by the TCLP to launch an inquiry into allegations of preferential treatment for Labour councillors in the allocation of council houses. The Executive was invited to adjudicate and a high-level team, comprising NEC members and the National Agent, was despatched to investigate.

The team dismissed the allegations which it saw as primarily a manifestation of the poor relations between group and Party. Its sympathies were wholly with the former. It reminded the TCLP that the group had prime responsibility for taking decisions on council matters, and reprimanded it for its attempts to influence the behaviour of individual councillors.[78] By its decision, the Executive signalled that in the jurisdictional clash between group and Party it stood firmly on the side of the former. The result was that, whilst the TCLP remained formally responsible for formulating election policy, effective power was increasingly concentrated in the hands of Labour councillors.[79]

Within the group, the leader, Jack Braddock, occupied a dominant position. This was further strengthened when Labour gained control of the council, for the first time, in 1958. Braddock developed a highly centralised style of policy-making in which he, and a few close associates, took the key decisions and – with the support of the majority of the group – swept aside any criticism.[80] Braddock dealt firmly with the anti-establishment councillors who queried his leadership. In 1957 he secured group approval for the development of vacant council premises as police quarters.[18] Eighteen councillors pressed for priority to be given to housing a school for the educationally sub-normal, bringing the matter to the floor of the council. Six of the 18 refused a group demand that they sign an undertaking to abide in future by majority decisions and were deprived of the whip.

One of the councillors appealed to the NEC. His appeal was upheld on the grounds that the Executive of the TCLP had not been properly consulted (as required by Standing Orders). Nevertheless, the national Party indicated its backing for Braddock's rigorous disciplinary regime by approving the group's strict interpretation of Standing Orders.[81]

The following year, an NEC team was back in Liverpool. Matters were brought to a head on an issue which, oddly, had cut across normal factional loyalties. In October 1958, ten councillors voted in council against a group decision to reject the application of the British Union of Fascists to hire St George's Hall. They claimed that this was a question of the right of free speech and the conscience clause ought to apply. The group disagreed and withdrew the whip from five of the ten councillors. Further, it requested them to resign from the council on the grounds that only nine months previously when they had broken the whip they proferred assurances of future good conduct.[82]

The matter itself was a politically marginal one. But – in Braddock's view at least – deeper issues were involved: the continued unity and effectiveness of the group in the face of the refusal of a minority to accept majority decisions. The Organisation Committee concurred and confirmed both the withdrawal of the whip and the 'request' that the rebels resign their seats.[83]

The judgment, with its upholding of the highly unusual call for councillors to vacate their seats, represented social-democratic centralism at its sternest. It proved too much for the NEC to swallow. It was extremely rare for the Executive to amend a recommendation of its Organisation Sub-committee but in this case Aneurin Bevan (now Shadow Foreign Secretary and deputy leader of the Party) successfully moved a motion to delete the 'request' to the appellants to quit the council.[84] The Organisation Committee then tried to negate this concession to liberality by ruling that retiring councillors who had been expelled from the group were not eligible for re-adoption as Labour candidates – in effect deselecting them.[85] The TCLP countered by declaring that they had already been placed on the panel and – with a major row in the offing on the eve of the local elections – the NEC agreed to Bevan's motion rescinding the minute.[86]

Hostilities, however, were soon resumed. As often in local politics, the flashpoint was rents policy. In January 1960, the TCLP passed a resolution 'instructing the Labour Group not to take the initiative in raising rents'. The group ignored this and voted to increase rents. The TCLP responded by warning the group that 'further measures'[87] would be considered if they failed to implement party policy. The group was not to be deflected from its course and pushed ahead with the rent increases. Five Labour councillors (including Crookes – Sefton was still whipless) voted against, in line with TCLP policy, and Braddock intimated his intention to recommend their expulsion from the group.[88]

Reg Wallis, the North West Regional Organiser, supported Braddock's plea for a stiffening of discipline[89] but, perhaps mindful of its own recent call for a liberalisation of group discipline,[90] the Executive deferred action.[91] At this point, Labour's fortunes in Liverpool plummeted. Severe losses in 1960 and 1961 restored control over the Council to the Conservatives, who promptly unseated many of Labour's aldermen – a serious blow to the Braddock establishment which relied heavily upon the aldermanic bench to keep its opponents at bay.[92]

Perhaps for this reason, a bid was now made to strike at the anti-establishment's power base, the TCLP. In January 1961 the North West Regional Committee of the TGWU requested an investigation into that body. The NEC agreed to despatch a high-level team, including the Chairman of the Organisation Committee (Ray Gunter) and the National Agent (Len Williams).[93]

It seems quite likely that the inspiration for the move came from Labour's able and influential Regional Organiser, Reg Wallis. He regarded the TCLP as 'completely unrepresentative of general Labour support' and 'dominated by a clique which is opposed to the official leadership locally and nationally'.[94] The only remedy, Wallis urged, was the immediate implementation of the Wilson Committee's recommendations.

The 1955 Wilson Committee's enquiry into party organisation had criticised weak organisation in many constituency parties, particularly in the cities. It attributed this in part to their neglect in favour of city-wide central parties (in places like Liverpool and Sheffield Trades Councils and Labour Parties). In 1957 the NEC agreed to a series of measures designed to strengthen CLPs at the expense of central parties.[95]

There is no doubt that the NEC genuinely believed that overly-strong central parties diminished the organisational effectiveness of the constituencies. On the other hand, it (or its officials) would not have been unaware that central or borough-wide units were the only bodies capable of articulating the views of the local party on municipal questions and hence of exerting pressure upon Labour groups. Whatever the major purpose of the change, a predictable consequence of reducing the status of the central organisation would be to buttress further the autonomy of the group.

The attraction of this course of action was evident where (as in Liverpool) the central party was controlled by forces hostile to the group establishment. Not surprisingly, the Liverpool TCLP objected to the NEC's organisational reforms, but was instructed to comply,[96] an instruction which it simply ignored.

This was the situation when, in November 1961, the NEC inquiry into the TCLP, headed by Organisation Committee Chairman, Ray

Gunter, convened.[97] The atmosphere was heavy with acrimony: more like a Star Chamber, Eric Heffer (a leading figure in the anti-establishment group) recalled, than an impartial tribunal.[98] As Sefton rose to object to the opening statement by Wallis as 'highly prejudiced', Gunter, who chaired the meeting, snapped back 'Sit down, I've already seen your dossier – I know all about you.'[99] Braddock denounced what he claimed to be a carefully planned campaign by an organised left faction to overthrow the leadership and virtually all trade union officials consulted displayed considerable hostility to the TCLP urging its dissolution into its constituent parts.[100] If the investigation offered an opportunity to clip the pretensions of the TCLP, the enquiry team seized it. It concluded that the organisation served no useful purpose, recommended that it be split into a Trades Council and Borough Labour Party, and instructed that the earlier decisions demoting it vis-a-vis the constituencies be implemented.

Ironically, within a year or so of the investigation Braddock had died and was succeeded by his erstwhile enemy, Bill Sefton, who, in the established Liverpool pattern, inherited much of his political stance as well as his position. Factionalism disappeared for a decade and, when it reappeared in the 1970s, it was in a radically different form.

It is difficult to assess with any precision the overall impact of NEC intervention upon the Liverpool dispute. But there is little doubt that the ability of the establishment to call upon the national Party for assistance was a valuable power resource. On two major issues, it received a helpful response. Firstly, in the clash over areas of competence between group and party: any effort by the latter to enforce control over Labour councillors – whether directly by seeking to impose its policy preferences or indirectly via the panel – earned it reprimands from the NEC. In the major row in 1960 over rents Braddock was able to treat the TCLP 'with contempt and escape unscathed',[101] safe in the knowledge that his reading of the rules would be upheld by the national Party.

Secondly, Braddock could rely upon the sympathy of the NEC in matters of group discipline. Even where the issue was tangential – as in the letting of a municipal hall to the BUF – the Executive approved expulsion from the group as a penalty for councillors who disobeyed the whip: less because of the issue than because of its anxiety to maintain the authority of the group leadership against its assailants.

But the case study also indicates the limits of central authority. The TCLP was allowed to defy clear NEC directives on its method of operation and funding for six years. Indeed its resistance to central authority continued beyond this. It persistently ignored the NEC's directive in 1962 to dismember itself into separate political and industrial organisations. Circumstances – particularly the general elections of 1964 and

1966 – provided plenty of excuses for delay, whilst the repairing of the breach with the group, following Sefton's accession to the leadership, removed much of the political impetus for the change. However – to place on the other side of the scales – the TUC, keen to disentangle Party and unions, became increasingly anxious to effect the separation.

One major reason for the NEC's failure to overcome the TCLP's stone-walling was the reluctance of its key official in the field, Reg Wallis, to implement the 1962 decision[102] – indicating the extent to which the Party relied upon its regional tier of officials to assert its authority. The way was only cleared with Wallis's resignation and his replacement by the equally strong-minded Paul Carmody. Even then the NEC had to threaten the TCLP with forcible re-organisation by the National Agent before it finally submitted.[103]

In the final instance, the NEC was able to assert its authority and overawe a defiant Party organisation. But the episode also discloses how time-consuming a process this could be. Indeed, it transpired that, in 1968 the TCLP was still disregarding a directive issued a decade earlier that it should meet less frequently and in separate industrial and political sections.[104] Even at a time when officials insistent upon the strict observance of the rules occupied the key positions in Transport House, local organisations could, if sufficiently determined (and with the complicity of regional office) thwart the will of the NEC for some considerable time. In the centralised, bureaucratic model of organisation envisaged by Michels, this could not have happened. We shall draw out the significance of this later.[105]

4.6 Nottingham and the Coates affair, 1965–69

Perhaps the most controversial disciplinary case in the final years of the social-democratic centralist regime was the expulsion, in 1966, of Ken Coates, President of the Nottingham Labour Party (and, in later years, an influential figure in left wing circles) and the disciplining of three other prominent left-wingers.

The affair was precipitated by an apparently minor incident. Jack Caughty, a Labour member of Nottingham Borough Council, was removed from the panel by the city party executive and replaced, as Labour candidate, by a leading left-winger, Peter Price, Vice-President of the Nottingham Party. Caughty charged that he was the victim of an increasingly influential Trotskyist faction and – with the backing of the Labour group and a number of unions – complained to the NEC.[106]

Caughty's ejection brought to the fore a simmering dispute between the right-wing Labour-controlled council and the more radical city party disenchanted by the former's lack of reforming zeal. The establishment immediately counter-attacked by striking at its foremost critic – city President, Ken Coates. Two senior members of the Labour group – the Leader and the Secretary – pushed through a resolution at Nottingham West CLP expelling Coates on the charges of seeking to discredit Nottingham's Labour Council and the Labour Government, and of active involvement in a Trotskyist organisation.[107]

Coates appealed to the NEC. At the same time a number of Nottingham councillors sought to drive their advantage home by urging the Executive to investigate the city party. The NEC agreed and despatched a senior inquiry team comprising two of its own members plus the National Agent, Sara Barker.[108] The enquiry into Coates's appeal and the state of the Nottingham party was conducted over three days in a grim atmosphere. Coates recalled his 'long and utterly barren wrangle with Miss Barker . . . this grey, implacable little old lady, who looked as if she ought to be selling toffees in a village shop, vested instead with all the dank, meaningless and mindless power of a great machine'.[109] The NEC upheld Coates's expulsion[110] and, in addition, banned three other leading left-wingers, Geoff Coggan, Bob Gregory and the acting President of the city party, Peter Price, from all Party office for the next three years.[111]

Coates was already well-known nationally, and his expulsion aroused an outcry amongst left-wing trade unionists and radical intellectuals. On what grounds had the NEC reached its verdict?

Firstly, he was held to have 'gone beyond fair criticism in both the written and spoken word' in his attacks on both the Labour council and Government. However, it was unusual, even in the social-democratic centralist era, for left-wingers to be expelled simply for their views. The first charge needs to be seen in the context of the second – that he did not accept 'the basic democratic beliefs of the Party' and had infiltrated its ranks, as leader of an organised faction, to promote the Trotskyist cause.

Coates vigorously defied all these charges at the hearing. The picture, however, was more complicated. He was a former Communist who joined the Labour Party in 1961. That same year he helped form the small, Nottingham-based Internationalist Group (the forerunner of the International Marxist Group – now Socialist League – the British affiliate of the Trotskyist Fourth International). He jointly edited *The Week* with Robin Blackburn, soon to become an intellectual luminary of the IMG, and worked closely with Pat Jordan, one of its most influential figures.

John Callaghan's recent study of British Trotskyism appears to confirm the charge that Coates was engaged in classic entryist tactics. 'The IMG tendency at first channelled its energies into the Nottingham City Labour Party where, according to Jordan, it "won hegemony" and elected Ken Coates to the Presidency.' This 'hegemony' was used to further the IMG's influence in the wider Party.[112]

This account, however, is misleading in a number of respects. Firstly, the International Group was less a disciplined faction than a small, ideologically heterogenous ginger group.[113] This, in turn, was part of a broader left caucus, a loose-knit association of people with disparate views held together by opposition to the ruling local establishment. Some of them later helped form the IMG whilst others were eventually to be assimilated into the establishment.[114]

As far as his beliefs were concerned, Coates was later to describe them as 'revisionist Trotskyism'. The term 'Trotskyist' did not, in the early 1960s, necessarily entail a hard and fast ideological position or espousal of anti-parliamentary politics; rather (for Coates at least) it more vaguely connoted an attachment to Marxism coupled with a repudiation of Soviet-style 'socialism'[115]

As far as Coates's opponents, both in the Nottingham Labour establishment and in Transport House, were concerned his unswerving, and often virulent, criticism of Labour policies both nationally and locally demonstrated that he lacked sufficient commitment to the Party's 'programme and principles'. The fact that Coates and his associates in the left caucus were evidently making headway (Coates's own incumbency of the Presidency, Price's replacement of Caughty as a council candidate) transformed an irritation into a potentially dangerous situation.

This brings us to Coates's third offence, and the underlying cause of the Nottingham dispute. According to the (Nottingham) *Guardian Journal*, 'control over the City affairs was seen to be the real issue at stake – the possibility of council policies being laid down by individuals having neither mandate nor civic responsibility'.[116] In its report the NEC sympathised with the group's 'ultra sensitivity' about safeguarding its position against pressure from 'outside bodies'.[117] The second inquiry, into the city party, found that dissension between Party and group had been 'incited by an organised group . . . led by Ken Coates'. Under its influence the city Party had encroached upon the proper domain of the group, the determination of council policy. This the NEC regarded as unacceptable and hence penalised three other prominent left-wingers (Coggan, Gregory and Price) for 'disruptive activities'.[118]

The episode offers some insight into the NEC's approach to adjudication in a politically highly-charged case. A key objective was to avoid electorally damaging splits. But such splits can be repaired either by seeking to reconcile the two sides or by imposing penalties on whoever was regarded as the guilty side. In this case, as in comparable ones, the NEC opted for the latter option (in contrast to practice in later years). Further, and consistent with a pattern of intervention we have previously depicted, the NEC brought its full weight to bear behind the group-based Nottingham establishment. By expelling Coates, one party worker[119] was quoted as saying, 'we removed the tongue and brain of the left wing . . . it is the beginning of the end of the left wing.[120]

The episode also sheds some light on the mechanisms of central control. It is worth looking first at the role of the Regional Organiser, Jim Cattermole, one of the most adroit in Labour's service. Years later he was to claim with some pride 'I got Ken Coates expelled'.[121] Rumours have for years abounded about Cattermole's infamous or celebrated ability – according to viewpoint – to manipulate events behind the scenes. Harder evidence is more difficult to come by. But from his own testimony as well as that of his critics there seems little doubt that he played an important role. He regarded Coates as an alien political element, a danger to the Party who ought to be removed as soon as was politically feasible. He was sympathetic to the Labour establishment in Nottingham[122] and certainly had discussions about how best to meet the threat of the left-leaning City party executive.[123]

In a letter to *Tribune*, Coggan queried the source of the allegations against Coates, speculating that it must have been a party official with access to 'the dusty vaults of Transport House'.[124] These dusty vaults have only recently disgorged their material including several fat files on Coates. One of these contained a collection of extracts from *The Week* with a cover note 'showing K. Coates' involvement, tactics and strategy'.[125] This indicates that Transport House was keeping close tabs upon those considered to be trouble-makers, and compiling dossiers which could form the basis of future disciplinary proceedings. This was not, as we shall see later, an isolated case.[126]

NEC intervention in Nottingham illustrates the capacity of the Executive to contain local left-wing challenges by the judicious exercise of its powers. The local establishment weathered the storm with, by later standards, remarkably little difficulty. The following decade the *New Statesman* described the Party in Nottingham as 'right-wing in complexion and heavily anti-Communist'.[127]

However, to conclude that the episode demonstrated the efficacy of central control would be premature, for it was also the point at which the tide began to turn. The affair did not end in 1966; in fact it was to drag on for another three years by which time the NEC had been forced to lift the disciplinary sanctions against Price, Coggan and Gregory and agreed to re-admit Coates.

None of the four disciplined left-wingers had been given the opportunity to examine, in advance, the charges upon which they were convicted. In the case of Coates's three allies, their only offence had been the nebulous one of engaging in 'disruptive activities'; furthermore, the court at which they had been tried had not been set up for that purpose. This procedure reflected the prevailing doctrine of constitutional centralism. Previously the doctrine had tended to escape rigorous scrutiny. This was now to change.

In September 1966 the four disciplined Nottingham left-wingers wrote to the NEC requesting the right to be heard by Conference. The NEC rejected this on the grounds that the Constitution made no provision for such appeals. It referred to clause VIII(4) which empowered it to adjudicate in disputes between party organisations, its decisions being binding on all concerned.[128] In their reply, Coggan, Gregory and Price denied that the NEC had any right, under this clause, to take disciplinary action. The only legitimate basis was clause II(b) which requires that any such action 'shall be reported to the next Annual Conference'. They complained that they had been 'deprived of a substantial part of our membership rights without the slightest trace of legality'.[129]

The NEC rejected the complaint and referred to clause VII(3) of the constitution which states that the NEC pronounce definitely upon 'the meaning and effect of . . . any part of this Constitution'.[130] Price and his colleagues, however, were not prepared to accept the Executive's ruling, and decided to seek legal redress.[131] Their solicitors wrote to Labour's General Secretary warning that, unless full membership rights were restored, proceedings would be instituted on the grounds that the NEC's decision was 'in accord neither with the Constitution nor with the principles of natural justice'.[132]

After a writ was served, the Executive consulted its own solicitors (Goodman, Derick and Co.) who obtained an Opinion from Lord Lloyd, Q.C. This was decisive. He advised that the Party might lose on both grounds: Clause VIII(4) made no provision for disciplinary action and procedurally the Party may well have been at fault since 'the plaintiffs had not been called upon to answer any specific charges made against them'.[133] In short, the NEC had both acted *ultra vires* and violated natural justice.

Several members of the Executive were loath to accept the Opinion and it was only 'with great reluctance and strong reservations' that the Committee finally agreed to rescind the sanctions on the three Nottingham members.[134]

The rebuff to the NEC was a seemingly minor one. But in fact it was a harbinger of later developments. Both the definition and exercise of Executive powers had been measured against established legal norms and found to be wanting. Two years later the legal challenge was repeated – this time in the courts – and the whole skein of constitutional centralism began to unravel.[135]

Coates also tried and failed to secure a hearing at Conference. His case in law was weaker, in that he was expelled by his constituency party not by the NEC, so the latter was under no obligation to report the matter to Conference. His efforts to secure readmission to his constituency party were, for the moment, fruitless.

There the matter rested until November 1968. By this time two of the leading protagonists in the drive to expel Coates had defected to the Conservatives.[136] Coates wrote to Labour's new General Secretary, Harry Nicholas, drawing his attention to the recent (and important) Pembroke judgment which had held that the NEC's (standard) disciplinary procedures flouted natural justice.[137] Coates noted that he had never been presented with specific charges – indeed he had never been informed of the verdict of the inquiry team. Intimating his reluctance to engage in litigation, he asked Nicholas to reopen the case.[138]

By this time, the climate within the Party had altered. The arch social-democratic centralist, Sara Barker, who had stubbornly fought to keep Coates out of the Party,[139] was replaced as National Agent by the much more liberal-minded Ron Hayward. Hayward was keen to secure the Nottingham left-winger's re-admittance as a sign of the new, more open managerial regime he wished to introduce and reversed the advice the NEC received from his predecessor.[140]

After some procrastination, the NEC sent a team comprising two NEC members (Jo Gormley and Jack Diamond) and the National Agent to interview Coates. The team questioned him about his activities and beliefs and his answers were deemed sufficiently satisfactory for the team to recommend his reinstatement.[141] With the imprimatur of two respected right-wingers, and with Ron Hayward using his considerable influence as National Agent in Coates's favour, NEC approval of the recommendation came readily. Coates was to be one of the first beneficiaries of the new, more liberal disciplinary regime and went on to play an active and influential role in left-wing politics.

Chapter Five

Parliamentary selection, 1951–70

5.1 The NEC's constitutional powers

As Ranney has observed, candidate selection offers 'one of the highest stakes in any internal struggle for control of a party's leadership and policy'.[1] In recognition of this, in this area, unlike others, the NEC's powers are spelt out in considerable detail in the constitution and in the Model Rules which, since 1930, all CLPs have been required to adopt.[2]

The Executive is alloted five main regulatory powers. Firstly, prior authorisation is required from the NEC before a constituency party can commence the selection process.[3] The original purpose of this clause was to give the Executive some discretion in determining which seats should be contested. After 1945 all seats in Britain have been fought, rendering this purpose redundant. However, the power was from time to time employed to influence the timing and order of selections.[4] The use of this power has not aroused any significant controversy and will not be further discussed.

Secondly, the NEC validates all nominations that a CLP receives for a candidature.[5] Validation has been treated as a technical exercise (i.e. that the nomination has been submitted in the proper way) and not as a form of control.[6]

Thirdly, the Party Constitution states that the selection procedure is not completed until the selection of the candidate has been 'duly endorsed' by the NEC.[7] This is the most formidable of the Executive's regulatory powers and will be discussed in more detail below.

Fourthly, in cases of by-elections, the NEC is given additional powers. CLP Rules stipulate that the normal procedure 'shall be suspended and the NEC shall co-operate with the Executive Committee of this Party in the nomination of a candidate. The NEC may, if it deems it necessary in the interests of the Labour Party, advise the Executive Committee of this Party to select a nomination it may submit to it.'[8]

Fifthly, the Executive is given special powers to suspend the normal procedure 'where no valid nominations are received, or when an emergency arises or the NEC are of the opinion that the interests of the Labour Party demand [it].' In any of these circumstances the NEC is empowered to dispense with the normal procedure.[9] These special powers are, obviously, potentially wide-ranging. In fact, the clause has very rarely been invoked.

In addition to these five stipulated powers, the NEC, in this period, could influence the selection process in two other ways: firstly, it acted as final arbiter in deselection disputes; its permission was, by convention, required before a constituency could set in motion the procedure to remove a sitting MP. Secondly it maintained two lists of candidates 'available' for selection. List A consisted of names forwarded by affiliated unions from their own panels of parliamentary aspirants; if adopted they would be sponsored by their union, which implied the provision of financial help. List B was introduced in 1948 after Conference, expressing regret at a tendency to select as candidates recent converts to the Party, had directed the NEC to 'create a national panel of possible Labour candidates' compiled from nominations received from CLPs and affiliated organisations. The sole condition was a minimum of one year's membership of the Party.[10] NEC agreement was required before a nominee was formally placed upon either list.[11] However, during the 1950s this did not imply any form of official approval; the Lists were 'only a source of information about members who are available for consideration as candidates.'[12] After 1960, and for the rest of that decade, B List was converted into a List of candidates deemed 'suitable' for adoption by CLPs.

The most potent of the NEC's powers were its control over the composition of the B List, its right to withhold endorsement and its ability to resist attempts to deselect sitting MPs. We shall now examine the use of these powers in the period 1951–9.

5.2   The B List in practice, 1951–9

Prior to the rule change of 1960, Ranney has written, Transport House did not 'interview or screen (applicants) in any way, and acted solely as a clearing house'.[13] This is inaccurate. As the NAD explained in 1955 'if nominees are not known to the office or if references are not satisfactory, they are usually interviewed by the National Agent or Assistant National Agent.'[14] Without exhaustive research, it is impossible to say for certain why some nominations were queried. But there was clearly an element of political vetting. Until 1955, this was rare; indeed between 1951 and 1955 there were only two definite cases of exclusion on these grounds: Gerry Healy, a well known Trotskyist leader, and

Konni Zilliacus, a persistent left-wing gadfly of the Party establishment.[15] Scrutiny of nominees' political credentials only began in earnest in 1958 as the NEC began discussing proposals to tighten control over candidate selection. Thus, in 1957 and 1958 the Chairmen's Sub-Committee reserved judgement on a number of nominations, pending a decision on the character of the list. They included Norman Atkinson, already well known in left-wing circles in Manchester, Dr N. Barnett, a former president of the Liverpool Trades Council and Labour Party and a prominent figure in the anti-establishment camp, and Dennis Hobden, later a left-wing MP for Brighton Kemptown.[16] Eventually Atkinson's application was approved but that of Barnett and Hobden rejected.[17] Similarly the nomination of G. Van Gelderen, a Trotskyist and keen ally of Gerry Healy was turned down.[18] The same fate initially befell Ronald Chamberlain, an MP on the left fringes of the PLP from 1945 to 1950. He was only accepted on to the list following an interview and after receiving, according to his own testimony, the 'vehement support' of some NEC members.[19]

In all these instances, it is fairly obvious that political criteria were being applied. But it would be misleading to infer that systematic political screening took place. Firstly, other factors – such as political inexperience and the brevity of Party membership – also played a part. Secondly, the actual numbers of nominations deferred or rejected was small. Since the names of most applicants were unfamiliar and since no reasons were ever given for exclusion from the list[20] a precise estimate of the prevalence of political vetting in this period is not possible.[21]

5.3 Endorsement

The power to withhold endorsement of a parliamentary candidate was potentially the most potent device available to the NEC to establish control over the selection process. Constitutionally, a candidate can be refused endorsement on the following grounds: non-membership, where eligible, of a trade union affiliated to or recognised by the TUC as a bona fide union; membership of a proscribed organisation; failure to 'accept and conform to the Constitution, Programme, Principles and Policy of the Party'; refusal to undertake to accept the Standing Orders of the PLP.[22] Of these, the first two and the last are clear-cut. The third is far more elastic; it provided the NEC, as Rush has pointed out, 'with extremely wide powers of discretion . . . Should a particular candidate be politically unacceptable to the NEC, this condition renders rejection of his selection a relatively simple matter.'[23]

NEC records indicate the political screening of candidates for endorsement was somewhat more widespread than previous accounts have suggested; it would appear that in the period 1951 to 1959 thirteen

candidates experienced difficulty on grounds of their beliefs or affiliations.[24]

The candidature of Bernard Floud (PPC for Chelmsford and, in his
student days, a member of the CP) was only endorsed after he managed
to dissipate suspicions of Communist associations: having served in the
Intelligence Corps during the War he told the NEC he had received a
security clearance.[25]

Three other candidates ran aground because of their alleged
Trotskyist connections. John Lawrence was selected as candidate for
the safe Tory seat of Woodford in 1953. He was a councillor and was
soon to be elected the controversial leader of St Pancras Council. He was
also a prominent Trotskyist and editor of the Trotskyist-controlled
magazine, *Socialist Outlook* (which was proscribed the following
year).[26] After being interviewed by the Elections Committee, his candidature was vetoed on the grounds of the 'unsatisfactory nature' of his
replies to questions on Party policy.[27]

Tom Braddock had been a far left MP from 1945 to 1950. He featured
prominently in backbench rebellions, particularly over foreign policy.
Shortly after, he became a leading figure in Socialist Fellowship, a
left-wing ginger group which eventually slipped into the Trotskyist
orbit and he worked closely with Gerry Healy's faction.[28] For these
reasons he fell foul of the NEC and was denied endorsement for
Mitcham (which he had represented as an MP) in 1952 and Wimbledon
two years later.[29] In 1957, he was selected for Kingston (as solidly Tory
as Wimbledon) again to find his path blocked by the NEC.[30] This time
perseverance paid off: a series of protests persuaded the NEC to grant
him an interview and he was endorsed after providing various assurances.[31]

Sam Goldberg was a Birmingham Labour Councillor and a senior
figure in the (Communist-run) Electricians Union. He had been
involved with *Socialist Outlook*. In 1956 he was selected as PPC for
Nottingham South, where the Regional Organiser reported adversely on
his speech. At an interview he was vetoed on grounds of his far left
beliefs and affiliations (both Trotskyist and, later, Communist).[32] Two
years later, his attempts to secure the nomination for Barking were
thwarted by the NEC which told the CLP that endorsement would be
withheld.[33]

Three other candidates – all well-known left-wingers, one of them
destined to rise to a senior position in the AEU and another to join the
NEC – had a narrow escape. Shortly before the general election of 1955 a
special meeting of the Elections Sub Committee was called to decide
upon the suitability of three candidates whose political position was
'doubtful'. Only three NEC members were able to attend the meeting,
one of whom was the leading Bevanite, Ian Mikardo. The first of the

doubtfuls was Konni Zilliacus, who had been readmitted into the Labour Party in 1952, his critical zeal unalloyed. The second was Ernie Roberts, a hard-line left-winger in the engineering union who worked closely with the Communists. He had been refused endorsement as a Labour candidate in 1945 and was later kept off the B List; however, he had been selected for Stockport North as an AEU-sponsored candidate. The third was Frank Allaun, a leading figure in left politics in Manchester. He had fought the Moss Side constituency in 1951 but – according to the minutes – 'doubt had been expressed about his full acceptance of Labour Party policy'.

According to Mikardo, Sara Barker opposed their endorsement, producing dossiers to list their various misdeeds. The left-wing MP riposted sharply that 'if the endorsements were withheld on the basis of that procedure, I would immediately resign from the NEC and announce publicly why I had done so'. After some heated discussion, the Committee approved the candidatures; in the subsequent poll both Allaun and Zilliacus were elected.[34]

In a number of other cases, candidates were only endorsed after having been called to interview and then having provided adequate reassurances.[35] Nevertheless, this screening process needs to be placed in context; during this period, hundreds of candidates were endorsed; only a proportion were scrutinised and a smaller number yet forfeited their candidatures. The Party did not operate a comprehensive system for vetting candidates. Many who held ideas or engaged in activities similar to those whose cases we have reviewed may well have escaped the attention of Transport House simply because it was unaware of them.[36] This was particularly likely for those who contested safe Tory seats where the difficulty was less in finding reliable candidates than in finding any at all – and who, anyway would not, by definition, affect the composition of the PLP. The candidates whose background was investigated fell into two categories; either they were well known (with dossiers ready to hand) like Zilliacus or Braddock, or the regional officers (who supervise all selection conferences) had reported adversely on their views.[37]

5.4   The deselection of MPs

The NEC can also affect the composition of the PLP not only by screening Parliamentary candidates but also by intervening when constituency parties seek to remove sitting MPs. In this period an MP was, under the rules, automatically re-adopted unless 'the General Committee on securing a mandate from its affiliated and Party organisations intimates by resolution its desire that he or she must retire'.[38]

Despite the severe dissension within the Party in the earlier half of the decade, attempts by constituency parties to deselect sitting MPs were, throughout the 1950s, rare. This was partly because the membership in staunch Labour areas tended to be more right wing than elsewhere and partly because of a general reluctance to part with an MP, even where views differed considerably. The exceptions were cases where relations had irretrievably broken down.

The best known example of this occurred in 1954 and 1955 when Liverpool Exchange strove to unseat its MP, the colourful and abrasive Bessie Braddock. In this case local cleavages intersected with national ones. Mrs Braddock was closely identified with the local right-wing establishment headed by her husband; she was also a fierce critic of Aneurin Bevan. She first incurred resentment within her local party when, as its delegate to the tumultuous Morecambe Conference, she offended many members by her vigorous advocacy of official national policy on contentious issues. Relations steadily deteriorated and in 1954 the GMC – by then solidly Bevanite in orientation[39] – decided to oust her. It asked all ward parties to take a view on a resolution calling upon the MP to retire at the next election. At this point Reg Wallis, the Regional Organiser, interceded and told the GC that its action was unconstitutional – though upon what grounds is not clear. The party reacted by passing a vote of no confidence in its MP and writing to the NEC requesting permission to activate Clause XII 7(b) of its rules empowering it to deselect Mrs Braddock.[40] Requests from a pro-Braddock ward party and from the member herself for an official enquiry were also before the Sub-Committee. It decided to despatch a team comprising two NEC members (Wilfred Burke and James Haworth) and the National Agent to investigate the party.[41]

The report commended Mrs Braddock's work as a constituency MP and criticised the organisation and administration of the party. The dispute, it noted, had arisen over policy differences and a misapprehension, on the CLP's part, that it could mandate its MP. Accordingly, it recommended that the NEC refuse Liverpool Exchange CLP permission to start deselection proceedings.[42]

There matters rested for a few months. Due to changes in constituency boundaries a selection conference was held in March 1955: it voted by 40 votes to 39 not to re-adopt Mrs. Braddock. The CLP Secretary wrote to the NEC asking to be allowed to select another candidate; at the same time Transport House received a number of protests alleging irregularities. The Elections Sub-Committee, in response, despatched Burke, Haworth and Williamson to conduct another investigation.[43]

The investigation, which uncovered a series of procedural irregularities concluded that opposition to the MP was due solely to her support of official Party policy and criticised the GC's attempt to mandate her. The NEC, after refusing the CLP permission to select another candidate, invoked its special powers under Clause XIII (4) of Constituency Rules to instruct Exchange to re-adopt Mrs Braddock.[44] Reg Wallis communicated the decision to an indignant GC Meeting adding the warning – to cries of 'Heil Hitler' – that failure to comply would lead to its disbandment. The GC gave way by 37 votes to 26 with CLP Secretary Brian Crookes complaining that 'we have accepted Mrs. Braddock with a gun at our heads'.[45] As Ranney has noted, 'Transport House's intervention had been decisive'.[46]

Mrs Braddock was not alone in facing constituency opposition. As we have seen, in the spring of 1955, opinion was inflamed throughout the Party by the bid to expel Bevan; a number of CLPs placed pressure upon their MPs to back the threatened left-winger and, in a few cases, failure by MPs to pay heed pushed to the brim long-standing political differences and precipitated attempts to remove them.

Coventry Borough Labour Party urged all three Coventry MPs to vote against the PLP Motion depriving Bevan of the whip. Two were, in fact Bevanites (Dick Crossman and Maurice Edelman) and readily complied. The third, Elaine Burton, right-wing MP for Coventry South, refused to do so. The Coventry Borough Party thereupon passed a motion of no confidence; Sara Barker and the West Midlands Regional Organiser, Reg Underhill, attended a meeting of the South party and warned that the NEC would not countenance any attempt to unseat the MP on the basis of the way she voted at the PLP and would, if need be, disaffiliate the party. The threat to Miss Burton receded and she was re-adopted.[47]

The NEC marched to the rescue of two other MPs. Herbert Butler, the right-wing MP for Hackney Central was narrowly deselected by his Bevanite local party on the grounds of his support for German rearmament. On Morgan Phillips' instructions, the London Regional Organiser told the CLP that the NEC would not tolerate the rejection of an MP for such a reason and, after a second meeting, Butler coasted safely to harbour.[48] Also in London Arthur Skefflington, MP for Hayes and Harlington (and an NEC member), overrode local resistance after Party officials intimated that the NEC would not stand idly by if he was evicted because of his views.[48]

These cases indicate the NEC's willingness to intervene vigorously to protect MPs in trouble with their local parties because of political disagreements. Indeed, it regarded any attempt by Party activists to influence the behaviour of MPs by threatening to remove them as unconstitutional and tantamount to intimidation.[50] The NEC stipulated that any constituency party seeking to remove its MP must first obtain its permission. In fact, the rules nowhere place such an obligation upon CLPs. Here, as elsewhere, the Executive's claims to broad regulatory powers rested upon its assumption of 'inherent' rights under the constitution, as sanctioned by the doctrine of constitutional centralism; such claims were not to survive the inspection of the Courts.[51]

5.5 The high point of central control: 1960–63

From time to time, in the late 1950s, the NEC had considered measures to tighten central control. In 1957, the Chairmen's Sub-Committee recommended a change in the meaning of 'validation', to embrace other than technical criteria.[52] The full NEC, however, effectively rejected the recommendation.[53] A second proposal was much more far-reaching. The National Agent suggested the conversion of the B List into (on the local government model) a fully-fledged parliamentary panel.[54] This would have restricted the chance of becoming a parliamentary candidate to individuals the NEC judged suitable to be members of the panel and would have represented a potentially major expansion of central control. Such a move would have been staunchly resisted[55] and, perhaps for this reason, evoked little enthusiasm on the NEC. A later NAD paper queried whether such a radical departure from 'long established practice' was justified by the relatively small number of 'really unsatisfactory candidates'[56] and the Executive finally rejected the idea in February 1958.[57]

The 1959 general election was followed by an outbreak of fierce factional strife. This rendered the right-wing dominated NEC more receptive to proposals for tighter control of the selection process. Len Williams toyed with the idea of resurrecting his suggestion for a parliamentary panel but doubted whether the defects of the existing system warranted such a drastic and controversial move.[58] Instead, in a paper submitted to the NEC, he opted for a lesser change transforming List B into a list of 'approved' names. He argued that under the present system, the NEC's rule was primarily negative – vetoing inclusion on to the List – an action which tended to incur the resentment of the nominating body. Furthermore, the NEC often did not have sufficient information about a nominee to reach an informed judgement and was inclined to err on the side of generosity. He urged, instead, that a more elaborate vetting procedure be established to enable the Executive to pronounce upon the suitability of a candidate.[59]

The organisation committee accepted the National Agent's view and decided that, henceforth, List B would become an Approved List of Candidates; that, where necessary, nominees would be interviewed; and that a panel of three would be set up by the Committee for that purpose.[60]

This fell short of establishing a parliamentary panel. Henceforth, nominees for the B List would be more thoroughly checked by the NEC; but

Harold Wilson, Chairman of the Organisation Sub Committee (and, at this point, no friend of the Party leadership) made a point of reassuring Conference that constituency parties were under no obligation to confine their choice to such 'approved' candidates.[61]

The Approved List established, for the first time, a systematic vetting procedure for the bulk of Labour's Parliamentary aspirants. In the six years in which it was in operation large numbers were interviewed,[62] the great majority of whom were accepted. In all, only fourteen nominees were rejected. With a couple of exceptions, the names are familiar and all were left-wingers. They included former MPs Tom Braddock and Ron Chamberlain;[63] prominent Liverpool left-wingers Bill Sefton and Brian Crookes,[64] and seasoned rank and file activists like Walter Wolfgang.[65] One of the more prominent victims was Jo Richardson, Secretary to Ian Mikardo and many left-wing ginger groups (including the Bevanites and Victory for Socialism). She was kept off the list for refusing to give an undertaking not to criticise the leader, Hugh Gaitskell, in public.[66]

Reasons were never given for exclusion from the B List, but there is no doubt that the main ground was political – in Sara Barker's phrase, questionable 'political stability'.[67] However, the criterion was applied in a somewhat haphazard manner. For example, Dennis Hobden was kept off the list but later endorsed for the highly marginal Brighton Kemptown seat.[68] Conversely, Iltyd Harrington, candidate for Wembley North in 1964, was rejected for the list a year later.[69]

Particularly in the early 1960s, when political tempers ran high, the new procedure was greatly resented on the left. *Tribune* denounced its manner of operation – a 'star chamber system';[70] and it met with 'fierce attack' at the 1961 Conference when it was accused of being used to weed out CND members.[71] In fact, most left-wingers (and CND members) were accepted on to the list. Why, then, were the minority kept off? It seems that two criteria were degree of leftness (into which category fell involvement or association with Trotskyists or Communists); and prominence – the NEC never risked turning down left-wingers with a national reputation. Also there was an arbitrary element. Many nominees were unknown to Transport House and a brief interview was not a very effective method of ascertaining their political stance. In fact, as we shall see, dissatisfaction with the way the new system operated steadily mounted and it was eventually discarded as much because it failed in its objective – to erect a viable vetting procedure – as because of opposition to the objective itself.

It is difficult to assess with any precision the impact of the new procedure. An obvious weakness was that it was not a panel – constituencies were not required to select members of the list. Further, membership of the list did not guarantee endorsement. On the other hand, exclusion from the list might well damage the prospects of a contender for a seat: opponents could hint that such a candidate would almost inevitably experience difficulties in securing endorsement. Such considerations might well have weighed with constituency parties, reluctant to risk having to repeat the time-consuming process of selecting a candidate.

The main significance of the Approved List, however, lay in the fact that it was not an isolated act but part of a general pattern. In 1962, a well-informed observer commented that 'there can be little doubt that in the last two years there has been a great strengthening of the official hand in the whole business of candidate selection'.[72] Harold Wilson was succeeded, as Chairman of the Organisation Committee, by tough-minded centralists who enjoyed the full-confidence of the leader, first Ray Gunter and, then – in a deliberate move to step up the importance of the post and place the Party machine more firmly at the service of the Parliamentary leadership – by George Brown, deputy leader of the Party (in March 1962).

As we have noted in other segments of the Party's internal life, the early 1960s witnessed a drive to tighten discipline.[73] This was reflected, in the field of candidate selection, not only in the institution of the Approved List, but also in the establishment of a more rigorous vetting process for endorsement. As the National Agent reported in December 1961, all cases for endorsement were scrutinised by the NAD and, in doubtful cases, by himself personally.[74] Where doubts lingered, candidates would be interviewed by a committee comprising representatives of the NEC and senior Party officials. In the period 1960 to 1965 (i.e. covering selections for the elections of 1964 and 1966) sixteen candidates were called to interview. All, or at least the bulk, were left-wingers.[75] Most were duly endorsed and a number were subsequently elected to Parliament.[76]

No explicit criteria were laid down or reasons given for deferring endorsement. Occasionally, however, details were provided. Thus Eric Varley, the candidate for Chesterfield had attended the Vienna Youth Festival, organised by the proscribed World Federation of Democratic Youth in 1959, as a delegate of Derbyshire NUM; he was endorsed after an interview.[77] In Bill Molloy's case, endorsement was deferred because he had criticised the leadership at his selection conference and was 'ambivalent' over whether he would accept the PLP's Standing Orders. (He, too, was eventually endorsed.)[78]

Others were less fortunate. The best known case was that of Iltyd Harrington, later to be deputy leader of the GLC under both Sir Reg Goodwin and Ken Livingstone. A left-winger, he was selected for the marginal Dover constituency. He was refused endorsement (after an interview with Ray Gunter, Chairman of the Organisation Committee, and Sara Barker) on the grounds, it appears, that he had refused to promise to cease writing articles for the (Communist) *Labour Monthly* and that he had spoken at a meeting organised by the Committee for Democracy in America (upon which Communists served).[79]

Ernie Roberts, by this time Assistant General Secretary of the Engineering Union, was selected in 1961 for the Tory marginal of Horsham but was denied endorsement by the NEC. No reason was given in his case, but he had for long been earmarked by Transport House as a politically dubious character and was known to hold hard-line left-wing views. His association with the powerful Communist faction in the AEU did not help; nor did the hint that its predominantly right-wing leadership would not be unduly perturbed by this affront to a senior union official.[80]

Another casualty in this period was John Palmer. He was endorsed as candidate for Croydon North West after providing written undertakings to uphold Party policy.[81] He was reselected for the Tory marginal in 1965 but called for an interview after the Regional Organiser had expressed doubts about his 'political stability'.[82] In the interview he was arraigned for his outspoken criticisms of the Labour Government's policies on Vietnam and immigration; he was rejected after he refused to sign a written undertaking to refrain from public criticism of the Government until after the next election.[83] The fourth, and final, casualty was Carol Lever, candidate for Epsom who was rejected (after an interview) following an 'unsatisfactory report' from the Regional Organiser concerning comments made at the selection conference.[84]

Why were some candidates endorsed only after an interview and why were some vetoed? As with the B List, the bulk of left-wing candidates safely navigated the vetting procedure. The credentials of the minority were subject to closer scrutiny it would seem, for three reasons. Firstly because Transport House had accumulated evidence of 'political unreliability'. Unless Head Office already had a file on an individual (as was undoubtedly the case with Ernie Roberts) it was dependent upon Regional Organisers' reports on the selection conference. Throughout the 1950s and 1960s, Regional Organisers were expected not only to ensure that procedures were properly followed at selection conferences but to inform Transport House if successful candidates deviated significantly from official policy; this certainly occurred in the cases of Eric Varley, Bill Molloy and Carol Lever. Presumably discretion in such matters paid off for other candidates.

Secondly, the NEC's judgement was probably influenced by the type of constituency: it was more likely to display leniency in a safe Tory seat than in a marginal or Labour one. This, presumably, is the explanation for the Executive's quirky decision to endorse Harrington as candidate for the safe Tory seat of Wembley North a year after evicting him from the Dover marginal.[85]

Thirdly, there is no doubt that in the four cases where endorsement was refused – Harrington, Roberts, Lever and Palmer – exception was taken primarily to their views. The NEC was empowered to withhold endorsement to any person who 'does not accept the Constitution, Programme, Principles and Policy of the Party';[86] so, constitutionally, it was within its rights to debar a candidate on grounds of belief. The fatal combination which seemed to place candidates beyond the pale was far left views and/or association with undesirable political groups, either Communist or Trotskyist.[87]

Finally, it appears that the NEC (more likely NAD officials) made a rough cost–benefit analysis when assessing borderline cases. A key ingredient in the analysis was the amount of trouble a rejection might cause. Where a constituency dug in its heels, and where a candidate was vigorously espoused by the left on the NEC or in its organs, like Tribune, judgment might swing in his or her favour. This happened with James Kerr, a councillor and active member of CND who was vetoed as candidate for Edinburgh South on the grounds of his refusal to promote a non-unilateralist defence policy. His fate drew loud protests from the left, and both the CLP and the Edinburgh Party actively championed him. As a result a compromise was cobbled together and he was endorsed.[88] Hugh Jenkins, the candidate for Putney (and a well known mainstream left-winger) more narrowly surived. He was endorsed after the recommendation of the Sub-Committee's Chairman (Ray Gunter) had been overturned by one vote.[89] Again the outcry his rejection would have occasioned may well have swung the waverers around.

5.6   The constraints on central control

Though there was a drift towards greater central involvement in candidate selection in the late 1950s and early 1960s, this stopped well short of a centralist system. Overall, constituencies continued to enjoy a large measure of autonomy; and, as we shall see, the major conduits through which NEC influence flowed were informal in character. A number of senior figures in the Party hierarchy – Hugh Gaitskell, Len Williams, George Brown and Ray Gunter – would have preferred a greater measure of national Party control, partly for political reasons, partly, also, to improve the calibre of new recruits to the PLP. But the steps taken in this direction were tentative and, in due time, reversed. Compared to continental sister parties, local rights in the selection of candidates remained firmly entrenched. Why? There were three main reasons, each of which afford insight into the limits to centralisation.

The trade union dimension

The first, and most important, was the trade union dimension. The NEC's capacity to exert control in the field of candidate selection was crucially mediated by this connection in two respects, the constitutional and the political. Constitutionally, the unions were powerfully represented at all levels of the Party; in the NEC itself, two thirds of its members owed their places to trade union votes. Elsewhere we have noted that, constitutionally, Labour embodied both confederal and unitary principle, and that the latter manifested itself most strongly in the relationship between the NEC and local parties.[90] But even here the scope of central authority was limited. Though formally subject to the NEC's authority, CLPs replicated the national Party's hybrid constitutional structure; they, too, consisted of a combination of individual membership units and affiliated trade union organisations. Often, particularly in staunch Labour areas, the latter were entitled to the majority of seats on the constituency GC. Levels of participation amongst trade union delegates tended to be low, except when a parliamentary selection was in the offing. In a considerable proportion of Labour-held seats, trade unions had come to regard the constituency as one of their own.

This notion was particularly firmly implanted in areas – like South Wales or parts of Yorkshire – where Labour Party organisation had developed as an off shoot of the unions, and where one union was powerfully entrenched (classically in mining areas). Rooted in tradition, sustained by convention and rendered effective by numbers and cash the assumption that a seat – like a Victorian benefice – lay in the gift of the locally dominant union was not easily shaken.

The effect of this was to place a major impediment to the expansion of central power in this most crucial area. Its importance was, paradoxically, enhanced by the slipping hold (reflecting their falling membership) of unions like the NUM and NUR who traditionally sponsored large numbers of MPs, as they became increasingly sensitive to developments which might further erode their influence.

This faced the Party leadership with something of a dilemma. Both Hugh Gaitskell and the senior official responsible for overseeing parliamentary selection, National Agent Len Williams, favoured greater centralisation, and the latter certainly was drawn to the idea of a parliamentary panel. As we have seen, two motives lay behind this – to improve the quality of candidates and to guard against the selection of 'unsuitable' individuals. Most trade union officials were sympathetic to the latter but suspected – rightly – that the former was directed against the adoption of dull, ageing and uninspired trade unionists.

As a result, many trade unionists were bound to look askance at any move designed to extend the NEC's say in the selection process. The point was explicitly acknowledged by a NAD paper on the topic. It noted that efforts to improve the selection procedure were 'likely to come up against sectional interests in marginal and Labour seats, and Head Office insistence that there should be several nominees of a high standard is almost certain to be regarded by interested unions as unwarranted interference'.[91]

Naturally, members of the trade union section of the NEC were not unaware of the concerns of their organisations. As a result, schemes for centralising the selection process risked alienating trade union loyalists as well as left-wing constituency representatives; further, if they required rule changes, they might well run aground on the block vote reefs at Conference. Indeed, an examination of NEC intervention in selection contests indicates that it was more responsive to the susceptibilities of trade unions than to the priorities of the Party leadership.

On three occasions in the late 1950s and the 1960s, trade union NEC members formally complained that nominees from unions traditionally strong in constituencies had been excluded from selections where by-elections were to be held. Under the rules, the Executive was empowered, in by-elections, to make a nomination to the short list. Prodded by the aggrieved union the NEC invoked this power though in none of the three contests was the nominee successful.[92] On another occasion — where the circumstances are more obscure – considerably more drastic central intervention appears to have been prompted by trade union indignation over the defeat of its nominee. In Newark – a traditionally trade union seat – the selection of a left-wing teacher was invalidated on grounds of irregularities (the successful candidate had canvassed for support) although the irregularity was neither uncommon nor was it technically a breach of rules.[93]

In April 1958, the Chairman's Sub-Committee decided to nominate Tom Driberg, on behalf of the NEC, for the forthcoming St Helens by-election. The choice of a veteran left-winger and rebel was unusual, partly explained by the convention that the NEC only nominated ex-MPs who had recently lost their seats and partly by the fact that Driberg happened, that year, to be Chairman of the Party and hence the beneficiary of a certain deference towards holders of that office. It proved to be a singularly unfortunate step. St Helens snubbed the NEC by excluding Driberg from the short list; and at the NEC, Walter Padley, leader of the shopworkers union, USDAW, moved an angry resolution berating the Chairman's Sub-Committee for the 'utterly intolerable position' into which it had placed the unions and their representatives on the National Executive.[94] Shortly after, probably to sooth ruffled union feelings, the NEC decided that in future informal consultation should take place with the leaders of trade unions likely to be affected by the retirement of sponsored MPs.[95]

But perhaps the most dramatic example of union resentment at any attempt to intrude upon their traditional fiefdoms is the fate meted out to the Party's top official, Morgan Phillips, in 1959. Without consulting any national leader he decided to seek adoption as candidate for the safe seat of Derbyshire North East. The Area NUM – which regarded the constituency as its own – was affronted, and moblised sufficient NUM delegates at the selection conference to elect its nominee, thus inflicting a humiliating rebuff on the Party's General Secretary[96] – a step it is difficult to imagine occurring in any Labour's continental sister parties.

If the union's organic link with the Party erected a constitutional barrier to centralisation, political factors also urged circumspection. Whilst the leadership genuinely wished to better the quality of its parliamentary representation, it could not ignore the impact of any change on the balance of forces within the Party. The trade union bloc of MPs might not provide a treasure of talent for future Labour cabinets but, composed largely of right-wing loyalists, it was a bulwark for the leadership against the left. Curbing the supply of such material might hold hidden dangers, since abler non-sponsored MPs might also be more left-wing. Secondly, trade union participants in selections, especially in safer Labour areas, constituted a major artery through which (as we shall see in more detail below) Transport House influenced coursed. Any steps which might discourage that participation would damage the artery and diminish the ability of Party officials to influence selection outcomes.

Constituency party autonomy
By the 1950s the right of constituency parties to choose their own candidates was firmly ingrained. As a NAD paper commented, 'the basic assumption of the electoral procedure is that the local party is the body which decides which member is suitable to be its parliamentary candidate.'[97] This assumption was reinforced by two features of the British political process.

The first was the single ballot, single-member constituency electoral system. Proportional representation, where members are elected from multi-member constituency or national party lists, facilitates a greater measure of central control because (at least in the absence of a powerful regional tier of Party authority) the task of deciding the composition and (more crucially) the ordering of candidates is almost inevitably appropriated by national organs. In these circumstances, the temptation to exclude or demote dissident elements is not easily resisted.[98] Conversely, the British system inhibits central control because of the assumption – well established in the practice of the older parties – that a candidate who contested a constituency should be selected within it. Constituency autonomy was further reinforced by the reliance of the national Party upon voluntary local activists to man the electoral machine. The required input of effort could only be elicited if a co-operative relationship existed between such local Party workers and the central authorities. If a candidate was forced upon an unwilling CLP, activists would not participate in election work with any enthusiasm.[99]

One further factor buttressed CLP autonomy – a resentment against any overt national interference. This did not derive – as Ranney has argued – primarily from 'a suspicion of all forms of party authority';[100] on the contrary, as we shall argue, respect for authority was an important feature of Labour's culture in the centralist era.[101] Rather it stemmed from a parochial outlook which looked askance at attempts by interlopers from London to meddle in their affairs.[102]

Administrative constraints
The final restraint upon centralisation of candidate selection was an administrative one. The creation of an Approved List of candidates and tighter procedures for vetting candidates laid the groundwork for a larger measure of national control. But the potential was never fully realised due to the weakness of the Party's administrative machinery. This point can best be demonstrated by examining the fate of the Approved List.

The new system never worked particularly well. The left had always opposed it and, within a couple of years, right-wingers began expressing doubts; it was agreed to review the procedure after the next election.[103] In January 1965 the National Agent produced a paper which – anticipating objections – staunchly defended the procedure and, indeed, suggested it be tightened up.[104] As we have seen, large numbers of nominees continued to be interviewed throughout that year. But in June 1966, after the election held in that year, Ian Mikardo raised the matter again. He argued that the vetting procedure was both too time-consuming and too shallow and recommended that it be abandoned.[105]

Mikardo had for years been a vigorous critic of central interference in candidate selection but had rarely made much headway against the NEC's entrenched right-wing majority. But this time he prevailed; the B List reverted to a list of available, rather than approved candidates and the elaborate interviewing schedule was discontinued. Mikardo succeeded because his doubts were shared by those who, whilst agreeing with the principle of an Approved List, accepted that, in practice, it did not work. Few NEC members volunteered to serve on the interviewing panel and too little time was available to interview nominees (ten minutes was allocated per person) to properly assess their views. As a result the system proved incapable of meeting its objectives.[106]

This need not have formed an insurmountable obstacle if the Party had possessed the administrative resources to institute a systematic checking procedure, but it did not. The whole weight of administering the system – and much of the burden of interviewing – fell upon already overstretched senior officials like the National and Assistant National Agents.

In fact, the NEC did not simply revert to the pre-1960 system; it effectively ceased to exercise any political control whatsoever over the B List, a practice formalised in 1970 when the NEC decided that it be reduced to the status of a 'non-approved file' of people nominated by CLPs and affiliated organisations. This reflected a general easing of central controls in the late 1960s, illustrated by the fact that the practice of excluding nominees for the B List on political grounds ended[107] and only one candidate failed to secure endorsement.[108]

5.7 The placing of parliamentary candidates

So far, we have focussed upon the formal authority of the NEC. As we have seen, this was deployed, from time to time, to influence the range of choice available to constituencies and, on occasion, to block candidatures.[109] The Executive also possessed some limited powers to place candidates. It could suspend normal procedures in an emergency or when, in its judgement, 'the interests of the Labour Party demand'; and it had the right to make a nomination to the short list for by-election contests.[110] These powers were, however, rarely used. It is understandable, therefore, that Rush reached the conclusion that the NEC's role is primarily negative: 'no part of the selection machinery at its disposal is conducive to ensuring the selection of a particular individual'.[111] But whilst true in a formal sense, this comment misses out a key dimension in the selection process, the exercise of influence. By influence we mean the ability to affect behaviour by means other than the application of rules or the enforcement of commands. We shall argue that the relative weakness of central authority in the field of candidate selection was, in this period, more than compensated by the influence that regional officials exerted on its behalf.

Regional Organisers were key figures in both Labour's organisational and power structure. They formed the administrative arm of the Party's machine and were invested with the delegated authority of the NEC. But, as we shall attempt to show, they were also wielders of influence in their own right and played a key role in the impression of leadership preferences on the selection process.

Regional Organisers and the selection process
The rules governing Labour's parliamentary selections are detailed and, although the Regional Organiser is charged with ensuring that selection conferences conform to them (and this might give a little leeway), they

tightly restrict the role he can play. Indeed one can say that once the selection conference has begun, the capacity of regional officials to exercise influence is minimal. All the key points of leverage lie prior to this stage.

Suggesting nominations
It was a common practice for most Regional Organisers to compile their own lists of suitable candidates.[112] This might contain as many as 150 names, only a minority of whom might be living within the region (nor would they all necessarily be on either the A or B Lists). Regional Organisers kept their eyes open for attractive candidates: one commented that he regarded himself as a talent spotter.[113] Trade union officials might suggest names and occasionally aspiring candidates would visit regional offices and if judged suitable material would earn themselves a place on the list. What were the criteria of suitability? Here practice varied somewhat. One former organiser looked back with considerable satisfaction to the string of capable right-wingers whom he had assisted;[114] another denied that political standpoint was a factor and instanced others such as ability, experience in the Labour movement and general presentability.[115]

As a result, when a vacancy occurred, an Organiser usually had in mind one or more appropriate names. How, then, did he promote him/them (rarely her)? It is at this point that power models can lead to a total misconstruction of the role of regional officials. For the measure of their influence was not the ability to induce a constituency even against its resistance to accept a favoured candidate, but rather the alacrity with which they were approached by constituency members seeking their advice.[116] The average CLP (in a winnable seat) would have very little experience in selecting a candidate. Unless there was a local 'favourite son', the members would have little idea who to consider for selection and, given the defects of the formal rules, they were unlikely to learn a great deal once the procedure got under way.[117] Whether they turned to the Regional Organiser for advice depended upon the quality of the relationships he had established with parties in his region. If Party members (particularly officers) trusted him, regarded him as fair, well-informed and sympathetic, they would solicit and act upon his advice. The crucial factor, then, was not his power, or even his role as representative of the NEC but his general political standing and prestige.

Timetable and procedure
Regional officials, we have seen, were formally responsible for overseeing the whole selection process. Due to the complexity of the rules, and the inexperience of most Party members, constituency parties were

heavily reliant upon the guidance of full-time officials. This was encouraged by the NEC when, in 1960, it made consultation with the Regional Office mandatory before a CLP initiated the selection process.[118] In theory (and to a large extent in practice) the regional official carried out his duties in an impartial manner, simply checking that at all stages the constituency complied with the rules. Yet his role as custodian of the rules afforded him a certain latitude in interpreting and applying them in ways that could advance his own political goals. Regional Organisers varied in both their willingness and their ability to engage in such procedural management. The astute and more politically minded official was aware of the resources at his disposal. His technical expertise (both practical experience and thorough grounding in the rules) particularly when compared to the lack of political sophistication of most Party activists furnished him with opportunities – if he had the confidence of senior CLP officers – to organise the procedure in such a way as to benefit a favoured candidate – which most Regional Organisers tended to have.[119] As representative of the NEC, he was responsible for arranging the timetable, which could have a bearing on the eventual results. Some Organisers (who were not necessarily typical) were quick to take advantage of this. For example, in 1965, Jim Cattermole, the East Midlands Regional Organiser and the Secretary of Grantham CLP 'agreed to defer looking at the timetable until we had established two or three new parties in the constituency. I (i.e. Cattermole) said that I would let him have the names of people he might look at before the selection process was put into operation'.[120] In another case (and another region) some years later the Regional Organiser kept the selection process 'completely under wraps': aside from a few constituency notables, nobody was aware that a selection conference was shortly to be held, enabling the preferred candidate (a senior local councillor) with the help of the Regional Organiser, to do much valuable groundwork which gave him a decided edge over his rivals.[121]

The Regional Organiser's role as advisor on procedure could also be used to further a preferred candidate. For example one CLP Secretary, at the Regional Officer's prompting, refused to circulate any information to people seeking nominations (for example the names and addresses of the Secretaries of local branches and affiliated organisations), to distribute their CVs or indeed to answer their correspondence, greatly hampering their ability to communicate with or even make known their existence to the CLP: all the while a favoured candidate quietly mustered support.[122]

One should not exaggerate the Regional Organiser's discretion here: if he abused his position he could easily earn himself a rap over the knuckles from Transport House. Further regional officials took their duty to supervise the selection process seriously and the great majority would avoid any overt manipulation of the rules. Yet between overt manipulation and absolute neutrality lay sufficient territory to allow organisers if they so chose to exert a significant degree of influence.

Short-Listing

The range of choice presented to a constituency at the selection conference was set by the composition of the short-list.[123] Two well-tested devices to influence the final outcome were to exclude a strong challenger from the list, or to ensure that it did not include anyone of unpalatable political opinions. If a Regional Organiser held the confidence of the constituency executive, he was well placed to influence its short-listing decisions. He might draw the attention of Executive members to any nominee who had been rejected for the B List (or, indeed, to others with dubious political beliefs or affiliations) and intimate that such a candidate might experience difficulties obtaining endorsement; he might devise a composite image of the ideal candidate for the constituency – horses for courses – an image to which some nominees might bear a closer resemblance than others.[124] Key variables included the Regional Officer's persuasive skills and the executive's readiness to listen to his advice, and these obviously varied considerably. At one extreme was stood Jim Cattermole, the highly capable East Midlands Organiser. He told Ranney that 'the main reason why so few anti-leadership candidates were adopted by the CLPs in his region was that he made it his business to see they were kept off short-lists whenever he could prevent it. Any Regional Organiser who does not do the same, he felt, is not doing his job properly'.[125] One notable example was his success in ensuring the absence of a strong candidate from the left in the Lincoln constituency in 1962; faced with a choice of three right-wingers, it opted for the most attractive, Dick Taverne.[126] Others might have been less assiduous, less politically committed and less successful. But the practice was not uncommon and it represented probably the most important method for influencing selection outcomes available to Regional Organisers.[127]

The selection conference

In theory, delegates at a selection conference approached the coming contest with a free mind and made their decision on the basis of the merits of the various performances. In practice (at least in Labour seats or marginals) this rarely happened. Merit was an important factor but it was by no means the only one; others included whether a nominee was sponsored, the composition of the GC and the political leanings of the contenders. But particularly relevant, in closely fought selection battles, was the organising ability of the nominees and their backers.

Organising ability is a major power resource in any voluntary association; but it was (and is) particularly so in the Labour Party because of the composition of the body responsible for candidate selection, the GC. It consists of delegates from ward parties, women's and Young Socialist sections (if any) and affiliated trade unions and socialist societies. The key to success for an aspiring Parliamentarian was often less his capacity to impress existing regular attenders at GC's than to secure the appointment to that body of as many supporters as possible.

The structure of GC's was ideally fixed for such an exercise in (what may be called) organisational politics. The rules for affiliation and delegate entitlement were (and are) complex. But, for our purposes, only certain essential elements need to be borne in mind. Firstly, the potential for building up delegate strength was (in this period) almost boundless: women's sections and Young Socialists branches could be set up specifically for the purpose; trade union branches could be persuaded to affiliate. Secondly, only a handful of people need be involved, whether to form a new women's section or a branch of a nationally affiliated socialist society (e.g. the Fabian Society or the Socialist Education Association); or to induce a (usually sparsely attended) trade union branch to affiliate or, if affiliated, to send its full delegate entitlement, committed to the 'right' nominee. Thirdly, Labour clubs, if associated with a ward party, could literally buy up membership cards and hence boost the ward's delegation to the GC.

Finally, CLP rules lent themselves to the packing of GC's. This last point merits elaboration. Three rules (all since modified or abolished) catered in particular for those with a flair for organisational manipulation. Firstly, any union branch with members in a constituency (even if it was located miles away) could affiliate to a CLP if it was part of a nationally affiliated organisation. Secondly, until 1965, delegates from such affiliated union branches were not required to be individual Party members: this created a reservoir of politically indifferent union members who could be corralled to attend a selection conference.[128] Thirdly a delegate who had never attended before was free to appear at a selection conference, cast his vote and then vanish again.[129]

As a result of these factors, participation rates at GC meetings were highly elastic. This elasticity created a situation in which organisational politics could flourish. Success at a selection conference, then, as often as not, rested more upon mobilisation than upon persuasion, encouraging the resort to a range of organisational stratagems: forming or securing the affiliation of bodies eligible to send delegates to the GC; pushing for the appointment of 'reliable' people as delegates; briefing them over tactics; ensuring that they turned up on the day.

Anyone with the time, aptitude and flair could engage in organisational politics. But Regional Organisers (and other full-time Party and trade union officials)[130] were especially well qualified. Partly this was for the negative reason that, in the 1950s and 1960s, few rank and file Party members (especially on the left) appreciated the crucial character of the organisational dimension. But more importantly, Party officials possessed a number of crucial resources not available to ordinary activists: these included their full-time status (which gave them time and enabled them to amass valuable political experience and skills) technical expertise, and access to useful information.[131] We shall now examine the ways in which the regional staff could accumulate and deploy these resources.

The trade union connection

Trade unions, in the 1950s and 1960s, were key factors in the selection process. We have already noted that a high proportion of Labour's safer seats were regarded as trade union benefices. This reflected (as well as tradition and convention) the preponderance of trade union delegates on many GCs (much more a characteristic of constituency parties in this period than in the last decade or so). A representative sample of local parties compiled by the NAD in 1955 indicated that, in Labour areas, trade union delegates usually equalled or outnumbered those from the branches.[132]

Trade union delegates were less prone to participate – often affiliated branches did not even fill up their delegate entitlement – than their political counterparts. But it was precisely this fact which rendered organisational politics so central a feature of candidate selection. Regional Organisers were well aware of this. The nature of their work – their various electoral, organisational and administrative responsibilities – encouraged them to cultivate good relations with as wide a spread of trade unions in their areas as possible. Harmonious relationships between Party and union officials was facilitated, in this period, by a number of factors. Firstly, Regional Organisers possessed a status which placed them on a par with their counterparts in union hierarchies. Secondly, they generally saw eye to eye on the main political issues; often sharing a right-wing and pro-(Labour) leadership orientation. Thirdly, the relationship provided mutual benefits. This last point is worth amplifying.

If Regional Organisers were keen to advance particular candidates, so too were unions. Most unions maintained a parliamentary panel and, naturally, wished to see its members selected. Hence the relationship between Party and union officials was, in this respect at least, a reciprocal one. One example may illustrate this. The National Union of Seamen was eager to secure the adoption of one of its abler young members, John Prescott. When it became evident that one of Hull's MPs was ailing and was unlikely to contest his seat again, the local Regional

Organiser, Harold Sims, was contacted by the NUS official in the city's docks. The two men knew each other, the atmosphere was 'convivial' when they met, and both were impressed by Prescott's calibre. Sims helped smooth the way for Prescott by arranging for him to attend meetings and make contacts in the constituency, *prior* to a vacancy being announced. As a result, when selection proceedings were formally instituted, the NUS man was already well known in the area.[133]

Some (perhaps most) Regional Organisers made a point of establishing a close and regular liaison with one or two top regional union officials – usually from the strongest union (or unions) in the vicinity. Jim Cattermole, for example, worked closely with Arthur Hayday, a prominent figure in the GMWU; Paul Carmody, in a somewhat later period, collaborated with Barney Donnaghy, President of the Lancashire NUM. In these cases, the trade unionist acted as key intermediary in organising 'the union side of things' in selection contests. For example, when a by-election occurred in Leicester, Cattermole and Hayday jointly agreed to promote the candidature of Tom Bradley, an official of the Transport Salaried Staff Association (TSSA). Hayday helped rally support amongst affiliated union branches whilst the Regional Organiser concentrated upon his constituency contacts.[134]

The technique of mobilising usually dormant trade union delegates was, of course, available to others as well as Regional Organisers. But they enjoyed multiple advantages, including experience, a grasp of the rules governing trade union affiliation and – via their relationship with trade union leaders – an access to branch officers which few others could equal. Perhaps alone, or one of a few, aware that a parliamentary vacancy would soon arise, they might arrange for the affiliation of union branches; mobilise support, through their contacts, for favoured candidates; and spur affiliated branches to fill up their delegate entitlements for selection conferences.[135]

The effects of this might be to alter the political composition of GC as regular attenders suddenly found themselves outnumbered by newcomers – a phenomenon often much resented,[136] but about which local activists could do little.

Constituency Contacts

The importance of the trade union connection did not lead to the neglect of the political wing of the Party. The shrewder Organisers recognised that their influence and their ability to do their jobs effectively, depended upon the amassing of two valuable resources: information and esteem.[137] For this reason, they strove to cultivate the trust and confidence of local activists, particularly office holders and other Party notables. They regarded 'contact work' as a vital part of their job: endless visits to constituency party meetings, getting to know the local officers, discussing their problems, proffering advice. The more adept Regional Organisers sought to be as unobtrusive as possible at meetings, perhaps not participating at all. The object was not to impress members with his authority but to establish good working relations, particularly with the local officers. Hence the experienced organiser would make a point of meeting them privately before a meeting. 'You could do more with a private chat over a drink than through attendance at a formal meeting,' one former organiser commented. Another noted the usefulness of regional summer schools, where he would get to know and earn the respect of Party activists as a result of which they might later contact him seeking his counsel.[138]

Organisers were particularly keen to foster good relations with CLP secretaries. This was the key post in any constituency party. The secretary managed constituency business (and controlled the flow of information); and was responsible, in conjunction with Regional Office, for arranging the selection procedure. He (rarely she) was the repository of vital information for putative Parliamentary candidates – the name and addresses of offices of ward parties, lists of affiliated organisations as well as general knowledge of the politics of his party.

Constituency secretaries were not always representative of the politics of their parties – certainly less so than today.[139] Within the predominantly working class membership of CLPs (in Labour areas) administrative and clerical skills, vital for the proper discharge of the secretary's duties, were in short supply. Hence secretaries were usually selected for their ability, rather than their politics, and often enjoyed lengthy tenures. Partly as a result of their role responsibilities, they tended to be somewhat more right-wing (or 'apolitical') in outlook, displaying more interest in organisational than in policy or doctrinal questions. For these reasons (and in contrast to the last decade) they were for the most part instinctively well-disposed to regional officials. In addition a much higher proportion of secretaries were full-time agents[140] (though still only a minority). Although not directly under the authority of either Transport House or Regional Office,[141] secretary/agents had closer contacts with regional officials than their lay counterparts, might aspire to promotion to a regional post, and, hence, might well be particularly receptive to the Regional Organiser's counsel.

Whether a full-time agent or not, most secretaries enjoyed relationships of trust and mutual understanding with the Regional Organiser and were an important source of information. Their importance, however, was primarily as part of a broader network of contacts that the able and more assiduous Regional Organisers sought to establish in their regions. To the extent that they succeeded – and this varied considerably – they built up a collection of people upon whom they could rely and who, conversely, looked to them for advice. As a result, they would generally be well briefed about the affairs of most CLPs in their region: the political outlook of local notables, their idiosyncracies and rivalries; the extent to which ward parties were active and the numbers and orientation of affiliated union branches. All this was valuable information for an aspiring candidate and its selective disbursement by the adroit Regional Organiser could give the favoured contender a considerable competitive edge over his rivals.

It is impossible to determine with any precision the extent to which Regional Organisers shaped selection decisions. Wilson claims that in one (un-named) region about one half the sitting MPs obtained their seats with the help of behind-the-scenes manoeuvring from the regional staff.[142] If so, this would not be typical. Regional Organisers differed both in their skills and their inclination to promote particular candidates. Some certainly enjoyed the reputation of successful parliamentary king-makers – notably Reg Wallis and Paul Carmody (both in the North West) and Jim Cattermole.[143] Others 'sticklers for the rules' were either unwilling to get involved in candidate selection beyond what their official duties required (e.g. Reg Underhill in the West Midlands in the 1950s')[144] or lacked the adroitness of a Wallis or a Cattermole. But there is little doubt that, overall, Regional Organisers did possess a substantial degree of influence.[145]

Regional influence and central control

To what extent did Regional Organisers, in their efforts to affect selection outcomes, act as agents of the centre? The formal position was unambiguous: they were appointed, paid by and under the authority of the NEC and Head Office; hence they were duty bound to comply with whatever directives emanated from Transport House. However, this formal position needs to be qualified for two reasons.

Firstly, in practice, Regional Organisers were afforded a considerable amount of discretion in defining their own roles. This was built into the role expectations of both Organisers and their official superiors (almost invariably former Regional Organisers themselves). Secondly, their efforts to shape the selection process were, in large part, exercises of influence rather than of formal authority; and influence was a commodity which was, in substantial measures, accumulated on their own behalf.

Nevertheless, the regional staff did operate as an institutional channel through which Transport House could indirectly (and unobtrusively) regulate candidate selection. Now and again, Regional Organisers would receive requests to promote the Parliamentary careers of particular individuals.[146] One particular Organiser recalled that from time to time Gaitskell would tell him privately 'Look, young X is a very able chap and we could use him to good purpose in the House. Would you see what you can do for him.'[147] Occasionally Regional Organisers would be asked by Transport House to use their influence to keep particular nominees off a short-list.[148]

Generally speaking, however, Transport House (and the leadership) were content to rely upon the judgement and good works of Regional Organisers in assisting deserving candidates. This was partly because of the mutual trust and a certain *esprit de corps* that bound together regional and national officials; but it was also due to the community of outlook between all senior officials, the NEC and the Parliamentary leadership. In following their own instincts, Regional Organisers were also acting as loyal servants of their political masters (the NEC) and working in the interests of the leadership.

In the early 1960s – a time of acute infra-party strife – some regional officials do appear to have become unusually embroiled in factional activities. During these years regular meetings of an informal Committee, consisting of the Party Leader, the Chief Whip, Bill Rodgers, the secretary of the right-wing ginger group the Campaign for Democratic Socialism and other influential figures met regularly to secure the selection of right-wing candidates for winnable constituencies.[149] This relied upon the co-operation of at least some Regional Organisers; indeed Seyd suggests that Gaitskell's private militia, the CDS, received help from no less than seven out of twelve organisers.[150]

However, relations between the CDS and the NAD were uneasy (which presumably influenced the disposition of regional officials to co-operate) due to the latter's distaste for factional involvement in candidate selection; and Sara Barker was only dissuaded from raising the issue of CDS activities at the NEC at Gaitskell's personal request.[151]

This period of the early 1960s was probably not typical. The more common pattern was for Transport House to leave the sensitive, but crucial, arena of candidate selection to the good sense and discretion of its regional staff. But it did reflect both the determination of the right-wing leadership, at a moment of internal crisis, to tighten its hold upon the Party and the amenability of much of the Party machine. It may well be that only Gaitskell's untimely death in early 1963, and his replacement by the much more liberal-minded Harold Wilson reversed the momentum towards firmer central control.

Chapter Six

Labour's response to Trotskyism, 1951 to the late 1960s

An analysis of the response of the Labour Party to Trotskyism within its ranks is highly germane to this study for three reasons. Firstly, as a case study, it offers insight into two key facets of the social-democratic centralist regime: the range of its claims to regulate the behaviour (and beliefs) of Party members, and the way in which these claims were enforced. Secondly, the experience of Labour's handling of the Trotskyist 'problem' helped mould the attitudes of the left and determine their behaviour in later years. Thirdly, despite frequent and highly-charged references (especially recently) to the 'witch-hunts' of the 1950s, they have never been treated to a detailed and systematic analysis.

6.1 The early history of Trotskyism

Scattered groups of Trotskyists had existed in Britain since the mid 1930s. Initially, they opted to work within the ILP; however, the rapid decline of that body after its departure from the Labour Party persuaded Trotsky and his British supporters to look for more fertile pastures: in the circumstances this could only mean the Labour Party. However, despite being minuscule in numbers, the Trotskyist movement was severely divided over strategy and tactics, in particular over the value of work in the Labour Party. In 1944, the various groups achieved a rare unity when they were induced to coalesce into the Revolutionary Communist Party.[1] But the unity was fragile. From the beginning, a minority group within the RCP, led by Gerry Healy, had practised entryism. It came to be known as 'The Club' and began fostering contacts with left-wing elements in the Labour Party. By 1949, riven with internal dissension and disappointed in its expectations of a revolutionary upsurge, the RCP decided to disband. It instructed its members to join the Labour Party.[2]

This appeared to justify Healy's espousal of 'entryism'. The tactic of 'entryism' was interpreted in different ways by the various Trotskyist groups. But its essential features were simple enough. Trotskyists should join the Labour Party, but only as part of a secret, tightly organised group. This group should, at all times, maintain its separate identity, its own leadership and an organisation parallel to the 'host' party. Members of the group would be rigorously bound by its directives, enforced by a strict internal disciplinary system, following the democratic centralist model.

From this perspective, entrance into the Labour Party was viewed simply as a tactic. It implied no sense of normative commitment, no real engagement in the Party as a distinct 'political community' with its own norms, rules and principles. This represented a key distinction with other left-wing groups, like the Socialist League, the Bevanites and Victory for Socialism. These groups might dissent strongly from Labour's official policies and leadership, but their final loyalty was to the Party as a distinct political entity. In contrast, for 'entryists' the value of membership was judged on utilitarian grounds: the opportunities it furnished to enlist new recruits, disseminate propaganda, expose the 'bankruptcy' and 'betrayal' of the leadership (and the mainstream left) and, ultimately, to construct from within the host organisation a new, truly socialist party.

This was the tactic that, from the late 1940s onwards, the Healyite faction pursued. In 1948 Healy joined forces with John Lawrence, another prominent Trotskyist and co-operated with a number of 'hard left' members of the Labour Party to found *Socialist Outlook*. It was edited by John Lawrence and regular contributors included MPs Tom Braddock, Ron Chamberlain, Harold Davies and Ellis Smith and trade unionists Jack Stanley, Ernie Roberts and Jim Figgins of the NUR.[3]

Healy envisaged *Socialist Outlook* as a conduit through which Trotskyist ideas could spread into the Labour Party. Although the journal was effectively controlled by The Club it opened its pages to other currents within the left and diluted its message in order to extend its influence.[4] Its establishment did not go unnoticed in Smith Square. In July 1950, the Organisation Sub-Committee received a document which provided details of its management, contributors and political line. However, the Committee was not unduly perturbed and was content to advise CLPs to discourage circulation.[5]

The Club may well have interpreted this as an encouraging signal. A further opportunity to promote its tactic of co-operation with non-Trotskyist leftists had already presented itself. In 1949 two MPs on the left fringes of the PLP, Ellis Smith and Fenner Brockway, founded

Socialist Fellowship. Unlike the Keep Left group of MPs, Socialist Fellowship sought to enlist the support of Party activists and trade unionists as well as Parliamentarians. Socialist Outlook welcomed the new group and members of The Club participated actively in the founding conference of Socialist Fellowship in November 1949. Ellis Smith was elected President and the other office-holders included Lawrence, Brockway, Tom Braddock and Chamberlain.[6] Active local branches were established in a number of areas, such as Manchester and Liverpool although (certainly in the latter case) connections with the centre were often tenuous.[7]

Initially, the Socialist Fellowship was a 'hard left' rather than a Trotskyist organisation. However, it soon fell under the Healyites' sway, after Smith and Brockway quit over its support for Communist forces in the Korean War and increasing Trotskyist influence.[8] By this time, too, the period of NEC tolerance had ended. By the spring of 1951 Bevan and two other Ministers had resigned in protest over the rearmament programme. Assuming its role as guardian of the Government, and with its patience already taxed by Bevan's attacks, the NEC proscribed Socialist Fellowship on the grounds of its 'disturbing' impact on the Party.[9]

Socialist Fellowship reacted by dissolving to avoid further disciplinary action. *Socialist Outlook* attempted to step into the gap, holding readers meetings and organising a network of contacts. However, a split within its ranks occurred in 1953/4. A minority, led by Lawrence and Braddock supported the formation of a 'united front' with Communists and the non-Trotskyist left and, in 1954 resigned from the editorial board.[10] Healy did not long enjoy his ascendancy, since within a few months *Socialist Outlook* was proscribed and ceased publication.[11]

The Club continued to be active. It published a journal *Labour Review* and could count on a small body of adherents concentrated in South London, Leeds, Birmingham and Liverpool. It received a significant boost to its strength in 1956/7 when it recruited a number of disaffected Communists who had quit (or had been expelled from) the Party over the Soviet invasion of Hungary. In 1957 the Healyites and the ex-Communists pooled their forces to launch *Newsletter*. The following year, the Trotskyists felt sufficiently emboldened to form the Socialist Labour League.[12]

By this time, The Club was left with a largely clear field (aside from small groups led by further RCP members Ted Grant and Tony Cliff). The Lawrence group, which had entrenched itself in Holborn and St. Pancras, had provoked the ire of Transport House, and Lawrence and a number of supporters were expelled from the Labour Party, mostly to join the Communist Party. The SLL sought to broaden its base by participating actively in industrial disputes, some of which received extensive press coverage. Its life within the Labour Party, however, was short-lived.

In 1959 both the SLL and *Newsletter* were proscribed, constituency parties in Streatham and Norwood were reorganised and leading Trotskyists in Leeds and Birmingham and elsewhere were expelled. The SLL reacted to these major reverses by concentrating, in the early 1960s, upon the reconstituted Young Socialist organisation. By 1964 it had fallen under Healyite control and was used to gain footholds in a number of constituency parties. There followed another wave of expulsions and disaffiliations in 1965 which effectively eliminated organised Trotskyism from the Labour Party. Shortly after, Healy renounced entryist tactics in favour of building an independent revolutionary party, which was to surface in the following decade as the Workers Revolutionary Party. As a result, until the rise of Militant in the mid 1970s, Trotskyist involvement in the Labour Party was minimal for a decade.

6.2 The response of Transport House

The response at Transport House (i.e. senior NEC members and Head Office officials) to Trotskyism can best be understood as a conjunction of two factors: their attitudes towards Trotskyism as a political creed and their perception of the managerial requirements of the Party, as mediated by social-democratic centralist principles.

Attitudes towards Trotskyism were a product of both experience and ideological dispositions. The formative period of the post-war generation of Labour politicians and officials was the interwar years – a time of envenomed hostility between Social Democracy and Communism. Both politicians and trade union leaders had fought resolutely against Communist attempts to infiltrate the Party.[13] During the period of the Labour Government and particularly after the onset of the Cold War in 1947, the NEC's main concern was the threat of Communist infiltration. Compared to the perceived threat posed by Moscow and the forces under its command, Trotskyism appeared to be an insignificant and marginal phenomenon. But this was a purely pragmatic judgement. The objections to Communism also applied to Trotskyism, and Transport House did not hesitate to utilise against the latter the mechanisms of containment which had evolved in the struggle to repulse the former.

Policy towards Trotskyists was also shaped by the perceived managerial needs of the Party. The NEC regarded Trotskyism as an alien political creed, and the efforts of its adherents to gain a foothold within the Party as acts of political subversion. In a managerial regime governed by the precepts of social-democratic centralism there was no place for a phenomenon construed in this light. What mechanisms were available to counter Trotskyism? How were they utilised? How effective were they? The rest of this chapter will be devoted to answering these questions.

6.3 Mechanisms of control

Information gathering and monitoring
A prerequisite of an effective control capability is the possession of a facility for information gathering and monitoring. This was less a mechanism in itself than a requirement upon which the feasibility of other mechanisms depended (as we shall see). We have already noted that the Party lacked an intelligence section: no member of staff was specifically entrusted with the task of compiling information in a systematic way. Much depended upon the interests and inclinations of individuals. Len Williams, for example, for many years a top Party official, read widely in Trotskyist and Communist literature and was well-informed.[14] The main sources of information were as follows: firstly Trotskyist publications themselves; second Communist publications – a useful source of information, since the Communists kept a sharp eye on their rivals; thirdly, reports from regional officials. This last was the most important, providing the main means for the monitoring of Trotskyist work in the constituencies. National officials were heavily reliant on the information supplied by the regional staff for the compilation of their reports.[15] The regional staff, in turn kept in close contact with each other, exchanging information about known or suspected Trotskyists. Most of this correspondence is not available for public inspection; however access has been obtained to the relevant records of the London Labour Party covering the early 1960s.

These records indicate that regional officials took seriously the task of gathering information about the identity, whereabouts and activities of Trotskyists.[16] Such information was important for two main reasons: firstly to keep Head Office and the regions alert to developments on the left fringes of politics, helping them to anticipate problems that might arise in particular constituencies. Secondly, information about the backgrounds, identities and activities of individual Trotskyists was required if effective disciplinary action was to be taken. Correspondence between the London and other Regional Offices give some indication as to the type of material that was being sought and accumulated.

In May 1960 John Anson, Yorkshire Regional Organiser, reported to his counterpart in London, Len Sims, that Mr and Mrs John Archer had recently moved to his area 'a particularly dangerous couple because they are . . . attached to the top layer of the SLL'. The following February, in response to requests from Sims, various Regional Organisers supplied information on individuals suspected of association with the (proscribed) SLL, noting details of their political leanings, activities and connections. Anson, for example, observed that all active unilateralists in Leeds 'appear to be working in close association with the SLL'.[17] In his reply, Emrys Jones, West Midlands Regional Organiser, noted of members of the Coventry Young Socialists that, although there was no hard data about their links with the SLL 'they certainly speak and act as if they were connected with it.'[18] Similarly, a North West regional official wrote to Sims of 'a Mr Knight' a full-time SLL official who had organised a group of sympathisers. He added that 'a careful watch is being kept on their activities'.[20]

Aside from their own efforts, how did Regional Organisers obtain their information? Undoubtedly, the bulk was provided by their, usually extensive, network of contacts in their area – agents, party officers, trade union officials and ex-Trotskyists.[21] There is some evidence that they obtained additional information from outside bodies. For example, Sims despatched a document on the 'Socialist Review Group' prepared by Industrial Relations Information Services, an organisation which gathered information upon leftists and industrial militants for use by their opponents in industry and the unions.[22] It would also seem that there were contacts with more official sources.

In May 1959 (during the height of the action against the SLL) the London Regional Women's Organiser wrote to Len Williams about a conversation with Mr Nodes, agent in Putney Labour Party, who 'gave me information of such a grave character that I feel it should be the subject of a special report to you'. It appears that Nodes was visited by an officer from Scotland Yard who informed him that a 'highly influential and important member of the Trotskyists', George Ellis, had moved into the area. According to the officer, Ellis had been secretary of the 'South West London Group of Trotskyists'. Nodes was able to provide the police with his address and they agreed to 'keep in touch with each other in this matter'.[23] From the wording and tone of the letter, one can surmise that contacts of this nature with Scotland Yard were not regarded as extraordinary. The question immediately arises as to how representative the few files available from the London Labour party archive are. They may well exaggerate the information gathering and surveillance work of Party officials for two reasons. Firstly, the period 1959–65 was one of unusually intense Trotskyist activity (until, that is, the rise of Militant in the 1970s).[24] Secondly, there was inevitably a concentration of that activity in the London area. With these two qualifications, it seems clear that monitoring Trotskyism was a normal part of the work of the regional staff – indeed the very accuracy of NAD documents submitted to the NEC would appear to confirm this. It would, however, be wrong to conclude that an elaborate machinery of surveillance existed. Transport House lacked the requisite manpower, resources and professional expertise. Much depended on the interest, ability and order of priorities of Party organisers. Not least, officials relied heavily upon contacts within the constituencies – locally employed agents, lay officers etc. – to supply them with information.

Proscriptions

In earlier chapters we have discussed the origins and functioning of proscription as a general method of control;[25] here we shall consider its specific employment against Trotskyists. 'Proscription' meant a formal declaration by the NEC, under Clause II 4(b) of the Constitution, that an organisation was ineligible for affiliation to the Labour Party. Membership of a proscribed organisation was incompatible with that of the Labour Party, hence the effect of proscribing an organisation was to render its members liable to expulsion.

Under Clause VIII Section 2(b) of the Constitution, the NEC was required to enforce the Constitution and rules of the party and 'to take any action it deems necessary for such purpose whether by way of disaffiliation of an organisation or of an individual, or otherwise'.[26] This, particularly the final clause, provided a broad constitutional mandate for the NEC to proscribe an organisation. Clause II (3) of the Constitution identified four organisational characteristics *any* of which rendered an organisation ineligible for affiliation: having their own 'Programme, Principles and Policy for distinctive and separate propaganda; possessing branches in the constituencies; promoting their own candidates for public office; and, finally, owing allegiance to any political organisations situated abroad.[27] The generous wording of clause VIII 2(b) offered further latitude to the NEC, in that it could (and did) claim that it was authorised by this clause to take any steps it saw fit to uphold the Constitution, including proscription, without having to provide a specific reason.

These clauses afforded the NEC its constitutional armoury. It does not follow that it used the broad powers vested in it indiscriminately; thus it did not automatically ban bodies once they had been ascertained to be Trotskyist. Other criteria had to be satisfied. These can best be identified by briefly analysing the history of Trotskyist proscriptions.

The first Trotskyist group to come to the attention of the NEC was the RCP. The Executive decided not to proscribe it, on the grounds that it did not present a significant threat.[28] Four years later, however, the NEC proscribed Socialist Fellowship (by then under Trotskyist control), because 'the factional activities it organised had a disturbing effect on many [constituency] parties', distracting them from their electoral functions.[29]

As we have seen, this had little effect on the Trotskyists, particularly

The Club, then beginning to operate in a number of constituencies. Presumably for this reason, and perhaps also because of the general increase in factional strife within the Party, the NEC determined on further action. In July 1954 the Organisation Sub-Committee resolved that 'persons associated with or supporting *Socialist Outlook* are declared to be ineligible for membership of the Labour Party'.[30] Unlike the earlier case of Socialist Fellowship, this step caused an outcry. The grounds given by the General Secretary for proscribing the paper were the involvement of a number of regular contributors in the RCP and the promotion by the paper of 'propaganda hostile to the declared policy of the Party'.[31]

As many on the left pointed out, the NEC was interpreting its powers in a very expansive manner. *Socialist Outlook* was a magazine and not an organisation and hence, in theory, could not be proscribed; if it did indeed conceal the operation of an organisation, no attempt was made to prove its existence. Michael Foot, writing in *Tribune*, delivered a heavy broadside at the Executive: a 'stupid, cowardly and totalitarian edict . . . novel and sinister . . . Such a device might fittingly be issued within a Fascist or Communist Party.'[32] The *New Statesman* joined in the chorus of condemnation and masses of resolutions protesting against the decision poured into Transport House.[33]

It is worth dwelling upon the nature of this response, since it was to have significant repercussions in later years. The broader context needs to be appreciated: it was at the height of the Bevanite controversy: indeed, some Bevanites suspected that it foreshadowed a similar move against *Tribune*. The proscription was widely regarded on the left as yet another instance of the dominant right's intolerance, its propensity to resort to authoritarian methods to quell dissent: 'miserable witch hunts' and acts of 'totalitarian suppression', in Michael Foot's words.[34] At the time, the left could do little more than protest. But the repugnance it felt for these methods of Party control was to have consequences when two decades later a more left-wing Executive refused to utilise them to curb the growing influence of the Militant Tendency.[35]

The NEC's action was effective to the extent that it induced *Socialist Outlook* to cease publication, but it did not extinguish or even noticeably hamper a slow, highly localised growth in Trotskyist influence. This was kept under scrutiny by Transport House, which became increasingly disturbed by Trotskyist penetration in a number of constituencies.[36] Healy's rather reckless decision to form the SLL in 1959 both convinced senior Labour officials that action was necessary and provided the justification for it. Within a few weeks the new organisation was proscribed.

It is pertinent at this point to reflect upon the rationale of proscriptions as an instrument of control. At the 1959 Party Conference, Harry

Nicholas, on behalf of the NEC, advanced two reasons for the proscription of *Newsletter* and the SLL. The first was ideological. Both bodies, Nicholas explained, 'stand for policies which are fundamentally opposed to the policies of the Labour Party',[37] and envisaged the use of revolutionary methods.[38] This particular ground for proscription will be discussed in more detail below. The second was organisational. Both *Newsletter* and SLL were charged with fomenting 'disruption'. The term was frequently employed as a warrant for imposing disciplinary penalties. Its imprecision exasperated left-wing critics: it appeared to justify disciplinary measures whenever the Executive chose to employ them with the victims left bewildered as to the exact nature of the offence. The reluctance to define the term – 'it is rather like an elephant', Harry Nicholas unhelpfully observed, quoting Attlee, 'you cannot define it, but you know one when you see it'[39] – in fact reflected more the insensitivity of Transport House, than Communist-style arbitrariness. For the term did have a fairly precise meaning or, rather, range of meanings.

Firstly, it referred to the tactic of infiltration, or entryism. Whilst not unduly exercised by individual Trotskyists within the Party the NEC did take exception to the suborning or manipulation of the constituency machinery of the Party by outside bodies, particularly where these bodies were seen to be ideologically offensive. Secondly, any form of factional activity was viewed with disfavour (as we have seen).[40] Where factions were centrally directed and with their own internal disciplinary system they were considered to be beyond the pale. The term 'disruption' also encompassed unacceptable types of behaviour, of which there were two sorts: firstly, actions which embarrassed the Party publicly and inflicted damage upon it internally and, secondly, various types of misconduct ranging from the use of irregular or unconstitutional practices to the intimidation and abuse of opponents.[41]

The NEC did not automatically proscribe an organisation found guilty of 'disruption'. One episode illustrates this. In 1962, the NEC investigated 'Young Guard' a faction within the Young Socialists directed by the 'International Socialism' group. Although the enquiry team did find Young Guard 'disruptive' in some of the senses of the term, it accepted its avowals of loyalty to the Party and decided not to proscribe.[42] Political judgements were involved here – Young Guard was seen as a possible counterweight to the SLL dominated Keep Left group – yet this does indicate that a degree of leeway was afforded.

What, then, would finally determine a decision to proscribe? One must recall here that any form of Trotskyist activity was regarded as illicit. Transport House, during this period, never accepted the right of Trotskyists to enjoy the benefits of membership – hence their residence within the Party was always a precarious one. Indeed success was likely to be self-defeating in that it would, sooner or later provoke the NEC into taking action. Secondly some types of 'disruption' were seen as more dangerous than others: tightly-knit, disciplined bodies with branches throughout the country and which sought to gain control of constituency parties to promote their own ends (ideological and organisational) were treated as serious transgressors and – as the case of the SLL in 1959 – were given short shrift.

In fact, proscription was only to be used once more in this period as a weapon against Trotskyism, when action was taken against *Keep Left*, the kernel of a Healyite group[43] – a step which failed in its purposes since three years later the *Young Socialist*, by now under total SLL control, was disbanded.[44] This particular act again contradicts the view that the NEC remorselessly hunted Trotskyist heretics, particularly in the youth movement, in this period. For a number of years the Assistant National Agent fed the Executive with reports of the SLL's gradual seizure of control of the Young Socialists, but many of its members were reluctant to act, until the Young Socialist's denunciations of Party policy took on a particularly strident tone in 1964, when an election was imminent.[45]

How useful was proscription as a method of control? Constitutionally, the proscription of an organisation greatly facilitated the expulsion of its members. As the National Agent explained: 'When the NEC proscribes an organisation, members of it no longer conform to the conditions of Party membership . . . and are not eligible to be individual members'. It followed that a constituency party need not embark upon the protracted and difficult process of expulsion, since '*such individuals have been expelled by the NEC's act of proscription*'. Its sole responsibility was to establish whether or not a person had been a member of a proscribed body.[46] By simplifying the process of expulsion proscription rendered it more credible. The behaviour of Trotskyists was undoubtedly influenced by their calculation as to the likelihood of sanctions being invoked against them. The easier it was to deploy sanctions, the more likely they would be deployed and hence the greater their deterrent value. This assumes that (unlike in democratic centralist parties) expulsions and purges were not easy operations – that Transport House was not the ruthless, capricious machine it was sometimes portrayed. Hence the value of the constitutional device of proscription. Those points are well illustrated by what *Tribune* called 'the incredible Sedler case'.[47]

Leeds had, for a number of years, been a centre of Trotskyist activity. In April 1959, in response to the NEC's proscription of the SLL and *Newsletter*, the city party executive rather peremptorily expelled nine party members for 'known association' with the two bodies.[48] One of the expelled, councillors Ron Sedler (a solicitor) instituted legal proceedings for a declaration that the expulsions were unlawful, since the executive had both infringed its own rules (only the General Committee was empowered to expel) and natural justice (the defendents had been denied the right to be heard in their own defence).[49] The executive had been careless in disregarding its own rules, but otherwise its behaviour was not exceptional.[50] But with the threat of a court case, the NEC (after consulting its own lawyers) advised the Leeds executive to rescind the expulsions (it also accepted liability for Sedler's costs).[51]

The Leeds party recommended disciplinary proceedings, this time taking care to conform to its own rules. The accused, however, protested at the procedure adopted. They were given insufficient time (five minutes) to present their case and their witnesses were not called. Tempers became frayed, 'wild and tumultuous scenes' erupted, and eight of the nine (including Sedler) stalked out. Of the four defendants dealt with at the meeting, Sedler and two others were expelled in their absence.[52]

The affair was, however, by no means over. Sedler warned that he would instigate further legal action; the NEC (on legal advice) decided, once more, to abrogate his expulsion and by agreement with his solicitors to despatch an enquiry team consisting of NEC members (James Griffiths and Ray Gunter) to hear the case anew.

Sedler's reprieve was short-lived. The hearing took place on 8th July and the enquiry team considered a lengthy charge sheet against the Leeds solicitor. The charges fell into three groups: firstly that Sedler had consistently spurned Party policy in word and deed; secondly that he knowingly had consorted over a number of years with members of proscribed organisations; thirdly, and most importantly, that he was intimately involved with the SLL.[53] The panel was convinced by the evidence that Sedler did not genuinely accept the 'principles and policy' of the Party and had persistently engaged in 'dissident and disruptive activities' and accordingly expelled him.[54]

Sedler, finally, after three attempts, was evicted. Transport House and the NEC doubtless appraised the sheer amount of time, effort and money (in legal costs and other expenses) in securing the expulsion of one man. It could be claimed that the willingness of the Party to invest all these resources in itself had a salutory effect in strengthening its credibility; and there is little doubt that Transport House's reputation for toughness did constrain the behaviour of Trotskyists within the Party.[55] Nevertheless the balance was a fine one.

Of all the charges levelled against Sedler, the most formidable, and the most difficult to refute, were the allegations of his connections with proscribed organisations. Once a member was found to be associated with such an organisation he was, according to Morgan Phillips 'henceforth ineligible for membership of the Labour Party'.[56] Without the

power of proscription, the long and arduous path to the Leeds Councill-
or's expulsion would have been strewn with yet more impediments.
This confirms its value as a control mechanism which could swiftly be
pressed into service in the battle against Trotskyist elements.

In fact, Transport House's interpretations of the meaning and implications of proscription rested on rather shaky legal foundations. As a
result of the Sedler legal imbroglio, the NEC had taken counsel's advice.
Lynn Ungoed-Thomas, QC, MP, submitted some pertinent observations. Firstly, the phrases 'associated with' and 'henceforth ineligible
for' were 'somewhat lacking in precision, particularly for the purpose of
automatically terminating membership of the Labour Party as seems to
have been suggested'. To what extent did 'associated with' extend
beyond mere membership and what, legally, would be the test of such an
association? Secondly, did 'henceforth ineligible for' apply to the date of
the appropriate NEC resolution or from the time when a member
associated with a proscribed organisation refused to surrender that
association?

Thomas concluded that, in his view, the NEC was fully entitled to
proscribe an organisation, but any subsequent expulsions had to be in
accordance with the principles of natural justice 'which require notice
of the charge and a reasonable opportunity of being heard, and as far as I
can judge on the information before me, *the opportunity of ceasing
association with the proscribed organisation.*'[57]

In the official NEC hearing (and in a departure from practice) some
steps were taken towards fulfilling the first two conditions, but not the
third; Sedler was disciplined primarily for his associations *prior to* the
proscriptions and despite his insistence that he had severed his connection with the SLL when the NEC issued its circular. Why did Transport
House not take full account of Ungoed-Thomas' opinion? The most
likely reason is that it ran against the grain of established Party practice.
Labour's disciplinary rules and procedures took little account of the
principles of natural justice, as ennumerated by Ungoed-Thomas. To
have done so would have considerably added to the time and effort
involved in disciplinary action; furthermore, it would have been quite at
odds with the centralist doctrine which underscored the normal exercise of NEC powers. In addition, it was easy to dismiss the Sedler case as
an isolated instance. There were, after all, few Trotskyist solicitors
active in Labour's ranks and, even if they had been familiar with the law,
the great majority of members would have regarded taking the Party to
the courts as dishonourable conduct. Finally the courts themselves, at
the time, showed little disposition to intervene in the internal affairs of
political parties. Several more years were to elapse before the Party
began to be troubled by considerations of natural justice.

Ideological Regulation
As we have seen, a central tenet of social-democratic centralist doctrine
was the protection of Labour's ideological identity as a social-democratic party and throughout the 1950s and early 1960s this formed a key
managerial precept. This was clearly articulated by the National Agent,
Len Williams. Replying to charges that members were being driven out
of the Party for their beliefs, he dismissed as 'incredibly naive' the belief
that a person can hold any opinion he likes and yet be a member. 'An
organisation is formed to fulfil certain purposes; anybody who joins
with a view to winning the organisation for other purposes is always in
danger of expulsion'.[58]

Labour's purpose were shaped, according to Williams, by its 'social-
democratic principles'. These he defined as 'the use of constitutional
means to achieve socialism'. He logically inferred from this that the
Party was 'quite justified in refusing to accept as members those who
believe in the revolutionary way'.[59] Consistent with this understanding, the NEC gave as one reason for the proscription of the SLL its
declaration that it was 'an organisation of Marxists' and that 'as distinct
from others who call themselves socialists, Marxists do not believe that
it is possible to reform capitalism out of existence or to change it into
Socialism by peaceful means'.[60]

Aside from involvement in proscribed organisations, ideological
deviation was the main lever for removing Trotskyists (and other
unwanted elements) from the Party. It was not uncommon for the NEC
to cite as one ground for disciplinary action evidence that the defendants
did not conform to the 'programme, principles and policy of the Party'.
Occasionally the NEC went further, requiring that it be established
that defendants 'no longer advanced views contrary to the principles of
the Labour Party',[61] or that they had 'fundamentally changed their
political principles'[62] before they could be readmitted into the Party.

Ideological regulation, as a form of control, derived its constitutional
mandate from the clause that required each individual member to
conform to the 'programme, principles and policy of the Party';[64] this
was understood to entail, we have noted, adherence to parliamentary
institutions and the electoral road to socialism. The problem with this
understanding is that it had no clear constitutional grounding. As Morgan Phillips himself pointed out, the Constitution nowhere defined the
'principles, policy and programme' of the Party. Indeed, he implicitly
conceded that commitment to parliamentary democracy could not be
regarded as a fundamental principle by urging the NEC to revise the
Constitution to include it.[65]

How do we explain the failure to give some ideological flesh and blood
to the concept of 'the principles of the Labour Party or of 'democratic
socialism'? There are a number of reasons for this. Firstly (and despite

the complaints of rampant witch-hunting) the leadership was not interested in establishing standards of ideological conformity; they merely wished to rid the Party of people they considered to be inveterate troublemakers. Since most of these fell at the bar of proper respect for parliamentary institutions, they were satisfied that the existing rules were adequate. To many (particularly trade unionists) devoting too much attention to the fine detail of ideology was to stir up a hornets nest, and for no reason. (It was for this reason that many on the centre-right of the Party regarded Gaitskell's attempt to open the question of Labour's aims as irresponsible and provocative.)

This pragmatic mentality was, in turn, an outgrowth of the Party's history, its origins as a *party of labour* designed to promote the material interests of the working class by utilising the existing Parliamentary machinery, rather than as a social-democratic party propagating an ideology. This characteristic remained even after the Party, in the inter-war years, clothed itself with items of social-democratic doctrine. Indeed it was reinforced by the type of member the Party enrolled (or retained) in its urban heartlands: people motivated less by beliefs than by sentiments of class solidarity who envisaged Labour primarily as a vehicle for working-class representation.

But ideology has multiple purposes: a programme on the model of the SPD's Heidelburg (1925) and Bad Godesberg (1959) statements not only outlined what the party stood for but what it stood against. It laid down boundaries between social democracy and rival creeds, and offered a coherent set of principles to which members were expected to adhere. Ideology imparts a sense of direction and evokes loyalty and commitment; but it is also an instrument of control. Thus Bad Godesberg equipped the SPD leadership was a solid basis for ideological regulation and could be (and was) employed to remove left-wing dissenters who appeared to deviate from the programme.[66]

The Labour Party lacked a comparable instrument. The equation of a Len Williams or Morgan Phillips of democratic socialism with the parliamentary road, but a road without a destination, was philosphically unsatisfying. The system of ideological regulation, as it operated in the 1950s and 1960s, never amounted to rigorous ideological *regimentation* on the communist (or Trotskyist) model. Most of those who fell foul of it were people whose loyalty to the Party was, at its best, divided and many of them embraced doctrines from which the bulk of membership would have instinctively recoiled. Nevertheless, the absence of an explicit and convincing ideological rationale for evicting people for holding views 'incompatible with the principles of the Labour Party' convinced many people, especially on the left, that ideological regulation was no more than crude thought control. The skein of ideological regulation was unravelled so rapidly in the 1970s precisely because of its threadbare quality. Indeed one can go further; the force of ideological integrity as a key managerial requirement was bound sooner or later to abate in the age of Wilsonian pragmatism. It was as if builders, having erected the scaffolding, decided that bricks and mortar were superfluous. One senior Party official sensed the fragility of the structure. Writing at the height of the constitutional crises, in 1960, Morgan Phillips urged that the constitution be revised to incorporate clear statements spelling out 'what [the Party] is, what are its aims; what are the principles it will adopt in achieving its aims'.[67]

The advice was not taken;[68] ideological disputation of this order probably struck the practical trade union representatives on the NEC (and their political allies, like Wilson) as an unwanted distraction from the real business of politics – the modern equivalent of medieval scholastic debates. In consequence, support for parliamentary democracy remained the sole tenet defining Transport House's understanding of 'the principles of the Labour Party'. This served its control purpose in that it erected a barrier to 'infiltration' by far-left elements. But, by its very nature, it could not furnish an ideological identity for the Party, a series of principles to which all or most members would subscribe and demarcating it from all other political organisations. A tenet which was so *transparently* designed to exclude a specific group of people rather than as a basis of affirmation lacked conviction: it inevitably alienated left-wingers who were consistently irked by the spectacle of stolid individuals like Ray Gunter, not known for their socialist fervour, interrogating others about their socialist credentials.[69] The whole system of ideological regulation, rooted so obviously in right-wing political hegemony and, indeed, geared to sustaining it, lacked legitimacy. It had never acquired the support of the left and was therefore vulnerable to a shift in the balance of political forces. By the 1970s when organised Trotskyism on a significant scale reappeared, it had become a cardinal maxim of a much stronger NEC left that no party member should be penalised for his beliefs. And the following decade, when action was once more taken against a Trotskyist group, successive Party General Secretaries (Ron Hayward, Jim Mortimer, Larry Whitty) were at pains to stress that nobody would be penalised for their beliefs.

Reorganisation of constituency parties
Under Clause VIII Section 2(c) of the Constitution, the NEC was authorised, as part of its role as upholder of the rules, to disaffiliate party organisations. This was the most drastic sanction in the Executive's armoury, and one only sparingly used in the contest against Trotskyism – on six occasions. We will briefly examine the sequence of events which prompted reorganisation in each of the occasions.

Norwood 1954   In September 1954, shortly after the proscription of Socialist Outlook, Transport House received a request from members of Norwood CLP for an enquiry into its affairs. The NEC responded positively.[70] The main evidence considered by the enquiry team consisted of a document, drawn up by members of Norwood CLP, presenting a detailed, and quite varied, list of charges against three individuals: T. Mercer, D. Finch and E. R. (Ted) Knight. These ranged from general accusations – the three 'conducted a conspiracy to promote the policies of the Revolutionary Communist Party (Trotskyists) – to quite specific ones – highly provocative attacks on royalty in the local party paper, obtaining the closure of one ward party and so on. The main burden of the charges were that the three used the machinery of the Party to propagate Trotskyist views, that they incessantly attacked Labour's policy and leadership, engaged in highly divisive factional activity and employed ruthless and dishonest methods and, generally, brought discredit upon the party in a marginal constituency.[71]

The enquiry accepted the validity of the charges, finding the three guilty of using 'disruptive and vicious methods' and of advocating 'political principles which are opposed to those of the Labour Party'. It recommended that they be expelled and the party be reorganised by the National Agent.[72]

Islington East 1954   Trotskyists had been active for a number of years in this constituency. The two most influential, Mr and Mrs Hunter, were close associates of Gerry Healy, former members of the RCP and subsequently involved in *Socialist Outlook*. By 1954 they had attracted much support on Islington East's GC, though the constituency Executive was hostile. It complained that the Trotskyist group, directed by the Hunters, had for a number of years, fomented disruption in the party, launching venomous attacks on their opponents, denouncing official Labour policy and dominating the agenda of GC meetings.[73] The GC ignored Morgan Phillip's circular on the proscription of *Socialist Outlook* but the Executive, encouraged by its able full-time secretary-agent, Bill Jones, determined to act and expelled the Hunters. This 'bent the rules a bit' (since the Executive was only empowered to make recommendations to the GC) and uproar followed at the next GC.[74] The NEC decided to hold an inquiry. The report acknowledged that the proper disciplinary procedures had not been adopted, but, notwithstanding, the expulsions were upheld on the grounds that the Hunters had disrupted the work of the CLP and advanced views 'not in accord with those of the Labour Party'. Further, the NEC responded to Islington East GC's opposition to the expulsion of the two Trotskyists by ordering the reorganisation of the party,[75] in the course of which several more members were expelled.[76]

Holborn and St Pancras South 1958   In the spring of 1958, Transport House received a letter, signed by twenty members of the GMC of Holborn and St Pancras South CLP. It complained of the activities of a group headed by councillor John Lawrence which had disrupted the work of the constituency, and requested Transport House intervention. Lawrence was a veteran of the RCP and a variety of Trotskyist groups who had broken from his former associates as he gravitated more closely to the Communist Party (he was an enthusiastic defender of the Soviet invasion of Hungary). He was also the highly controversial leader of the council in the borough of St Pancras.[77]

The major complaints contained in the letter were as follows: firstly that the Lawrence group has propagated views closer in spirit to the Communist than the Labour Party: secondly, that it operated as a tightly organised and disciplined faction allowing it to subvert the real wishes of the majority; thirdly, that Lawrence personally worked closely with Communist-controlled organisations and, fourthly, that his group used tactics of intimidation and manipulation to cower its opponents and to seize control of the Labour Group on St Pancras Council.[78] The activities of Lawrence as leader of St Pancras Council had caused the Party leadership a considerable degree of embarrassment, generating much unfavourable publicity. Hence, the Executive pounced upon this opportunity to act with alacrity and decided to suspend Lawrence and re-organise the party. The party was accordingly reconstructed and the leading members of the Lawrence group, including Lawrence himself, were expelled.[79]

Norwood 1959   The earlier reorganisation of Norwood had not achieved its objective. Gerry Healy's club continued to exert considerable influence behind the scenes. By early 1959, Party officials were convinced that only forceful national intervention would resolve what they clearly perceived as a serious problem. Proscription of the SLL and *Newsletter* provided the go-ahead. In April, Len Sims, London Regional Organiser, met the officers of the CLP and drew up a list of prominent members definitely or probably associated with the SLL.[80] However, both the Norwood Executive and General Committee demurred; it was apparent that a majority of both bodies were opposed to expulsion and were not prepared to comply with NEC directives. After receiving a request from Norwood's senior officers, the NEC authorised the National Agent to reorganise the Party and a number of expulsions followed.[81]

Streatham 1959   Together with Norwood, Streatham was the epicentre of Trotskyist activity – Gerry Healy himself was a leading member.

As in the neighbouring constituency, Streatham's General Committee refused to take action against members alleged to be associated with the SLL. After a stormy session during which the GC refused to accept the Regional Organiser's 'advice' that as a known member of the SLL Healy was automatically excluded and had no right to attend Party meetings, Sims declared the meeting 'unconstitutional' and effectively suspended Streatham on his own authority.[82] The NEC promptly ratified his action and instructed the National Agent to reorganise the party.[83] In both Norwood and Streatham dissident members formed unofficial 'suspended' parties but these soon faded away.

Paddington South 1965 The sequence of events was rather different in this, the last constituency to be reorganised. Throughout 1964, according to the Regional Organiser, John Keys, the SLL tightened its grip on Paddington South CLP. With the approval of the constituency the SLL-controlled Young Socialist branch engaged in a number of activities which disturbed Party officials, including involvement in industrial disputes (which drew a protest from the Union of Postal Workers). Eventually, John Keys received a letter from a number of disenchanted local party members urging NEC intervention.

Keys compiled a detailed report for the Executive, noting that Paddington South had fallen into the hands of the Trotskyists, had allowed its Young Socialist branch to engage in many 'disruptive activities' and had distributed literature and an election address which had 'viciously attacked' Harold Wilson, Labour's new Prime Minister. Furthermore, the dominant clique was using irregular and intimidatory practices to maintain its hold on the constituency. The NEC responded by authorising the reorganisation of the Party.[84]

Looking at the six organisations as a whole, one can identify two main factors prompting NEC action. Firstly, wilful non-compliance with NEC rulings. Top officials, of the Williams-Barker school, recognised that rule by discipline and by consent were not alternatives, but interconnected. If duly constituted authority – authority based on consent enshrined in freely accepted rules – was shown to be ineffective, then regard for it would falter, rebelliousness, appearing to be rewarded, would flourish and its legitimacy would begin to be questioned. This was the rationale for what struck many critics for the unnecessarily heavy-handedness of discipline in the social-democratic centralist period.

The second factor was evidence that a dominant group within a constituency was promoting 'disruptive activities'. As we have seen, this term covered a variety of conduct, ranging from the exploitation of the machinery of the Party to further the ends of an outside group to the use of unconstitutional and intimidatory practices. This latter figured in Norwood in 1954, Holborn and St Pancras South in 1958 and, in particular, in Paddington South in 1964–5.[85] In each case, reorganisation was prompted by requests from a significant number of local members. It may well have been that the requests were encouraged, even suggested, by Party officials.[86] But this in itself was significant. Transport House was fully aware that Trotskyists would seek to portray NEC intervention as a threat to local rights (and that local resentment could easily be ignited if it trod too clumsily). It preferred the garb of an arbiter, invited by local party members to restore *their* rights being threatened by an unrepresentative and autocratic minority. To its critics this garb was no more than a disguise; but it could be contended that, as custodian of the Party's rules, the NEC was under an obligation, both constitutional and moral, to intervene, even to disaffiliate, if a constituency had fallen under the sway of a group prepared to use any means, however improper, to remain in control.

The procedure of reorganisation

Disaffiliation or reorganisation was the ultimate exercise of managerial control, a potent sanction which effectively blocked the implantation of Trotskyism as a significant force in the 1950s and 1960s. Rather surprisingly, the actual procedure used has never been an object of academic study.

The decision to reorganise consisted of two directives: the constituency party would be told that it was suspended and the National Agent 'given authority under the Constitution' to carry out the reorganisation.[87] The procedure the National Agent then followed was a standard one. Constituency parties were always reconstituted from the base upwards. The first stage was to compile as accurate a set as possible of membership records. Members were placed in two categories: those whose loyalty was in question and those whose loyalty was not. The second stage was to write to all in the second category informing them of the fact of suspension and of details of ward meetings to be held as part of the process of reorganisation. Those attending the meeting were asked to sign and hand over a form to the steward at the door reaffirming their acceptance of the conditions of membership and expressing willingness to accept the NEC decision to reorganise, and assist in the re-establishment of ward committees.[88]

The ward meetings were chaired by senior Party officials (the National or Assistant National Agent) accompanied by other officials. The agenda consisted of the election of ward officers and General Committee delegates and nominations for constituency party officers. The chairman explained to the meeting the reasons for reorganisation and members were then asked to vote upon a resolution indicating willingness to co-operate in the reconstitution of the party.[89] The same pattern was followed throughout the constituency with the purpose of electing a 'sound and representative' General Committee. As part of this stage, all organisations affiliated to the constituency (mainly trade union branches) were contacted. They were asked to reaffirm their affiliations and appoint delegates to the GC. These delegates were required to sign a declaration that they conformed to the conditions governing the appointment of delegates. When the cycle of branch meetings was completed, the third stage was reached – the newly elected delegates to the GC were called to a meeting, under the supervision of Party officials, which proceeded to affirm its support for reorganisation and to elect constituency officers. Finally a report was submitted to the appropriate sub-committee of the NEC (Organisation or Chairmen) which considered and almost invariably approved its recommendations, usually involving disciplinary action.

The decisive step in the whole procedure was the selection for differential treatment of those whose loyalty was in doubt. This list would feature only a small number of names, at most 30. Transport House reckoned that the expulsion of relatively few could have broader political ramifications, probably changing the whole political complexion of a party.[90] This was because the Trotskyists, and to a lesser degree their supporters, were by no means typical of the membership at large. They were often distinguished by their energy, their dedication, their verbal skills and assertiveness and not least in importance, their assiduousness in attending meetings. By sheer persistence, force of personality and, often, political adeptness, a relatively small proportion of the overall membership of a branch or constituency Party could gain effective control and erect so invincible a position as to convince opponents that they could only be ousted by central intervention.

Critics of Transport House sometimes gave the impression that apparatchiks from Head Office were let loose upon a constituency party running amok with machetes, and lopping off the heads of anyone who could be suspected of disloyal thoughts. This was quite wrong. Officials, in conjunction with local loyalists, took pains to discriminate between Trotskyists and their associates (albeit a term broadly defined) and ordinary left-wingers. This was partly out of a sense of fairness, partly out of a calculation that drastic purges were unnecessary: if the officers and NCOs were removed, the trouble-making capacity of the rest would be sharply curtailed.

Not all who were placed on the suspect list were expelled – indeed they were given the opportunity to redeem themselves. The purpose of the list was otherwise – effectively to remove from the process of reorganisation (though not initially or necessarily from the Party) all those who could be expected to offer stiff resistance to Transport House. No members who figured on the list were notified of the holding of branch meetings (i.e. they were in practice excluded); instead they received a registered letter asking for a written undertaking that they accepted the conditions of membership and assurances that they did 'not belong to or were actively associated with any proscribed organisation' and would 'co-operate with the NEC in the re-establishment of the Party'.[91]

The wording was specifically designed to sift out Trotskyists. It was assumed (with some justification) that while they might have little hesitation in reaffirming their loyalty to the 'programme, principles and policy' of the Party, and in denying involvement in proscribed organisations, they would be loath to swallow their pride by publicly recanting and agreeing, in writing, to co-operate with reorganisation.[92] The reports presented to the NEC on reorganisation (usually after the completion of the operation) gave details of these responses and contained recommendations for expulsion or suspension when they were deemed to be unsatisfactory.[93]

The significance of this procedure was twofold. Firstly, as we have noted, it removed from the scene (in some cases temporarily) anyone who might create difficulties in the course of the reconstitution of the party. Secondly, it was a mechanism (a loyalty oath, its critics claimed) to single out the 'disloyal' and offer grounds for expulsion – the grounds presumably (they were not actually specified) being either failure to provide appropriate assurances to abide by Party rules and/or membership of or active association with a proscribed organisation. It was hoped, by using this mechanism, to overcome the problems caused by the willingness of some members of the SLL to deny any connection with it.[94]

The standard procedure was criticised not only by Trotskyists but by the mainstream left. *Tribune*, in particular, constantly reproved Transport House for its unfairness – it was arbitrary, it denied a proper hearing to the accused and it failed to specify charges in advance.[95] The procedure of reorganisation was, however, justified on two grounds. Firstly – pragmatically – because it was effective. It achieved its objective, of eliminating disruptive and ideologically hostile forces with a reasonable economy of effort, avoiding long and tiresome disciplinary hearings. But, secondly, it was justified on normative grounds. Disciplinary action may have been distasteful but it was not arbitrary. The NEC was fulfilling its duty to uphold the constitution in a perfectly proper manner by ridding the Party of troublesome and parasitical elements.[96] Normative justification was also afforded by the precepts of social democratic centralism. Given that the unity of the party, and the disciplined pooling of effort were key managerial needs, the NEC was fully warranted in penalising those who it believed sabotaged those needs. Further, the principles of majoritarian democracy legitimated decisions to reorganise, since outside groups were using their command of constituency machinery to defy the will of the majority as articulated in NEC decisions and directives.

Screening
A subsidiary but not insignificant instrument of control was screening, that is the checking by Transport House of the credentials of individuals seeking entry into the Party. Here a distinction needs to be made between applications to join and applications (by expelled members) for readmission. Responsibility for accepting into membership lay with constituency parties (though individuals whose applications were refused could appeal to the NEC). Whether or not known Trotskyists were allowed to join depended very much on the vigilance and/or inclination of the constituencies: if turned down they could on appeal expect little succour from the NEC.[97] This included those who were only transferring membership.

The case of Gus Macdonald (later of Granada and Scottish TV fame) affords an interesting example. A member of Glasgow Gorbals CLP, on moving to London he sought to transfer his Party card to Islington East. His application was rejected and he appealed to the NEC. The London Regional Organiser, asked to check his background and affiliations, was told by his Scottish counterpart that Macdonald had been involved in the Trotskyist Young Guard organisation and had caused 'much trouble' in the Gorbals party.[98] At the enquiry hearing Macdonald acknowledged his participation in Young Guard, though he noted that it had not been proscribed. The enquiry team, after mildly admonishing Islington East's 'unbending attitude' (the Islington parties were well known for their lack of enthusiasm for new, radically minded members[99]) upheld its decision to refuse Macdonald admission, presumably – no grounds were given, indeed no charge had been levelled – on the basis of his connection with the (non-proscribed) Young Guard, and his Trotskyist views.[100]

Throughout much of the rest of the decade the NEC continued to uphold the ideological bar operated by the Islington East, and a number of other CLPs.[101] But it is unlikely that this was typical. Outside those urban bastions where local Labour establishments were strongly entrenched, few constituency parties either had the means or the inclination to screen applicants; the frontiers of the Labour Party have always been permeable.

The case of ex-members seeking readmission was different. The prior approval of the NEC was required before requests by them to re-enter the Party were acceded to. Take the example of Ted Knight, expelled as a very young man from Norwood Labour Party in 1954. He applied for reinstatement on several occasions over a lengthy period. Generally, the applications were dismissed automatically, but from time to time investigations were held. These revealed that Party officials continued to monitor Knight's political activities and attitudes, enabling them to present sufficient evidence to convince the NEC that he remained (whatever his protestations of loyalty) a convinced and committed Healyite.[102]

What were the NEC's criteria in deciding whether or not to reinstate into membership? Firstly, the view of the CLP to which the request was made was important; the NEC rarely agreed to re-entry against local opposition. However, support by an applicant's constituency by no means guaranteed success.[103] Secondly, account was taken of the effects upon a CLP of an individual's re-entry; for example if revived dissension or 'disruptive activity' was anticipated the prospect of a successful application was remote. Thirdly, applicants were expected to display a genuine contrition for their earlier actions and to have renounced revolutionary views. Where a person's record since expulsion was 'clean' and where the NEC was persuaded of the sincerity of affirmations of loyalty, he or she would normally be reinstated.[104] In cases of doubt, applicants would be interviewed and questioned about his/her beliefs and involvements. Where there was evidence that a person continued to consort with a proscribed organisation, the NEC would refuse readmission.

Occasionally, there would be a grey area, where an individual had associations with an unproscribed, though politically suspect group. One example was the long saga for readmission of Roger Protz (later to win fame and acclaim as editor of the *Good Beer Guide*). He was originally expelled for attacking the NEC whilst a member of the Party's staff and for his editorship of the proscribed paper *Keep Left*, and made numerous and strenuous attempts – including instigating legal proceedings – to rejoin. He was finally interviewed in 1968 but rejected largely on the grounds of his editorship of *Labour Worker* (now *Socialist Worker*) the organ of the Trotskyist, though not proscribed, International Socialism group.[105]

It is difficult to judge the effectiveness of screening as an instrument of control. It seems unlikely that Transport House kept track of more than a small minority of potential 'trouble-makers': many of the more obscure must have crept in/back to the Party, except in those areas where city machines maintained their own vetting procedures. However, one should not underestimate the impact of the experienced, able and energetic which could be out of all proportion to their numbers – the rapid rise to prominence of Ted Knight when he finally won his battle for readmission illustrates this.[106] This suggests that the screening process did indeed have an effect in preventing the revival of Trotskyist activity, particularly in areas where it had earlier sunk roots.

The role of Party officials

In the campaign against Trotskyism, regional officials played a central part. Formally they were Party bureaucrats charged with implementing NEC decisions. But, given the virtual absence of a proper administrative machine, this does not accurately describe their role. They were as much political brokers as civil servants. In conjunction with top NAD officials, they had a large amount of discretion in determining how NEC directives were executed. Further, in order to extract as large a measure of co-operation as they could from the mixture of recalcitrant and compliant attitudes they often encountered, they had to supplement the delegated authority of the NEC with other methods of influencing behaviour. We have already indicated the importance of information-gathering in the struggle against Trotskyism. Reorganising constituency parties posed specific problems, requiring the compiling of particular types of information. The most important was the identification of Trotskyist supporters, both because this provided vital political intelligence and also because of the procedures used to isolate and eliminate them; as we have seen, suspected Trotskyists were treated differently from other members in parties undergoing reorganisation: unlike the latter they had to demonstrate innocence rather than rebut charges of guilt. The task of officials was thus like that of continental investigating magistrates amassing evidence for prima facie cases of wrongdoing. In performing this task, they relied heavily upon the assistance of local contacts. For example, Len Sims, the London regional organiser drew up with the aid of two local opponents of Healy a list of members consisting of his outright followers and of sympathisers who objected to expulsions, broken down ward by ward.[107] This enabled Transport House firstly to compile its list of suspects and, secondly, identify the wards where they could anticipate most trouble in the process of reorganisation. Particularly helpful in providing accurate information were disenchanted ex-Trotskyists who were well-placed to pierce the web of disinformation spun by Trotskyist groups as a means of self-protection.[108]

Constituency officers were especially useful as allies. Where circumstances permitted, officials worked closely with them in deciding how best to reconstitute a party.[109] They were often experienced, knew the local terrain and were well versed in the political attitudes and personal idiosyncracies of constituency activists. Where constituency officers (especially the Chairman and Secretary) were unsympathetic, the task of officials was considerably harder. This was the case in Streatham and Paddington South, where senior office holders obstructed regional officials (e.g. refusing to hand over party records) and, helped to organise resistance to the NEC.[110]

However, in all six cases of reorganisation, Transport House could rely upon help from local loyalists. This was of critical importance. Local loyalists furnished information, co-operated in the reformation of branches, filled offices at branch and constituency level and generally ensured that, even after the eviction (or desertion) of a substantial number of activities, the constituency remained a going concern.[111] Without a fair measure of support from within, the task of reorganisation would have been far more demanding. Faced with the adamant resistance of the bulk of activists, Transport House would either have had to draft in more officials (which it could ill-afford) or allow local organisation to lapse. But, during this period, it never had to confront this possibility. It always undertook disaffiliation in the knowledge that a higher proportion (nearly always a majority) of activists would rally round. Put simply, the less co-operation officials received from local members, the more time and energy they had to invest themselves and the more strain was placed upon the Party machine. There was thus a positive link between the degree of co-operation elicited and the efficiency of central control.

Information was a resource provided by others and then utilised by officials. Expertise was a resource which they possessed and could use to good effect in influencing the course of events. It took two forms: firstly a technical expertise deriving from a much better grasp of Party rules than that possessed by the average activist. Aware that direct and overt intervention in General Committee debates might be resented as interference and might, therefore, be counterproductive, officials preferred an indirect mode of intervention: they hoped to affect the outcome of debates by offering formally 'objective' interpretations of the rules, but ones not infrequently slanted towards the desired objective – and not always self-evidently correct. For example, they might advise on the eligibility to vote of delegates (or the constitutionality of a meeting).[112] Their advice was not always accepted, but was a significant influence, since there were always Party members who were undecided about the issues at stake but were anxious to keep within the rules.[113]

The potency of technical expertise as an influence resource varied according to two main factors. Firstly upon the shrewdness and ability of the practitioner; secondly upon his standing in the eyes of Party members. Those two factors also operated in the second type of expertise, which can be labelled political insight: an understanding of how the Party operated. This could be at least as important as technical expertise, for, unlike ordinary Party members, officials were professionals in politics. Employed full time, they were afforded plenty of opportunity to sharpen their political antennae, to develop an intuitive feel for what course of action might be most feasible in a given set of circumstances. The fact that the Trotskyists were often more adept and politically experienced than their local opponents enhanced the value of the advice of Party officials[114] – which was freely given and usually acted upon. This had a broader political ramification: as we have seen, the NEC was reluctant to initiate intervention – it preferred to respond to local requests for assistance. But these 'local requests' were in fact often inspired by officials. For example, the NEC's decision to suspend Norwood CLP was, formally at least, triggered off by a petition, signed by its senior officers and a number of other GC members calling upon the NEC to intervene. In fact the petition was originally drafted by Bill Jones who also helped to gather signatories.[115]

6.4　The containment of Trotskyism

Trotskyism in the 1950s and 1960s never represented a significant threat to the integrity and cohesion of the Labour Party. It was a highly localised phenomenon, and its adherents rarely numbered more than a handful. Nevertheless, the NEC never hesitated about bringing its full weight to bear to eradicate Trotskyist organisations. The reason for this, put at its simplest, was that a Party organisation governed by social-democratic centralist principles, could not absorb either Trotskyist ideas or modes of organisation into its bloodstream. The odd individual might be tolerated; but the Party's authorities would not countenance organised activity especially if it succeeded in seizing control of the Party's constituency machinery. The Party's organisational frontiers were strictly defined and patrolled, and forays by bands of hostile warriors were always punished.[116]

The various mechanisms of control were adequate for this task. The Party machine was run by tough and capable officials, wholly committed to social-democratic centralist principles who enjoyed the full-hearted support of their political masters, the NEC. They were prepared to utilise the Party's disciplinary powers with energy and resolution. But, it would be inaccurate to conclude that their success in extruding Trotskyism was a result of this alone. Social-democratic centralism was widely diffused throughout the Party. Members averse to the use of discipline as a method of resolving political differences were often swayed by the call to comply with majority decisions. Left-wingers often criticised the methods used, but few were prepared to deny the right of the NEC to expel Trotskyists – even to disband constituency parties – once Conference had pronounced its view. Not least of all, the NEC's work was eased by its ability to enlist the co-operation of Party members. Without the willingness of activists to proffer assistance to Party officials, and to man constituency organisations once Trotskyists had been ejected, the Executive's task would have been far more arduous.

Chapter Seven

The basis of social-democratic centralism

7.1 The power of the machine

Our analysis in the preceding chapters has disclosed a high measure of managerial control bolstered by a stringent disciplinary regime. What were the underlying conditions that sustained this system of social-democratic centralism?

From many activists the explanation lay in what John Rex called 'the powerful system of bureaucratic control which operates within the Party today'.[1] Crossman, one of the Party's most perceptive commentators, was convinced that Labour was succumbing to 'the law of increasing oligarchy'.[2] That law, as Crossman acknowledged, found its fullest and most eloquent expression in the work of Michels.

Oligarchy, Michels claimed, was 'a matter of technical and practical necessity'. In its efforts to mobilise the masses, the socialist party creates and continually seeks to perfect an elaborate organisational structure. The drive to organisational effectiveness demands a complex and intricate division of labour, specialisation and 'a rigorously defined and hierarchial bureaucracy'. At the summit of this complex organisation stands a bureaucratic leadership stratum; because it alone possesses the experience and the mastery of technical and political detail, it rapidly renders itself indispensible. With its command over the party machine, its superior skills, and its capacity for co-ordinated action, this stratum is able to elude popular control and to manipulate the amorphus mass membership to serve its own ends. Oligarchy, a massive concentration of power at the centre is, then, 'an essential postulate of the regular functioning of the party machine'.[3]

Subsequent studies of the SPD have provided some confirmation of Michels' propositions. The size of the administrative apparatus steadily expanded, with full-time, centrally appointed officials filling an ever-widening spread of strategic positions throughout the party. Since they were under the direction of the centre, and their pay and their careers depended upon head office, central authority expanded *pari passu* with the growth of their numbers. And the very nature of their tasks as administrators, primarily interested in the efficient working of the party machine, helped generate a mentality averse to radical and dissident ideas which might distract attention from electoral and organisational tasks and undermine party unity.[4]

The SPD's elaborate organisational structure attracted admirers in Britain, foremost amongst whom was Herbert Morrison; he endeavoured to apply the same 'sound principles of organisation' to the London Labour Party (of which he was, for many years, secretary).[5] Morrison rapidly rose to national eminence and, during his prolonged tenure on the NEC, took a keen interest in organisational matters.

It was understandable, then, that finding their political aspirations constantly thwarted, and with an ever-vigilant Transport House ready to punish transgressions, many left-wingers and constituency activists should attribute their importance to the power of the 'party machine'. Yet Labour's machine was far from the impressive bureaucratic structure that Michels envisaged: it was, in reality, weak, ramshackle and rudimentary.

Full-time agents[6] (who numbered over 200 in the 1950s and early 1960s) constituted the bulk of Labour's organisational staff. But they were in no sense part of a bureaucratically-arranged administrative apparatus. They were poorly paid, inadequately trained, and suffered from chronic insecurity 'scraping round to find the current month's salary';[7] not surprisingly, they were of uneven calibre. Indeed the very notion of a full-time agency 'service' was misleading. There was no proper career structure, agency posts were continually collapsing and their occupants spent on average (according to the Wilson Report on Party Organisation) no more than one day a week on organisation. Finally, the agency system was not ordered in a hierarchical manner, with a clear chain of command reaching to the centre. They were appointed and were, for the most part, paid by constituency parties. Naturally it was to them, not Head Office, that they owed their first loyalty.[8]

Agents did figure as a significant element in Regional Organisers' networks, but these, though important, lacked the solidity and dependability of a bureaucratic structure. Regional officials themselves did constitute part of a Labour civil service and did carry the authority and status and possess the skills that so many agents lacked. But they were few in number, underpaid and overstretched.[9] Their power was, as we have seen, rooted as much in their own range of contacts, and the personal authority they acquired, as in their place in the organisational hierarchy.[10]

The absence of a formidable party machine did not prevent the establishment of a centralised power system, but it rendered it both less durable and less effective. We can illustrate the latter point by pondering upon a hypothetical situation. What would have been the consequences of the introduction of the Approved List of Parliamentary candidates in 1960 if the Party had been equipped with the resources to administer it properly? The change in the character of the B List had occurred at a time when Labour's leadership was actively considering ways of tightening central control.[11] The experiment, it will be recalled, was discontinued largely because it could never be made to work effectively. If the administrative machinery had existed, it would have been possible to monitor, more systematically, the attitudes and activities of putative parliamentary candidates. On the principle of functional specialisation, the officials charged with this task would have developed expertise and experience, and been able to accumulate a reliable body of information Given the well established dynamics of bureaucratic expansion it would not have been long, once political circumstances were propitious, before the Approved List would have been converted into a full-blooded Parliamentary Panel granting the NEC greater powers to vet candidates.[12]

The relationship between the calibre of the Party machine and the balance of power between centre and periphery did not pass unnoticed. For example, the *New Statesman* found the proposal for a nationally financed and directed agency service mooted in the Wilson Report (but discarded for financial reasons) administratively sensible. But it added that such an extension of Transport House authority 'would almost certainly have proved totally unacceptable to most constituency parties, once its implications were understood – the more so since some of the more loquacious trade union leaders have openly claimed the extension of their control over the local parties as one of the merits of such a system'.[13]

Why did the process of bureaucratisation not occur in the Labour Party; why were Morrison's 'sound principles of organisation' never fully applied? The prime purpose of the Party machine was not, of course, to enforce discipline but to win elections. But, given the shoddy and decrepit organisation which the Wilson Report uncovered – and held responsible for the loss of many seats – one could anticipate that a serious effort would be made to improve it. This, of course, was precisely Michels' point: bureaucratisation was a matter of 'technical and practical necessity'. But in politics, unlike the pure sciences, 'iron laws' do not grind away with spendid indifference to mere mortals: they have to be apprehended as necessities in the first place. Why did this not happen in the Labour Party?

The obvious reason – and the one always given – was lack of finance.

Successive reports bewailed Labour's tottering organisation but reluctantly conceded that the Party's impoverished state placed strict limits upon what could be achieved. But why not boost income? The answer was that the trade unions, Labour's chief financiers, whilst prepared to provide funds for election campaigns, wanted to keep hold of the purse-strings and determine for themselves how their money should be spent. Why not, then, increase the meagre sums raised from individual members? This option was discussed from time to time, but always dismissed on the grounds that the membership was simply unprepared to pay much more for the privilege of membership. This might have been so, but it does not explain why many of Labour's sister parties abroad managed to retain, proportionately, at least as large a membership whilst requiring the payment of much higher dues.

The superficial answer was that expectations as to the proper level of subscription varied considerably between Britain on the one hand and such countries as West Germany and Sweden on the other – superficial because it does not account for the variations. The deeper answer lies in Labour's origins and rationale.

Most continental socialist parties were established with the avowed intention of transforming the existing social order. They were not simply electoral parties but, in Neumann's term, parties of democratic integration.[14] Because they defined their purpose as the mobilisation of the working class in order to seize power and construct a radically different society they set out to establish veritable counter-communities which could encapsulate much of the lives of their members. Hence they established many newspapers, publishing houses and a host of ancillary organisations like sports clubs, leisure centres, educational institutes and so forth. All of this required a massive and sustained organisational effort, from which many of the consequences that Michels analysed flowed. Once the effort had been made, the elaborate structures created, they proved self-sustaining – even after the original project of system-transformation had been displaced.[15]

In contrast, Labour's aims were always more modest. Its original purpose was to secure improved parliamentary representation for working people; even after 1918 its horizons were for all practical purposes restricted to achieving reform within the contours of the existing social order and it never engaged in the type of ideological and social mobilisation undertaken by other European socialist parties. Hence the impulse towards organisational expansion to be found in parties of democratic integration was absent.

The modern political party, Michels wrote, was 'the methodical organisation of the electoral masses'. This had two integrally related facets: 'parliamentarianism', which 'signifies the aspiration for the greatest number of votes'; and 'party organisation', which signifies the aspiration for the greatest number of members'. The 'vital interest' of the socialist party, he concluded, lay in simultaneously recruiting both.[16] Duverger makes the additional essential point that membership recruitment is a functional imperative for the mass socialist party, not only for the ideological mobilisation of the working class, but also for financial reasons: given the relative poverty of its constituency, it was necessary to 'spread the burden' of revenue-raising as broadly as possible.[17] Means had to be found for enrolling and maintaining a mass membership; and this imparted another powerful impulse towards organisational growth.

Labour's origins as a trade union sponsored party with a readily available external source of cash blunted the financial imperative of mass enrolment. Because contributions to the Labour Party (via the political fund, after 1913) were collected as an increment – in practice – to normal subscription, it was always administratively easier for the Party to raise additional sums by appealing to the unions rather by internal organisational improvements. Further, its financial reliance upon the unions deflected any attempt to alter membership expectations as to the proper level of subscriptions – hence reluctance to pay much became ingrained, hallowed by custom and tradition.

If the ideological and financial impulses towards bureaucratisation were lacking, so too were the political. For the protection afforded by the massed vote of the trade unions at Conference lessened the leadership's vulnerability to rank and file insurgency. In contrast in, say, the French and German parties, the leadership, to retain control of the party, had to maintain a solid base of support within the local organisations. Central direction was not only administratively preferable, it was also politically highly desirable: hence the institution of various organisational methods to counterbalance the weight of the more radically-minded activists.[18] In Britain, this would have been a superfluous expenditure of effort since the leadership could always rally the massed battalions of the unions to quell any rank and file challenge – as happened in the Bevanite period.

Nonetheless, in the generation from the early 1930s to the mid 1960s, Labour's internal life was presided over by a centralised and tightly disciplined power structure. Upon what, then, was it based, and why did it prove to be far less immutable than it appeared at the time? To understand both what sustained social-democratic centralism and the process of its dissolution it is essential to grasp that this structure was to a large extent the product of contingent circumstances, a complex of arrangements, attitudes and relationships which were by no means endemic to a mass working class party. It is to these that we shall now turn.

7.2 The basis of managerial control

Types of control
To explore more fully the basis of Labour's centralised managerial regime it is necessary, as a first step, to distinguish between the various types of control available to the leadership of a political party. We can identify three types: imperative, instrumental and normative. Imperative control refers to a relation where the right to exert control is derived from a party's rules and where compliance can be enforced by sanctions; it consists, in other words, of an exercise of formal authority. Instrumental control refers to a relation where compliance is obtained through the provision of rewards (material or intangible benefits). Normative control refers to a relation in which the right of an authority holder to issue commands is accepted, and where the recipient feels under some obligation to obey.

Imperative control resembles de Crespigny's concept of 'de jure power', that is 'power prescribed by a system of rules'.[19] We have suggested earlier that the NEC's 'de jure power' was reinforced by the prevailing doctrine of constitutional centralism, which sanctioned a high degree of centralisation. Nevertheless, there were inherent limits to the effectiveness of imperative control.

The most salient of these was Labour's character as a voluntary organisation. If they so wished, disenchanted Party members could simply escape central control by relinquishing membership. Some political parties – most notably Communist Parties in western countries in the heyday of democratic centralism – were prepared to pay this price to maintain strict Party discipline. But this option was not one that appealed to Labour. The effectiveness of the Party's electoral machine was seen to depend on the willingness of Party workers to undertake time-consuming chores: canvassing, leafletting, knocking up on election day and so forth. Such a heavy reliance upon voluntary contribution necessarily restricted the utility of imperative control as a way of sustaining central authority.

The absence of an efficient machinery of enforcement further reduced its attraction. This factor reflected the weakness of Labour's organisational apparatus, to which we have already alluded. Transport House was not in a position to police, in any comprehensive and rigorous fashion, the conduct of Party members; and resort to disciplinary action, when undertaken on a significant scale, always placed a substantial strain upon the Party's slender organisational resources. Indeed, as we have seen, when Transport House did engage in such action – for example the reorganisation of constituency parties – it leant heavily upon the co-operation, or, at least, acquiescence of local activists.

The fallibility of imperative control in political parties has been remedied, in some political parties, by utilising instrumental control: the classic example is the American city machine. But the reliance upon inducements to enforce leadership authority was by no means confined to Tammany Hall in Chicago. In Labour's continental sister parties (including the SPD and the French and Italian Socialists) the ability to reward members with material or intangible benefits facilitated leadership control. For example, the system of political vetting of senior appointments to public sector organisations, as it operated in SPD strongholds like the city states of West Berlin, Hamburg and Bremen, gave the leadership considerable powers of patronage. Activists working in local administration who criticised the leadership did so at a possible risk to their own careers; conversely loyalists could earn appropriate rewards.[20] In Italy patronage as a basis of leadership control has been taken much further, both in the dominant Christian Democratic party and (since the early 1960s) within the Socialist Party.

Because of the different political environment in which the Labour Party operates (both locally and nationally) it has never been in the position to disburse benefits on anything like the scale of some of its sister parties – although, as we shall see, the scope for instrumental control was somewhat wider in the 1950s and 1960s than it has become subsequently.

This brings us to the third form of control. We shall argue that a crucial factor sustaining social-democratic centralism was the capacity of Party authorities to exercise a substantial degree of normative control.

Normative control in the Labour Party
The extent and availability of normative control in a political organisation is a function of the orientation to authority of its members. This, in turn, is shaped by their mode of involvement, that is their motives for participating in party affairs. We can distinguish between three modes: the remunerative, the purposive and the solidaristic.[21]

The remunerative mode refers to involvement based on the expectation of benefits. These can either be tangible ones – positions, promotions etc. – or intangible ones, like status or sociability. Reliable evidence on modes of involvement in the Labour party is scanty, but what we do have suggests that the remunerative was more pronounced in the 1950s and 1960s than today. Particularly in Labour strongholds, where such benefits were available, a significant number of members were motivated (*inter alia*) by the struggle for position – seats on the council, a place on the Aldermanic bench or the mayoralty. In his study of Labour groups, Bulpitt found that control over positions was at least as important a source of partisan conflict as policy differences: 'the predominance of patronage disputes suggests a preoccupation with the possession of power, not the use of it for policy purposes'.[22] Many working-class Party members in urban areas, caught in poorly paid, low-status, manual work turned to politics as a means of self-advancement. Speaking of activists in the more deprived areas of Liverpool (in the 1950s) Baxter comments 'Great issues meant nothing, for their concern was with becoming the local Councillor, being the ward secretary and gaining prestige from local politics which was denied most of them in their jobs'.[23]

By no means all members shared these ambitions. Some – whatever their original reason for joining the Party – continued to participate because it offered a social outlet. One (rare) piece of research into local Labour parties (in Manchester) concluded that, particularly in safe wards, local parties were 'social rather than political organisations. Between elections, people attend meetings rather as they would go to a club; to meet their friends and discuss the business of running a club.'[24]

The remunerative mode of involvement fostered a disposition to accept authority for two reasons. Firstly, it faciliated instrumental control; whether at the local or national level it was, almost invariably, a right-wing political establishment which disbursed the rewards, whether in the form of positions or status. Secondly, because those drawn to political activity in the hope of personal satisfaction tended to display little interest in other than parochial issues, they made few demands upon the Party; they were often right-wing (Labour) in inclination and looked askance at radicals whose behaviour risked the Party's electoral prospects, hence diminishing the supply of rewards.[25]

The remunerative mode was always a minority stand. Far more common was the solidaristic. Purposive participants consist, as we shall see, of members who make a conscious decision to join the Party; those who participated for solidaristic reasons did so because it appeared a natural step. They consisted of participants drawn to Labour because involvement seemed a logical extension of class loyalties: thus many politically aware manual workers gravitated to it simply because it was seen as the party of the working class.

Two facets of solidarism were conducive to normative control: the social status of solidaristic participants and their general outlook. By definition, they were predominantly working class and, since they were attracted to the Party less by ideology than by class identification, they were more imbued with prevailing social values. Notable amongst these was deference: a respect for those who occupied senior positions in established hierarchies. To this extent the Labour Party was a microcosm of the wider (working class) social milieu.[26]

Deference within the Party, however, fell short of the 'adulation of the leadership' and the 'cult of veneration among the masses' which Michels discerned in the pre–1914 SPD.[27] It more closely resembled what Dennis Wrong calls 'competent authority'. This he defines as 'a power relation in which the subject obeys the directives of the authority out of a belief in the authority's superior competence or expertise to decide which action will best serve the subject's interests and goals.'[28]

Competent authority was rooted in the social and intellectual distance between the bulk of (working class) Party members on the one hand, and Party leaders and officials on the other; it was particularly evident in Labour-held strongholds where the working class composition of the membership was most pronounced. Since the authority of the Party was primarily encountered through the Regional Organisers, it was in the relationship between them and the rank and file that competent authority was most obviously manifest.

Regional Organisers were regarded – both by Head Office and by the constituencies – as 'the custodians of the Party in the region'.[29] Hence the authority (or 'de jure power') vested in the NEC devolved upon them. But their ability to secure compliance was as much a function of their competent authority as of their de jure powers.

Whatever their social background, by virtue both of their ability and of the experience acquired in their work organisers gained manifold skills which widened the social and intellectual distance between themselves and ordinary party members; they were generally articulate, well informed, armed with a considerable grasp of organisational and constitutional complexities, and, often, endowed with a feel for the intricacies of political life. Here there was a dialectic between office and the incumbent. The office carried considerable prestige because attached to it was the delegated authority of the NEC. This provided a framework for respect. Insofar as the incumbent possessed the requisite qualities expected of him (or her) – verbal skills, organisational profficiency, expertise and a wide understanding of the world of politics – he could build upon that respect.

Respect for competent authority, as embodied in Regional Organisers (and, of course, Transport House officials) engendered what Ian Mikardo has called an 'awe of officials' and 'aura of priestcraft' – the deference of laymen towards the holders of office, the possessors of knowledge and authority.[30]. This 'awe of officials' was reinforced by the trade union ethos, with its premium upon solidarity, discipline and loyalty, which impregnated the outlook of many solidaristic participants. Here a comparison with more ideologically oriented, purposive participants may be illuminating. For such members, loyalty was primarily to an ideal or a cause and allegiance to the Party was tempered by the degree to which the ideal or cause was advanced.[31]

For the solidaristic participant the Party (like its progenitor, the trade union movement) was seen as more than a means, but as the collective creation of the working class and, as such, an object of loyalty in its own right. It was envisaged less as the bearer of any particular set of ideas or policies than as the irreplaceable instrument for the betterment of the working class. As long as such a perception seemed credible, solidaristic involvement gave rise to a powerful sense of attachment to the Party, as party. And this, in turn, could easily be transmuted into loyalism – a propensity to rally behind the leadership and respect authority in its own right.

The purposive mode refers to participation in party life animated primarily by the desire to achieve favoured goals or realise cherished values. However important the element of solidaristic involvement the Labour Party, as a reforming organisation, inevitably enlisted the support and active participation of the purposive-minded. Purposive participants, we have suggested, formed a smaller proportion of the active membership in the 1950s and 1960s than in later years. Nevertheless, because of their skills, their sense of political commitment and, often, their greater enthusiasm, they figured prominently in many sections of the Party.

Purposive participants (whether middle or working class) tended – for obvious reasons – to be more left-wing: to make greater demands upon the leadership, to feel disenchantment with the tepidity of its socialism and to enrol in left-wing ginger groups. Purposive involvement gives rise to a conditional orientation to authority.

Formal authority (or de jure power) authorises those invested with it to issue commands and take decisions; it does not guarantee they will be obeyed. The power to inflict penalities for non-compliance is attached to formal authority but, as we have seen, this form of control has definite limits in a voluntary organisation. The single most decisive factor converting de jure power into effective control is legitimation: the belief that patterns of authority are rightly constituted and worthy of support and, hence, that authority-holders have the right to issue commands and members the obligation to obey.

Respect for the constitution and rules, and willingness to abide by decisions if reached in the properly authorised manner was a marked feature of membership attitudes and behaviour. National Agent Len Williams commented in a paper on disciplinary questions upon 'the almost invariable acceptance of [NEC] decisions *without question* following enquiries'. This he attributed to the 'prestige with which the National Executive is held in these matters'.[32]

Legitimation of Labour's authority structure rested upon two, interlinked factors: procedural and substantive consensus. The former refers to agreement over the ground-rules and norms which structured and regulated the way power was distributed and decisions taken. In this period it was embodied in the widespread endorsement of key social – democratic principles, in particular, majority rule. Insofar as the

Party's decision-making process appeared to be governed by this principle the bulk of members felt constrained to swallow their reservations and to accept official pronouncements and directives. Conference promulgated the majority will and a refusal to abide by it – in the eyes of most members – amounted to a defiance of democratic norms.

Social-democratic centralist doctrine formed in this period what Easton has called a 'legitimating ideology', that is a pattern of 'ethical principles that justify the way power is organised, used, and limited and that define the broad responsibilities expected of the participants in the particular political relationships'.[33] As long as the behaviour of Party authorities conformed to these principles, then their decisions carried a moral imperative.

At one crisis point, the leadership itself seemed on the verge of repudiating majority rule, when Gaitskell defied (and many of his supporters derided) conference sovereignty on the issue of unilateral nuclear disarmament in 1960. But, for a time at least, it seemed a brief (if furiously fought) departure from established convention, as Gaitskell succeeded in persuading conference to reverse its earlier support for unilateralism. It took the more emollient leadership of the adroit Harold Wilson to finally emasculate the doctrine of majority rule.

Consensus over procedural norms was coupled with, and to a considerable degree, sustained by consensus over substantive values. This neither precluded nor, indeed, prevented wide and persistent differences of opinion over policies and programme. Rather, substantive consensus described a broad agreement over the fundamental purposes and role of the Party reinforced by a common pride in the achievements of the Attlee government. Labour, of course, was troubled by chronic strife, particularly in the early 1950s and early 1960s. But, although fierce passions were aroused, this strife did not encompass the bedrock values or raison d'etre of the Party.[34] It took the experience of two further Labour governments to call this into question.

This was for the future. The high measure of consensus prevailing within Labour's ranks in the 1950s and early 1960s legitimated the Party's authority structure. Even when the content of NEC directives was unpalatable, as long as they had been processed in the proper way, in conformity with Party rules and norms, the bulk of the rank and file felt obligated to comply. The official secret of social-democratic centralism was less the stick it brandished than the aura of legitimacy that surrounded it.

The potent combination of solidarism and legitimation furnished the basis of normative control. It generated a powerful feeling of attachment to the Party, moral and emotional, as well as rational and a disposition to identify Party with leadership. For many activists Labour was more than an association established to achieve particular goals: it was also a community whose members felt part of a collective political enterprise, linked together by bonds of solidarity and fellow feeling and sharing in a common political destiny.[35] This sense of community – what the French called a party patriotism – generated a fund of loyalty which was harnessed to undergird and sustain the social-democratic centralist regime.[36]

Integrated organisational control

One further factor has to be considered before concluding this discussion. The paradox of Labour's centralised regime was that it rested upon a pluralist foundation. The Party's authority structure, far from being pyrammidical in character, possed certain characteristics conducive to a pluralistic spread of powers.

The first was its confederal nature. The leadership's ability to concentrate power in its hands was checked by the constitutionally entrenched autonomy of key units – the affiliated trade unions. The repercussions of this for Labour's policy-making process have been thoroughly explored.[37] Confederalism, however, also has implications for the management and control of the party. In unitary parties, the leadership may well have the capacity to extinguish all organised centres of opposition. In the Labour Party the authority of the centre stopped at the frontiers of the unions. Potentially, at least, they could operate as bases of opposition and, unlike rank and file ginger groups, could not readily be brought to heel by the leadership.

The second pluralist feature was the separation of powers between the Parliamentary and extra-Parliamentary components of the Party. In the policy sphere the voice of the former has always tended to predominate. In contrast, the bulk of managerial powers are vested in the NEC (subject to conference endorsement) – and there is no guarantee that those will be used to uphold the authority of the PLP leadership.

Neither of these features prevented the full development of a centralised system of control. Two characteristics of the Party in this period arrested its centrifugal tendencies. The first was elite consensus.

The intersection of confederalism and the separation of powers created three separate, though interlinked, elites – the trade union, the Parliamentary and the wider Party (i.e. the NEC). In this period (until the late 1960s) each elite was predominantly right-wing in orientation. This pattern of concurrent majorities engendered a broad community of outlook and interest. It was strengthened by three further elements: firstly a system of overlapping personnel; this centred on the NEC where representatives of both the trade union and PLP elites sat; secondly, a shared acceptance of the principle tenets of social-democratic centralism; and thirdly, a common aversion to the left – a term which enclosed both Communists and Labour leftists (often seen, especially by trade unions, to be allies in the same camp). Elite consensus fostered co-ordination between the three power centres and guaranteed a wide measure of agreement over the Party's principal managerial tasks.

The second characteristic was the principle of functional differentiation – articulated in a series of unwritten conventions and understandings – which shaped the Party-Union relationship. On the one hand, the Party undertook to respect the vital industrial and organisational interests of the unions, including the effective closure of the key policy area of industrial relations from unilateral Party action. On the other, the unions both refrained from taking policy initiatives and volunteered to defend the leadership from left-wing dissidents. This second, managerial facet, obtruded most visibly in the early 1950s when major trade unions acted as the 'Praetorian Guard' of the political leadership, but was a general characteristic of the period.

The combination of elite consensus and functional differentiation facilitated a high level of integration within Labour's diverse institutional structure, rendering possible the development and effective functioning of a single Party centre. The NEC defined its managerial role to conform with the requirements and expectations of the Parliamentary leadership. It deployed its powers to contain and repel challenges to the leadership, secure in the knowledge that the trade union barons and the block votes at Conference stood full square behind it.

The social-democratic centralist regime survived until the second half of the 1960s. The Party then underwent a two-stage process of managerial change. The first stage which covered the period of the late 1960s and early 1970s was one of liberalisation from above – a deliberate experiment by Party managers in both the PLP and the wider Party to relax the managerial regime. This is covered by the following chapter. In the second stage, the sytem of integrated organisational control crumbled from within. Now under left-wing control the NEC, in the late 1970s and early 1980s, ceased to operate as the shield of the Parliamentary leadership and redefined its managerial role. This is discussed in Chapters nine and ten. In the early 1980s Labour succumbed to a veritable crisis of party management; a leadership which sought to re-establish a more rigorous regime, primarily in an effort to combat the Trotskyist Militant Tendency, encountered almost insurmountable barriers; the conditions which had sustained social-democratic centralism no longer operated. This is the theme of Chapter eleven. The final chapter discusses the Party's second assault (under new leadership) against Militant and its efforts to reconstruct an effective managerial regime.

Chapter Eight

Liberalisation, 1966–74

8.1 Introduction

In the previous chapter, we suggested that the social-democratic centralist regime was sustained primarily by a combination of conditions, rather than by inherent organisational characteristics. From the late 1960s to the early 1970s, the Party underwent a process of liberalisation, due, in large part, to a conscious decision to loosen the managerial regime both inside and outside Parliament. In retrospect, we can see this period as one of transition, from the tight discipline of social-democratic centralism to the more drastic overhaul of Labour's managerial regime in the late 1970s. This chapter attempts both to describe and account for this process.

Managerial powers and responsibilities are divided between different institutions (primarily the Parliamentary leadership and the NEC) and one feature of the liberalisation process was its lack of uniformity. An easing of the control regime was evident in the PLP before it manifested itself in the wider party. Further, it exhibited different features, reflecting the variety of factors which contributed to it, as well as the peculiarities of Labour's organisational structure.

The first section of this chapter discusses the institution of a more liberal regime in the PLP in the formative years of the late 1960s; the second traces a similar process in the wider Party.

8.2 The liberalisation of parliamentary discipline, 1966–1970

To place the liberalisation measures of the late 1960s in context, it is necessary to review briefly the PLP's disciplinary regime in the years following the collapse of the Bevanite insurgency.

PLP discipline, 1955–64
The disciplinary regime established in the early 1950's continued to operate for another decade.[1] Its intensity varied primarily according to the ebb and flow of strife within the Party. Thus the period 1955–59 was one of relative tranquility, with the left grieviously weakened by the co-opting of prominent former Bevanites, particularly Wilson and Crossman, into the leadership and by Bevan's own defection in 1957.

The climate in the Party abruptly changed after the 1959 election, Labour's third successive defeat: there followed three years of bitter hostilities as Hugh Gaitskell, determined to remould the Party in his image, encountered a resurgent left.

Initially, a slight gesture was made towards liberalisation. In December 1959 in one of his final acts before succumbing to cancer, Aneurin Bevan, by now deputy leader, suggested the suspension of the 1952 Standing Orders. His colleagues in the Shadow Cabinet (including Gaitskell) only grudgingly agreed; and much of the effect was negated by the adoption of a Code of Conduct that only slightly extended the frontiers of liberty.[2]

Shortly after, the Party was engulfed in a tidal wave of dissension over the issue of nuclear weapons. The major arena was Conference, where the left swept to an unprecedented victory by persuading delegates at Scarborough in 1960 to vote for unilateral nuclear disarmament. But the battle spilled over to Westminster where the leadership faced two major revolts. In March 1960 43 MPs defied a three-line whip and abstained on an official opposition amendment to the Government's Defence White Paper.[3] At the end of the year, 60 MPs abstained on an opposition censure motion over Government defence policy, which reiterated the policy that Conference had shortly before repudiated.[4]

Whilst in both cases the behaviour of the dissenters was deplored, the very size of the rebellions precluded disciplinary action, and the PLP majority contented itself with reprimands. This, however, was a purely pragmatic response. Elements within the leadership – particularly Bevan's successor as deputy leader, George Brown – were baying for blood. In March 1961 five MPs (including Michael Foot) defied a Party decision to abstain and voted against the defence estimates. The numbers this time were manageable and the five were promptly expelled from the PLP. A few months later seven other MPs were severely censured for breaching the whip on the minor issue of the training of West German troops in Wales.[5]

Two other former Bevanites fell victim to this disciplinary drive. Dick Crossman was forced to resign as a front-bench spokesman for refusing to give an assurance to desist from 'persistent and public advocacy' of revisions in Labour defence policy,[6] somewhat ironically since within a few months Gaitskell openly and brazenly defied Conference's decision over unilateralism. Barbara Castle was also sacked as a front-bench spokesman for abstaining on the December 1960 motion.[7]

These moves were part of the by now well-established pattern in which the leadership resorted to discipline as a method of resolving internal differences. As in the early 1950s, there were few outright expulsions from the PLP, though the major restraint was the impracticability of harsh penalties where large numbers were involved. But the leadership signalled its intention to maintain as tight a rein as possible by pushing successfully, in December 1961, for the re-imposition of Standing Orders.[8]

By 1962 Gaitskell and the right had succeeded in vanquishing their opponents. The leader did not for long savour his triumph. Within a year he was dead and succeeded by the erstwhile Bevanite, Harold Wilson, who moved rapidly to soothe Labour's wounds and, in 1964, led a united Party to victory at the polls.

The introduction of the liberal regime: April 1966 – December 1967
Both Attlee and Gaitskell were convinced that strict Party discipline was essential if the PLP were to operate as an effective political force. Initially it appeared that the new Labour Government accepted this maxim. Between October 1964 and the Party's sweeping electoral triumph in the spring of 1966, the key managerial posts – chief whip, Leader of the House and Chairman of the PLP – were occupied by traditionalists[9] and Labour in the House ran a tight ship. In fact, there was little need to enforce discipline: Labour's tiny majority and the novelty of the return to power combined with the awareness that another election could not be long delayed to guarantee very considerable self-discipline.

In April 1966, the Party returned to power with a majority of almost 100 seats. The joy of triumph was soon marred as the Government was plagued by a series of crises which induced it to take measures unpalatable to many of its supporters. By this time new men had been appointed to cope with changed conditions. Manny Shinwell remained (for a while) elected Chairman of the PLP, but in July Ted Short was replaced by John Silkin (formerly his deputy) as Chief Whip (in July) and Herbert Bowden by Richard Crossman as Leader of the House in August. As was soon to become apparent, the changes reflected a considered decision to introduce a new style of party management.

In the twenty months from Labour's triumph at the polls in 1966 to the close of 1967 there were six major revolts: over Vietnam in July 1966; over prices and incomes legislation in August and then again in October 1966; over defence in March 1967; over the EEC in May 1967 and finally over prices and incomes once more in June 1967. In each case the pattern was broadly similar: a significant number of (mainly left-wing) MPs rebel over a major issue of policy; loyalists demand stiff penalities; PLP managers opt for lenient treatment, successfully resisting pressure for a return to more traditional methods. In reviewing this period, we shall analyse the character of the new regime and the reasons for its introduction.

Policy developments formed the context for the operation of managerial politics. Throughout the 1966–70 Parliament the Government grappled with a formidable array of economic problems, including balance of payments deficits, strikes and inflation. The response was to pursue a set of policies – cuts in public expenditure, wage restraint etc – which many of its supporters found hard to stomach. Thus within months of Labour's electoral triumph in April 1966 the Party was shaken, and many left-wingers dismayed by the Government's deflationary package introduced in July in response to a sterling crisis. However, the first major revolt in the Commons was, in the same month, over Vietnam. A growing disenchantment on the left with Labour's steady backing for America resulted in 32 MPs refusing to support the Government in the Commons. Four left-wingers who tabled a critical motion calling for the Government to disassociate itself from American policy were hauled before the new Chief Whip, only to be 'mildly surprised by his friendly tone'. He accepted that their abstention could be justified by invoking the hallowed 'conscience clause', though he warned that this not be extended to major pieces of legislation in line with Party decisions, like the recently drafted Prices and Incomes Bill.[10]

Vietnam was to arouse for the lifetime of the Government heated and passionate debate, but it was not a major item in its programme. Incomes policy, whether it took the form of voluntary or statutory restraint, in contrast, was the centrepiece of its economic strategy, designed to remedy the country's balance of payments deficit and to curb inflation. However, despite Silkin's admonitions, this did not deter its critics. Within weeks of the Vietnam vote, 26 Labour MPs demonstrated their hostility to wage restraint by ignoring a three-line whip and abstaining; most of them defied the whip in two more divisions in the following days. Loyalist backbenchers were indignant and demanded that the ringleaders (who included Michael Foot, Ian Mikardo and Frank Cousins, who had recently resigned from the Government over the issue) should be disciplined as an example to the others.[11]

Responsibility for PLP discipline was shared between the Chief Whip and the Liaison Committee. The latter consisted of the Chief Whip, the Leader of the House and three elected members – the Chairman of the PLP and his two deputies. The Chief Whip was responsible for recommending disciplinary action, subject to the approval of the Liaison

Committee. Any recommendation was discussed by the PLP, with whom the final decision rested. It was agreed to await the behaviour of the rebels on later stages of the prices and incomes legislation before considering what action to take.[12]

The dissenters were unrepentant. In October, 28 defied a three-line whip and abstained on an order activating Part 4 (the statutory element) of the Prices and Incomes Act. At the next Liaison Committee meeting all three elected members (Shinwell, Willie Hamilton and Malcolm MacPherson) demanded the withdrawal of the whip from the ringleaders. Silkin, however, refused to recommend any such action – to the fury of Shinwell and Hamilton; instead (since Standing Orders had not been renewed) it was agreed to present to the PLP new ground-rules for party discipline. These consisted of three parts: a ban on personal attacks, a prohibition of all organised groups, unless specifically recognised by the Chief Whip and – to balance this – a liberal interpretation of the traditional conscience clause. Despite the frustration of some loyalists these rules were approved by the PLP.[13]

Within months the new regime was to be placed under its severest test. In March, no less than 62 MPs – left-wingers reinforced by a number from the centre and right – abstained on the Government's Defence White Paper, in protest against the failure to transfer resources from military to social programmes.[14] Wilson reacted furiously. In an infelicitous analogy, he warned that whilst every dog was allowed 'one bite', if one continually bit 'not because of the dictates of conscience but because he is considered vicious', he might not get his licence renewed.[15] Wilson's outburst was uncharacteristic and, as we shall see below, counter-productive. Crossman, engaged in a bitter row with Shinwell over PLP discipline, threatened to resign unless the Prime Minister unambiguously came down in favour of the liberal regime – which he finally did.[16] Shinwell retreated from the fray and shortly afterwards resigned in some bitterness as Chairman of the PLP, to be replaced by the right-wing but liberal-minded Douglas Houghton. During the course of the highly-publicised controversy between Shinwell and Crossman, attention was diverted from the defence rebels. Crossman's victory confirmed that they would be spared the rigours of Party discipline.

Two months later 35 MPs defied a three-line whip over a vote approving the applications to join the EEC. Silkin, at an earlier PLP meeting, intimated that a rebellion would not be treated lightly and, indeed, seven PPSs were sacked for joining the revolt; the case of the others was deferred until after the recess – a calculated move to allow tempers to cool. Ignoring loyalist pressure, Silkin confined himself to chiding the rebels and warning that future misconduct might imperil their membership of the PLP. In fact, Silkin's letter amounted to a reaffirmation of the liberal regime. Whilst stating that a three-line whip must be observed on questions of confidence, he acknowledged the right of MPs to invoke the conscience clause on all policy issues. This confirmed that the earlier, strict interpretation of conscience had now been discarded.[17]

Shortly afterwards, 30 members took advantage of this to abstain on the second reading of a new Prices and Incomes Bill. The Liaison Committee deflected hard-line demands to penalise the rebels by announcing that it was engaged in formulating a new Code of Conduct. The announcement having served its purpose, work on the Code proceeded at a leisurely pace and, by the close of the year, it had yet to surface.

The liberal regime had now passed through 18 tumultuous months, more or less unscathed. Why was it introduced? What did it signify about party management? And why did it overcome both tradition and resistance?

The appointment of Crossman and Silkin in the two key Party roles reflected a willingness to experiment with new methods of party management. Both were convinced that a 'liberal philosophy' was 'the only way to run a modern left-wing party'.[18] All their predecessors were men of the right; both Crossman and Silkin identified themselves with the centre-left. Former party managers were traditional disciplinarians; both Crossman and Silkin were men of a more libertarian stamp.

Whereas the Chief Whip was a relative newcomer to Parliament, the Leader of the House had, by 1966, served as an MP for twenty years. A man of immense intellectual fertility combined with an effervescent personality and (at times) erratic judgement, Crossman had been usually consistent in his objections to social-democratic centralism. In an article in 1955 he suggested that 'loyalty to majority decisions' could be too easily abused 'to concentrate power in a few hands and change party democracy into party oligarchy'. He identified two oligarchical mechanisms. Firstly, 'using the powerful machinery of the whip's office to muster support for the line of the shadow cabinet, yet forbidding those who want the Party to modify that line any form of group activity or organisation'. Secondly, 'exploiting to the full the trade union sentiment that it is in all circumstances disloyal for the minority to oppose a majority decision once it has been taken'. He dismissed 'the system of "democracy" enforced by the PLP's Standing Orders' as 'little less ruthless than the Democratic Centralism of Leninist theory'. He argued for a more pluralist conception of party democracy which placed less emphasis upon the will of the majority and more upon the ability of minorities to challenge and replace the holders of power. This entailed extending to dissenters the rights to organise and publicise their views with minimum hindrance.[19]

To a large extent Crossman, as party manager, remained faithful to these views; they were, if anything, fortified by more immediate and practical considerations. Responding to criticism from traditional disciplinarians, like Shinwell, he insisted that 'old fashioned, rigid regimentation is unsuitable to a modern party'.[20] The intakes of 1964 and 1966 together comprised a majority of all backbenchers. They were more highly educated and more professional in occupational background than their colleagues, more critical and questioning in spirit and keener to participate in policy-making. Crucially, this outlook – always common amongst the more restless and rebellious elements on the left – had spread to the ranks of the 'loyalist' centre and right. Fewer of these were – in Ian Trethowan's words – 'bred in the unblinking clannish loyalties of the mining village or union branch'.[21] Crossman and Silkin were both acutely sensitive to these changes and recognised that styles of party management had to adjust to the new temper of the PLP.

Their first step was to widen the conscience clause. The function of the clause was to regulate conflict by reconciling party unity and discipline with the expression of minority views. It defined the scope of permissible dissent by delimiting the issues upon which the clause might be legitimately invoked.[22] A series of PLP Standing Orders (1952 Standing Orders, 1959 Code of Conduct, 1961 Standing Orders) stipulated that the clause may be invoked 'on matters of deeply held personal conscientious conviction'; this was interpreted as referring to questions of 'religion, temperance and pacifism'.[23]

Crossman rejected this definition of conscience. He postulated, as a basic tenet of the 'liberal philosophy' of party management, the 'assumption that every member of the Party may well on occasion have to abstain conscientiously; conscientious abstention won't in future be limited to pacifists and teetotallers, but will be recognised as *the right of every member*'.[24] Silkin shared the same view: in a 'deeply moving, simple speech' he told the PLP that it would be far better if it were recognised that conscience applied to all political issues and could not be cribbed by confining it to religion, temperance and pacifism.[25]

This redefinition of conscience represented a decisive break with older precepts. It abolished the distinction between 'conscientious' and 'political' convictions. But it left open the question about how dissent could properly be expressed. Conscience, Attlee had pronounced, should be 'a still, small voice and not a loudspeaker'.[26] It should be the act of an individual, consulting his or her own moral principles: an 'organised conscience' – concerted disobedience to Party decisions – was unacceptable, whilst sustained and orchestrated factional activity went well beyond the pale.

On this point, Crossman and Silkin trod more cautiously. Crossman appeared to endorse social-democratic centralist thinking when he warned left-wing MPs that, though committed to asserting 'the rule of conscience' in full, he 'wasn't going to tolerate a party within a party . . . conscience must be individual not collective'.[27] This was formalised when the PLP accepted the Liaison Committee recommendation reminding members that 'no organised group is acceptable which is not officially recognised by the PLP', the penalty being expulsion from the Parliamentary Party. It would be for the Chief Whip, Silkin explained, to decide whether 'alliances' were 'organised' and fell within the compass of the ban.[28] This re-assertion of the 1952 ban on groups was strongly attacked by the left,[29] and was indeed inconsistent with Crossman's earlier views. Whether Crossman seriously meant it or not is unclear, but Silkin did not. It was a gesture to pacify Shinwell[30] and was promptly nullified when Silkin authorised all eleven groups (including the recently founded Tribune group) which applied for recognition, to the surprise and delight of their members.[31]

Both men also disappointed those traditionalists who had hoped that the liberalised groundrules would be strictly enforced. Here, again, they broke with social-democratic centralism which insisted that cohesion depended upon a willingness to discipline perennial rebels: failure to do so would signal to others that they were free to flout Party rules and decisions.[32] Instead they consciously set out to copy the more relaxed Tory model of party management.[33] This involved relying more heavily on informal methods of control – pressure from colleagues, from constituency parties, and the pull of ambition. Secondly it called for improved lines of communication between the Government and its backbenchers, with ministers expending more effort in explaining and promoting their policy rather than expecting the Parliamentary rank and file simply to fall into line.[34]

Thirdly, it implied a different style of management. Party management was, in Silkin's phrase, a 'soft art'. Relying upon mechanical majorities to force dissidents to buckle under was counterproductive: it sharpened lines of cleavage and, in the heat of the battle, encouraged the adoption of intransigent positions. Silkin, as Chief Whip, preferred to rely upon the fostering of friendly relations and the power of persuasion. Even if this failed to prevent a revolt, it would mitigate its impact, countering the tendency of the Party to divide into entrenched and mutually hostile camps.[35]

This gelled with Wilson's style of leadership. Unlike Gaitskell, his power base did not rest upon one wing of the Party. Indeed, during his term of office between 1964 and 1970 he contrived the unusual feat of adopting policies identified with the right whilst relying upon the left to protect him from right-wing efforts to remove him. According to Silkin, he deliberately sought to run the Party on a 'two wings system' – balancing left and right, turning from one to another. This precluded a rigid disciplinary system which would completely alienate one wing –

in the circumstances, the left minority.[36] Instead, whilst adamantly resisting pressure from the left on policy matters, he devoted considerable effort to conciliating them. 'I am constantly astonished', David Wood wrote in *The Times*, 'by the number of left-wing parliamentary critics who claim they have just had a heart-to-heart private exchange with Mr. Wilson', who also displayed 'a sensitive understanding of their point of view' and (Wood added) a readiness to start left-wingers on 'the ladder of ministerial promotion'.[37] When the Prime Minister was forced to choose between liberals and disciplinarians in the clash between Crossman and Shinwell, he opted for the former.[38]

The consolidation of the liberal regime, 1968–70

By the close of 1967, the liberal regime was well in place. But it was only consolidated, in the face of multiple pressures, with difficulty. The task of party management, far from easing, became more complex and demanding as the managers struggled to cope with two, inter-related, challenges: firstly intensifying dissension over a range of key policy areas, in the context of growing left-wing disenchantment, massive electoral setbacks and collapsing morale; secondly, incessant attacks by loyalists on the failure to mete out harsh treatment of left-wing rebels.

A major row erupted in the first weeks of the new year. The Government introduced a package of public expenditure cuts fiercely assailed by the left. Twenty-five MPs abstained on a confidence motion approving the measures. At a prior PLP meeting, loyalists had been angered by Silkin's refusal to declare that abstainers would be punished, provoking stormy scenes. Of the 25 rebles, two (George Jeger and Carol Johnson) were right-wingers protesting against this laxity of discipline.[39] Responding to loyalist bitterness, Silkin despatched a letter to all 25 MPs banning them from attending any meeting of the PLP. This move – designed to take the heat of the row – in fact added more fuel; it was widely condemned – from both left and right – since the Chief Whip, inadvertently or not, had exceeded his authority.[40] Silkin hurriedly rescinded the letter and, in its place, it was announced that the Liaison Committee would shortly submit the (long delayed) draft code of conduct.[41]

The code was finally discussed and approved at two rather poorly attended meetings of the PLP.[42] In large part it merely codified recent decisions and practice. Thus the word 'conscientious' was dropped from the provision which granted members the right to abstain on 'matters of deeply held personal conviction', finally eradicating the distinction between conviction arising from 'conscience' and from beliefs. Labour MPs were still formally debarred from voting contrary to the decision of a Party meeting, or abstaining on a vote of confidence in a Labour Government.[43] The one new element was the additional sanction of 'suspension from privileges of the membership of the PLP'. The Liaison Committee was empowered, on the recommendations of the Chief Whip, to seek the approval of the Party meeting to ban for a specified period members from attending any meetings of the PLP.[44] Silkin later described it as 'absolute nonsense' – its only effect being to relieve MPs of the tedium of attending Party meetings. It was introduced primarily to accommodate the hardliners.[45]

The code had no discernible effect on stilling the tide of dissent. Later in the year there was a rash of revolts over government legislation establishing statutory wage controls. In one case – a vote to delete the penal provisions of the new Prices and Incomes Bill – 23 MPs clearly violated the new Code. Despite the 'outrage' of loyalists, this attracted only a (quite innocuous) censure.[46] The situation further deteriorated in the new year. Government plans for a reform of the House of Lords were effectively scuppered by backbench opposition, with Party managers wilting before a series of revolts.[47] Shortly afterwards, 40 Labour MPs rebelled over a bill to levy Selective Employment Tax.[48] But by this time the Government was engulfed by a veritable mutiny over its proposals for trade union reform, *In Place of Strife* which, amongst many other provisions, envisaged a compulsory cooling off period in certain disputes, compulsory strike ballots before some official stoppages and the right of the Government to impose settlements in serious inter-union disputes. Silkin was finally deposed for his apparent failure to master the Party and replaced by Bob Mellish on the understanding that he would institute much sharper discipline.[49]

If this was indeed Wilson's intention, it was to prove unavailing. For, by this time, the conditions which would have rendered feasible a return to severe methods of party management had largely vanished.

We have observed above that social democratic centralism drew sustenance from a syndrome of norms – loyalty to class and to the union, respect for majority decisions – all of which flowed from the collective experience of trade unionism. It was the trade union leader and the trade union MP who were most insistent upon maintaining unity enforced, if necessary, by discipline; and least sympathetic to the call of conscience and the rights of minorities.[50] But what if loyalty to one's union, one's class – to 'the movement' – came into conflict with loyalty to the Government? By the late 1960s solidarity – as a key norm in Labour's procedural consensus – was under threat from two quarters. The first was, the revisionist assault on class politics, with its claim that class loyalties were not only fraying in practice but obsolescent in principle, indeed a positive source of electoral disadvantage. 'The scales were weighed against the Labour Party', the ablest revisionist thinker, Tony Crosland, warned 'so long as it preserves its one-class image'. The message thus derived was that the Party should disengage from the working class, demarcate itself more sharply from the unions and present itself 'as a broadly-based, national people's party'.[51] This mode of reasoning, widely diffused amongst the upper echelons of the PLP, hacked away at the traditions of instinctive loyalty and solidarity which had bolstered Party discipline in the social democratic centralist era. It was taken one step further by Harold Wilson who, as Prime Minister, sought to establish Labour as 'the natural party of Government' and consistently denied a privileged connection with any one sector of the community.

Conceptions of loyalty and solidarity were also being rendered increasingly threadbare by the intensifying strains between Government and unions. The traditional functional differentiation between the political and industrial arms of 'the movement', which had welded together the various Party institutions, disintegrated in the late 1960s as the Government encroached upon the union's reserved domain of collective bargaining through successive measures of wage restraint. The trade union group of MPs – the bedrock of right-wing loyalism – found themselves cross-pressured between loyalty to the leadership and to the unions. In one of many ironies it was Manny Shinwell – manoeuvred from his chairmanship of the PLP because of his hostility towards the liberal regime – who highlighted the dilemma. Announcing his opposition to wage restraint he told his Parliamentary colleagues that, if confronted with the choice of loyalty to the Government or to the movement as a whole, he would unhesitatingly opt for the latter.[52] Most members of the trade union group continued to back the Government's incomes legislation, though with mounting reluctance. Their disaffection added to the burden of Party managers, yet guaranteed that their liberal regime would survive. Already assured of the sympathy of the left, and of younger, more liberal-minded (and middle class) right-wingers, the ranks of their critics began to dwindle as trade union attacks on incomes policy intensified.

Unrest within the trade union group finally exploded in 1969 with the publication of *In Place of Strife*. The episode appeared to terminate the life of the liberal regime – John Silkin was dismissed as Chief Whip and replaced by the tough-talking Bob Mellish.[53] In fact it demonstrated decisively that circumstances did not permit the rehabilitation of the older style of party management.

By 1969 the authority of the Government, tossed hither and thither by economic storms was badly dented. It had failed to deliver the economic goods; it had dismayed many of its supporters by despatching cherished principles – over social spending, prescription charges, wages restraint. Morale in the PLP was at a low ebb and now in the spring of 1969, the unity of the movement itself began to fracture. Trade unions signalled that their patience had expired: they swelled the ranks of customary left-wing rebels in the vote on *In Place of Strife*.[54] The nexus between Party and unions seemed in danger of being severed. Unity, Douglas Houghton, chairman of the PLP but also for many years the General Secretary of the Inland Revenue Staff Association, asserted meant 'full accord in the wider movements as well as in the PLP. The trade union movement is an integral part of the Labour Party. We must not be torn apart'.[55]

Unity and loyalty were not the only normative props of PLP discipline to be corroding from within. In the strife-torn early 1950s, Bevanite MPs were castigated time and again – particularly from trade union quarters – for their disregard of majority decisions. There was always a degree of ambiguity about precisely which institution – Conference or the PLP itself – expressed the majority will, to which all MPs were expected to conform. This never surfaced as a political dilemma because of the pattern of concurrent majorities in all key Party bodies: only, briefly, in 1960–61, did it intrude as a potential problem for PLP discipline.

But, by the late 1960s, the pattern was definitely disrupted. With the votes of the two biggest unions, the TGWU and the AEU, available for mobilisation by the left, the right's hold upon Conference was broken. The effect was to add a political charge to the tricky question of whose will, according to the traditional canons of majoritarian democracy, was binding upon MPs – the PLP or Conference. The MPs who defied the whip over prices and incomes legislation could claim that they were acting in conformity with the will of the Party as articulated by its sovereign body, the Annual Conference.[56]

Loyalists could, and did, riposte that, under the rules, MPs were required to conform to the Standing Orders of the PLP. As Houghton observed (when ruling out of order amendments to the Parliamentary Party's Code of Conduct which would have absolved members from discipline if they were supporting Conference decisions) the PLP had the 'right to order its own affairs, decide its own policies and impose its own discipline'.[57]

However, this argument blurred the distinction between the right of the PLP, under its rules, to demand loyalty to its decisions and its ability to exact it. Thus, firstly, the ultimate and most fearsome punishment against Parliamentary dissidents – the right to expel from the Party – was available only to the NEC and not the PLP. It clearly was inoperable when the dissident could claim to be complying with the will of Conference. Secondly, PLP discipline, in practice, depended more upon the sense of obligation than the fear of penalties. This was impaired – for those who took majoritarian democracy seriously – by the sight of the Government (and the bulk of Labour MPs) so openly disdaining the authority of Conference (over prices and incomes and other major issues).

In practice, when Labour was in office, the overriding claim upon

Labour MPs was their duty to 'sustain the Government'. They had, after all, been elected not because of their personal qualities but to return a Labour Government. This claim even the most persistent left-wing rebel willingly acknowledged.[58] But for the hardliners – in the cabinet[59] as well as the backbenches – this did not suffice. A defeat in the House, precipitating an election, was not the only way in which the Government could be damaged. The well publicised spectacle of intra-Party 'wrangling' weakened, it was claimed, the morale of the PLP, impeded the passage of legislation, diminished the authority of the Government and alienated voters. Not only – so the complaint rang – did such behaviour, licensed by the Crossman-Silkin regime, go unpunished; disloyalty was actually rewarded as dissidents were hailed in the constituencies as people of courage and integrity whilst the loyalists – whose votes kept the Government in being, allowing their left-wing colleagues to flaunt their consciences – were mocked as time-servers.

The hardliners, however, failed to grasp that, in a Party where obedience rested ultimately upon loyalty, and where MPs were subject to conflicting obligations, the threat or actual imposition of sanctions was of limited value. Once more, it was the liberalisers who were more attuned to political realities. 'We have to realise', Crossman averred 'that when a Government suddenly does things which are not in the Party manifesto and which are profoundly controversial, then members have the right to challenge that Government and in the last resort to abstain conscientiously'.[60]

By the end of the decade, the normative standards of social democratic centralism, which had held sway for a generation, were in disarray. This breakdown of older conventions was, ironically, reflected in the conduct of the hardliners themselves. Why should they feel obliged to conform to the rules when Silkin's idea of combating left-wing indiscipline was (in Peter Jenkins' metaphor) 'a bottle of wine with Stan Orme'.[61] Disengagement from traditional modes of behaviour (on the part of hardliners) first manifested itself in defiance of the whip in protest at the failure of party managers to punish the unruly.[62] But the process soon went further as disciplinarians began to savour the forbidden fruit of revolt. Willie Hamilton, a vice-chairman of the PLP, and hence a member of the Liaison Committee, and formerly a bitter critic of Silkin–Crossman permissiveness, rebelled over expenditure cuts[63] soon to be followed by the sternest disciplinarian of all, Manny Shinwell, who openly boasted his willingness to break ranks over prices and incomes legislation.[64]

John Silkin may have been replaced by a disciplinarian as Chief Whip. But – as a decade in that post was to demonstrate – it was Bob Mellish's destiny to preside over the continuation of the liberal regime. As Alan Watkins pointed out, the victory of the disciplinarians was more apparent than real: 'it will be impossible to go back to the old ways'.[65] The liberal regime survived because only a flexible system of party management could cope with wide differences of opinion over policies, principles and loyalties.

Coda: the 1971 EEC revolt
The last nail had yet to be hammered in the coffin of the older regime. This occurred in 1971 when its moral basis was repudiated by those who had been amongst its most ardent champions.

Party discipline in the House of Commons derived its ultimate justification from the status of MPs as representatives, collectively, of the Labour Party. 'The candidate of one of the major Parties' Attlee wrote 'stands for a connected policy and for a certain body of men who, if a majority can be obtained, will form a Government. This is well understood by the electors. If the member fails to support the Government *or fails to act with the opposition in their efforts to turn the government out*, he is acting contrary to the expectations of those who have put their trust in him'.[66] It was this principle of collective representation which was decisively repudiated in the early 1970s by a substantial minority of the PLP, including many who had figured in the past as its most eager proponents.

In 1971 the Party Conference rejected entry into the Common Market on the terms negotiated by the Conservative Government. The PLP concurred with this view. This created a situation similar to that in 1954 on German rearmament though, in this case, majorities in both bodies were far larger. In 1954 only a handful of MPs defied the majority view, broke ranks in the House of Commons and were promptly expelled.[67] In 1971 a very substantial minority (69) not only violated the whip but – renouncing Attlee's injunction – actually helped sustain the Conservative Government in office.[68]

This precipitated prolonged and acrimonious dissension within the Party as the left accused pro-marketeers of betraying Labour by succouring the Government and were, in turn, condemned for their intolerance. Both left and right shifted position somewhat. Earlier enthusiasm in the left for the MP who stood by the dictates of his conscience[69] was increasingly displaced by calls to stand by Conference decisions.[70] The shift of outlook on the right was more radical. This may be illustrated by a number of examples. George Lawson, who resigned as a whip during the previous Labour Government in protest against lax party discipline, abstained on every single division (62) on European legislation. Ted Short, a former chief whip of the traditional stamp abstained on the vote on the principle of entry.[71] MPs who had steadfastly resisted the widening of the conscience clause now invoked it as their birthright.[72]

To justify their conduct most of the pro-marketeers embraced

Burkean notions of the role of the MP. An MP should not allow loyalty to the Party to smother his deeply-held convictions; he was ultimately accountable to the voters who elected him and his own conscience: indeed, they claimed, voters respected the integrity of the MP who stood by his principles and resisted the threats and blandishments of Party. This conception of the role of the MP amounted to a rupture, not only with the idea of Conference sovereignty but, more pertinently, with the Attlee–Gaitskell doctrine of Party loyalty. In the 1950s and early 1960s right-wingers had berated dissident left-wing MPs who had refused to acknowledge their status as servants of the Party.[73] By the early 1970s often the same MPs were quick to scorn those who placed loyalty to the Party higher than those to that of individual conscience.[74]

The effect of this spectacle of the ardent disciplinarians and fervent Party loyalists of the recent past[75] avidly expanding a libertarian view of the rights of MPs was to completely discredit the traditional doctrine of PLP management and to finally demolish any prospects of its revival. Both in government and in opposition the PLP in the 1970s and 1980s was to be run on a much tighter rein.[76]

8.3   Liberalisation in the wider party, 1968–74

Liberalisation in the wider Party commenced rather later than in the PLP, but was to have, with the passage of time, more profound consequences. It was also part of a broader process of change: two other ingredients were decentralisation, the transfer of powers from the centre to subordinate units, and deconcentration, the emergence of a more pluralist set of arrangements at the centre.

Liberalisation (1) the Pembroke judgment, 1968–9
The first important step in the liberalisation process was unplanned, but it was to have, in due course, the most far-reaching consequences.

Desmond Donnelly, the MP for Pembroke, had for long been a maverick. Originally a Bevanite, he soon switched his allegiance and by the 1960s had drifted to the extreme right fringes of the Party. In early 1968 he resigned the whip and, after he had expressed his repugnance for both Labour's leader and its policies, he was expelled by the NEC.[77]

However, Donnelly retained the support of many Party members in his constituency who threatened to unilaterally withdraw from Labour's national organisation (taking with them substantial assets). Reg Underhill, the Assistant National Agent, was despatched to Pembroke to sort matters out. He asked the party's GC to pass a resolution reaffirming its willingness to abide by the rules; then 'pandemonium broke loose'.[78] The (loyalist) chairman adjourned the meeting and left, followed by thirty others. The remaining seventy present then carried a motion disaffiliating from the Labour Party. The NEC responded by authorising the National Agent to reorganise the CLP.[79]

The Executive followed normal procedures. It invoked clause VIII 2(b) of the Constitution which empowered it to disaffiliate a constituency organisation and then set in motion the established process of reorganisation.[80] Thus it invited all Pembroke's members, except those alleged to be involved in the dissident group, to attend branch meetings, called by national officials, requesting them to re-affirm, in writing, their acceptance of the conditions of membership and expressing their readiness to co-operate with the NEC in re-establishing the Party. The 26 people 'alleged to have played a leading role in the dissident group' received a special letter stating that before any recommendations were made to the NEC about their continued membership they should provide a written undertaking accepting the conditions of membership, confirming they were not members of proscribed bodies and indicating a willingness to co-operate in the reorganisation of the CLP. They were not informed of the branch meetings – hence debarred from participating in Party affairs.[81]

At this point, the normal course of events was interrupted. Both sides had resorted to the Courts – the NEC to repossess the assets of the Pembroke party, the CLP to uphold its claim to the right to secede by challenging the legal authority of the National Executive to intervene in its affairs.

Traditionally, the Courts had been reluctant to involve themselves in the internal life of political parties.[82] But in recent years the Courts had exhibited an increasing disposition to review administrative decisions to ensure that they were properly taken and that the precepts of natural justice had been respected. As it happened, the Pembroke case was heard by Justice Megarry, a judge sympathetic to this trend towards judicial activism.[83]

Megarry addressed himself to two main questions: the first was whether a CLP had the right to disaffiliate itself from the Labour Party. This can be dealt with briefly. He held that every constituency party was bound by the Constitution and Rules of the Party (including CLP rules) and any action taken by a CLP to sever itself from the national organisation was in breach of its own rules and hence invalid.[84] This judgment was vital in the negative sense that, if Megarry had found otherwise, then the right of the national Party to exercise control over local branches would have been demolished; but this, however, merely confirmed the status quo.

The second question was the more crucial one. This dealt with the validity of the NEC's decision to deprive members of the 'dissident group' of membership or the rights of membership by preventing them from attending meetings of the reconstituted party. After some prevarication upon the question whether the barred members had or had not in fact been expelled, the NEC's counsel elected to contend (for legal reasons) that they had terminated their own membership by failing to provide the requisite undertakings: 'by their unconstitutional action and demonstration of disloyalty they had repudiated their membership'.[85] For this reason they had been barred from taking any further part in the affairs of the CLP.

The NEC's right to reorganise a constituency party and expel members flowed from clause VIII 2(b) of the Constitution, which equipped it with wide-ranging powers to uphold the Constitution. Previously, as we have seen, it construed these powers loosely to take any action which it believed appropriate to defend the rules and interests of the Party. It was on this point that Megarry made his crucial intervention. He contended that, in the exercise of its powers, the NEC was bound by the principle of natural justice. This principle had three irreducible elements. '(1) The right to be heard by an unbiased tribunal (2); the right to have notice of charges of misconduct; (3) the right to be heard in answer to these charges'. Neither the initial decision to reorganise the Pembroke party, nor the denial of membership rights which issued from it, had conformed to natural justice in that 'the process of giving notice of the charges and giving those concerned the right to be heard in answer to the charges was plainly not followed'.[86] On these grounds the NEC's actions in disaffiliating the CLP and penalising its dissident members were invalidated.

What were the consequences of the Pembroke judgment? We can distinguish between the immediate and the long term. Two NEC decisions fall into the first category. Firstly, on legal advice, the Executive held another, and extremely painstaking and time-consuming enquiry into the Pembroke party which revealed a ramshackle organisation which operated with scant regard for Party rules (e.g. most members of the GC which voted to defy the NEC were not properly accredited delegates); this assisted the Party to resolve the dispute in a reasonably satisfactory manner.[87] Secondly, the NEC amended CLP rules giving any person charged with disciplinary offences the right to be heard in answer to charges by the executive and GC of his Party.[88]

The long-term consequences were both more important and more wide-ranging. In their summary of Megarry's judgment, the Party's solicitors guardedly commented 'the whole thing is in some ways very unsatisfactory since it suggests that there are flaws in the procedure which has on past occasion been successfully carried out by the Labour Party'.[89] This put the matter tactfully. Whilst Megarry's judgment did not bind other judges hearing similar cases in the future it was a definite augury since it reflected a general drift towards greater activism by the Courts to uphold the right to natural justice.

In the social democratic centralist era, the NEC had not been unduly troubled by considerations of natural justice. It was not, as we have seen, wholly uncommon for Party members to be tried, found guilty and sentenced without ever being told of the precise charges for which they were being arraigned. Several of the methods and procedures routinely deployed against Trotskyist and other dissidents in the 1950s and early 1960s might not, if employed again, survive scrutiny by the Courts.[90]

From a purely formal view, the judgment did not subtract from the NEC's powers. Its rights to disband parties and expel members remained intact; in future it merely had to take care that its methods and procedures conformed to natural justice. But, in practice, (if the new accent of natural justice was maintained by the Courts) its powers *were* diminished. Natural justice demanded that the Party proceed in a much more laborious and meticulous way than it had previously been accustomed to do. This would have encumbered any voluntary organisation. To one as stripped of cash and of organisational resources as the Labour Party it was a serious handicap. In future in taking disciplinary measures the NEC might find itself either accruing hefty legal expenses or adding substantially to Transport House's workload, or both.[91]

The repercussions (or, at least, potential repercussions)[92] of the Pembroke rulings extended even further. Previously the NEC had been free (within reasonable limits, and subject to Conference endorsement) to determine for itself the 'meaning and effect' of the Constitution and, hence, the character and reach of its own powers. This now ceased to be automatically so. For not only did the Megarry judgment if followed in the future constrain the manner in which the NEC could, in future, exercise its powers; it also, in effect, removed the NEC from its status as a final appeals court by establishing a precedent for the judicial review of its own actions.

Liberalisation (2) changes at the top

The Pembroke judgment, as it happened, came at the right moment.[93] The pendulum on the NEC, having for so many years been stuck on the right, was already swinging to a left keen to ease Party discipline. The liberalisation process received a further impetus with the departure in 1968 and 1969 of the two staunch social-democratic centralists, Len Williams, the General Secretary, and Sara Barker, the National Agent, to be replaced respectively by Harry Nicholas, formerly number two at the TGWU and Ron Hayward, the Southern Regional Organiser. The latter was to prove the more notable of the two appointments.

It had been widely expected that Reg Underhill, the experienced and highly capable Assistant National Agent, would succeed to the vacant position.[94] It was precisely because Underhill was a man in high standing that Hayward's selection was a significant political development.

He was unusual amongst Regional Organisers in not being identified with the right of the Party; and he was known to favour a relaxation of party discipline.[95] However, left-wing votes alone would not have been sufficient to elect Hayward. His rival was closely identified with the old guard at Transport House which, many felt, had become stale and organisationally ineffective; as an outsider, the Southern Regional Organiser capitalised on a desire for change.[96]

Hayward made plain at his interview his distaste for the traditional managerial style; and one of his first acts in his new post was to consign to the flames a stack of disciplinary dossiers.[97] Unlike his two predecessors, he objected to the use of discipline as an instrument of party management feeling it to be unnecessary and counterproductive. Like his counterparts in the PLP, Crossman and Silkin, he preferred a more emollient approach. Too rigid an insistence upon imposing rules, too obtrusive a presence inflamed feelings and sharpened differences; he regarded conciliation, the smoothing of differences and the accomodation of divergent views as a superior method of resolving conflicts.[98]

Hence his years as National Agent (and, after 1973, as General Secretary) witnessed a discarding of traditional controls. No attempts were made to crib the activities of left-wing groups who were given the freedom to organise and mobilise which they had not enjoyed to the full in the past; and the period[99] saw a seepage back of individuals – the best known was Ted Knight – who had earlier been expelled for Trotskyist affiliations.[100]

By the turn of the decade, the new, more tolerant, regime at Transport House was being acclaimed in left-wing circles.[101] Hayward succeeded in liberalising discipline because his views matched those of the steadily growing left-wing contingent on the NEC, and reflected (as we have seen in the PLP) a generally more relaxed atmosphere in the Party. A notable consequence of the new mood of tolerance was the decision to abolish the Proscribed List.

Liberalisation (3): the abolition of the Proscribed List
The list had been devised as a rampart of the Party's organisational and ideological defences. In the 1950s and early 1960s it had two main purposes: to discourage involvement of Labour Party members in pro-Soviet and anti-NATO organisations and to combat Trotskyist penetration.[102] In 1962, the credibility of proscription had been badly damaged by the bungled attempt to remove Russell and others from the Party.[103] From that point onwards the list was in a state of stasis; whilst unwilling to abolish it, the Executive rebuffed all proposals to add to it. Thus in 1967 it turned down a request from two CLPs to proscribe the predominantly far-left Vietnam Solidarity campaign.[104] In 1969 it rejected Sara Barker's advice to ban the curious 'Radical Action Movement'.[105]

In June 1967 the Organisation Sub-Committee received a request from the Clerical Workers Union, CAWU (now APEX), a union with impeccable 'moderate' credentials, to remove the Labour Research Department from the List.[106] The LRD had originally been set up by left-wing Fabians (like G. D. H. Cole) but in the early 1920s fell under Communist control and was subsequently proscribed.[107] By the late 1960s, however, it was primarily a research organisation, providing useful information for trade unions, several of which were affiliated to it. For whatever reason, CAWU (unlike other unions) was unwilling to acquiesce in the anomaly of a proscribed body with whom 'some trade unionists and members of the NEC had associations'.[108] It made a series of attempts to persuade the Executive to either lift or enforce the ban. For several years (to CAWU's mounting exasperation) it refused to do either.[109] No final decision was reached until early 1972, ostensibly because of the difficulty in obtaining information about the LRD, particularly its (unpublished) list of affiliates. Finally Ron Hayward cut this particular Gordian Knot by simply asking trade union NEC members how many of their organisations were affiliated: it transpired, a majority.[110] In these circumstances, the decision to lift the proscription was inevitable.[111]

A breach had been made, and was soon exploited. In October 1972, Frank Allaun raised the question of the status of the Medical Aid Committee for Vietnam (MACV).[112] The NEC had decided, in 1965, not to proscribe it but to discourage party organisations from associating with it. It now 'in view of the changing situation in Vietnam' agreed to reconsider the matter.[113] The original 1965 document – which concluded that Communist influence in MACV was 'strong' – was reproduced, together with a sharp rejoinder by a left wing NEC member, Renee Short, who happened to be Vice-Chairman of the body. This argued that the 1965 document was incorrect and misleading, hence the decision ought to be rescinded. The sting in the tail of Short's paper was its suggestion that since 'incorrect information circulated about MACV' the NEC ought to reassure itself that similar misapprehensions were not held about other proscribed organisations[114] by reviewing the whole list.[115]

The NEC agreed to delete the 1965 decision and to take up Mrs Short's suggestion. A series of documents were produced providing details about the aims and governing bodies of various proscribed organisations.[116] These demonstrated how ineffective proscription had become. The list of individuals occupying posts within the organisations – and, hence, ineligible for membership of the Party – included several influential trade union leaders (e.g. Bob Wright of the AEU, Bill Jones of the T&G), a number of Labour MPs – and two members of the NEC, Joan Maynard and Renee Short.

This evidence of an open and blatant disregard of Party rules was embarrassing. Initially the NEC responded by deleting organisations from the List,[117] but then decided to take the bull by the horns and commissioned a paper from the National Agent about its continued value.[118]

The paper by the new National Agent, Reg Underhill, did not actually propose the abolition of the list; but by arguing that it was unnecessary, impracticable and even counterproductive, he made this appear the logical step.[119] After a discussion (in which no vote was taken) the organisational committee took this step, which was ratified by the full NEC; it was also agreed to despatch a circular to all Party and affiliated organisations notifying them of the decision.[120]

The circular reflected the reasoning in Underhill's paper. It emphasised that the ending of the List did 'not represent any change in policy', but merely recognised the problems in maintaining an up-to-date record of suspect organisations; and was at pains to point out that adequate constitutional safeguards remained. It concluded by urging all party and affiliated bodies 'to continue to refrain from associating with other political organisations whose aims and objects are not consistent with those of the Labour Party'.[121]

Paul McCormick has dismissed all this as 'political rhetoric' and suggests that the termination of the list was solely a product of the newfound strength of the left on the NEC.[12] Similarly, Philip Williams interpreted it as a factional move by the left to weaken the right by encouraging extreme left infiltration.[123]

In fact this interpretation misconstrues both the reasons for the decision to end the list and its constitutional effect. The crucial point to grasp is that the decision, when it was finally taken, was not a controversial one. Some regional organisers harboured doubts, but the majority of both NEC members and Party officials were quite content to phase out the list. Of the six members present at the Organisation Committee meeting which discussed the matter, three were right-wingers (John Cartwright, Shirley Williams – both now in the SDP – and Denis Healey) and three were from the left (Tony Benn, Michael Foot and Alex Kitson).[124] No vote was ever taken, and Cartwright, who chaired the meeting, did not even feel it necessary to draw the full NEC's attention to the item when presenting the Committee's minutes.[125]

It is probably misleading even to think in terms of a decision, if by this is meant a conscious act of deliberation. There was a widespread feeling in the early 1970s that the list was obsolescent; indeed it could be argued that a policy which was so completely evaded only undermined the authority of the NEC. But if there was a general consensus that the list, as constituted at the time, served no useful purpose the motives of those who favoured (or acquiesced in) dispensing with it varied.

One can distinguish two strands of opinion. The first, held by Party officials (and perhaps shared by right-wing NEC members) objected not to the principle of proscription but to its mode of operation, namely the list. This was the position taken by Reg Underhill, in his influential paper. He believed that there were adequate constitutional safeguards against far left infiltration. Under clauses II(3) of the Constitution organisations with their own 'Programme, Principles and Policy for distinctive and separate propaganda' were ineligible for affiliation to the Party; and under clause II(4) membership of such organisations was incompatible with membership of the Party. 'Thus if an organisation is covered by the provision of section (3) there is no necessity for it to be proscribed. Its members are *automatically debarred* from Party membership'.[126]

Secondly, Underhill suggested that the existence of the list actually diminished vigilance, since local parties often laboured under the 'misapprehension that because an organisation is not included in the List therefore it must be a bona fide organisation'. For example, it was wrongly assumed that because a particular Trotskyist organisation did not figure on the list, association with it was 'in order'.[127] Thirdly, there were practical problems in compiling an adequate, up to date, list – it was, for example, simple for a banned organisation simply to change its name.[128]

The second strand of opinion was represented mainly by left-wingers (and by the new liberal-minded General Secretary Ron Hayward) who saw the ending of the list as part of a general process of liberalisation. By 1973 the left had effective parity on the Executive. Since their eagerness to get rid of the list was matched by no comparable enthusiasm to retain it, the result was a foregone conclusion.

An analysis of what, in fact, did prove to be a seminal act must however, go beyond motive. There was a general agreement that the list was both ineffective and obsolescent, because the conditions which sustained it had largely vanished. Its prime function, it should be recalled, was to repel Communist attempts to penetrate the Labour Party, and reflected a time when the boundary between Communism and Social Democracy was tightly drawn, and the bulk of trade unions were run by fiercely anti-Communist right-wingers. The hold of such men on the union movement had been snapped by the late 1960s. The decisive change was the emergence of a powerful, non-Communist, left which, in the very able forms of Jack Jones[129] and Hugh Scanlon, was strongly entrenched in the two largest unions. Left-wingers from both the Communist and Labour Parties often co-operated in challenging the right in loose 'broad left' alliances which by the early 1970s formed a highly influential nexus in the trade union movement. The effect of this was to destroy both the basis of support and much of the rationale of the Proscribed List. It became completely unenforceable when the occasional senior trade union leader occupied a prominent position in a proscribed body.[130] To this extent Underhill and others were making a wholly realistic assessment of the situation.

Far from the left seeking to enlist the support of revolutionaries[131] the period of the late 60s/early 70s was a somnolent one on the Trotskyist front. Trotskyism was actually experiencing a marked revival – but the bulk of recruits and energy flowed into organisations which would have no truck with the Labour Party – IS, IMG and SLL; few people had heard of Militant which, indeed, (outside the LPYS) had a shadowy presence.

The effect of the list's abolition on the NEC's control capability was shrouded in misunderstandings and miscalculations. Firstly, many people assumed that the Executive was no longer empowered to proscribe organisations. This view confused the *constitutional power* to proscribe (i.e. to declare an organisation ineligible for affiliation to the Labour Party), with the existence of the list, which was merely a compilation of banned organisations. The effect of dissolving the list was to 'unban' all such organisations. It in no way removed from the NEC its power to proscribe in the future; this would have required a constitutional amendment.

Underhill himself unwittingly contributed to the confusion by his misreading (or, more accurately, his traditional, centralist reading) of the constitution. He argued, it will be recalled, that Trotskyist groups not on the list, like IS and IMG, were 'automatically debarred from affiliation' – hence their members were ineligible to join the Labour Party – 'within the meaning of the 1946 amendment' (i.e. clause II(3)) because they had their own 'Programme, Principles and Policy' and so forth.[132] This was incorrect; such organisations *did* have to be proscribed (*declared* ineligible for affiliation) before their members were barred.[133] The impression[134] left by Underhill's argument was that the ending of the list also ended (because it was redundant) the power to proscribe.

In strict constitutional terms, the Executive suffered no net loss of powers; it was not stripped of the right to proscribe organisations. But, in political terms, the abolition of the list did lead to a significant contraction of Labour's control capability. The true significance of the move was a symbolic one: it symbolised (as, indeed, both the left and the General Secretary had intended) the installation of a more lenient managerial regime. For this reason, the power to proscribe, whilst never revoked, became more difficult to use; a precedent had been set: in the future (unlike in the past) the onus would be on those who wish to invoke it. And any such step inevitably brought cries of protest that its instigation would be a return to the days of 'bans, proscriptions and witch-hunting'.

Decentralisation: the McKay case and the 1970 rule-changes
The liberalisation of Party discipline was matched by a shift towards decentralisation; this was primarily evident in the key area of parliamentary selection. But, paradoxically, the first significant alteration in the selection procedure was designed to consolidate rather than curtail the powers of the centre.

Mrs Margaret McKay, MP for Clapham, had for a number of years enjoyed uneasy relations with her constituency party. Mounting disaffection over a range of issues – the MP's alleged neglect of her constituency and hostility towards local activists, and her outspoken championship of the Arab cause in the Middle East (coupled with charges of anti-semitism) – came to a head in the winter of 1969–70. After a stormy meeting of the Clapham GC a resolution was carried seeking 'the permission of the NEC for the holding of a mandated meeting as provided for in Clause XII 7(b) of the Rules'.[135]

The Clapham party was (on the advice of John Keys, a London regional official) following the standard procedure for instigating the deselection process.[136] In the past, as we have seen, the NEC's reluctance to allow constituency parties to depose their MPs prompted it to withhold its permission. It was now told, to its suprise, that it had no such powers. The new National Agent, Ron Hayward, explained that 'under the constitution the permission of the NEC for a constituency party to hold a mandated meeting was not, in fact, required'.[137]

Presumably, Hayward's predecessors, Len Williams and Sara Barker, were as familiar as he with the wording of the constitution. So the National Agent's intervention represented a considered departure. Hayward did not share the centralist caste of mind of the two earlier incumbents; but it would seem at least as likely that his action displayed an awareness of the recent Pembroke judgment. Previously the Executive had felt able to claim certain 'inherent' powers derived from its role as authoritative interpreter of the constitution. In the wake of the Pembroke case, it was now evident that such a claim rested on fragile legal foundations.

The NEC still retained its duty to uphold the Party's rules. On this point it was found that the Clapham party had carried out the correct procedure; hence it was free to commence deselection proceedings. However, the Organisation Committee, which considered the matter, was clearly unhappy with the existing rules covering deselection. It was agreed to recommend two changes. The first, on the suggestion of two left-wingers, Ian Mikardo and Tom Driberg[138], was designed to formally establish the right of an MP to a fair hearing (in line with the precepts on natural justice); the second, more contentious, change aimed to restore to the NEC the broad powers to adjudicate in deselection cases which it had customarily exerted but now found it did not, under the rules, possess.[139]

The 1970 Conference endorsed both changes. It established a new detailed procedure (not incorporated into the rules but binding upon CLPs) guaranteeing MPs facing deselection the right to a fair hearing at constituency level. Secondly it approved a rule change giving such MPs the right of appeal to the NEC which, in turn, was empowered to 'confirm, vary or reverse the decision taken by the General Committee'.[140]

This clause proved, predictably, highly controversial. Eric Heffer, an influential left-wing MP, charged that it gave the NEC 'unprecedented and unnecessary powers' and in *Tribune's* words, effectively transformed the NEC into 'the supreme arbiter' in any attempt to oust a sitting MP.[141] The amendment was carried – but only by a narrow margin, reflecting the much greater voting strength the left now wielded at Conference. And, within a year, the opportunity arose to decide whether the Executive had, indeed, now become – or, more accurately still remained – 'the supreme arbiter' in deselection disputes.[142]

The Taverne case

Dick Taverne had been, as we have seen, a beneficiary of the patronage of Party officials.[143] He was urged in 1962 to stand for the Lincoln seat, vacated by the resignation of Sir Geoffrey de Freitas, by John Harris, Transport House's head of publicity and a Gaitskell aide. Astute manoeuvrings by Jim Cattermole, the Regional Organiser, deprived a GC with only a slight right-wing margin of a left-wing contender. At the selection conference, four left-wingers walked out in protest at the lack of choice.[144] Gradually, however, the balance in the GMC tilted to the left and Taverne found himself totally at odds with a constituency party dominated 'by a small group of very determined left-wingers'.[145] Despite the CLP's bitter opposition to a range of Labour Government policies in the 1960s – over Vietnam, pay policy and *In Place of Strife*, Taverne's position was not immediately endangered. But the disenchantment of many within Lincoln fostered a mood which, a decade later, was to envelop much of the Party. Activists were expected to undertake much demanding doorstep activity. 'Yet when they came to exercise their democratic rights' as Taverne himself candidly acknowledged 'to express their views and to formulate policy through resolutions submitted to the Party's annual conference, the Government simply pushed them aside. They were cannon fodder and no more . . . No wonder they felt bolshy'.[146]

But it was the row over Common Market entry that provoked the open split between the Party and its MP. Taverne was a dedicated pro-marketeer. He was one of 69 MPs who voted in favour of the principle of entry and one of the smaller number who helped the passage of consequential legislation by abstaining on selected votes.[147] His constituency party was solidly against entry and appealed to him to abstain rather than vote for the Government on the first, crucial vote. A meeting of the GC had already been held a couple of months earlier to discuss the unsatisfactory relationship with the MP and the party reacted to his backing for the Government by passing a motion of no-confidence by 55 votes to 51 (with five abstentions).[148] The following month the constituency agreed to suspend any further action (a motion to drop the matter altogether was only lost by the casting vote of the Chairman).[149] In April 1972 Taverne resigned as a front-bench spokesman; the following month the EC decided by 18 votes to 2 to call for a special GC to consider a motion whether the MP should retire at the next election.[150]

This activated the new procedure established by the 1970 Conference. A special meeting of the GC was called in May to discuss the EC motion; it was approved by 58 votes to 37. In accordance with the amended procedure, a further meeting of the GC was held in June. By 75 votes to 50 it carried a resolution that the MP should retire at the next election. Taverne then exercised his right to appeal to the NEC.[151]

An enquiry committee, comprising the Chairman of the Organisation Committee, John Chalmers, plus two other right-wingers, Tom Bradley and Jack Diamond (both, incidentally, later joined Taverne in the SDP) was despatched to Lincoln. Taverne appealed against his dismissal by the Lincoln party on two main grounds.[152] The first was procedural. The new procedure had stipulated a four week gap between the two meetings of the GC required to consider a resolution to deselect an MP. This was clearly intended, Taverne claimed, to allow for full consultation of members through the cycle of branch meetings. Such consultations had not taken place – hence the CLP had acted in breach of the rules.

The second ground concerned the rights and responsibilities of an MP and his relationship with his local party. He argued that his eviction denied MPs the right to dissent 'on all great issues of conscience and principle and deeply held conviction' long established in the Party.[153] Further, if allowed to stand, it would lend official sanction to the doctrine that an MP was no more than a delegate, beholden to his local party. This, he argued, violated long-standing constitutional conventions as to the proper relationship between a Labour MP and his constituency organisation.

Anticipating objections, Taverne asserted the relevance of these broader considerations by drawing attention to the 1970 rule change which he argued empowered the NEC to over-rule a CLP decision on grounds other than procedural ones.

The enquiry team side-stepped these politically more delicate issues and chose to concentrate on the MP's first objection. The NAD's interpretation of the four week gap was that it was designed to provide, firstly, a 'cooling-off period' and, second, sufficient time for all accredited delegates to attend the final GC meeting. The committee concluded that the CLP properly discharged its requirements laid down by the revised 1970 procedure, but then suggested that the procedure itself was at fault. Failure to furnish all members an opportunity to discuss the issue was, the team claimed, in breach of natural justice. In the light of this, it recommended that the appeal be upheld.

The enquiry report's conclusion indicated the extent to which the concept of natural justice had permeated the Party's thinking. But it also stretched the term to encompass matters which did not fall within the established legal definition.[154] The report was, in fact, arguing not that natural justice had been violated but that the procedure itself was defective. This – Ian Mikardo reasoned at the special meeting of the Organisation Committee held to consider the report – was not an adequate ground for upholding the appeal.[155] The Sub-Committee approved the recommendation, though only by the casting vote of the Chairman; it was, however, rejected by the full Executive by a margin of twelve votes to eight.[156]

Taverne had anticipated that the NEC would rally to his aid, and precedent justified him in that belief. In the past the NEC had not hesitated to defend loyalist MPs in danger of deposition by their local parties.[157] The Lincoln MP was in a slightly equivocal position – he had rebelled on the issue of EEC entry, defying both Conference and the PLP. But this – as he was at pains to point out[158] – was an isolated incident: his record was otherwise unblemished. He was also correct in arguing that his dismissal violated accepted (Labour) constitutional conventions as to the appropriate relationship between an MP and his party. Further, he was on strong grounds in voicing the view that the 1970 rule change was expressly intended to empower the NEC to 'confirm, vary or reverse' a CLP decision on other than procedural grounds; indeed it was precisely for this reason that it aroused the ire of the left (and was so narrowly approved).

Why, then, had the Executive chosen not to employ powers it had so recently laid claim to? Its shifting political balance played a part. But the left, for so long critical of excessive central control, still fell short of a majority. Here contingent political circumstances played a part. Anti-marketeers on the right and centre of the Party were not enamoured of a staunch pro-marketeer who, as a deliberate act, helped the Government navigate EEC membership legislation through the Commons. More seriously, in the eyes of trade union loyalists, he had helped succour a Tory administration in the process of enacting restrictive trade union legislation.

The Lincoln decision signalled a significant contraction of managerial control. Three aspects are particularly noteworthy. Firstly the role of Transport House officials. In the past, beleaguered right-wing MPs could often count upon their support. In stark contrast to his predecessor (who helped secure the seat for Taverne in the first place) East Midlands Regional Organiser, Les Bridges, confined himself to his official responsibilities as a watch-dog of the rules. Further, whereas Sara Barker had operated as a 'part-time protector of MPs'[159] Ron Hayward saw his role as a conciliator – and what sympathy he felt for the MP's plight was soon extinguished.[160] In other words, Taverne was not afforded the assistance that, for example, Bessie Braddock had enjoyed *prior* to the final decision being taken.

Secondly, and even more importantly, the NEC revised the established constitutional convention governing relations between an MP and his CLP. In the social democratic centralist era the Executive had responded harshly to any attempt by constituency parties to exert pressure on an MP. Ian Mikardo, on the Committee's behalf, now sought a midway position between this traditional 'representational' model of the relationship and the 'delegate' alternative. Instead, he propounded what may be called the 'compatibility' view: there ought to be a reasonable understanding between a constituency party and its elected member; where this broke down the party was quite within its rights in seeking a 'divorce'.[161]

Thirdly, the NEC reinterpreted its own managerial prerogatives. The 1970 rule change was designed to give constitutional recognition to powers of intervention that the Executive had traditionally wielded. The Lincoln decision saw it divest itself of those powers. In effect it argued that the power to 'confirm, vary or reverse' a CLP decision applied only where the rules, or the procedure laid down in the same year, were infringed. Shortly afterwards this received formal acknowledgement in the enunciation of what was dubbed 'the Mikardo doctrine'. Speaking on behalf of the NEC, the MP for Bethnall Green and Bow assured Conference that, if a CLP chose to deselect its MP, there would be 'no interference from the NEC so long as the proper constitutional provisions are carried out'.[162]

The Mikardo doctrine significantly widened the sphere of discretion of constituency organisations in the sphere of candidate selection. But, in leaving CLPs freer to set in motion the deselection procedure it was to demonstrate how cumbersome and stressful it was; hence the new doctrine was to have the unanticipated effect of spurring the movement for (what came to be known as) mandatory reselection.

Deconcentration: the trend towards polycentrism

The liberalisation and decentralisation of Labour's political system occurred at a time when the centralised system of control was corroding from within. The system was rooted, as we have seen,[163] in a high level of institutional integration. This, in turn, was sustained by elite consensus and by a pattern of functional differentiation with its agreed division of roles and responsibilities between the Party and the unions. From the late 1960s onwards, both these conditions came to an end.

During the Attlee administration, the NEC and the party machine it commanded, unhesitatingly and systematically deployed its powers to buttress the Government against its critics.[164] This pattern carried over into the 1950s and early 1960s. Trade union leaders, both inside and outside the NEC, were amongst the sternest disciplinarians.[165] 'In 1951', Minkin has written 'there was a solid block of trade union supporters who identified sympathetically with the political values and strategy of the parliamentary leadership.'[166] This elite consensus, which knitted together the main centres of power within the Party, was given added thrust by a shared attachment to the precepts of social democratic centralism.

The rise of left-wing trade unionism broke up the old consensus. The voice of the unions no longer spoke unambiguously in the accent of a authoritarian right-wing eager to clamp down on left-wing dissidents. Not only had the trade union right lost their automatic prerogative to speak on behalf of the majority; the doctrine of majority rule, the central tenet of social-democratic centralism, had become discredited as the Government forcefully repudiated any notion of Conference sovereignty. By the 1970s, roles had been neatly reversed: it was now the powerful spokesmen of the trade union left, like Hugh Scanlon, who demanded of *right-wing* dissidents that Conference decisions be 'binding on us all, and that includes every MP in the Party'.[167]

The radically altered balance of forces within the unions transformed the climate within the Party. 'The change in the atmosphere was immense' according to Jim Mortimer, formerly a left-wing trade union official, later to become Labour's General Secretary. The emergence of a powerful union left 'brought to an end the right-wing disciplinary regime'.[168] Much of the political drive and moral energy which nourished social-democratic centralism evaporated.

The shift of the unions to the left was bound, in due course, to alter the composition of the NEC. But the process was retarded by the convention (at the time) of life tenancy for Executive members in the trade union sector; and by the various deals and arrangements which cut across political considerations in NEC elections.[169] Although the size of the left contingent steadily grew, it was not until the mid 1970s (after the end of the period covered in this chapter) that it secured a clear majority. Nevertheless its influence steadily mounted and, in conjunction with the rift between the unions and the Government, effected a significant alteration in the relationship between the NEC and the Parliamentary leadership.

Right-wing trade unionists were still well entrenched on the NEC, particularly the Organisation Committee which they traditionally dominated; but any enthusiasm they might have had for shielding the Wilson Government against its critics soon ebbed away, as their own organisations became increasingly embattled with the Government. Successive phases of prices and incomes legislation broke down the system of functional differentiation. At a key meeting of the NEC it was two right-wing trade union members, John Chalmers of the boilermakers and Andy Cunningham of the GMWU who moved support for Frank Cousins' Conference resolution calling for the repeal of Labour's income legislation.[170] Relations further deteriorated with the Government's proposals for trade union reform *In Place of Strife*. It was the Chairman of the Organisation Committee, Joe Gormley (the right-wing miners leader) who moved the resolution setting the NEC at loggerheads with the Government over the issue;[171] and it was Gormley, again, who a year later proposed a motion criticising the Government for failing to consult adequately with the NEC.[172]

By the late 1960s, the Executive had come to operate increasingly as an independent pressure upon rather than as a buffer of the Government.[173] The growing gap between Government and the wider Party, Wilson's open disdain for critical Conference resolutions, complaints that ministers took little or no account of NEC representations all prompted a reappraisal of the proper role of Labour's senior body. A process of disaggregation between the Executive and the Parliamentary leadership was set in motion.

Wilson himself appears to have favoured a clearer demarcation of roles between the two. He resisted any attempt by the NEC to intervene in what he regarded as the proper sphere of government. Conversely – and perhaps in reaction to the conduct of his predecessor – he detached himself from managerial matters. On being elected leader in 1963 he told the Executive that he 'would not be involved in any matter affecting party organisation, the selection or endorsement of parliamentary candidates, disciplinary questions or appointments'.[174] He remained faithful to this self-denying ordinance.[175]

In 1967 the Simpson Report on Party Organisation recommended an upgrading of the political role of the General Secretary, who was envisaged as a 'secondary focus of power'.[176] This was another step towards institutional differentiation between the parliamentary and extra-parliamentary party. In fact, it had little immediate consequence, and only really took effect with the election of Ron Hayward to the post in 1972.

His (narrow) victory[177] in 1972 was (in part) a reflection of the desire of the NEC for a more assertive incumbent role; and the new General Secretary's job description (which he often quoted) departed from tradition in emphasising his responsibility to promote Party policy (as laid down by Conference and the NEC). Hayward executed it with alacrity: henceforth the General Secretary was an 'unambiguous servant of the Party rather than of the Parliamentary leadership.'[178]

These developments heralded the end of a period when the Party machine was fully at the disposal of the parliamentary leadership. Managerial goals were no longer automatically defined in a way to serve the needs and interests of the PLP majority. By 1974 – when Labour returned to office – institutional pluralism was well established. The concept of a Party 'centre', for so long unproblematic, had now ceased to be so. The new polycentric system was to have profound consequences as Labour entered a decade of unparalleled turbulence.

Chapter Nine

Parliamentary selection from the Mikardo doctrine to mandatory reselection, 1974–80

9.1 The Mikardo doctrine and deselection controversies

In the previous chapter, we traced the liberalisation of Labour's managerial regime from the late 1960s to the Party's return to office in 1974. This more relaxed approach nevertheless left more or less intact Labour's existing authority structure, and the pattern of relations between the various Party institutions. Both were now to undergo major alteration.

Two key impulses behind liberalisation, the rising influence of the left on the NEC and the more pluralist power system, had by no means exhausted themselves. Indeed, both were to be impelled further forward by the Party's response to another, and even more stressful, period of office. By the end of the decade, the left had, for the first time in Labour's history, achieved a position of ascendency on the NEC; and relations between the Executive and the Government had deteriorated so sharply as to threaten to replace the polycentric system of the early 1970s by an adversarial one.

'Who controls selections', Ranney wrote in the 1960s, 'controls the Party'.[1] No period in its history bears stronger testimony of the truth of this statement than the six years in the life of the Labour Party from 1974 to 1980. Both left and right came to regard it as the central terrain of conflict; efforts to reach a settled compromise were constantly thwarted; and the eventual triumph of the drive to subject each MP to mandatory reselection in each Parliament effected the most far-reaching change in Labour's constitution and power-structure for many years.

Parliamentary selection procedures – a seemingly obscure set of rules few cared about and even fewer understood – had been thrust on to the political agenda in 1972 with the deselection of Dick Taverne. One immediate consequence was to encourage other constituencies dissatisfied with their MP's performance. Within months of Labour's resumption of office, Eddie Griffiths was unseated by his local party. Complaining that he was the victim of 'a well planned coup by extremists'[2] he appealed to the NEC. But the CLP had taken considerable care to follow the rules. A special meeting of the Organisation Committee hurriedly held because of the impending general election dismissed the MP's appeal after the Regional Organiser, Harold Sims (who supervised the procedure) confirmed there had been no irregularities: 'there is nothing for the meeting to consider' Ian Mikardo – who chaired it – briskly told the infuriated MP.[3]

The question of parliamentary selection procedures figured in the agenda of that year's Conference. One of the items to be debated was a proposal, from Rushcliffe CLP, calling for mandatory reselection of MPs. Ian Mikardo siezed the opportunity to secure formal NEC endorsement for 'his' doctrine. After a heated discussion, he managed to persuade his colleagues that unless this was placed on record the Rushcliffe proposal might well be carried (a view, in fact, he did not hold).[4] Many years of championing constituency rights had at last brought forth results.[5] With the authority of the NEC, he was able to inform Conference that 'our only function as National Executive [in deselection disputes] is to determine whether the procedure has been carried out'.[6]

The purpose of the Mikardo doctrine was both to liberate CLPs from excessive central interference; and to establish relations between constituency parties and their MPs upon a more stable and equal footing by encouraging a greater responsiveness by members to local party opinion. The second objective was not achieved. Instead, within a year, the relationship had became a flashpoint of political controversy.

Reg Prentice had been a comparatively obscure (though, in the PLP, well respected[7]) MP until 1972 when, as shadow employment spokesman, he angered many left-wingers by a series of unflattering observations on 'extremists' and 'marxists' (in which categories he included the Tribune group of MPs) in the Party and unions. His forthright and abrasive style did not commend him to those who did not share his views. This included many within his own party in Newham North East – gravitating to the left as it received an influx of radical middle-class recruits in the early 1970s – which formally disassociated itself from one particularly outspoken speech in 1973.[8]

Prentice was unwilling to temper his views to placate critics. In 1975 – by then Education Secretary – he delivered a highly publicised speech accusing the unions of 'welshing' on the social contract, earning himself a censure motion from his CLP's Executive Committee.[9] Three months later, Newham North East formally instigated deselection proceedings. The Executive voted by 12 to 8 to recommend the GC to convene a special meeting to consider a motion that Prentice retire at the next election. This was accepted by the GC by 30 votes to 6. The special meeting was held in July and by 29 votes to 19 it called upon the MP to retire.[10] Prentice's dismissal attracted widespread public attention. To appreciate its significance, one must place it in a broader political context.

The Labour Government's shift to the right in 1975 – its shunting aside of the interventionist industrial strategy devised in opposition, its retreat from commitments to full employment and expanding welfare services – disenchanted many Party activists. The extra-parliamentary organs – Conference and the NEC – seemed impotent in the face of the Government's determination to press ahead with orthodox deflationary policies in response to the country's mounting economic difficulties. This inevitably focussed attention upon the effective autonomy of the Parliamentary party, stimulating, in due course, a drive for constitutional reform. The immediate effort was to intensify pressure on MPs already in difficulties with their constituencies.

Prentice was a man of unyielding temperament, prone to outspoken accusations which not only angered his opponents but also, as time wore on, alienated his friends. But the political significance of his deselection – as, to a lesser degree, that of Frank Tomney, Sir Arthur Irvine and, earlier, Eddie Griffiths – was that, unlike Dick Taverne, he was a loyalist who had never stood out publicly against a major plank of Party policy, or defied the Whip in Parliament. Indeed, all the deselected MPs in this period could – and did – legitimately claim that a major fault, in the eyes of their critics, was precisely their steadfast loyalty to the Government.

Prentice's case was by far the most controversial, because of his status as a cabinet minister, his high public profile and his reputation as a hammer of the militants. It soon became standard to portray his fate – and that of those who shared it – as part of a concerted left-wing strategy to reduce Labour MPs to the status of servants of their local caucuses.[11] Before the final decision was taken to dismiss him, he attracted a flood of support from his parliamentary colleagues. Well over one-half of the PLP (180 MPs) including 12 cabinet ministers and 35 junior ministers signed a letter praising the Newham North East MP's 'uncompromising support' for socialist measures as Education and more latterly Overseas Development minister and urging his CLP to desist from its 'extremely damaging' attempt to evict him.[12] The Prime Minister himself stepped into the arena with a sharply worded letter castigating 'small and unrepresentative cliques' acting in a constitutionally improper manner to evict their MPs.[13]

The Newham North East Party remained unmoved by the mounting pressure, compounded by extremely hostile and (in some cases) personally abusive media coverage and proceeded to deselect its MP by 29 votes to 19. His appeal to the NEC was heard by an enquiry committee, comprising two right-wingers (John Chalmers, Chairman of the Organisation Committee and Tom Bradley) and one left-winger (Alex Kitson of the TGWU) plus the National Agent, Reg Underhill.[14] In his evidence, Prentice detailed a number of procedural irregularities, but these did not comprise the burden of his case. The NEC, he stated, should consider two other factors: firstly the precepts of natural justice; secondly, the wider political and constitutional ramifications.

On the first point, Prentice argued that his removal was orchestrated by a small, organised group of 'hardline intolerant people associated with Militant and its backers' who had infiltrated the constituency and consciously set about manipulating its machine. Even if the rules themselves had been observed (which he questioned) their spirit had been violated and the decision in no way reflected opinion in the Newham North East party.[15] The second point represented the kernal of Prentice's case. He had been deposed not because of any dissatisfaction with his performance as an MP, either in his constituency or Parliament, but simply because of his beliefs. He adduced three reasons why the decision to dismiss him should be set aside: firstly, the views of his opponents were utterly unrepresentative of Labour Party members and voters both in Newham North East and nationally; secondly, it was part of a concerted drive by extreme left-wing elements to alter the composition of the PLP; thirdly, it imperilled the system of parliamentary democracy by seeking to convert MPs into cyphers of local party caucuses.

Much of the evidence (including questions by members of the enquiry panel) was taken up by a consideration of those wider issues. But, in its judgment, the panel reverted to the Mikardo doctrine – that its sole responsibility was to ensure the correct procedures had been followed – and the appeal was dismissed. However, the panel was uneasy with a strict adherence to the doctrine and could not have been unaware of the storm of criticism, in the PLP and the media, the decision to sanction Prentice's removal would provoke. In view 'of all the circumstances set out in the report' it urged a genuine attempt to be made to reconcile the MP and his GC.

At the Organisation Committee, Shirley Williams attempted to delete the recommendation to dismiss the appeal, pending a possible reconciliation. This was defeated by nine votes to two – a significant vote because there were only six left-wingers present.[16] This showed that the Mikardo doctrine commanded broad support on the Executive. A further amendment deputing the General Secretary, Ron Hayward, to act as conciliator was agreed.

The following NEC was – even by the standards of the time – an unusually full and contentious one. Its agenda covered, besides the

Prentice case, the Underhill Report on 'entryism', a move by Ian Mikardo to push mandatory reselection of MPs and a motion by Judith Hart reprimanding the failure of the Government to pursue Party policy on economic and industrial questions. It also witnessed a (rare) and vigorous intervention by the Prime Minister. Earlier, he had appeared to pledge his full support behind his cabinet colleague, even proposing to depart from his rule not to intervene in organisational and disciplinary matters 'to raise the whole question of action by small and certainly not necessarily representative groups who have secured a degree of power within a constituency'.[17] His contribution, it transpired, was to be more nuanced. Performing a typical Wilson manoeuvre, he chose to balance tough reproofs for the NEC's attacks on his Government and its failure to act on entryism by reprimanding Prentice for his associations with the extreme right.[18] This did little for Prentice's prospects for reprieve, which were probably slight anyway. The attempt at reconciliation was to go ahead but the rejection of his appeal was confirmed.[19]

The General Secretary attempted to bring the two sides together, but with both sides obdurate, the reconciliation attempt soon petered out. Annoyed in particular by the MP's unwillingness to desist from exploiting a hostile media to belabour his enemies and embarrass the Party, Hayward advised the Organisation Committee of the futility of his mission, which was henceforth abandoned.[20] Within a year Prentice had, to the distress of his supporters and the gratification of his critics, defected to the Conservative Party; he was to serve loyally, as a junior minister, in the Thatcher administration.

Other casualties of the deselection process were less well known. Frank Tomney had for long had an uneasy relationship with his party in Hammersmith North. In his struggle to survive he enjoyed the generous patronage of *The Times* which depicted him – in the now established imagery – as the sturdy moderate, the exemplar of proletarian decency and good sense, battling a clique of left-wing extremists.[21] In fact, Tomney had a reputation as a poor MP, on the extreme right of the Party, with some notably illiberal views on homosexuality, race and capital punishment.[22] The Hammersmith North party was politically mixed rather than being uniformly left-wing. Already past his political prime (he was 71 by the time the next election was held) the MP had escaped several attempts to dislodge him, in some cases by employing the tried and tested methods for which his (and Prentice's) opponents were severely admonished.[23]

Finally, in February 1976, after protracted efforts which had commenced 18 months earlier, the constituency GC voted to unseat him, and the MP appealed to the NEC.[24] At the enquiry, Tomney demanded that regard should be given to 'service, devotion and loyalty' as well as procedure. The enquiry team, however, interpreted its remit in the by now accepted sense and, no evidence of rule infringements being found, the appeal was dismissed.

Sir Arthur Irvine, MP for Liverpool Edge Hill, had, earlier in his Commons career, figured amongst Aneurin Bevan's supporters. But, with the passage of years, the liveliness of his interest in left-wing causes (and, indeed, as a QC with a flourishing London practice, in his Parliamentary work) had dimmed. Like Tomney he was past retiring age and had survived earlier attempts to displace him. In 1977, he was finally unseated but, perhaps anticipating the likely response, rather than appeal to the NEC he resigned his seat, paving the way for the electoral triumph of a young and energetic Liberal, David Alton.[25]

The NEC's unwillingness to overturn local deselection decisions except on procedural grounds aroused considerable disquiet in the PLP. Many agreed with Tomney that the Mikardo doctrine deprived MPs of 'any procedure to ensure fair and democratic treatment'.[26] However, the Executive was unresponsive to PLP calls to discard the doctrine and, indeed, in a motion proposed by Mikardo in 1976 formally reaffirmed its commitment to it.[27]

But how hard and fast was this distinction between procedure and substance? Rule-infringements of some sort are almost inevitable in voluntary organisations with complex and not easily decipherable rule books. It becomes, in these circumstances, a matter of judgement whether the infringement is sufficiently serious to merit the attention of the NEC. And this judgement – as was clearly the case in the earlier period – may easily be influenced by political considerations.

Paul McCormick has taken this argument a step further. Far from signifying a reduction of central control, the Mikardo doctrine, he suggests, actually extends it, by investing 'the NEC with a peculiar kind of elastic power that can be extended almost to the full degree of the original formal powers', whilst masquerading as restricted and neutral. It enabled the NEC to disclaim any power to save MPs of whom it disapproves (like Prentice and Tomney) whilst stepping in to protect those it favours. An example of this, he suggests, was the case of Maureen Colquhoun, MP for Northampton North.[28]

This case has a number of distinctive features. Firstly Mrs Colquhoun was a left-of-centre MP, indeed the Treasurer of the Tribune group. Secondly, unravelling the reasons behind the attempt to unseat her is even more difficult than usual in such cases. She was widely criticised for a speech which (her critics claimed and she denied) intimated some sympathy for Enoch Powell's views on race. She asserted (and her critics denied) that the main objection to her was her lesbianism. Charges and counter-charges were rife, wrapped up in an atmosphere of personal animosity and rendered the more sensitive by the extreme marginality of her seat (taken by the Conservatives in 1979).

Whatever the motives of her critics, by the autumn of 1977 she had clearly lost the confidence of her GC, which deselected her by 23 votes to 18. She appealed to the NEC, and her case was heard by a panel consisting of Brian Stanley, Tom Bradley, Harold Hickling (all right-wing trade unionists) and Eric Heffer, with Reg Underhill as secretary.[29] At the enquiry the Chairman made it clear that the Committee's terms of reference were simply to investigate whether the rules had been fully observed and (unlike in the Prentice case) the report consisted entirely of the hearing of evidence on alleged procedural irregularities. No major ones were found. However, it was discovered that the original resolution calling upon Mrs Colquhoun to retire, which precipitated the process of deselection, was not given prior notice at the branch at which it was initially carried; it had been simply moved from the floor during the branch meeting. This, the enquiry committee concluded, violated natural justice and, for this reason, the appeal was upheld. The Committee's recommendation was approved by the NEC.[30]

The judgment is significant in that the failure to provide prior notice was not, technically, a rule infringement. The irregularity itself was so minor and common (it is not at all unusual for branch meetings not to circulate in advance resolutions which are debated and then passed to the GC) that it hardly justified revoking Northampton North's decision.[31] Indeed, the enquiry team conceded this by resting its judgment not on the irregularity itself but on the argument that, since the resolution initiated deselection proceedings, the failure to notify members of its terms constituted a violation of natural justice. Yet this was one of the arguments which, in the Taverne case, the NEC had disallowed, presumably on the grounds that, unless the meaning of the term was strictly defined and incorporated into the rules it would drive a coach and horses through the Mikardo doctrine, effectively reinstating the pre-1972 position.

How, then, do we explain the NEC's action? According to McCormick, it illustrates the calculated deception of the Mikardo doctrine, whose function was to 'camouflage and enhance the powers of the NEC ... whilst ostensibly diminishing them' and, furthermore 'to create a form of power that lends itself to partisan application when the left-wing dominates the NEC'.[32] Hence, the NEC was able both to seal the fate of Prentice and other right-wingers whilst saving Mrs Colquhoun, a left-winger, all in the convenient guise of impartially upholding the rules.

The argument is partly inaccurate and partly misleading. Firstly, the principle of intervening only on procedural grounds was first invoked by a right-wing NEC in the case of a left-wing MP – John Bird of Wolverhampton North East – facing deselection; although, as we have seen, the Executive never imposed such restraints upon itself when right-wing Parliamentarians found themselves in the same predicament.[33]

Secondly, McCormick's claim that the Mikardo doctrine was 'an ideal weapon in the political armoury for it is potent yet largely concealed'[34] is unconvincing. The origins of the doctrine lay in left-wing resentment at the behaviour of the NEC in the 1950s and early 1960s when it used its powers to curb constituency autonomy in the selection process. It was designed to curtail, not to extend, the Executive's power. Also it is by no means evident what purpose would be served by camouflaging the NEC's power. Right-wingers were hardly likely to be, and, in fact, were not assuaged by the Executive's claim to be powerless to save embattled Parliamentary colleagues. Finally, his assertion – supported only by the Colquhoun case – of 'partisan application' is factually inaccurate. As we have seen, of the four members of the enquiry team hearing the Colquhoun appeal, three were on the right of the Party – further the recommendation was unanimous and was not disputed by the NEC. The Colquhoun case was far more intricate than McCormick allows and certainly cannot be reduced to a simple left-right conflict; indeed Colquhoun's leading opponents were mainly left-wing themselves, and all were supporters of the 'hard left' ginger group, the Campaign for Labour Party Democracy.[35] (CLPD itself was unsympathetic to Mrs. Colquhoun; the journal *Tribune* adopted a neutral position. Other factors were more germane – some NEC members were probably sensitive about sanctioning a decision which was allegedly influenced by the MP's lesbianism; and none could be unaware of the risks attached to (possibly) precipitating a by-election in an extremely marginal seat when the Government already lacked an overall majority.

All of this is to accept that the Mikardo doctrine was by no means automatic in its operation – that it did, indeed, grant the NEC a certain leeway. But it does not follow that this discretion would necessarily be utilised for partisan advantage. Indeed, the case would appear to suggest the opposite: that NEC powers, under the Mikardo doctrine, were at their most elastic where there was a broad consensus between left and right, and, hence, were not available for factional advancement.

The Mikardo doctrine represented the most important, but not the sole, example of the retraction of central control. Indeed, formal and direct NEC intervention does not (as we argued earlier) offer an accurate measure of centralisation. A series of changes in the mid-1970s – ranging from rule revisions and shifts in the balance of political forces to alterations in outlook and expectation – combined to diminish the centre's capacity to influence the selection process.

The rule revisions originated in the comprehensive consultation exercise undertaken in 1973 as part of the compilation of a report on Party structure submitted by the NEC to the 1974 Conference.[36] This uncovered considerable dissatisfaction with existing practices, particularly the packing of selection conferences by delegates (usually from affiliated organisations) 'who have never previously attended General Committee meetings and are not seen afterwards', or who have been specially appointed for the purpose.[37] The report recommended a rule change preventing branches and affiliated organisations 'topping-up' their delegations for a selection conference but otherwise left the status quo intact.[38] In his speech, on behalf of the NEC, on Party reorganisation, however, Mikardo cast his net wider. He attacked past practices 'when there were a lot of carve-ups and ... when the machine was brought to bear to try and prevent CLPs selecting the person they wanted, or to push someone else'. He promised to propose to the NEC a change stipulating prior attendance at a GC as a condition of eligibility to vote at a selection conference[39] – a proposal later incorporated in the rules.[40]

These minor rule revisions were designed to restrict the room for lobbying or 'fiddle faddle' in Mikardo's phrase,[41] on the part of regional officials, or others. More important was the change in political climate occasioned by the growing strength of the left on the NEC. Regional officials[42] could no longer feel assured that their efforts to promote right-wing candidates (or discourage CLPs from ousting right-wing MPs) would have the endorsement of either the NEC or Transport House. Too overt involvement in the selection process now ran the risk of a reprimand from the left-wing NEC if it came to light.[43] Ron Hayward, the General Secretary, was politically identified with the new majority; and Reg Underhill, the National Agent, had always believed that regional organisers should confine themselves to their official duties.[44]

Inevitably (and often quite legitimately) regional officials continued to exercise influence. But, responding to different cues and pressures that influence was now less likely to be deployed in one political direction. The career of Frank Tomney illustrates this point.

Years before he was actually deselected he had forfeited the confidence of his local party. His ability to survive was at least in part due to aid from the Regional Organiser. As often happened, rank and file members lacked an adequate grasp of the rules. The Regional Organiser was selectively helpful, ready to volunteer advice and assistance to the MP and his supporters, much less so to anti-Tomney elements. As a result, several deselection efforts foundered upon failure to observe fully the proper procedures.[45]

By the mid 1970s, adroit manoeuvring by regional officers to forestall deselections was no longer favoured by the NEC. They were expected to proffer impartial guidance. Some officials welcomed this new climate, having tired of protecting MPs who they did not regard as assets to the

Party. This was certainly the view held of Tomney by Bill Jones, Deputy General Secretary of the London Labour Party who, by this time was thoroughly disenchanted with the Hammersmith MP and, indeed 'suggested he could save a great deal of trouble if he would consider retiring.'[46] He would not, and Jones accordingly provided his CLP with detailed advice as to proper procedures for dispensing with his services.[47]

9.2 The campaign for mandatory reselection

Mounting disenchantment with the Labour Government's performance – rising unemployment, cuts in social spending and the repudiation of the economic and industrial policies laboriously worked out in opposition – fuelled a campaign to alter the structure of power and authority within the Party. Years earlier Richard Crossman had pinpointed the efficient secret of Labour's constitution: 'the concession in principle of sovereign powers to the delegates at the annual conference and the removal in practice of most of this sovereignty through the trade union block vote on the one hand, and the complete independence of the PLP on the other'.[48] The first of these pillars had crumbled in the late 1960s and Conference approval had been secured in the early 1970s for a radical set of policies. The ease with which the 1974–1979 government was able (after an early spurt of reform) to discard these policies and the helplessness of the wider Party – including the NEC – to arrest the process convinced many constituency activists that the main barrier to radical change lay in Crossman's second condition, the independence of the PLP. The demand for greater accountability swiftly became the chief rallying cry of left-wingers in the constituencies.

How was this to be accomplished? Conference might endorse socialist policies but the Party lacked any effective mechanism to impel a Labour cabinet to implement them. What the Party did possess, however, was control over its own internal arrangements. If the independence of the PLP, as a collective body, appeared to be impregnable it was wholly within the power of the wider Party to alter the relationship between a CLP and individual MPs.

In the mid 1960s Ranney described selection conferences as 'far more significant battlegrounds than annual Conferences' adding his 'distinct impression that the right have understood this fact of life better than the left'.[49] It was to be the signal contribution of the Campaign for Labour Party Democracy (CLPD), set up in 1973, to the cause of the left that it educated constituency activists to this 'fact of life'. Early on in the life of the new Labour Government it adopted as the spearhead of its campaign for democratisation the call for mandatory reselection of MPs; with great tactical skill and political acumen its leaders, with growing success, sought to mobilise support for this goal in all sections of the movement.[50]

The drive for mandatory reselection was given added impetus from the experience of the deselections of the 1970s. Whilst many MPs complained about the lack of adequate safeguards afforded to their colleagues by the NEC, most activists drew the opposite conclusion: the procedure was too cumbersome, too time-consuming and too vulnerable to exploitation by opponents of the Party. CLPs which had undergone the experience had been bitterly divided, battered by a barrage of hostile media attention and, in some cases, denounced and derided by senior Party figures. Those feelings were not confined to radical activists; a substantial minority of the regional staff, in 1974, favoured a modification in the rules to enable constituencies to debate removing MPs 'in less unpleasant circumstances'.[51]

Mikardo had, on behalf of the NEC, rejected a motion calling for mandatory reselection at the 1974 Conference. Although personally sympathetic, he was aware that opinion as a whole on the Executive was not and, in any case, felt reasonably confidant that the rights of CLPs to unseat their MPs were adequately protected by the doctrine he expounded that year. Within a year he had changed his mind, primarily in response to the Prentice affair. The vigour of the efforts of the right, including NEC members, to persuade the Executive to overturn Newham North East's decision demonstrated that the survival of the Mikardo doctrine rested precariously on the balance of political forces within it. Secondly, the avalanche of damaging publicity and the ill feeling generated, spotlighted the defects of the existing procedure.[52]

Accordingly, at the November 1975 NEC – the same meeting which rejected Prentice's appeal – Mikardo proposed that a constitutional amendment providing for mandatory reselection be submitted to the next Conference.[53] There followed months of debate in an evenly divided executive in which alignments followed left-right lines. Finally, the Mikardo resolution was defeated by fourteen votes to eleven[54] and there, as far as the NEC was concerned, the matter rested for the next year or so.

Why did an ostensibly left-wing NEC reject a proposal whose passage would modify the correlation of forces in the Party to its advantage? Firstly – when the right turned out in force – the Executive was in fact more or less evenly balanced. Secondly, a minority of left-wingers was either lukewarm or hostile to mandatory reselection. Thirdly, and probably most importantly, multiple pressures were brought to bear upon the NEC urging maintenance of the status quo.

Firstly, an NAD paper commissioned by the Organisation Committee came out strongly against change. Using the well-honed bureaucratic technique of questioning the feasibility of a reform rather than the principle, it listed a battery of practical and administrative complications whilst refraining from suggesting how they could be overcome.[55] Secondly, and predictably, the PLP lobbied energetically against the proposal. Its Chairman, Cledwyn Hughes – rehearsing arguments that were to become familiar – claimed that mandatory reselection would, by undermining the security of MPs, damage their morale, discourage able people from seeking a Parliamentary career (in particular manual workers without a profession to fall back on), place unions sponsoring MPs at a disadvantage, provoke 'unnecessary bickering' and incur damaging press publicity.[56]

Thirdly, trade unions were mobilised to resist the measure; sponsored MPs, they were urged, might be unseated and unions would be deprived of the opportunity to forward alternative nominees.[57] Finally, the Party leader and Premier, Harold Wilson, and his soon to be elected successor, Jim Callaghan, warned of the danger of Militant full-timers being drafted into constituencies to oust sitting MPs.[58]

But momentum for change was sweeping the constituencies. A significant number of resolutions calling for mandatory resolution were put to the 1976 Conference; but these were ruled out of order by the Conference Arrangements Committee because of the three year rule (the issue was last debated in 1974).[59] The following year there was a positive torrent of resolutions and constitutional amendments (over 90) – by far the largest number for any single issue. Nevertheless, a combination of mistakes by the CLPD (whose model constitutional amendment commanded most support) and adroit manoeuvring by the opponents of change almost kept the matter off the agenda. It is here that the NEC played a key role as faciliter of change – opening the sluice gates which could easily have been slammed shut.

The Conference Arrangements Committee, in a deft piece of agenda management, removed the bulk of the resolutions from the agenda by applying an obscure rule introduced in 1968: this stated that any constitutional amendment must first be referred to the NEC for a year before being debated. The number of resolutions having been drastically pruned, the CAC then fixed the debate on reselection late on Thursday afternoon, when it might easily have been crowded out, on the grounds that the small number of remaining resolutions on the topic indicated that it did not merit high priority. The alert and experienced Ian Mikardo promptly circumvented this by persuading the NEC to urge the CAC to alter the agenda (which it did) guaranteeing the item would be reached.[60]

The sword-playing continued and became more intricate. The NEC had voted to support the (CLPD backed) Rushcliffe resolution. The resolution, for whatever reason, did not survive the compositing meeting and was replaced by another proposal (favoured by Militant). This

was important because, whereas the Rushcliffe resolution would probably have passed, the composite was highly unlikely to, since it would
have exposed an MP to a constant threat of deselection, more or less at
any time.

The NEC opposed the composite and, if it were not remitted, would
have asked Conference to vote it down (which, under the three year rule,
could have excluded further deliberation until 1980, by which time the
political balance at Conference might have altered). The next thrust of
the sword came from Mikardo, speaking on behalf of the NEC. Having
stated that the NEC could not support the composite, he then spoke
strongly in favour of the principle of reselection and concluded by
pledging that, in the event of remittance, the NEC would present a
constitutional amendment to provide for mandatory reselection 'in the
way and in the sense that the sponsors of the 60 odd resolutions want'.
He assured delegates (in words often to be quoted) that there was not 'the
least chance of the Executive reneging on that undertaking'.[61]

If the NEC had enacted its traditional role – of shield to the Parliamentary leadership – it could have deployed a range of techniques to
sidetrack the demand for mandatory reselection.[62] Instead, its sympathetic response guaranteed that the demand would survive. Aware of
this, the Party establishment set about restoring the shield.

Mikardo argued that the NEC had a simple and limited task before it:
to produce the appropriate constitutional amendment, in the light of his
pledge to Conference. Opposition to this soon surfaced. Callaghan
claimed that remission was in fact tantamount to defeat; others argued
that one NEC could not bind its successor – in other words the pledge
was valueless. The NAD submitted a paper which pushed for a re-open-
ing of the debate by suggesting that the NEC consider the basic principles. This was accepted by the Organisation Committee which, on the
casting vote of its right-wing Chairman recommended the setting-up of
a working party.[63]

Mikardo strongly resisted the proposal, which he rightly interpreted
as a retreat from his pledge and moved the reference back at the NEC.
This was defeated by fourteen votes to eleven after Callaghan had
thrown his weight behind the recommendation.[64] The composition of
the working party, as suggested by an office paper, would have afforded
the right a built-in majority;[65] however it was altered somewhat by the
Organisation Committee to produce a broadly even balance between
left and right.[66]

The PLP and the right of the Party (with some discreet assistance from
the NAD) were exerting all their energy to stall the campaign for
mandatory reselection. But by now feeling in its favour was running so
strongly in the wider Party that its opponents were prepared to settle for
a compromise. For this reason proposals advanced by Joe Ashton, the

voluble MP for Bassetlaw, met a ready reponse amongst his colleagues. These suggested a two-stage procedure: in each Parliament every CLP with a sitting Labour member would initially vote upon whether to re-adopt the MP or carry out a new selection; formal selection procedures would only be activated if the latter course was agreed.[67]

After a series of meetings, the working party elected for this compromise. It made two other recommendations: a CLP was to retain the existing right, in event of changed circumstances, to reconsider the position of its MP, even if formally reselected, though with the important qualification that it must obtain the prior approval of the NEC. Secondly, the Mikardo doctrine was formally incorporated into the rules.[68]

This retreat from mandatory reselection was unacceptable to three members of the Working Party, Jo Richardson MP, Ray Apps (the mover of the 1977 composite) and Bernard Kissen of the Labour Parliamentary Association (Eric Heffer signed the majority Report but added a note of reservation). More formidably, CLPD was up in arms against the Report. However, the two most influential left-wing members, Moss Evans of the TGWU, and Ian Mikardo, signed it.

Ian Mikardo's change of heart caused most controversy and was a factor in his deposition from the NEC later in the year, after almost 30 years' membership. It was strictly a pragmatic judgment. He was convinced that mandatory reselection could not secure a majority at Conference, since Moss Evans (and, he presumed, his union) had been swayed by the arguments over sponsorship. Secondly, John Cartwright, an NEC member of the Working Party, had attracted considerable support for a proposal to extend the basis of appeal: the quid pro quo for the Ashton compromise was the formal codification of the Mikardo doctrine.[69] The Working Party recommendations were endorsed by the NEC by a large majority – several other left-wingers joining Mikardo in approving them.[70]

Mikardo was one of Labour's shrewdest and deftest political operators. He had also been the NEC's most consistent and ablest advocate of mandatory reselection. But, for once, his judgment was faulty. He (and other erstwhile supporters of the constitutional reform) had assumed that the disposition of the unions block votes would reflect their leaders' preferences. This was a miscalculation: the days of effortless leadership domination had passed in the unions as well as the Party. As Conference came to debate the issue, it became evident that the TGWU delegation favoured mandatory reselection; so too (despite the efforts of Hugh Scanlon and the new President-elect, the right-wing Terry Duffy, to dissuade it) did the AUEW. This guaranteed it a majority.

Or so it seemed. When the time came to cast his union's vote Hugh

Scanlon was overcome with confusion and failed to drop his million-card vote into the ballot box – which ensured that mandatory reselection would be defeated. Uproar followed, but the Party Chairman, Joan Lestor, refused calls for a re-vote.[71]

This might have brought down the gates on reselection. The three year rule barred discussion of the issue until 1981 – by which time, it seemed, Terry Duffy's oft-made promise to sort out his union's Labour Party delegation would surely be fulfilled. The shift of the engineering union to the right, which catapulted Duffy to the presidency in 1978 was bound, sooner or later, to reverberate on the political balance in the NEC. But this was to take some time. Meanwhile, the NEC elections in 1978 registered another slight shift to the left. This was to prove important. In February 1979, the Organisation Committee received a request from Frank Allaun to waive the three year rule and allow the Conference to debate reselection once more. Against the advice of the General Secretary, the Committee decided, by five votes to four, to recommend that the NEC 'inform' the CAC that an opportunity should be found for Conference to debate the issue. This was referred back – very narrowly – by the NEC.[72] The following month, however, it was agreed to set up a committee of five (four of whom could be expected to back Allaun's proposal) to discuss the matter with the CAC.[73]

At this point the election intervened – and radically altered the political climate. Labour's defeat, and the ensuing acrimony, deepened and embittered differences between left and right which, in turn, effected a further change in the NEC's role. Between 1974 and 1979 it had operated less as an initiator of reform than as an arena of struggle. The interests and preferences of the Parliamentary leadership had ceased to be the major factor determining how it performed its managerial function but it was as yet unwilling to act, in a forthright manner, as the voice of those in the constituencies demanding constitutional reform. Its indecisive behaviour – its oscillations between one side of the argument to the other – reflected not only the even balance of forces within it but also the impact of external pressures – the Government, the PLP, the unions and, indeed, from within Transport House itself.

This altered in the wake of the 1979 election defeat. Within weeks, a newly emboldened Executive had placed itself in the forefront of a sweeping three-pronged programme of constitutional reform: proposals for extending the franchise, for electing the leader of the Party and vesting the framing of the manifesto into the hands of the NEC were added to the earlier call for mandatory reselection. In a long, tumultuous session in July it insisted that the latter be placed on the agenda of the forthcoming Conference.[74] Stubborn resistance from the CAC – whose voice traditionally determined such matters – was overcome with the NEC displaying a determination it had not previously shown.[75]

The NEC having swept aside the procedural barriers its predecessors had previously deployed to protect the Parliamentary leadership, Conference was free to debate – and approve – mandatory reselection, a decision confirmed the following year.[76] This accomplished the most substantial alteration in the Party's constitution and power structure for many years, effecting a major decentralisation of Labour's political system. It placed a potent weapon in the hands of constituency parties which – virtually disenfranchised by the block vote at Conference – they had never before possessed.

A comparison with the early 1950s is illuminating. In both periods the Party witnessed a veritable insurgency of the rank and file. In the Bevanite years it was effectively crushed, whilst 25 years later it achieved a fair measure of what it sought. Two factors were, above all, critical in its success. The first and most visible was the role of the unions: in the 1950s, most of the biggest unions acted as the leadership's Praetorian Guard; a quarter of a century later, the majority were, if not accomplices in the insurgency, totally unwilling to suppress it at the leadership's behest.

The second was the role of the NEC. As we have shown, in the Bevanite period it placed the Party machine fully at the disposal of the Parliamentary leadership, protecting its extra-parliamentary flank and maintaining a stringent managerial regime which exposed persistent dissidents to the lash of Party discipline. By the late 1970s it was wholly disinclined to perpetuate this role and, indeed, was far more receptive to rank and file sentiment.

The effect was to strip the leadership of an effective control capability. The interlocking between the two centres of power – the PLP and the NEC – had provided the basis of the social-democratic centralist regime. The two were, by the close of the 1970s, split asunder. The Executive alone had access to the various managerial powers and techniques which could have succoured besieged MPs and blocked the drive for mandatory reselection. Deprived of them, the capacity of the leadership to subdue the grass-roots rebellion was fatally damaged.

Indeed, by the close of the 1970s, the integrated control system of the earlier period had been replaced by a pattern of institutionalised conflict between the Parliamentary leadership and a National Executive displaying an unprecedented responsiveness to rank and file sentiment, with the loyalties of a divided trade union movement almost equally split between the two. The NEC's espousal of constitutional reform, and the left's success in mobilising sufficient trade union votes to secure the passage of two of the three constitutional changes (mandatory reselection and the electoral college[77]) was fiercely resented by the bulk of Labour's Parliamentarians.[78] The game-keeper had turned poacher.

Chapter Ten

The pattern of adjudication, 1970–82

10.1 The transitional phase, 1970–1978

(1) Group discipline and group-party conflicts
From the late 1960s, discipline had been progressively relaxed. Last to be affected by the new spirit of liberalisation was the field of adjudication. Unlike other managerial tasks, this one was primarily undertaken by the regional executive committees and regional and national officials who manned the enquiry teams. Throughout the first half of the 1970s, the NEC rarely intervened in local controversies; it was generally content to accept the advice of officials and the recommendations of enquiry panels.

In the first year or two of the new decade, the traditional pattern of adjudication remained intact. The Executive continued to endorse the often rigid disciplinary regimes which prevailed in many Labour Groups in local authorities;[1] and was vigilant in protecting Councillors against pressures from their own party organisations.[2]

A more substantial shift is, however, evident from 1972. Before then, the NEC had been faced with few politically charged disputes. That year, the Heath Government pushed through a Housing Finance Act which required a substantial increase in council rents and was bitterly opposed by Labour, both nationally and locally. Failure to comply with the Act brought penalties, including surcharge and disqualification from office.

The resulting conflict became, in a sense, a dress rehearsal for what was to occur on a much broader scale after 1979. Initially the Party, nationally and locally, could unite in resisting the proposed legislation. But when it finally reached the statute book, ruling Labour Councils were forced to make hard choices: were they to reverse their position and implement the Act, or were they to risk surcharge and refuse to comply?[3] The result was a rash of disputes which brought in their train a host of appeals to the NEC.

The appeals were of two types: firstly, appeals by Councillors who had been disciplined for defying Group decisions by voting in Council against the implementation of the Act; secondly, appeals by Councillors excluded from the panel for refusing to persist in their opposition to the Act to the point of non-compliance. Given the prominence of the issue, it was inevitable that the NEC would take a greater interest in enquiry appeals than was normally the case. The right remained strongly entrenched in the Organisation Sub-Committee[4] and Regional Executive Committees. On the other hand, the left was now nearing parity on the full Executive; and the conversion of many right-wing MPs to the cause of toleration, as they found themselves in a pro-EEC minority, naturally influenced attitudes to the enforcement of majority decisions at local level.

Hence, in the clashes over the Housing Finance Act, the NEC typically advocating greater toleration of minority opinion. Most disputes which came to appeal fell into the first category – the disciplining of Councillors unwilling to toe the line on implementation. The NEC, whilst still largely accepting the traditional view of the duty of Councillors to abide by majority decisions, urged a lenient approach. For example, in its judgment on the dispute in Newham Labour Group (a Council where Labour held an overwhelming majority) the enquiry team reaffirmed the right of the Group to require all members to vote in conformity with its decisions, whilst recommending that the penalty for rebellion be lightened.[5]

The second type of appeal arising from the Housing Finance Act was the exclusion from the election panel of those Councillors who refused to support local party policy of non-implementation. The NEC was unwilling to condone the punishment of Councillors for rejecting defiance of the law and insisted upon their reinstatement. This was consistent with earlier practice, but the grounds the Executive invoked were different. In the past, it simply declared that it would not accept the removal of sitting Councillors for political reasons.[6] By the early 1970s it was less willing to railroad local sentiment in this fashion. Instead it invoked natural justice – a term in much wider usage after the Pembroke case – to over-rule local party decisions.[7]

The controversy over the Housing Finance Act helped stir the NEC into looking anew at the question of Group discipline. Disciplinary regimes continued to vary widely. Writing in 1977 Gyford and Baker commented: 'Some Groups operate a draconian system of discipline over a wide range of issues; others function without taking a binding Group decision from one meeting to another'.[8] Discipline tended to be most exacting in the cities and larger towns. Here it was often combined with an autocratic system of policy-making, which afforded Group members few opportunities to participate but imposed 'a very rigid

Group whip'.[9]

In the social-democratic centralist era, this ran with the national grain. By the early 1970s, the climate had altered, with the growing strength of the left on the NEC and the liberalising efforts of Ron Hayward, first as National Agent and then as General Secretary. In July 1973, Tony Benn (who had now emerged as an influential force on the National Executive) urged the Organisation Committee to modify the 'too rigid and inflexible' disciplinary procedures operated by many Labour Groups.[10] As a result, the General Secretary despatched a circular to all Group members requesting them to ensure that their Standing Orders were applied 'with flexibility'. 'It is desirable', the circular continued 'that Group members are given every opportunity to speak and in other ways to act with the utmost individual freedom on matters which do not involve policy questions on which Group decisions have been made.'[11] In effect, the NEC sought to distinguish between significant matters of policy, where Group decisions should continue to be binding, and other items of Council business, where discipline was inappropriate.

In the next couple of years, the Party was embarrassed by a series of corruption scandals in Labour controlled councils. As a result, it set up a special committee into 'The Conduct of the Party in Local Government'. The Committee interpreted its remit to include all aspects of the organisation of Labour Groups and, in the course of its report, it criticised 'unnecessarily rigid discipline'. However, its recommendations were cautious. It urged 'maximum flexibility' in allowing Group members to 'raise local issues which are not contrary to Party or group policy', provided that the Group or the Group Leaders were first consulted. It also suggested that Groups should 'consider' permitting free votes on 'non-political issues' – though it left this category undefined.[12] This represented a shift in emphasis rather than substance and the Report rejected any alteration in Standing Orders.

The NEC's deliberations as a court of appeal in the years of the Labour Government (1974–79) were very much imbued with this spirit. Generally speaking, enquiry recommendations (still rarely altered by the NEC in this period) dismissed appeals against disciplinary action by dissident Councillors, but softened the penalty imposed. Thus, in 1976, four Labour Councillors in Newham were disciplined for voting against a Group decision to comply with a (Labour) Government circular to reduce spending. The NEC commended the Group for its 'restraint and judgment' in handling a sensitive issue, but reduced the severity of the punishment.[13]

Two years later, Newham Labour Group faced another rebellion. Six members voted against a Group decision to approve plans for a new civic centre. Of these two, who were previous offenders, were suspended. One of the appellants justified his act of dissent by invoking the conscience clause. By the 1970s the Crossman-Silkin redefinition of 'conscience' to encompass all matters of strong conviction was firmly implanted in the PLP. But the older view continued to apply at local level. Although Labour's majority was impregnable in Newham (57 out of 60 Council seats), the enquiry report commented that the issue was one of 'judgment' rather than conscience. Again the appeal was dismissed but the penalty was reduced.[14]

This combination of dismissing appeals whilst lightening sentences was designed to sustain the authority of Labour Groups whilst prodding them towards a more relaxed application of Standing Orders.[15] It reflected both the NEC's preference for a more flexible system of discipline and an awareness that Group leaderships must adapt their behaviour to changing circumstances. As the second Newham report observed, the 1978 dispute was an example of 'the increasingly common experience of young guard resenting the rigid application of rigid Standing Orders by old guard'.[16] During the 1970s, both Executive members and officials agreed that leniency within the existing framework of rules was the most appropriate response.

(2) Constituency discipline

However, friction between the young guard and the old extended beyond the Council Chamber. The old guards – local Labour establishments in Labour's urban bastions – had, from time to time, been troubled by assorted radicals and newcomers. Generally, they had been able to brush them off; where the challenge assumed more formidable proportions, the NEC was usually willing to step in and quell the insurgents. By the late 1960s oligarchial tendencies in Labour's urban heartlands had become pronounced with power frequently concentrated in the hands of a narrow clique of Councillors. Left-wing activists, drawn to the grand issues of national debate, evinced (in most areas) little interest in local government and, anyway, were numerically weakest in staunch Labour areas. As a result, the political complexion of the great majority of Labour local authorities was right-wing; and the supremacy of Group-based local establishments was rarely contested.

A series of developments from the late 1960s – which, however, operated at a highly uneven pace and intensity across the country – began to corrode the ascendancy of these establishments. The massive anti-Labour swings in the local elections of 1967 and 1968 decimated the ranks of Labour Councillors. According to Gyford, the scale of these losses undermined the position of 'hitherto long-entrenched Labour Councillors and of the traditional right-wing Leadership which had dominated many Labour controlled authorities'.[17] The major reorganisation of local government in the early years of the following decade further disturbed settled patterns of power.[18] Around the same time, the composition of Labour's membership began, slowly at first, to change. A new breed of activists began to appear – young, well-educated, self-confident and predominantly left-wing, many of them veterans of the radical sixties generation. Initially, their impact was felt primarily in national politics. But, in the second half of the 1970s, they started to make an impression at local level, firstly in London, then in the provincial cities. As a result, the incidence of conflicts between traditional Labour elites and more radical elements steadily grew.

In the past, as we have seen, the NEC exhibited a considerable sympathy for local, Group-based, establishments. From the late 1970s, this ceased to be so. This was partly because the steady shift to the left had, by then, furnished them with an outright majority and partly because left-wingers started to display more interest in the Organisation Committee. In the past (with one or two exceptions, most notably Ian Mikardo) the left tended to neglect this Committee. By 1974, the two policy committees (Home Policy and International), both chaired by leading left-wingers (Tony Benn and Ian Mikardo) had left-wing majorities; it was not until near the end of the decade that the Organisation Committee followed suit (Eric Heffer was elected Chairman in 1978). Nevertheless, from about 1975–6 the Executive's more radical members were attending more closely to the work of the Organisation Committee. This was mainly because of the growing prominence of constitutional issues – especially the drive for mandatory reselection – coupled with the controversies over the deselection of Prentice and other MPs which fell within the remit of the Committee. Its effect, however, was to awaken the left to the significance of the Executive's adjudicating function.

Traditionally, the Party officials, REC members, and the few NEC members (mainly trade unionists) who staffed Labour's disciplinary and appeals machinery had enjoyed very considerable autonomy. Scrutiny of enquiry reports by the Organisation Committee, or the NEC itself, tended to be rather perfunctory. Their recommendations were very rarely questioned or altered and usually went through 'on the nod'.[19] As in earlier years, most reports dealt with parochial matters; but the minority of more political cases were now examined more closely. In a number of controversial judgments (often overturning enquiry recommendations) the NEC upheld the appeals of left-wing rebels disciplined by the local party machine.

One example illustrates the altered pattern of NEC intervention. We have discussed at length the Executive's earlier, decisive intervention in Nottingham labour politics. In the mid 1970s there was a revival of left-wing activity. One Councillor – Stephen Evans – had proved particularly bothersome. He was first suspended from the Labour Group;[20]

undeterred, he persisted in campaigning publicly against the ruling Labour administration, charging the local MP (Jack Dunnett) with corruption and claiming that his 'machine' ran the city party. Eventually on these (and other) grounds he was expelled from the Party.[21] The incident bore a certain resemblance to the Coates affair, a decade earlier (though on a small scale). The recommendations of the enquiry team (composed of the East Midlands Regional Organiser, Les Bridges and two REC members) followed the established pattern. The appeal was dismissed on the grounds that Evans was unwilling to conform to collective responsibility.[22] But here the similarity ends. Splitting on left-right lines, the Organisation Committee diluted the penalty to a reprimand.[23]

A not dissimilar case was the protracted (and much more heavily publicised) row over the expulsion of Keith Veness from Islington North CLP. The politics of Islington Labour Party had long been familiar to the NEC; as in the past, the interminable strife that beset Islington Labour politics in the late 1970s (in particular in Islington North CLP) could not be reduced to a classic left-right conflict: party life was complicated by large doses of parochial (and perhaps religious) rivalries and personality clashes. Furthermore, although policy and ideological differences were never absent, the factors which precipitated each row tended to be a tangle of allegations of malpractices, abuse and intimidation often exceedingly difficult to unravel.[24]

In the past, as we have seen, the NEC had protected Islington's Labour establishment against its critics, though not always enthusiastically.[25] This was no longer so. Islington Council, with its fondness for patronage and perquisites, its timidity and inertia, and its aversion to any radical ideas (or members) symbolised the pattern of local Labour politics from which the left NEC recoiled.

The Islington establishment had always relied more heavily upon discipline as a political weapon than most local parties. In January 1976, the right-dominated Islington North party expelled Veness, one of its most persistent and vociferous critics, for a virulent attack on its MP, Michael O'Halloran, and on local borough leaders. This soon become a *cause celebre*, generating a welter of charges and counter-charges about abuses of the rules, corruption and intimidation.

The enquiry team (comprising London Party General Secretary, John Keys, and two members of the REC) which heard Veness's appeal produced recommendations in line with the previous pattern of NEC adjudication. It commended the CLP's officers, criticised Veness for his attempt to undermine the MP (O'Halloran) and the constituency party, concluding that his publicly expressed 'extreme views . . . cannot be condoned and that decency and tolerance are essential'. His appeal was dismissed.[26]

However, many questioned the extent to which the CLP exemplified a reasonable standard of 'decency and tolerance'. The Veness expulsion, and the publicity it earned, provoked an avalanche of allegations about maladministration and vote-rigging. The NEC – to the considerable annoyance of John Keys – deferred judgment upon Veness and instead decided to hold an investigation into the CLP.[27] There then followed a procession of painstaking and time-consuming investigations which disclosed so many irregularities and so faction-ridden and acrimonious a party that, eventually, the NEC seconded a senior official (London Deputy General Secretary, Bill Jones) to preside over its affairs.[28]

Veness's case was held in abeyance for two years whilst the CLP was being investigated. By this time, the question of his expulsion had become a touchstone of the battle between the old guard and the new. The NEC's eventual decision to permit his readmittance was bitterly resented by the ruling faction in Islington North and it was only after the Executive threatened to reorganise the party that it finally agreed to comply.[29]

The significance of the NEC's decision transcended the fate of an individual. It signalled that the increasingly beleaguered establishment – faced with a growing number of left-wing critics on the Council as well as within the three constituencies – could no longer expect assistance from Transport House; and it doubtless raised the morale of the insurgents. The Executive's stance, then, may well have affected the eventual outcome of years of trench warfare in Islington – the mass defection of the old establishment to (the less than welcoming arms of) the SDP in 1981 and the triumph of the left.[30]

The Islington case was a harbinger of later developments. Until the late 1970s, the NEC had pursued a policy of liberalisation, within the established framework of rules, and conventions. After 1979, that framework came increasingly to be challenged.

10.2 The pluralist pattern of adjudication, 1979–82

Serious politically-charged disputes at local level remained infrequent throughout the 1970s. This altered with the turn of the decade: they multiplied in number, severity and scale. This was due to a whole range of factors, which interacted with each other to transpose Labour's chronic national political differences to the local level.

The most important was the dual-pronged offensive, launched by the new Conservative Government, against the autonomy and the finances of local authorities. This dramatically reduced the room for manoeuvre available to Labour local authorities, confronting them with unpalatable choices which greatly aggravated internal Party differences. Labour local authorities had to grapple with a host of increasingly severe problems – urban decay, unemployment, housing shortages and mounting demands on the social services, all with a steadily contracting financial base. Most Labour authorities sought to adjust as best they could to the new situation, deferring plans for improvements, curbing expenditure, reducing their workforces. This approach was bitterly resented by left-wing elements which counterposed a strategy of resistance to any cuts in jobs and services, and a willingness to confront the Government. The outcome was a rash of disputes, both within Labour Groups and between Group and party.

At the same time, the growth of the left's participation in local politics, evident since the 1970s, became more pronounced. The local left was encouraged by their national counterpart's success, particularly between 1979 and 1981: the adoption of mandatory reselection, the broadening of the franchise for the election of the leader and the adoption of a radical programme. Acute polarisation at national level also spread into local politics, inflaming suspicions and hardening attitudes.

Further, the composition of Labour Groups began to alter with the election of growing numbers of young, often well-educated, left-wing Councillors in the major urban centres. They were impatient with the traditional paternalist and unimaginative approaches to local government which prevailed in most Groups and were impressed with new ideas of local socialism which assigned to municipal administrations a much more energetic and innovative role.[31] Friction within the usually rather right-wing, predominantly middle-aged and working class Labour Groups was inevitable. Most Labour establishments in Labour-controlled Councils were wary about injecting partisan considerations and ideological passion into the management of local government. The disputes that erupted – firstly in London boroughs (like Newham, Islington, Southwark) and then in the provinces (Manchester, Bristol, Coventry, etc.) – were multi-faceted in character: conflicts between left and right, ins and outs, the new and old (in sociological terms) types of Councillors and, increasingly, between local parties and Labour Groups.

How did the NEC respond? From 1979 to 1982 the left was firmly in the saddle. Although, as we shall see, differences existed within the left camp, it was united in rejecting the traditional pattern of adjudication. Its most prominent members – Eric Heffer, Chairman of the Organisation Committee, and Tony Benn – together with the General Secretary, adopted a pluralist approach. Its basic presuppositions were that disagreement was inevitable in a democratic party, that different strands of opinions were fully entitled to express and promote their views; and that the task of the NEC was not to impose its own solutions but to facilitate the orderly resolution of conflict through compromise and mutual restraint.

Pluralism, as a managerial doctrine, represented a rupture with social-democratic centralism, with its more unitary conception of the Party, its impatience with dissent and its accent on discipline. However, no sudden or sharp break occurred. Rather pluralism, increasingly influential from the early 1970s onwards, became steadily more salient until it was formally codified in 1979 in an NEC resolution on 'tolerance within the Party'. This called upon all protagonists to a dispute to display an understanding of the views of others; urged that the rights of minorities be fully protected and cautioned office-holders (and majorities in general) to refrain from using sanctions to impose their will.[32]

As applied to the adjudicatory process, one can discern four pluralist principles: the liberalisation of Group discipline; the democratisation of Group decision-making procedures; power sharing between Group and Party; and conciliation. Each of these will be discussed in turn.

Liberalisation of group discipline
In a paper submitted to the Organisation Committee, the National Agent, David Hughes (who had replaced Reg Underhill in 1979) noted that of 13 appeals against withdrawals of the whip between November 1978 and January 1981, the NEC had reversed enquiry recommendations in six cases.[33] This pattern continued until 1982 and reflected a shift in the NEC's position, from one of urging leniency in the implementation of established disciplinary rules to a questioning of the whole basis of traditional Group discipline in favour of a much larger dose of liberalisation.

This had two main elements. Firstly, the degree to which individual Councillors should be constrained by Group decisions should be lessened. The whip should be applied much more selectively – primarily in major policy matters; otherwise Group members should be allowed discretion in the way they cast their votes. In Ron Hayward's words: 'We are not machine men and women; we do not demand total uncritical acceptance of what the Group is doing'.[34] Thus in one case the NEC upheld the appeals (overturning the enquiry recommendation) of two Scunthorpe Labour Councillors who had been deprived of the whip for disobeying a Group decision to support a particular candidate for the mayoralty.[35] In another case, the Executive upheld the appeals of ten Coventry Councillors expelled for voting against a Group decision to raise the price of school meals.[36]

But even on major policy matters, the NEC was reluctant to endorse disciplinary action. This brings us to the second main element: whilst the Executive accepted that cohesion was vital if a Group was to operate effectively, it did not regard the application of sanctions as an appropriate method of maintaining it, except in exceptional cases. It recognised that Conservative policies were placing great strains upon Labour local authorities and exacerbating divisions within them; but precisely for this reason it urged that tolerance of divergent views was essential. In two controversial judgments (which both reversed enquiry recommendations) the NEC upheld the appeals of Manchester and Bristol Councillors expelled from the Group for opposing the Labour controlled authorities' budgets.[37] The Bristol decision was vigorously contested at the Organisation Committee meeting by the Assistant National Agent, Walter Brown, who had served on the enquiry team, and denounced by the Secretary of Bristol's Labour Group as 'tantamount to tearing up the rule book'. The NEC's act, it was claimed, seriously undermined the authority of the Group, the integrity of its democratic procedures and its ability to sustain unity, by denying it the right to sanction those who defied the will of the majority on a vital issue of policy. Similar criticisms were made in the Manchester case[38] but the decisions reflected the conviction of left-wing NEC members that discipline was a wholly inappropriate way of resolving internal differences and that unity could best be maintained within a climate of tolerance.[39]

Democratisation of group decision-making
Rigidity in discipline was not uncommonly associated with limited opportunities for ordinary Group members to participate in decision-making. Appelants in enquiry reports frequently complained that they were expected to support policies formulated in a closed and oligarchial manner.

In the 1970s it was not unusual for control over Group decision-making to be vested in the hands of a small number of office-holders: and for this elite to sustain itself through the exploitation of the considerable powers of patronage available to a Council leader and his closest associates.[40] In the social-democratic centralist era, the NEC had not betrayed much concern with the growth of oligarchy in Labour Groups[41] (nor, indeed, did many Labour Councillors). But with the recruitment of better educated, more policy-oriented and radical Councillors from the 1970s onwards, the demand for change mounted: an underlying cause of many disputes in Labour Groups was the resentment of newer Councillors towards a system which demanded a high level of loyalty but disparaged their contribution to policy-making.

Unlike its predecessors, the left NEC in this period[42] regarded the calibre of a Group's decision-making procedures as a major criterion guiding its judgments on disciplinary cases. It expected that plentiful opportunities should be afforded for discussion; that adequate information should be made available and that a wide measure of participation amongst all Group members should be fostered. Where these conditions did not obtain, it was reluctant to endorse sanctions against minorities, even when they had defied Group decisions on major issues. The NEC's response to the opening scene of the embittered Southwark dispute illustrates this. In 1978, 17 Group members had voted against a Group decision to approve plans for an expensive new Town Hall; of these, ten were suspended for refusing to give satisfactory assurances as to their future behaviour. The enquiry team, however, criticised the Group (led by the tough and autocratic Jim O'Grady) for not allowing full and informed discussion and recommended that (on receipt of undertakings to abide by Standing orders) the whip be restored.[43]

Power sharing
The third pluralist principle dealt with the relationship between Group and party. As we have seen, the rules entrusted the latter with the task of formulating the local election manifesto whilst the former was responsible for taking decisions on all matters of Council business. The scope for jurisdictional disputes was obvious but, in fact, such disputes were relatively rare until the 1980s, partly because local parties were often content to leave policy-making to the Group and partly because, in many Labour areas, the Group leadership effectively controlled the party;[44] where it did not it was usually able to ignore it.[45]

Many of these Group-based local establishments survived into the 1980s, but they came under increasing challenge. Three interlinked factors were particularly relevant. Firstly, the Conservative onslaught politicised local government and awakened a much greater measure of activist interest. Secondly, the new Labour left of the late 1970s and early 1980s (many of whose adherents were professionally involved in work falling under the jurisdiction of local authorities) was much readier than the left in earlier years to see involvement in local government politics as a worthwhile pursuit.[46]

Thirdly, left-wing elements began increasingly to displace often long-standing incumbents in urban party organisations. In some areas of the country (e.g. Manchester, Liverpool, the GLC and a number of London boroughs) the hold of right-wing Council leaderships upon the party had been snapped by the early 1980s; elsewhere (e.g. Coventry, Birmingham, Wakefield) the left's progress was slower and more halting. Overall the trend was unmistakable: the incidence of disputes between Group and party steadily mounted as more radical and assertive party organisations flexed their muscles and demanded a larger share in the formulation of policy in Labour-controlled local authorities.

Similar political trends were influencing the composition of Labour Groups themselves. A growing number of left-wing newcomers defied Group decisions, justifying their conduct by invoking a higher loyalty to local (and sometimes national) party policy. The combination of clashes between Group and party and internal Group strife sometimes engendered serious and protracted conflicts.

In adjudicating these conflicts the NEC was inevitably influenced by its understanding of the proper relationship between Group and party. In fact, no one view commanded the adherence of the Executive. Instead one can identify three perspectives. The traditional one insisted upon the autonomy of the Group and the inadmissibility of 'outside' party pressure. The second favoured a radical alteration in the balance between Group and party. The party shoud have primary responsibility for policy-making in all its stages; and the Group should be unequivocally accountable to the party for the way it conducted its business. For one brief moment in 1980 (as we shall see below) the radical perspective rallied substantial support on the NEC. But, in this period, it was the third perspective which was most influential. This we have called the 'power sharing' approach.

This was a mid-way position. It insisted upon two propositions: that the party, via the local election manifesto, should be responsible for setting the policy framework within which the Group conducted its work; and that the Group should be fully accountable to the party for its actions. It did not, however, believe that total control over policy, and the day to day operations of the Group, should pass to the party. Rather it emphasised the need for a partnership, or a power-sharing arrangement, between the two. The local manifesto – over which the party had the final say – must be binding upon a Labour local authority: within this context a spirit of co-operation and mutual understanding was essential.[47]

This perspective underlay the NEC's adjudicatory judgments in the period 1979–82. Only briefly, in 1980, did the more radical approach sieze the initiative. Tony Benn proposed a series of amendments to Group Standing Orders designed to greatly enlarge the power of the local party at the expense of the Group.[48] These were initially agreed by the Organisation Committee but provoked a furious response from Labour Group leaders. Manchester Council leader Norman Morris expressed himself 'absolutely disgusted' with such 'dangerous and sinister' proposals[49] and a number of Labour's most influential figures in local government wrote in protest to the NEC.[50] Tony Benn himself recognised the force of the charge that there had been an almost total lack of consultation of interested parties and moved the reference back of his own proposals.[51] It was agreed to establish a special sub-committee to consider the matter.[52]

A combination of internal disagreements, the pressure of more urgent business and bureaucratic inertia delayed the submission of a report for four years.[53] By this time, the pendulum had swung decisively against the radical innovators. The alterations to Standing Orders proposed by the NEC to the 1984 Conference envisaged only a limited shift of the balance between Group and party in favour of the latter. These were described by David Blunkett, who moved them on behalf of the Executive as 'very minimum changes'.[54]

Some of the most tumultuous local disputes raged over the issue of the competing claims of Group and party. The corollary of the power-sharing perspective was that since policy making and implementation was (or ought to be) a joint endeavour, it could only be properly undertaken in an atmosphere of collaboration and mutual respect. The NEC was unimpressed by the insistence of many Labour Groups in traditional Party strongholds upon complete autonomy in the policy sphere. It actively promoted the right of local parties to determine election policy, and the responsibility of Groups to implement it. As a result, where appellants in appeal cases could credibly argue that their actions in defying the whip were actuated by loyalty to district policy (as embodied in the local manifesto), or to national Conference policy, or even that they enjoyed the full-hearted support of the local party, they were assured of an understanding response from the NEC.[55]

Conciliation

One can distinguish two mechanisms for resolving conflict: discipline and conciliation. Although, under the social-democratic regime, both mechanisms were used, the accent was on the former.[56] This was underpinned by what may be called a 'mechanical doctrine' of adjudication, which was espoused by senior Party officials like Len Williams and Sara Barker, and shared by the bulk of Regional Organisers and REC members (who staffed most of the enquiry teams) as well as by the NEC majority. The mechanical theory regarded the task of adjudication as an objective one: discover the facts of the case, identify any rule infringements and derive from the rule book the appropriate action to be taken. In practice, its practitioners acknowledged that matters were rarely this straightforward, and exercises of judgement were required, but they denied that this damaged the impartiality of the process.

The left had never accepted the truth of this picture. Throughout the 1950s and early 1960s it had castigated the established pattern of adjudication geared, it claimed, more to sustaining the right's ascendency, both nationally and locally, than simply upholding the rules.

One response could have been to alter the whole system of adjudication; to separate the political and quasi-judicial responsibilities of the NEC and to install an independent appeals tribunal, entrusted with all adjudicatory and disciplinary matters. Indeed, particularly in the 1960s, this solution was frequently advocated by the left. However – doubtless not unconnected with their growing strength in the NEC – most left-wingers lost interest in this idea by the 1970s. Instead, the left NEC's handling of adjudication was governed by its advocacy of pluralism.

This approach held that disagreement was inevitable, and a legitimate aspect of the life of a mass democratic party. The first priority of the NEC, therefore, should be the orderly management of differences, to ensure that they were conducted in a tolerant fashion and to facilitate their resolution. The rigid enforcement of Party rules was more likely to inflame feelings and harden cleavages. The task of the NEC, as adjudicator, should be to bring the protagonists together and to construct agreed frameworks through which their differences could be negotiated and which both sides would feel honour bound to observe.

Not all the left on the NEC embraced this approach. Some members (like Dennis Skinner, Joan Maynard and Les Huckfield) placed local disputes in the broader context of the struggle between left and right, then raging nationally with great ferocity and urged that the NEC should back 'its' side. However, from 1978 to 1982, key posts within the party were occupied by conciliators: Ron Hayward, whose managerial perspective we have already discussed,[57] and Eric Heffer, the Chairman of the Organisation Committee.

To an extent that may have surprised many not fully appraised of his work as Chairman, Heffer was a conciliator by inclination. He strove hard (though, in the circumstances, not always successfully) to propitiate the protagonists where dissension was particularly acute. He had, as Jim Mortimer observed, a 'very strong desire to resolve problems and antagonisms in the Party' by a process of give and take.[58] He believed that most local disputes could be settled by mutual accommodation, and he regarded it as the NEC's responsibility to foster a spirit of tolerance and compromise[59] – an approach not always appreciated either by officials or by more hardline left-wingers.

This accent on conciliation is illustrated by the NEC's role in the venemous Southwark dispute. Tension had been steadily mounting between rival left and right-wing groups since the late 1970s. Southwark was a staunch Labour stronghold in the grip of a tough and intransigent right-wing leadership headed, for more than a decade, by Jim O'Grady. There was, however, growing resistance from an increasingly energetic and well-organised left which, by the opening of the new decade, had gained control of most Party organisations in the borough. An eruption finally occurred towards the end of 1981. Eleven Councillors were suspended for persistent disregard of Standing Orders whilst a number of right-wing Councillors (including O'Grady and other senior figures) were excluded from the panel.[60] The issue, however, was complicated by the defection of 14 further Councillors to the SDP, and rumours that more were to follow.

Before the NEC had fully considered the matter, the Tatchell affair exploded in its face.[61] Although not directly relevant, it raised the temperature of the dispute to a fever pitch. In particular, the NEC decision not to endorse Tatchell infuriated the local left (of which he was a well-known member) and damaged its standing as a mediator.

In December, the Organisation Committee voted both to uphold the appeals of the eleven disciplined Councillors and to freeze the selection of local candidates whilst the NEC tried to resolve the dispute over the panel.[62] The following month, Eric Heffer, Chairman of the Organisation Sub, and National Agent, David Hughes, met the EC of Southwark's Local Government Committee (LGC).[63] It was a lively meeting. Heffer presented the NEC's compromise: all Councillors to return to the Group in return for the reinstatement of those kept off the panel. He appealed insistently for a *'modus vivendi'* between the warring factions exclaiming at one point 'I don't give a damn about the rules, Bishops Stortford [the national bid to reconcile left and right] determines everything'.[64] The audience was not receptive. The following evening the full LGC voted to reject the Heffer compromise and to defy the NEC.[65] The Executive reacted by charging Party Chairman, Judith Hart, with another attempt at conciliation overriding the opposition of a number of left-wingers (including Benn, Jo Richardson and Skinner) but with the support of others (including Heffer, Kinnock and Judith Hart). It added that, failing a settlement, the Organisation Committee would be authorised to instruct Southwark to reinstate all Councillors excluded from the panel.[66]

By this time the London REC had agreed to uphold the appeals of four Councillors rejected for the panel; but Southwark dug in its heels over the remaining four (including O'Grady) claiming (correctly) that it was acting wholly within its rights. The NEC, this time, brushed aside all objections and instructed that all four be placed on the panel – two of whom (including O'Grady) were subsequently re-elected.[67]

This left much ill-feeling in Southwark.[68] The NEC's decision to override Southwark's constitutional rights on this issue reflected the particularly fraught circumstances – the clash over the Tatchell candidature and what everyone anticipated would be a very tough by-election. But it was consistent with action taken in other major disputes in Manchester and Coventry and reflected its belief that destructive conflicts could only be defused by compromise and mutual restraint.

10.3   NEC adjudication 1979–82: the impact

What were the effects of the left's conduct of adjudication? The first was the strain it placed on relations between the NEC and the Party's officials. Many Regional Organisers felt deeply aggrieved by what they saw as the cavalier disregard of their work as the Executive overturned enquiry recommendations.[69]

Regional officials saw their enquiry work as guided by two main considerations: their duty to uphold Party rules and their desire to reach fair and equitable decisions. The NEC, they charged, after about 1975 (and especially in the period 1979–82) had politicised the whole process. Too many reversals of enquiry recommendations, they alleged, represented no more than off-the-cuff political judgments.

Secondly, they complained that the conduct of several NEC members reflected a lack of faith in the impartiality and ability of Party officials. This manifested itself primarily (in the words of a report compiled by the regional staff) in the 'susceptibility of some NEC members to canvassing in relation to internal disputes and the leaking . . . of confidential reports prepared by organisers'.[70] The growth of lobbying of NEC members was undoubtedly a feature of the period. Left-wing party activists who felt they had not received a fair hearing from enquiry panels would directly approach NEC members who often proved sympathetic. They realised that the National Executive was almost entirely reliant upon enquiry reports (and supplementary information supplied by Party officials) for furnishing the factual background to a dispute; given the right-wing and disciplinarian leanings widely attributed, by the left, to both the regional staff and the NAD,[71] they were keen to provide the Executive with an alternative view of events. As lobbying became more common, so did the leaking of reports.[72] By the early 1980s relations between the NEC and the regional staff had so far deteriorated that a number threatened to refuse to conduct any further enquiries (one carried out the threat).

The frequent overturning by the NEC of enquiry recommendations was particularly resented by regional officials because it undermined their political standing. By suggesting that they did not enjoy the full confidence of their masters, it diminished their authority; it signalled to local Party activists that rulings by Regional Organisers might not fully reflect the view of the NEC. Similarly, the influence of regional officials suffered, as their better informed critics realised that they could be by-passed or outmanoeuvred by direct approaches to the Executive. The doubts that persistent questioning of enquiry recommendations cast upon the impartiality and judgment of organisers compounded this, since their influence depended heavily upon their stock of prestige: their reputation for fairness, political acumen and expertise. But the shrinking political weight of the regional staff had broader consequences. Regional Organisers were the principal means through which the NEC exercised its authority. Any diminution in their power inevitably weakened that of Labour's chief directive organ too and, as we shall see, contributed to what, in the early 1980s, developed into a major crisis of authority in the Party.

The left's pluralist approach met with only limited success in that it rarely managed to reconcile antagonists in local disputes. This was probably inevitable.

The NEC, however, was not successful in reconciling the two sides; nor was this failure atypical of the Executive's experience in similar disputes. The approach, to prevail, presupposed conditions which, in Manchester, Bristol and Southwark and elsewhere, were absent: a reasonable measure of agreement over decision rules and procedures; and a degree of trust which would oil the search for a settlement. Instead both left and right contestants generally held radically different ideas over the proper locus of power and balance of policy-making rights between Group and party; and the disputes were almost invariably wrapped in an atmosphere of rancour and suspicion where neither believed a compromise was feasible. (Although it ought to be added that, in the circumstances, it is highly unlikely that any other approaches could have enjoyed any more success.)

However, the left's mode of adjudication did have a significant impact upon the balance of political forces throughout the Party. In the social-democratic centralist era the fear (and, occasionally, the fact) of Transport House intervention to succour right-wing local establishments inhibited left-wing offensives. As it happened, the years in which the pluralist pattern of adjudication was in the ascendent – a brief but vital period – witnessed the most pervasive, sustained and successful left-wing assault on right-wing hegemony in local government. Even a right-wing Executive could not have entirely stemmed the radical tide in many parts of the country. However, there is little doubt that, particularly in the early stages of a contest, the NEC's adjudicating response did have a notable effect. Thus in four major disputes (in Southwark, Manchester, Bristol and Coventry) the Executive initially refused to endorse disciplinary action against rebel left-wing Councillors. This raised their morale, whilst discouraging their opponents and diminishing the utility of discipline as a mechanism of control. The (usually exaggerated) awe of 'Transport House' was dispelled; and the upholding by the NEC of appeals helped galvanise support amongst those who sympathised politically with the rebels but were reluctant to endorse violations of Party rules. Overall, there seems little doubt that the pluralist mode of adjudication contributed to the unprecedented success of the left in local government.

Chapter Eleven

The militant tendency and the crisis of party management

11.1 Prologue: The left NEC and Militant, 1975–1980

In the early 1970s, the issue of Trotskyism was one that evoked little attention in the Labour Party. In the 1960s the major Trotskyist groups – the SLL, the International Socialists and the International Marxist Group – had all elected to work outside the Party. Only one small group survived in Labour's ranks – the so-called Militant Tendency, headed by a veteran Trotskyist, Ted Grant.

Militant had its origins in the Revolutionary Socialist League, the least successful of the various Trotskyist sects in the 1950s and 1960s. Unlike its larger rivals, it was not discouraged by the tough anti-Trotskyist regime in these years. 'The Labour Party', an internal document argued in 1964, 'is not a political party in the normal (even Social-Democratic) sense, it is rather a Federation of Groups and, in spite of increasing bureaucratic action and an ever growing list of proscriptions, expulsions and restrictions, it is this very looseness of the Labour Party which allows one in the words of George Brown to "drive a horse and cart through the Constitution".'[1]

That same year, the RSL decided to launch a new paper, to be called *Militant*. It was to be a 'Tendency Paper' by which it meant an 'entrist propaganda paper, applying the programme of Trotskyism within the Labour Party and the Trade Unions'.[2] The entrist tactic, the RSL was at pains to point out, was 'a tactical question and not one concerning our political principle'.[3] Nevertheless, the RSL was unique amongst Trotskyist groups in the single-mindedness and determination with which it pursued entryism.

For a decade, Militant[4] went quietly about its work. Within three years of the establishment of Labour's new youth organisation in 1967, the Labour Party Young Socialists (LPYS)[5] it had fallen under Militant's control; and it gained useful footholds in a number of constituencies.

The abolition of the Proscribed List in 1973 and the more liberal regime introduced in the early 1970s removed from Militant the threat of disciplinary measures.

In 1975, the issue of 'Trotskyist infiltration' suddenly became newsworthy, primarily because of Militant's alleged role in masterminding the removal of Reg Prentice.[6] In September, the NEC agreed to allow the National Agent, Reg Underhill, to prepare a report on Trotskyism in the Party. Entitled 'Entryist Activities' this was presented to the Organisation Committee in November. For some time Underhill had been collecting information on the Tendency, provided by regional officials, Militant defectors and anonymous sources. He was worried by its success in gaining command of the LPYS, which was proving to be a valuable source of recruits. But what finally propelled him into action was a copy he had recently obtained of a Militant document called 'British Perspectives and Tasks 1974'; its contents, he later recalled 'horrified me'.[7] It provided the centrepiece of his report to the NEC.

He discussed a range of Trotskyist groups but his primary focus was on Militant. He explained its origins in the RSL and its pursuit of the entryist tactic. This he defined as 'the tactic adopted by an organisation which because it is ineligible for affiliation to the Labour Party, decides that its members, or some of them, shall enter the Labour Party as individual members to carry out activities within the Labour Party as directed by the outside organisation'.[8] He then quoted extensively from 'British Perspectives' which spelt out candidly Militant's methods and objectives: its intention to secure the election of a small group of MPs to promote Militant's viewpoint; to extend its activities from the LPYS to the constituencies 'many of which are still shells dominated by politically dead old men and women . . . ossified little cliques'; its view that, at present 'the main struggle would be between us and the Tribunite Left'; and details of its mode of operation.

Underhill concluded that 'British Perspectives' confirmed 'beyond any doubt whatever that there is a central organisation associated with Militant with its own membership and full-time organisers'. However, his intention at the time was not to win expulsion of the organisation, but simply to alert the Party to the problem.[9]

The meeting which discussed the paper was poorly attended. Eric Heffer suggested that Trotskyism could best be combatted by political persuasion; Ian Mikardo dismissed Militant as 'more of a nuisance than a danger'; and the LPYS representative (and Militant member) Nick Bradley avowed that Militant was no more than a pressure group like Tribune.[10] 'Reg', he commiserated 'you've been conned'.[11] Shirley Williams's call for further investigation was rejected and it was decided to leave the matter on the table.[12] A move to refer back the minutes at the NEC was defeated by 16 votes to 12, on a straight left-right vote.[13]

The matter remained dormant for a year and then flared up again. The intervening twelve months witnessed mounting aggravation within the Party: bitter exchanges between left and right over Government policies and (as we have seen) a series of well-publicised bids by constituency parties to remove their MPs. Many on the right of the Party (and much of the Press) ascribed these to the conspiratorial work of a growing number of extremists, and began to urge that action be taken to eliminate them. Several regional organisers worried by (in their view) a rapid expansion in Militant's influence pressed for reconsideration of the Underhill Report.[14]

But, as so often happens in the Labour Party, it was a quirk of fortune which thrust the whole issue back into public view. In the autumn of 1976, a leading Militant activist, Andy Bevan, was appointed as the Party's Youth Officer, by an NEC Sub-Committee attended by two right-wing trade unionists and the General Secretary.[15] There was an immediate uproar, with the press upbraiding Labour for choosing an 'extremist' and Labour's National Union of Labour Organisers up in arms. The right tried to reverse the decision but eventually Bevan was confirmed in his position.

The effect of the Bevan row was to re-ignite media interest in Militant. The Underhill Report was leaked – by Labour right-wingers – to the press. The Prime Minister and his predecessor, Sir Harold Wilson, delivered well-publicised speeches castigating 'extremism' in the Party;[16] and right-winger Tom Bradley tabled a motion for the NEC instructing the National Agent to update his report.

By this time, the NEC and the Parliamentary leadership had drifted so far apart that the Prime Minister's urgent call for action to clear out 'left-wing infiltrations' made absolutely no impression.[17] Instead the NEC accepted unanimously a resolution moved by Eric Heffer and seconded by Joan Lestor denouncing the 'calculated campaign' to instigate a 'frenzied witch-hunt'. Bradley's motion was deferred until after the end of the Christmas season.[18]

The NEC returned to the motion in January. Reg Underhill, perturbed by the fate of his report the previous year, weighed in strongly, asserting that, in its role as custodian of the Constitution, the Executive was under an obligation to give proper consideration to his report. It was agreed – on Michael Foot's initiative – to set up a sub-committee to examine the Underhill documents, comprising Foot, Heffer, Tom Bradley and John Chalmers (both right-wingers) and General Secretary, Ron Hayward.[19]

Of the five members, Bradley and Chalmers favoured disciplinary action against Militant; Heffer and Foot were opposed. Hayward strove for a compromise. He had no sympathy for Militant, regarding its activities as harmful but, equally, he objected to disciplinary action. He doubted whether the Tendency represented any real danger to the Party; further he felt that the term 'Trotskyist' was too freely employed as a term of abuse to discredit 'the awkward squad'. But, above all, he was, as a matter of principle, opposed to reviving the methods of the 1950s and wished to preserve the liberal regime which he helped to construct.[20]

Whilst attempting to accommodate the two viewpoints, the report primarily reflected that of Heffer, Foot and Hayward. It expressed opposition to the use of discipline as a method of settling political arguments but it accepted that some effort should be made to combat Militant's influence. It recommended a membership drive, improved political education and a greater openess in the way the LPYS ('claimed' to be under the control of the Tendency) operated.[21]

The report was sufficiently anodyne to please almost all (only the LPYS member voted against it).[22] The recommendations succeeded in their major function of taking the heat out of the controversy so nobody felt under any pressure to implement them. There the matter stood until after the fall of the Labour Government in 1979.

Shortly after the election, Reg Underhill retired and was elevated to the House of Lords. Almost at once he came under 'intense pressure' from right-wing Labour MPs and journalists to publicise his work on Militant.[23] He decided to update his 1975 report which he despatched to the General Secretary. The press, supplied with fresh information by right-wing MPs eagerly siezed the opportunity to highlight extremism in the Labour Party. The NEC, however, stood firm and, after an idiosyncratic recommendation from the Organisation Committee to investigate both Militant and the CIA had been unceremoniously dumped, simply agreed to invite Underhill to publish his documents. It also asked all groups within the Party to submit details about their organisation, membership and finances.[24] Militant readily complied, producing a document as revealing as could be expected in the circumstances.[25]

The new National Agent, David Hughes, then presented a report urging the NEC to implement the largely ignored recommendations of the 1977 report.[26] His advice was disregarded[27] and, with the Party embroiled in fierce internal strife over firstly the constitutional reforms and then the deputy leadership contest between Benn and Healey, the question of Militant slipped off the agenda for over a year.

The right bitterly resented the NEC's failure to nip Militant in the bud in the 1970s. Certainly, Militant used the respite profitably to expand its organisation and influence. By the opening of the new decade it was a significant force in a number of areas, and a dominant one in Liverpool. When action was taken, the Tendency was to prove a far harder nut to crack.

In fact, there was never any prospect that Militant would be suppressed in the 1970s. The NEC's left majority was adamantly opposed to the use of discipline to quell far-left dissent. The left was not entirely like-minded. Some prominent left-wingers, like Benn and Heffer, were reluctant to engage in any serious public criticism of Militant. They regarded many of its views as mistaken and disliked its intemperate sectarian tone; on the other hand – like most left-wingers in the constituencies – they tended to regard Militant supporters as erring comrades, their faults due more to the exuberance of youth than to any fundamental flaws in their outlook. Others – like Ian Mikardo (and Tribune editor, Richard Clements) were less indulgent. Mikardo accepted much of Underhill's analysis (unlike some of his colleagues like Eric Heffer he never cast doubts upon the authenticity of the Underhill documents) dismissing the Tendency as a parasitical body.[28] Nevertheless, the left was at one in rejecting tough measures.[29]

In adopting this position, the NEC pursued an approach to party management which differed radically from social-democratic centralism. It had two key components, which we can call 'pluralism' and 'libertarianism'.

11.2 The Left NEC and Party Management

(1) Pluralism

Social-democratic centralism regarded 'factions' or Party pressure groups with suspicion and hostility. The left, in contrast, saw organisational pluralism as positively conducive to intra-party democracy. Left-wing groups proliferated as never before in the late 1970s: the Campaign for Labour Party Democracy, the Labour Co-ordinating Committee (LCC) and several, less influential ones. The NEC never made any attempt to restrict their activities. This was not only a matter of shared views. Left-wingers – unlike the earlier social-democratic centralists – looked upon Party pressure groups as a sign of democratic vitality; far from interposing themselves between official institutions and the rank and file, such intermediary organisations played a vital role in articulating opinion and mobilising effective grass-root pressures.

But what of bodies like the Militant Tendency, which were something more than internal Party ginger groups? Underhill was careful in his report to distinguish entryist organisations from 'bona fide pressure groups' which sought, wholly legitimately, to promote their own policies and views.[30] There was widespread ignorance in the constituencies about the true nature of Militant but most leading left-wingers were better informed and recognised that the secretive, democratic centralist mode of organisation of the Tendency set it apart from other non-Trotskyist groups. Nevertheless, their approval of pluralism encompassed Militant.

Senior Party officials, like Underhill and the bulk of the regional staff felt strongly that, in taking this view, the NEC was neglecting its responsibilities since Militant was blatantly in breach of Clause II of the Constitution.[31] Most left-wing NEC members acknowledged that, technically, the Tendency infringed Clause II of the Constitution. But, they argued, the clause was couched in such all-embracing terms that, if rigorously applied, it would entrap a whole range of Party pressure groups (like CLPD, the LCC etc.) which possessed their own programmes and propaganda machinery, plus the formal structure and membership which Militant professed to lack. For the well-being of party democracy, the left NEC concluded, the constitution should be operated in a flexible and liberal spirit.

(2) Libertarianism
By the late 1970s, the bulk of the left had become ardent protagonists of majority rule. Earlier hesitations and ambivalences about Conference sovereignty had been largely abandoned. However, adherence to majority rule was (for most left-wingers) never pressed into the service of a centralist doctrine. It became an article of faith for the left NEC that discipline should never be used to suppress minority opinion. In an important resolution on 'tolerance within the Party' the Executive affirmed its belief 'in the right of all members . . . to speak and write freely and to seek to persuade others to adopt their views'. It appealed to the Party at all levels to respect Labour's 'tradition of tolerance and not resort to expulsion against those who differ from majority views'.[32]

The NEC was as unwilling to confirm expulsions carried out by CLPs as it was to initiate them itself. On a number of occasions it quoshed the expulsion at constituency level of individuals charged with Trotskyist views or organisational affiliations – decisions which, at times, were deeply resented by the constituency involved.[33] The NEC was accused by the right of failing in its duties to safeguard the constitution and defend Labour's organisational and ideological integrity. It was unreceptive to such criticism. Senior figures like Mikardo remembered all too vividly the harsh and oppressive regime in the 1950s and early 1960s. Revulsion against the regime was now so deeply ingrained on the left as to form a part of its collective consciousness. The left NEC objected particularly strongly to any regulation of belief. The views of Party members were, Tony Benn held, a matter of 'individual conscience'.[34] The left were unimpressed by demands from the right that adherence to democratic socialism should be established as a condition of membership,[35] not least because of an understandable scepticism of the right's commitment to any type of socialism whatsoever. More positively, left-wingers espoused the notion of Labour as a 'broad church' with no rigidly demarcated ideological frontiers. Right from the

Party's inception, members had drawn their inspiration from multiple sources – Owenism, christian socialism, Marxism and so forth. Its rich ideological tapestry was a source of strength not of weakness and Marxism, whether represented by Militant or any other current, a wholly legitimate strand within it.[36] This view was coupled with the left's conception of the Party. Like their forebears in the inter-war years, many left-wingers viewed Labour as primarily the political vehicle of the organised working class. Anyone who aligned with Labour in the contest with capital had, from this perspective, a right to join the Party.

11.3 The right-wing counter-offensive

The years 1979 to 1981 were a period of unprecedented left advance. The Party adopted radical policies on such key issues as the extension of public ownership, the management of the economy and, with the acceptance of unilateral nuclear disarmament, on defence. The left's campaign for constitutional reform equally scored major triumphs with the acceptance of mandatory reselection and a wider franchise for electing the leader (via an electoral college). But in 1981, the year the second of these triumphs was clinched, the tide was already beginning to turn. After several abortive bids in the past, the right was able to muster its trade union battalions and five left-wingers were eliminated from the Executive. The left still retained a slight edge, but the balance of power belonged to a new grouping on the centre left.

This first emerged with the election of Michael Foot to the Party leadership in November 1980. Ostensibly a victory for the left, in practice it encouraged a rapprochement between the right and an element on the left which had never shared the general left-wing enthusiasm for either constitutional changes or Tony Benn. As long as the right-wing Jim Callaghan remained leader this element (which included NEC members like Neil Kinnock and Joan Lestor) felt that its natural habitat lay with the rest of the left. This altered with Foot's election; henceforth the centre-leftists were primarily Foot loyalists and detached themselves from the rest of the left.

Alignments remained fluid until the highly acrimonious contest between Benn and Healey for the deputy leadership. Foot appealed to Benn not to stand in the interests of Party unity. However, Benn was determined to go ahead. The centre-left could not stomach either of the two leading contenders and rallied behind John Silkin's candidature; sufficient of its members abstained on the second, decisive ballot to deprive Benn of victory. By this time relations between the Foot loyalists and (what may be called for short) the Bennite left were so envenomed that the left was irreparably split. An increasing number of centre-leftists were now prepared to work with the right to clip the wings of the Bennites.[37] Foot himself was initially reluctant to place himself at the fore of such an alliance and, as a result, Heffer and Benn survived as Chairmen of the two key NEC Committees, Organisation and Home Policy. But relations between the leader and his successor as darling of the constituencies continued to sour. By the close of 1981 a rapprochement between the right and the centre-left under Foot's aegis had been achieved.

The emergence of this new bloc was highly significant for it meant that, for the first time in a decade, the leader had an NEC willing to consider sympathetically his managerial goals. The dislocation of the centre, which had so hampered the efforts of Foot's predecessors to strengthen leadership control, was now largely remedied.

Rarely are Party leaders the free agents the media likes to portray – and none less so than Michael Foot. From the moment he assumed the leadership he was engaged in a desperate struggle to hold the Party together and to preserve it as a credible electoral force. One blow followed another. Early in 1981 a group of leading right-wingers, Roy Jenkins, David Owen, Shirley Williams and Bill Rodgers, had, to a tremendous fanfare of publicity announced the formation of the Social Democratic Party. Their public rationale was that Labour had now fallen into the clutches of the extreme left and, from that point on, the issue of extremism in the Labour Party was relentlessly exploited by its political opponents and the media. Then, almost immediately after the creation of the new party, Labour embarked upon the fraticidal deputy leadership contest. In the course of 1981 its electoral support collapsed. Foot found himself presiding over a strife-torn, increasingly demoral-ised, organisation unable to staunch a politically highly damaging flow of defections to the SDP and presenting a spectacle of a body incapable of governing itself, not to mention the country.[38]

With the polls indicating that Labour supporters, repelled at the image of a hopelessly divided and (as depicted by the media) an increas-ingly extreme Party, were deserting it in droves, the right clamoured for firm action to restore order within the Party and to repel the advance of the 'hard' or 'extreme' left. To many on the right and, increasingly, the centre-left the first and essential step to reassure Labour's frightened voters (and those MPs still contemplating defection to the SDP) was a new, much tougher, line on Militant.

Initially, Foot resisted the pressure. Whilst he deplored the Trotskyist organisation as 'a pestilential nuisance' he objected to reviving the 'near Communist discipline' imposed by the right of the Party in the past.[39] But, in December 1981, he reversed his position and moved a resolution at the Organisation Committee calling for an enquiry into the organi-sation and operations of Militant.[40] This reversal seems to have been due to a number of factors. Firstly, the Tendency's growing influence, reflected in the rising number of Militant Parliamentary candidates, convinced him that, more than a mere nuisance, it was now inflicting serious harm on Labour's electoral prospects.[41] Secondly, he was disturbed by the 'hordes' of Party members – many of them old comrades in arms from his Aldermaston days – who wrote to him complaining of Militant's behaviour – its intolerance, abuse of its opponents and conspirational methods.[42] Thirdly, the pressure from the PLP was becoming difficult to contain with the right, who had for years agitated for tough measures against the Trotskyist group now being joined by centre-left MPs like Jack Straw and Jeff Rooker.[43] They too were desperately worried by Labour's derisory showing in the opinion polls, and by the evidence that its increasingly left-wing image was propelling millions of its supporters into the arms of the SDP. Finally, there were hints of further defections to the SDP by MPs, several of whom feared that Militant orchestrated activity might deprive them of their Parliamentary seats.

In the past, the NEC had blocked any action against the Tendency. But, with the soldering of a new right/centre-left alliance disposing of a clear majority and supportive of the leader, Foot's call for an enquiry into Militant was approved by a handsome margin of 19 votes to 10. The Party's General Secretary, Ron Hayward, and National Agent, David Hughes, were appointed to conduct the investigation.[45]

The report took six months to compile. In the meantime, Foot's drive to restore his authority had claimed another victim. Bermondsey CLP had selected as successor to its long-serving MP, the bluff and popular Bob Mellish, its own secretary, a young Australian of staunch left-wing views, Peter Tatchell.[45] It was a controversial choice. Tatchell, who had relatively little political experience, was a prominent figure within the Southwark left which was embroiled in a furious struggle with the traditional right-wing establishment. Mellish had close links with the Southwark right and was extremely unhappy at Tatchell's selection. There were rumours he would resign and precipitate a by-election in the formerly rock-solid Labour seat – which, many MPs feared could be captured by the newly-formed Liberal-SDP alliance thereby inflicting a devastating blow on Labour's sagging morale.

Labour's plight – many urged – was also Foot's opportunity to demonstrate that the Party would no longer have any truck with extremism. Foot seized it. In an extraordinary, but premeditated outburst in the House of Commons, he proclaimed that Tatchell was not yet an endorsed candidate 'and so far as I am concerned never will be'. Castigating Tatchell as an exponent of anti-Parliamentary politics, he announced to his colleagues in the PLP that 'Parliamentary democracy is at stake. There can be no wavering on that'.[46]

Tatchell himself was stunned by Foot's denunciation. Politically he was polls apart from Trotskyism, much closer to the Bennite camp, favouring extra-Parliamentary mobilisation but wholly committed to the electoral road to power. It does appear that Foot genuinely misunderstood (or was misled about) Tatchell's beliefs. But even then his behaviour was inconsistent since he had acquiesced in the endorsement of a number of Militant Parliamentary candidates; and, indeed, he remained opposed to the penalisation of any Party member on account of their views.

But Foot had staked his leadership on the issue. The Organisation Committee voted by twelve to seven not to endorse Tatchell, brushing aside the efforts of its Chairman, Eric Heffer, to reach a face-saving compromise.[47] Many on the left were dismayed. Dick Clements, Tribune's Editor and a close associate of Foot for many years (and shortly to be appointed his political advisor) admonished the leader for gratuitously stoking up the fires within the Party. 'There will be justified outrage from those who believe that he has severely undermined the constitutional rights of local Labour parties in selecting candidates of their own choice.'[48] As the Party's own paper, Labour Weekly pointed out, the decision not to endorse Tatchell purely on political grounds represented a regression to the rigid practices of the 1950s[49] – against which Foot had fought so hard.

Foot's act was widely commended in the PLP and by the media as a display of courage and resolution; in fact it reflected his fragile grip on the Party. He was badgered by outside pressures into a step which later he must have deeply regretted. As was soon disclosed, Mellish (who, throughout a long political career had boasted his loyalty to the Party) had threatened to resign immediately if the young Australian was endorsed. 'Mellish' the *New Statesman* commented 'effectively blackmailed Michael Foot into a public repudiation of Tatchell'.[50] But wider issues were at stake. As the right-wing NEC member, Betty Boothroyd, pointed out: 'This was not just about one man. It was about the direction of the Labour Party'.[51] Tatchell's rejection was, in the words of a man with ready access to many senior Labour politicians, *The Guardian's* Political Editor, Ian Aitken, 'the first engagement' in Foot's 'campaign to halt the advance of the far left's grip on the Labour Party'.[52] As such, it was part of a three-pronged counter-offensive, launched in December 1981, along with the enquiry into Militant and the refusal to admit Tariq Ali into the Party.[53] To many Labour MPs, on the centre-left as well as the right, Foot's handling of Tatchell was a test of his determination to take on the far left.[54] Thus the young Australian's candidature was never discussed simply on its merits. Austin Mitchell, the right-wing MP for Grimsby explained: Tatchell 'had become a symbol for all the headbanger candidates local parties were selecting . . . As the more exposed he had to be made an example for the others'.[55]

As a test of Foot's ability to stamp his authority on the Party, the disowning of Tatchell was a dismal failure. His support on the NEC almost immediately began to crumble as his natural allies on the centre left – perhaps now alert to the misrepresentation of the Bermondsey candidate's views, and doubtless aware of the mounting anger in the constituencies – deserted him. Whilst extremely anxious not to undermine his leadership, nevertheless all but Neil Kinnock felt themselves unable to back him and in the key vote on the Executive he only avoided a humiliating rebuff by the narrowest margin.[56]

It was a pyrrhic victory, divested by its narrowness of any real authority. Feeling amongst the Party's activists was outraged by what many saw as an arbitrary and wilful act. The NEC was deluged by resolutions demanding that it endorse Tatchell – 65 in February alone.[57] The Bermondsey party dug its heels in, refusing to abandon its candidate, leaving the NEC little option, if it persisted in its line, but disbanding the CLP – a step calculated to provoke uproar. The Executive ordered a new selection but in fact effectively capitulated by agreeing to Tatchell's right to contest it. Foot himself may well have come to recognise that his repudiation of the Australian was – in the words of one of his oldest comrades in arms, Ian Mikardo – 'a gross error of judgement'.[58] Any lingering inclination on his part to stand by his original decision was probably dissipated by Mellish's failure to honour his side of the bargain struck in December, not to embarrass the Party if Tatchell was cast to the wolves.[59] With the leader's approval, the NEC voted to approve the Bermondsey left-winger's renomination[60] and he was re-adopted by an overwhelming majority early the following year.[61]

Foot had staked his authority as leader on the rejection of Tatchell and he had been rebuffed. In the past, leaders had been able, with the backing of the NEC, to impress their will on a reluctant Party; those days had now passed. The authority of the centre had reached its nadir. Foot had little option but to swallow his words (and his pride) and offer full support to the Australian as Labour's official standard-bearer. But the worst was by no means over. There followed, after Mellish's resignation, perhaps the most unseemly by-election in recent history, with Tatchell subjected to (in the words of the President of the National Union of Journalists) an 'appalling' torrent of 'personal abuse, vilification and lies' by the right-wing tabloids.[62] The election result was a humiliation for Labour. Its vote collapsed and the Liberal Simon Hughes swept to an overwhelming victory.

11.4   The Pat Wall incident

Torn apart by fierce internal strife and with electoral nemesis beckoning, a desperate bid was made to pull the Party together. A joint meeting of the NEC and TULV (Trade Unions for a Labour Victory) at the ASTMS retreat in Bishops Stortford, attended by all the major protagonists in January 1982, called a truce. But the respite was short-lived. Whilst Ron Hayward and David Hughes were patiently compiling their report, apprehension within the PLP swelled as Militant notched up more triumphs in selection contests. By February 1982, eight Tendency members had been selected, most in winnable seats. Amongst these was Pat Wall, the only one to oust a sitting MP, Ben Ford, in Bradforth North. Wall, a founder-member of Militant, had beaten Ford by 35 votes to 28.[63] The MP appealed to the NEC and the case was heard in January 1982 by an enquiry panel comprising two right-wing NEC members, John Golding and Alan Hadden, and the Assistant National Agent Walter Brown.[64] Under the rules, the NEC could only invalidate a selection on grounds of procedural improprieties and these formed the thrust of Ford's complaints.

The enquiry team uncovered a number of irregularities which did not materially affect the result. Nevertheless, on these grounds it recommended that Pat Wall be denied endorsement and a fresh selection be held. The judgment underlined the problem of separating political and procedural grounds for rescinding a constituency decision since it is doubtful whether the irregularities would have been considered of sufficient seriousness to warrant nullifying the selection if the candidate had been politically more palatable. Golding removed any doubts on this score by stating publicly that in his view no member of Militant could be considered suitable to stand as a Labour candidate. Left-wing NEC members immediately charged that this statement brought into question the impartiality of the enquiry and the Organisation Committee rejected its recommendation by eight votes to six, and by ten to five voted to endorse Wall.[65]

Foot was unhappy with the decision, preferring to defer consideration of the matter until the completion of the Hayward/Hughes report. At the full NEC, the Organisation Committee's minute was referred back, by a narrow margin of 15 votes to 13.[66] The day before the Organisation Committee was due to meet to reconsider the matter, the *Sunday Times* tossed a grenade into the proceedings. It taped a debate between Wall and the SWP (Socialist Workers Party) in which the former was reported as calling for the abolition of the monarchy and the House of Lords, and the sacking of top military personnel, senior civil servants and judges. Furthermore, he was quoted as forecasting in lurid terms 'the possibility in Britain of a civil war and the terrible death and destruction and bloodshed that would mean' unless a Labour Government moved rapidly to disarm a ruling class which would not peacefully surrender its privileges.[67]

Though Wall may well have geared his rhetoric to suit the occasion, his speech, predictably and understandably, horrified many in Labour's ranks and the clamour of the right and centre-left for tough action against Militant rose appreciably. In the wake of what *The Guardian* dubbed 'the most damaging crisis' since the peace pact of Bishop Stortford, senior right-wingers demanded Wall's repudiation.[68] The Organisation Committee ordered a re-run of the selection (though this was inevitable after the NEC's referral back of its earlier decision); but a move to prevent the endorsement of other Militant candidates until Hayward and Hughes had reported was thrown out.[69]

Yet no attempt was made to debar Wall from standing again and he was selected with a bigger majority (49 votes to 12) in the new selection than in the original one.[70] By then the Hayward-Hughes report had been submitted. Foot sought to delay the decision on endorsement until after Conference by which time, it was anticipated, Militant members would be precluded from standing as Parliamentary candidates. But – underlining again Foot's lack of authority – the NEC voted to accept Wall.[71] By this time, however, the limelight had shifted to wider issues.

11.5 The Hayward–Hughes report

The Hayward–Hughes report was submitted in June 1982.[72] It was a brief document consisting almost entirely of conclusions and recommendations; it included no extracts or precis of the evidence upon which these were based. Its key finding was that the Militant Tendency was a 'well-organised caucus centrally controlled ... with its own programme and policy for separate and distinctive propaganda'. This placed it in conflict with Clause II Section 3 of the Constitution.[73] Hayward and Hughes, however, were careful to distinguish between two types of Militant supporters: the first consisted of an 'indeterminate number who are aware of the nature and objectives of the Militant organisation' and the second of a 'larger group who are not fully aware of that nature and those objectives and believe themselves to be working for socialist objectives and the Party'.

Having defined the problem, Hayward and Hughes recommended a rather circuitous method for resolving it. They proposed a 'Register of non-affiliated groups to be recognised and allowed to operate within the Party'. All such groups had to apply for inclusion on the Register to the NEC, whose decision would be final. The Register would contain details of the aims and organisation of groups included on it. A number of ground-rules of eligibility were laid down; groups must be open and democratic; should not be allowed to operate their own internal discipline or be associated with any international organisation not supported by the Labour Party or Socialist International. Any group found to be in breach of these rules would be given a three-month period of grace to place their house in order. Failure to satisfy the NEC would put them in violation of the constitution.

Rather inconsistently, instead of suggesting that Militant, like all other groups, should be invited to apply for registration and judged by the above criteria, the authors stated that 'it is our opinion that the Militant Tendency as presently constituted would not be eligible to be included on the proposed Register in the light of our findings'.

The report pleased few. Many right-wingers, including senior figures like Healey and Shore, were disappointed by the failure to recommend immediate disciplinary action.[74] The Tribune Group, in a controversial decision, rallied behind its long-serving member Michael Foot and – very narrowly – approved the Report.[75] But the bulk of the left was unequivocally hostile. Influential non-Trotskyist bodies like the Labour Co-ordinating Committee (LCC) and the Campaign for Labour Party Democracy (CLPD) and most leading left-wingers denounced it as an unacceptable abridgement of the rights of Party members.[76] Notwithstanding, it was approved by the NEC by 16 votes to 10.[77]

Not only was the idea of a Register poorly received, events were soon to reveal it as unworkable and, indeed, unconstitutional. Why then was it adopted – bearing in mind that the Executive already possessed adequate disciplinary weapons in its armoury?

To answer this question, it is necessary to explore both the attitudes and goals of the chief protagonists (Hayward, his successor Jim Mortimer, Hughes and Foot) and the context in which they operated.

All shared a distaste for discipline as a method of managing the Party but were convinced that action was now unavoidable. Firstly they felt that Militant's infringement of the Constitution was too blatant to be ignored. Secondly, Foot was under heavy pressure from many MPs demanding a firm stance against 'extremism'. Here it may be useful to distinguish between symbolic and tangible action. The Party Leader agreed that Labour had to be *seen* to be doing something if the rattled nerves of many MPs were to be calmed and the electorate persuaded that the Labour Party would not countenance 'extremism'.[78] From this perspective, the ends the register was designed to serve were less important than the fact of its existence: it was a symbolic act of reassurance. The Register, finally, was designed to enable the NEC to perform a delicate balancing act: on the one hand to placate those on the right clamouring for tough measures and, indeed, viewing Foot's handling of the Militant issues as the 'crucial test of his leadership';[79] whilst on the other to reassure those on the left that they would not be next on the line by demarcating clearly between legitimate and illegitimate forms of group activity.[80]

Perhaps the greatest virtue of the Register, in the eyes of its advocates, was a negative one: it offered an alternative to the discredited instruments of the social-democratic centralist regime – the legacy of which hung like a pall over the present. The two main instruments employed then to contain Trotskyism were, as we have seen, ideological regulation and proscription.[81]

The constitutional basis of ideological regulation lay in Clause III 3(a) of the Constitution which states that each individual member must accept and conform to the constitution Programme, Principles and Policy of the Party'. This – in the centralist period from the 1930s to the 1960s – was read to entail a commitment to the existing Parliamentary system; members (or recruits) who advocated revolutionary methods were seen as disqualifying themselves from membership. The left of the 1970s, as part of its liberalising policy, had dismantled all ideological boundaries and embraced the doctrine of the 'broad church'. This open-door policy to the revolutionary left had never been acceptable to Labour's right, and, as the current in the Party began to flow in their direction, they agitated more vigorously for a return to older practices. 'We have a frontier both on the right and on the left' Peter Shore declared, 'and that frontier must be manned'.[82] The frontier post was fixed at the defence of parliamentary democracy; and that, Denis Healey insisted, excluded Trotskyists.[83] The appeal of this argument extended beyond the right. 'What else is the Labour Party about', enquired the Tribunite Bryan Gould, 'if not ideas? The notion that the party has no ideological boundaries is specious'.[84]

For a moment, in December 1981, the Party appeared to veer towards this view. Not only was Tatchell denied endorsement for his alleged anti-Parliamentary views; the NEC also refused to grant membership to a man who – in contrasts to Tatchell – did actually espouse revolutionary socialism, Tariq Ali. A celebrated student revolutionary of the 1960s, he had for over a decade been a prominent figure within the Trotskyist International Marxist Group, which was the (Trotskyist) Fourth International's official UK subsidiary. In a highly publicised move, he quit the IMG and announced his intention of joining the Labour Party. However, he also stressed that he remained true to his basic political beliefs including his rejection of the parliamentary road to socialism.[85]

David Hughes brought the matter to the NEC arguing that the Executive had a duty to ascertain whether Tariq Ali 'accepts the role of Parliament in achieving socialism as laid down in the Party Constitution'.[86] Hughes recommended that assurances be sought from the former student revolutionary but the Committee wanted immediate action and voted to exclude him from the Party.[87]

The matter was to drag on for two years as Hornsey CLP (to which Tariq Ali had applied) insisted upon accepting him into membership.[88] And, despite the heated debate the case aroused, it did not in fact signify a revival of ideological regulation. The real objection to Tariq Ali was less his views than his fame (or, for most of the media, his notoriety). His entrance into the Labour Party, the NEC majority feared, could be too easily exploited to symbolise the rising flood of extremism swamping it. In fact, several of Tariq Ali's political allies (like Robin Blackburn) had already slipped unnoticed into the Party and shortly after the IMG was to embrace entryism and move, more or less, en bloc and unhindered, into Labour's ranks.

In fact both Foot (despite his temporary aberration over Tatchell) and the new General Secretary, Jim Mortimer, were adamantly opposed to the resuscitation of ideological regulation. Both repeatedly insisted that no-one would be expelled for their views. Indeed, it would appear that this approach to handling Militant was never seriously considered.[89] Why not? Firstly, because Foot and Mortimer genuinely and fervently opposed any revival of 1950s-type 'witch-hunting'. This they defined, firstly, as the victimisation of the innocent and, secondly, (and more pertinently in this context) as the attempt to suppress minority opinion by disciplinary means.[90] Nobody, Mortimer assured Conference delegates in his speech on the Register, would be 'asked a question about their ideology'.[91]

This objection in principle to ideological regulation was reinforced by more pragmatic consideration. A number of trade unions (including the centre-right GMWU) had been mandated by their conference to oppose 'witch hunts'. A decision to expel Militant members on grounds of their views would certainly have been construed by many as such and would have exacerbated the NEC's problems in securing a convincing Conference majority for action against the Tendency. Similarly, it would have played into the hands of the Trotskyist group, whose propaganda machine increasingly churned out the message that 'Marxists' were being hounded for their beliefs.

But there were other, more fundamental, reasons why ideological borders could not be restored, without massive resistance. Where, exactly would the borders be located? The notion of a boundary implied the existence of some core body of principles, setting the fundamental purposes of the Party, which could thereby define the outer limits of the ideologically permissable. To the right (and some Tribunites like Gould) this core comprised democratic socialism, understood as the Parliamentary route to socialism. There were two problems with this, one constitutional the other political. Firstly, although all members were obliged to conform to the principles, programme and policy' of the Party, the meaning of the first term was nowhere defined in the Constitution; and, in the section on Party Objects, there was no mention of adherence to the Parliamentary system.[92] Secondly, subscribing to a doctrinal kernel as a condition of membership presupposed a reasonable degree of consensus over Labour's basic aims. But by the 1980s this was quite obviously lacking. Many on the left (and elsewhere), noted that the right's enthusiasm for Parliamentary institutions was not matched by any commensurate interest in socialist objectives;[93] and, indeed, that its insistence on applying the Constitution did not extend to its objects, as enshrined in the commitment to common ownership. Furthermore, left-wingers recalled that, until very recently, the most vociferous defenders of the Party's democratic socialist character had included Shirley Williams and David Owen, now widely regarded, particularly in the constituencies, as traitors to the cause. In these circumstances, any attempt to resurrect ideological regulation would have been deemed illegitimate by a wide spectrum of party opinion and, hence, calculated to provoke fierce resistance.

The second established method for combating Trotskyism was proscription. Eventually, and reluctantly, six months after the release of the Hayward–Hughes Report, the NEC did proscribe Militant. But in June 1982, the major appeal of the Register was precisely that it was an *alternative* to proscription. Why was the Party so chary about taking a step when delay was to inflict months of electorally very damaging infighting?

The first reason was again the shadow of the earlier centralist regime.[94] Left-Wingers, including Foot, had consistently castigated the right's use of the proscription to harass opponents and violate the rights of members. John Mortimer had actually been a victim – forced to quit the Party for his vice-chairmanship of a proscribed organisation, the Anglo-Chinese Friendship Society.[95] His predecessor, and joint-author of the Militant Report, Ron Hayward, had been instrumental in securing the abolition of the Proscribed List, and, in formulating his recommendations, had no wish to reinstate it in any shape or form.

These inhibitions were widely shared. To many, the very word 'proscription' was anathema; it conjured up images of ruthless apparatchiks suffocating dissent by imposing a stringent disciplinary regime. This may not have mattered so much if the political balance in the trade unions – the wielders of the bloc vote – had not altered so much since the 1950s. The fervour of the AUEW's Sir John Boyd to cleanse the Party 'a sewer with all sorts of rubbish floating in it'[96] was not widely shared. Even the centre-right GMWU as we have seen was bound by its conference to oppose all expulsions and witch/hunts;[97] more predictably, there was powerful opposition to any disciplinary action whatsoever in the giant left-wing Transport Union.

This last consideration was a vital one. Overwhelming endorsement by Conference of the drive against Militant would lend it a legitimacy that a narrow majority could not provide. It would inhibit or impair the credibility of those on the left who, whilst bitterly opposed to the disciplining of Militant, cherished Conference sovereignty as their ultimate credo.[98] In practical terms, this meant that the support of the TGWU, with its one million votes, was essential. As it happened, it was only with extreme difficulty that the union's leadership managed to swing it behind the Register.[99] They would probably have failed if the issue had been proscription, hence depriving the NEC of a Conference majority large enough to legitimate, in the eyes of many in the Party, the expulsion of Militant leaders.

11.6 The Register

The NEC in June 1982, formally approved the setting up of the Register.[100] How was it to operate? This was to prove far more tricky than anticipated. In a circular [101] despatched to all known groups active in the Labour Party, the new General Secretary, Jim Mortimer, set down the conditions of eligibility for the Register (as outlined in the Hayward–Hughes Report). He intimated that any organisation which failed to meet these conditions, or make appropriate adjustments would not only be excluded from the Register but put in breach of the constitution and hence liable to disciplinary action. Militant received an additional letter in which – alone – it was given a fixed time-limit of three months after the despatch of the letter (i.e. until the end of September) to send in its application for registration.[102]

In September, Conference, in a stormy session debated the issue. Two key decisions were taken. Firstly, the section of the NEC report dealing with the Register was approved by 5,173,000 votes to 1,565,000. Secondly, a composite resolution (Number 48) moved by APEX and seconded by EEPTU, with the support of the NEC, was passed by 5,087,000 votes to 1,857,000. The central passages of this resolution reminded the NEC of its 'obligations, under clause 1 X 2 (d) of the Constitution to enforce the Constitution', affirmed Conference's 'determination to uphold Clause II of the Constitution in respect of any un-constitutional activity within the Party structure' and reiterated the NEC's 'duty to declare that organisations not in conformity with that Constitution are incompatible with membership of the Labour Party'.[103] These two decisions were to be of critical importance in the subsequent combat with Militant as they furnished the Constitutional justification for the NEC's disciplinary drive.

The political setting for the anti-Militant drive also looked distinctly more favourable after the 1982 Conference. The right scored two further gains in the NEC elections giving it, for the first time in a decade, an outright, though slender, majority. This not only underlined the shift within the unions to the right but the right's superior organisational skills and unity, which enabled it to harness its votes far more effectively than the left.[104] The right on the NEC, ably led by John

Golding, celebrated its triumph by ousting Benn from the chair of the Home Policy (replaced by Golding himself) and Heffer from the Organisation Committee (in favour of Russel Tuck). They appeared to be firmly in the driving seat.

Conference endorsement of the Register gave the go-ahead for moves against Militant. Its three month's time-limit had now expired and no application for registration had been received – the Trotskyist organisation claiming that it was under no obligation to respond until Conference ratified the Hayward–Hughes Report. This, in theory, placed the Tendency in breach of the constitution. But difficulties for the NEC were already gathering.

Firstly, many left-wing groups were showing reluctance even to apply for the Register (some opted for an outright boycott).[105] The NEC's response was to extend the deadline until the end of the year. Secondly, two bodies which did apply, Labour Friends of Israel (LFI) and the Labour Movement for Europe (LME) were judged to be ineligible for registration on the grounds that they received funds from abroad.[106] The NEC contrived here to trip itself up. On Mortimer's recommendation it was agreed, in effect (as we shall see later) to sever the link between non-eligibility for the Register and liability to disciplinary action; and to introduce a fresh distinction between those non-registered organisations which infringed Clause II (3) of the Constitution (i.e. Militant) and those (like LFI and LME) which did not.[107] What then, critics might (and did) ask was the point of the Register? This decision, in effect, began the retreat for the Executive's original strategy.

The NEC had as yet to determine the scale of expulsions. The authors of the Hayward–Hughes Report, Mortimer and Foot all saw themselves as engaging in a balancing act; to launch a limited strike against Militant's organisational structure whilst deflecting right-wing pressure for an all-out purge. From the original Report onwards, a key distinction was made between (in Mortimer's words) the Tendency's 'inner organising group' and its 'wider circle of sympathisers'.[108] This was designed to identify a manageable number of disciplinary targets, whose removal would enfeeble the Trotskyist group, whilst insulating the rank and file from indiscriminate attack.

There was some disagreement about who, precisely, formed the 'inner organising group', with the resurgent right on the NEC keen to catch as many in the net as possible. Mortimer, who took over from Hayward in July, preferred a restrictive definition. In a paper to the NEC, he proposed that the *Militant* paper's five-member editorial board be immediately expelled; its 34 full-time 'sellers'[109] (i.e. regional organisers) be asked to vacate their jobs or quit the Party, and that Militant's eight PPCs be required to desist helping 'the organised activity' of the Tendency.[110]

Right-wingers had hoped to mete out more punishing treatment.[111] But both they, and the Mortimer-Foot bloc had greatly under-rated the difficulties of the enterprise. This was now to become more evident. Prior to the Organisation Committee discussing his paper, Mortimer received Militant's belated response, written by the paper's editor, Peter Taaffe, to the letter set in July inviting it to apply for registration.[112]

It indicated that Militant had worked out a coherent strategic response to the NEC's offensive. This had three main elements. Firstly, in a tone of injured innocence, the Tendency simply denied all the allegations made against it: it had no membership, no organisation, no separate principles, policies and programme and no internal disciplinary systems. It was merely a current of opinion, like *Tribune* and the *New Statesman*. Militant's leaders knew, of course, that this declaration of unblemished purity would make little impression on the NEC.[113] But this was not its purpose. Rather, it was designed to achieve two objectives: firstly, to reassure the substantial body of constituency activists who did not (or did not want to) believe that Militant was a 'party within a party' and, secondly, to admit nothing that – to use a well-worn phrase – could be used as evidence against it (of which more later).

The second element was to depict the NEC's move as part of a concerted campaign to wrench the party to the right, divest it of its radical policies and intimidate the rest of the left into submission. This tactic aimed at – and to a large measure succeeded in – mobilising maximum left resistance to the NEC.

The NEC fully anticipated these two elements, but not the third. Taaffe wrote that Militant had been advised by its lawyers that the Register was unconstitutional, and, hence, any expulsions flowing from exclusion from the Register could be challenged in the Courts. The NEC, Militant claimed, was acting unlawfully in two ways. Firstly, on grounds of *ultra vires*. The Haywood-Hughes Report had concluded that the Tendency was in breach of Clause III (3) of the Constitution; this rendered it ineligible for inclusion on the Register and thus it (and its members) vulnerable to eviction from the Labour Party. Militant – having noted the Register's lack of a clear constitutional grounding – pointed out that Clause II (3) did not state that members of non-affiliated organisations could not be members of the Labour Party. The NEC itself had apparently conceded this by exempting non-affiliated bodies like CND and NCCL from the requirement to seek registration, and more damagingly, by declaring that the members of two organisations deemed not to qualify for the Register – LFI and LME – were not liable for disciplinary action. The only way in which the Executive could constitutionally act against Militant was by declaring it a proscribed organisation,[114] a step (Militant claimed) which Conference would not have approved.

The second ground was natural justice. Militant reminded the NEC that, in undertaking any disciplinary action it was required by law to abide by the principle of natural justice. This entailed granting defendants the rights to receive and comment upon specific charges, to examine the evidence upon which they were based, and to a full and impartial hearing – all of which had been denied to Militant.

Initially, Mortimer was unperturbed, assuming the Tendency was bluffing. Others were less sure. Labour front-bencher (and lawyer) John Smith consulted Alexander Irvine Q.C. Irvine advised that Militant had a strong case.[115] Irvine's advice which 'came out of the blue' to Head Office and the NEC[116] was that Militant had a strong case. That it should do so was surprising. The Pembroke judgment, a decade and a half earlier, had established two key principles: firstly that, in the exercise of its powers, the NEC must act in conformity with natural justice and, secondly, that it was not – as had earlier been supposed – the ultimate and sole arbiter of the rules but was, when engaging in actions which affected the rights of Party members, subject to judicial review.[117]

The Pembroke judgment had, in fact, been confirmed by a superior Court, the Court of Appeals, in 1978. Shortly after the deselection of Reg Prentice, two self-styled moderates, Paul McCormick (a man with legal training) and Julian Lewis, had launched a campaign from outside the constituency to save Newham North East from the 'extremists'. Within months the CLP was in such disarray that the NEC decided to suspend it, an action whose legality the litigatious duo promptly challenged in the Courts.[118] The matter was eventually considered by the Court of Appeal.

Lord Denning, the Master of the Rolls, reached two important conclusions.[119] Firstly, he accepted the NEC's contention that the Labour Party was a unitary organisation, with power emanating from the centre and not (as McCormick and Lewis claimed) a federation of units. But, secondly, he reaffirmed Megarry's earlier ruling that, in applying its powers, the Executive must comply with the precept of natural justice.[120] The full significance of this judgment eluded both the NEC and senior Party officials. Neither seemed fully aware that both the 1969 High Court and the 1977 Appeals Court rulings reflected a shift in judicial thinking – a greater disposition to intervene in voluntary organisations to protect their members against what could be construed as unfair or arbitrary disciplinary practices. So it was with surprise and dismay that the Executive discovered, on drawing its disciplinary weapons in 1982, that they had lost their edge.

The immediate effect of Militant's threat of legal action was to force Mortimer (on the advice of the Party's solicitors) to withdraw his original proposals. But the full impact was far more serious; the obligation both to act strictly within its own rules and, even more, to observe natural justice, was henceforth to sharply curtail the NEC's freedom of manoeuvre.[121] As a result the original intention of dealing the Tendency a short, sharp, shock was dashed and Labour was to be plunged into a highly-publicised, protracted and electorally debilitating battle with the Trotskyist group.

Mortimer's amended report to the NEC[122] spelt out in great detail the numerous legal reefs and barriers through which the Party had to steer and the lengthy and complex procedures it would now have to adopt. After discussing the operations of the Register (at some length), Mortimer effectively conceded that it was useless as a method for proceeding against Militant. In other words, what had seemed an ingenious device for launching a controlled strike against the Trotskyist organisation, rendering the unpleasant act of proscription unnecessary, was riddled with so many legal holes that (as a disciplinary instrument) it might just as well be scrapped.[123]

Henceforth (and in sharp contrast to the practices of the social-democratic centralist era) the NEC found itself hemmed in by legal restraints. All future proposals debated by the Executive had to be cleared (and were often drafted) by the Party's solicitors. The first (and crucial) step Labour's General Secretary recommended was one he had hoped to avoid but was now convinced was essential. He conceded that the NEC did not (as Militant claimed) have the power under Clause II (3) to act against the Trotskyist group. But it was given wide powers to enforce the constitution (Clause II (2)) and, more specifically, the right to proscribe organisations (Clause II (4) (b)). In the circumstances, there was no option but to declare Militant a proscribed organisation.

This was unpalatable, but it did overcome the ultra vires objection. The question of natural justice proved more tricky. Both the Foot/Mortimer and right-wing camps had hoped for speedy and incisive action against Militant; only this could achieve the multiple goals of weakening the organisation and restoring the Party's 'respectability' in the eyes of public opinion whilst limiting the damage inflicted by prolonged internal strife.

Legal obstacles demolished this hope. To act in conformity both with its own constitution and natural justice, the party had to adopt a two-stage approach. The first was to proscribe Militant; only then only could it contemplate the second, expulsions. But at both stages it had to afford the Tendency full rights to receive the comment upon specific charges, and to a full and fair hearing. This meant that, at a minimum, proceedings would stretch into January and February of 1983 – a likely election year.

Mortimer's recommendations were agreed by the NEC by a large majority.[124] Recognising that its imminent proscription placed the NEC on firmer constitutional grounds, Militant concentrated on its right to natural justice, claiming full access to all the evidence upon which the NEC's charges were based. This, on legal advice, the Executive refused. Militant promptly issued a writ seeking an interlocutory injunction to restrain the Party from proceeding against it.

In the Court hearing that followed Labour experienced a narrow escape. Mr Justice Nourse, delivering his judgment reaffirmed the earlier Pembroke ruling that the NEC's duty 'to act in accordance with natural justice was paramount'. Normally, this would entail right of access by defendants to all relevant evidence. But, on a technicality – that Militant should have applied for a writ on publication of the Hayward–Hughes Report six months earlier – the application was rejected.[125]

The NEC was free to proceed. In December by 18 votes to 9 it approved a motion proscribing Militant.[126] The step was of symbolic as well as practical significance. The 1973 decision abolishing the Proscribed List had not (despite Militant's claim to the contrary) impaired the NEC's right to proscribe. Nevertheless it did have consequences. The first, and immediate, one was to lift the ban on those groups which at the time figured on the list. The second, and more important effect was to strengthen (and lend a quasi-official recognition to) a growing inhibition against utilising this particular disciplinary sanction. The abandonment of proscription was, for many, symbolic of the lenient discipinary regime of the 1970s.[127] The NEC's decision to proscribe Militant broke a psychological barrier, easing the way to the installation of a tighter disciplinary regime.

The way was now clear for expulsions. But how many? The NEC had been prevaricating over this for months. Hardline right-wingers wanted to emasculate Militant's organisation and favoured wide-ranging expulsions. The bulk of the left was adamantly opposed to any. Neither group had a majority. The final decision, rested upon the middle group – a diverse array of centre-leftists leadership loyalists and cautious trade unionists who inclined towards limited expulsions.

This course was favoured by the General Secretary, who was responsible for overseeing the drive against Militant. He agreed that, as a party within a party, the Tendency had no right to operate within Labour's ranks and was fully committed to exposing its entryist and conspiratorial character. On the other hand – unlike many on the right (and in the media) – he did not regard Militant as a major problem for the Party; and he became increasingly frustrated by the sheer amount of time and energy the matter was consuming, to the neglect of more important policy, electoral and organisational needs. The legal quagmire into which the Party had fallen reinforced this cautious (at times tepid) approach.[128]

Mortimer had two advantages in pushing for acceptance of his approach. First and most importantly, he enjoyed the confidence of the Party leader; as we have seen he and Foot were in broad agreement over how the Militant issue should be handled. This meant that he could rely upon the support of the leadership loyalists who held the balance on the NEC.

Secondly, he possessed the power of the initiator: he drafted the reports and submitted the recommendations which, to a very large extent, set the Executive's agenda. His high standing within the Party, his considerable reputation as former chairman of the conciliation service ACAS, his grasp of detail and his lucidity as a drafter and speaker enabled him to exploit this power to the full. To be set against this, however, was the sheer weight of the constraints which pressed against him, which constantly thwarted his efforts to effect a speedy resolution of the matter and often gave the impression that he was being tossed about by events over which he had little control.

Nevertheless, at first glance it seems odd that Mortimer prevailed so easily against the right-wing NEC majority. Senior right-wingers, both on the political wing (Healey, Shore, Hattersley) and on the industrial (Terry Duffy of the Engineers, Sid Weighel of the NUR, Frank Chappel of the Electricians) would have relished an all-out onslaught on Militant. But, in reality, the trade union right (whose votes were crucial both at Conference and in the NEC) was a far from homogenous group. A significant proportion of the trade union section of the Executive (Sid Tierney of USDAW, Alan Hadden of the Boilermakers, David Williams of COHSE, and the centrist Sam McCluskie of the NUS) lacked the enthusiasm of their colleagues. This was for a range of reasons. Firstly, they were strongly loyalist in outlook, unwilling to take any steps that might embarass Michael Foot. This outlook was broadly shared, outside the NEC, by the highly influential leader of the GMWU (the third largest union affiliated to the Party) David Basnett, who had swung his traditionally solidly right-wing union on to a more centrist course.[129] As a result, Foot, never keen on mass expulsions, was able to set the pace. Secondly, many trade union officials (both inside and outside the NEC) accorded purely political issues a lower priority than industrial ones. Lacking both interest in and knowledge of Militant's scale and methods of operation (and nervous about unnecessarily upsetting left-wingers amongst their own activists) they felt that right-wingers in the PLP had over-reacted to the Militant threat.[130]

Unexpectedly, John Golding adopted a similarly cautious position. Golding occupied a key position on the NEC. He was, as Chairman of the Home Policy Committee, a leading light on the Executive. Furthermore, as both an MP and a senior union official (number two in his union, the Post Office Engineer Workers – now the National Communication Union) he straddled the political and industrial worlds. He was also the right's ablest and most ruthless organiser – a man who instinctively preferred the bludgeon to the rapier, and one of the left's top bugbears (a role he enjoyed). But precisely because of his political acumen and his insight into trade union thinking, he urged a prudent approach. Though, personally extremely hostile towards Militant (he would have expelled the entire organisation lock, stock and barrel if he could) he realised that drastic measures were not feasible; that a solid anti-Militant bloc sufficient to delivery thumping majorities at Conference did not exist but had to be constructed; and that to force through measures against Foot's opposition could only damage his standing and, therefore, that of the Party, in the eyes of the electorate.[131]

With the right-wing majority divided, Mortimer (with Foot's backing) experienced little difficulty in winning approval for his strategy of selective expulsions (i.e. the paper's editorial board and the presumed thirty-odd full-time organisers). This strategy, however, was wrecked by legal problems revolving around the question of Militant's membership. According to the Constitution, members of proscribed organisations were ineligible to remain within the party – but Militant constantly denied having any members. Mortimer was entrusted with the task of producing a legally acceptable definition (in the absence of a formal list) of membership. Reluctant to expose the Trotskyist group's rank and file to expulsion, he proposed a restrictive definition more or less equating membership with the holding of a senior position in the Tendency's hierarchy.[132]

The law once more intruded. Barristers Alexander Irvine Q.C. and Anthony Blair advised that Mortimer's definition was too restrictive: membership of an organisation meant precisely that, and not involvement in its inner core. The barristers stressed that constitutionally the NEC was 'obliged to expel all Militant Tendency members once the Militant Tendency had been declared ineligible to affiliate to the Party'.[133] Formulated in such a way as to comply with legal requirements, the definition finally approved by the NEC in January was wide-ranging. It stated that in seeking to establish membership of Militant, the Executive 'shall have regard, in particular, to their involvement in financial support for and/or the organisation of and/or the activities of the Militant tendency'.[134]

The result of the erasing of the distinction between 'organisers' and 'followers' was – as Mortimer and others had feared – to leave any adherent of Militant, however lowly his rank, vulnerable to expulsion (either by the NEC or by CLPs) once his or her membership had been established. Whatever the intentions of some of its members, the NEC had (as the left minority always claimed) sanctioned the use of discipline as a method of combating Trotskyism and opened the gates to the expulsion of ordinary rank and file Militants.

But this was for the future. In the immediate circumstances, the NEC felt it had no option but to retreat and abandon its original goal of eliminating Militant's inner core. The reasons for this were partly political (these will be discussed below) and partly legal. Having developed criteria for establishing membership of Militant, the Executive could only take action on the basis of evidence adequate to satisfy the Courts. This placed the presumed members of the Tendency's inner group in two categories: those – the five-person Militant editorial board – whose involvement in the organisation was avowed and acknowledged, and the rest (including the PPC's and the 'newspaper sellers') whose status was much less clear cut.[135] Proceeding against the former was much more straightforward than against the latter. Wishing to avoid a long legal tussle, with all the political and electoral difficulties this would bring in its wake, the NEC chose to confine its efforts to the editorial board.

Mortimer was instructed to prepare a case against its five members, giving them (in line with legal advice) the right to examine the particulars and to an interview before the Executive.[136] However, it transpired that the 'particulars' referred simply to Conference and NEC decisions authorising action against the Tendency, and the single allegation that the editorial board were members of the Trotskyist organisation.[137] The five denounced their continued denial of access to the evidence upon which the Hayward–Hughes Report was based as a violation of natural justice. Their solicitors issued a writ on the Party seeking an injunction restraining it from acting upon the proscription resolution, but Militant elected not to take the matter further.[138]

As arranged, the editorial board attended the February meeting of the NEC. They were allowed to make statements in response to the charge of membership of Militant and replied to questions from the NEC. Then the verdict: by 19 votes to 9, Peter Taaffe, Ted Grant, Keith Dickenson, Lynn Walsh and Clare Doyle were expelled from the Party.[139] Each were allowed to make a personal appeal to the 1983 Conference; as was expected the expulsions were confirmed by majorities of around five million to a little over one and half million.[140]

11.7 The drive against Militant: an appraisal

It had taken Labour fifteen months to procure the expulsion of five individuals. With electoral nemesis beginning to loom, there was little inclination to take the matter further. Militant did not pursue its writ – though it continued to hang over the Party if it opted for more expulsions. This reticence may well have reflected Militant's assessment

that, all in all, it had not fared too badly.[141] The right had waited ten
years to regain control over the NEC and its grip on the Party's disciplinary machinery. Yet – set against its own objectives – it achieved
remarkably little. Not surprisingly, the 'maximalists' on the right felt
cheated and deeply disgruntled.

But their disappointment was by no means universally shared
amongst those who had backed the campaign against Militant. The
'minimalists' like Foot and Mortimer had always lacked enthusiasm for
a full-scale assault. As far as the latter was concerned, the removal from
the Party of the editorial board had helped defuse pressure for sterner
measures; the Tendency had been formally placed beyond the pale but
widespread expulsions had been avoided. The Party, he hoped, could
now concentrate on more important and pressing matters.[142]

The pragmatists on the right, led by Golding, were also not too
disheartened. They, like the maximalists, wished to extirpate the Militant menace but had a shrewder feel for what was feasible at the time.
Golding was blamed by several right-wingers for the meagre pickings of
months of battling against Militant. But such criticism displayed a lack
of awareness of the constraints which hemmed in the Party at every
turn. The legal constraints we have already examined; it is to the
political ones that we now turn.

The resistance of the left

Action against Militant was a highly controversial move less because
the Tendency itself represented a large body of opinion than because it
could call upon the sympathy of the bulk of the left.[143] The left's
determined opposition to expulsions did not spring from any deep
sympathy for Militant's politics (not to mention its style and methods);
indeed, it was widely regarded (in Foot's phrase) as a 'pestilential nuisance'.[144] Yet there was a whole range of reasons for the left's hostility
to the attack on Militant.

Firstly, many feared a reversion to the heavy-handed methods and the
intolerance of the social-democratic centralist era. The image of this era
– whether derived from direct experience or as communicated via the
collective memory of the left – shaped the way in which the present was
perceived and understood. 'No return to the bans, proscriptions and
expulsions' of the 1950s was an emotive cry; and the point was insistently made that the pantheon of left-wing heroes – Cripps, Bevan, even
Foot himself, had all been victims of right-wing intolerance.

This objection in principle to expulsions was reinforced by a number
of other considerations. Those most critical of Militant argued that
attacking that organisation was actually self-defeating: it confirmed
exaggerated estimates of its strength and, by giving it massive publicity
and creating martyrs, endowed it with a credibility it did not deserve.

Further, most left-wingers saw the assault on Militant as actuated primarily by hostility to its ideas rather than by any alleged violation of the constitution. Charges that the Trotskyist organisation represented an alien element provoked the riposte that the real traitors were those who defected to form the SDP (and those who secretly sympathised with and might yet join them). The left also vigorously denounced the time-consuming and divisive campaign against Militant as an extremely damaging distraction from the Party's top priority – mobilising opposition to the Conservative Government. Far from placating the voters, it simply confirmed their perception of a strife-ridden Party and, hence, alienated them further.

Finally, Foot and Mortimer entirely failed to allay fears that the action against Militant 'would be the signal for a more widespread purge of other legitimate groupings which found themselves out of step with the leadership'.[145] This fear was perhaps the decisive consideration for those who felt least affinity for the Tendency. 'The right', Tribune's longstanding parliamentary correspondant, Hugh McPherson, wrote, 'was bent on a purge not of Trotskyists but against the left in the PLP and beyond'.[146] To understand why so many on the left (including many who were sharply critical of Militant) concurred with this assessment, it is necessary to place the Militant episode in a wider political setting, which shows that these fears were not groundless.

The years following Labour's defeat at the polls in June 1979 witnessed one of the most ferocious periods of internal strife that the Party has ever known. The right was seriously alarmed by the success of the campaign for constitutional reform and those who stayed within the Party fought back furiously to stem the left-wing tide. The right's main target was not the Militant Tendency but the broader coalition known as the Bennite left. It was the Bennites, not Militant, whom Roy Hattersley, co-chairman of the right-wing Labour Solidarity group, charged with organising 'purges and pogroms' against moderates.[147] 'The intolerant, fanatical and authoritarian zealots in Labour's ranks' corruscated by the oratory of Peter Shore were the members, not of any Trotskyist sect, but, in the Guardian's phrase 'the Bennite left'. And it was Benn himself, not Militant's guru, Ted Grant, whom Shore damned as a 'cuckoo in the nest'.[148]

Most right-wingers recognised that, alone, Militant represented no real threat. As Hattersley explained in an interview in 1981: 'The problem is not Militant, about whom we always talk, because Militant is so easily identifiable and so unpleasant that most people are prepared to squash it . . . the problem is those organisations who talk in the language of democratic socialism . . . CLPD and the Rank and File Mobilising Committee'.[149]

Thus, as the strife within the Party reached its apogee in 1981, the right more or less lost sight of Militant; their senior spokesmen, like Healey, Shore and Hattersley, were far more likely to lash at its non-Trotskyist rivals, like CLPD or the LCC, or the ranks of the Bennite left generally.[150] Benn himself was charged by Healey with encouraging 'a sort of People's Democracy the Russians set up in Eastern Europe after the war against which the Polish workers are now rebelling'.[150] The right, at least in its public pronouncements, adhered to a composite image of the hard left/far left/ultra left (the terms were used interchangeably) terms which appeared to embrace anyone to the left of Neil Kinnock.

More than any single incident, the Tatchell affair lent credence to the left's anxiety that, once a purge was begun, it would devour far more than a handful of Trotskyists. Commenting on Foot's repudiation of Tatchell, The Guardian's Ian Aitken wrote that 'he will now have to extend his campaign against the ultra left to cover their increasing control in constituency parties throughout London and in other metropolitan centres like Manchester, Liverpool and parts of Birmingham. It will be a long and bloody campaign, but he has now given notice that he does not intend to flinch from it.'[152] (Aitken often used the term 'ultra-left' to refer to the Bennites.)

In an ideal world, sections of the right may well have tried to discipline Benn and his lieutenants (following in the footsteps of their predecessors in the 1950s). But with Foot as leader and with powerful left-wing unions like the TGWU this was always improbable. The right aimed not to suppress, but to discredit and isolate the (Bennite) left by tarring it with the brush of extremism: hence the imagery of 'bully boys' the analogies with Eastern Europe and the accusations of intimidation and brutality. Few voters possessed either the knowledge or the inclination to distinguish between the Trotskyist and Bennite left. And the press made no attempt to enlighten them. The right-wing tabloids, like the *Sun*, *Mail* and *Express* were only too eager to malign and misrepresent Benn and the broad coalition he led as extremists determined to establish a Soviet-style dictatorship. But even the more sympathetic *Mirror* and *Guardian* (and much TV coverage) rarely if ever bothered to differentiate between the Trotskyist and mainstream left.[153] The right was undoubtedly aware of this and content that it be so. As Mark Hollingsworth observed 'the personal attacks by shadow cabinet members also gave credibility to the press accusations of extremism in Labour's ranks.'[154] Nor was this unintentional. Many senior right-wing Labour politicians possessed good contacts in the media and were only too ready to utilise them to mobilise opinion against the left.

The right's tactic was, in the next couple of years, to earn them significant political dividends, although at the expense of gravely harming the Party. It contributed to a public revulsion from the left; and the growing recognition that Labour's left-wing image was a serious electoral handicap greatly assisted the right in staging its come-back after the 1983 general election.[155] But its immediate effect was to infuriate the left and redouble their hostility to a purge.

It was the mass hostility of the rank and file coupled with the Party's legal problems that finally convinced the NEC that large-scale expulsions were not feasible.[156] The crucial factor here was not so much that most constituency activists disagreed with official Party decisions as that they were simply not prepared to be bound by them. Walworth Road was flooded with resolutions denouncing the 'witch-hunt' and bluntly refusing to implement NEC decisions.[157]

With this in mind it is important to appreciate that, whilst in its policy-making role the NEC can afford to discount constituency opinion, in its managerial role it cannot. To impose its authority effectively, it requires a fair measure of rank and file co-operation, or at least, acquiescence. It may expel a member, but that expulsion can only be enforced by his or her constituency party. Of course, the NEC is by no means helpless if its directives are ignored. It can, for example, threaten or actually disband a local party. This is a feasible option where defiance is isolated: precisely for that reason it was a powerful sanction in the social-democratic centralist era. But where it is widespread, such drastic measures are much riskier. This was the state of affairs in the early 1980s. The constituency left, which by then had secured a strong grip on local party organisation, was almost unanimous in rejecting expulsions. Most of the CLPs which contained Militant full-timers publicly declared that they would refuse to accept their eviction from the Party. The same problem existed in those constituencies which had adopted Militant PPCs.

Some – perhaps a majority – of the dominant centre-right bloc on the NEC were prepared to take on the constituency parties, whatever the consequences. But they lacked an overall majority; others (including the influential John Golding) reluctantly concluded that the price would be too high. Anticipated constituency party reaction was a major factor tempering the approach to Militant throughout the years 1981–1983.[158] It steadily mounted in importance as legal difficulties dragged out the whole process and as the electorally harmful effects of media focus on the Party's internal feuds struck home. The sight of pitched battles throughout the country with rebellious constituency parties in a likely election year could hardly have filled even the stoutest right-winger with confidence.

The use of sanctions to quell the rank and file resistance had other risks attached to it. The Party still relied upon local activists to man its constituency election machine and select parliamentary candidates. Antagonising them might well imperil Labour's electoral prospects in a number of areas. This was a decisive factor restraining action against the eight Militant PPCs, most of whom were, by any reckoning, part of the Tendency's "inner-core". Further, re-organisations of constituency parties were time-consuming and administratively very taxing exercises; with an election in the offing they would have placed an unbearable strain on Labour's exiguous organisational resources. Jim Mortimer put the matter squarely in a report to the NEC: 'Labour cannot afford to alienate large numbers of its activists or to come into collision with a significant number of constituency Labour Parties in the approach to the General Election'.[159]

The erosion of normative control
Widespread defiance of the NEC's authority then, was a major impediment inhibiting its offensive against Militant. In the social-democratic centralist age, large-scale rank and file opposition to the centre was mediated by a willingness, in the final resort, to accept its authority. Many might disagree with NEC decisions but, equally, they acknowledged its right to make them. This ability to exert a large measure of normative control was rooted in two crucial features of Labour's political culture in the 1950s and early 1960s – loyalist sentiment deriving from a widespread solidaristic attachment to the Party and a considerable measure of consensus which legitimated the structure and exercise of authority.[160] Both these conditions of normative control suffered serious erosion from the early 1970s onwards. Major changes in membership composition (which proceeded at an uneven pace throughout the country) undercut loyalism. There was a steady inflow of educated, assertive, younger recruits, often employed in professional occupations. The working class members who deserted the Party in droves in the late 1960s were never replaced. As a result, the social complexion of Labour's membership (particularly its activist component) underwent a substantial alteration.[161] The new cohorts of activists were considerably more likely to exhibit a purposive orientation than the older ones; they were often animated by a distinctively socialist matrix of ideas and values and entered the Party primarily to influence the policy process. In addition they tended to be radical in outlook and imbued with a participative ethos.

The educated, articulate activists of the 1980s possessed the self-confidence and the political skills which earlier generations of members had often lacked to challenge authority figures at all levels of the Party.[162] Given their social background and occupational experience they were less influenced by solidaristic sentiments, and – this reflected broader societal trends – they were far less likely than older members to exhibit a generalised deference towards authority. The status and esteem in which the NEC's key intermediaries – the regional officials –

were held fell (often dramatically) as they lost their monopoly of skills, expertise and information. Middle-class activists rapidly acquired a mastery of how to operate within the Party. New channels of communications, outside the formal Party structure, emerged with the rapid development, from the mid 1970s onwards of Party pressure groups.[163] The 'aura of priestcraft' (in Ian Mikardo's phrase) in which Party officials once bathed all but vanished and they often found themselves confronted by activists who felt not the slightest inhibition about questioning their rulings or defying NEC directives.

Lacking any instinctive sense of loyalty or deference, the orientation to authority of purposive members tended to be conditional. In the social-democratic centralist era, authority had been respected because it was regarded as legitimate. Legitimacy, in turn, rested on a large measure of consensus, both substantive and procedural. By the early 1980s, this had collapsed.

In the Labour Party, as in other voluntary organisations, the respect in which the authorities were held varied to the extent to which they were seen to be promoting collective values and goals. The cumulative impact of the 1974–1979 Labour Government (on top of that of its predecessor in the 1960s) was one of the deep and pervasive disillusion. Left and right had always differed over the pace of reform, priorities and, indeed, the final destination. But common support for state intervention and Keynesian economic management to maintain full employment and promote equality and social justice through expanding welfare programmes had formed a kernel of consensus. When the leadership (and much of the right) abandoned these cherished tenets of Croslandite social-democracy, and with the left demanding the adoption of more radical economic strategies, the common ground between the two vanished. Large swathes of activist opinion became convinced that the Labour Government had betrayed the Party and all it stood for.

Hand in hand with this process of substantive or ideological polarisation went the crumbling of Labour's procedural consensus. Labour Governments compounded their betrayal (in the eyes of many activists) of the Party's core values by their persistent and, sometimes, contemptuous disregard of the voice of the majority, as articulated in Conference pronouncements. By this time, Labour's Parliamentary leadership had totally abandoned the doctrine of majority rule and Conference sovereignty. Indeed, ever since the right had lost its grip on Conference, many of its members had discovered previously unnoticed virtues in the Burkean notion of representation. The parliamentary leadership was able to cast off the fetters of Conference with ease, but the longer term consequences were serious. Social-democratic centralist principles had operated as a legitimating ideology justifying, in the eyes of the Party membership, the exisiting structure of authority and power. The rejection by the leadership of traditional majoritarian democracy called into question their right to rule.

The response of radical constituency activists to what they perceived as the derelictions of the 1974–1979 Government was to launch the drive for constitutional reform. This was stridently opposed by the right, several of whose luminaries deserted to form the SDP. The constitutional battle exposed to the public gaze the deep fractures within the Party. It was, at one and the same time, a clash of radically divergent conceptions of party democracy and a bitter struggle for power. To the left, party democracy entailed the collective accountability of the PLP to Conference, the individual accountability of MPs to their constituency parties and the right of Conference to determine the programme of the Party and of any Labour Government. To the right this was a recipe for oligarchy not democracy. It would transform Labour into a 'vanguard party' entrenching 'the supremacy of Party over the supremacy of Parliament'.[164] It demanded 'a mindless, mechanical obedience to Conference resolutions' transforming Labour's elected representatives into 'grovelling zombies'.[165] Even Michael Foot concurred: the left's constitutional project, he somberly warned, 'carried to its logical conclusion would destroy Parliament'.[166]

These claims were, of course, far-fetched. As Hine commented in his comparative survey of democracy within European social-democracy, the three constitutional reforms (mandatory reselection, a wider franchise for electing the leader and the right of the NEC to formulate the manifesto) 'envisaged changes long-accepted as normal in most European social-democratic parties' and 'were extremely difficult to refute by most standards of democracy'.[167] The charge (echoed in virtually the entire press) that the constitutional change would pave the way for an East European-style state was specious in the extreme, and not to be taken literally.

Its true significance is that it laid bare the absence, within the Party, of any agreement over decision-making rules and, yet more fundamental, the principles which should govern the way the party operated. With a radical form of majoritarian democracy counterposed to an almost Burkean reverance for the independence of MPs, Labour's normative infrastructure was torn apart. 'The rules', Peter Kellner of the *New Statesman* commented, 'far from being a civilising influence on party behaviour have become weapons . . . in a party at war with itself'.[168]

What were the effects of the collapse of consensus? Firstly, a massive estrangement between the mass of left-wing activists and the leadership. After two instalments of Labour Governments had failed to satisfy even their more modest aspirations, a deep disenchantment with those who ran the Party set in. After 1979, this became so ubiquitous, so palpable that it expanded from antagonism to particular leaders to an alienation from the very structure of authority within the Party. At its most extreme, leadership became almost synonymous with betrayal. Loyalism and the 'veneration of leadership' virtually vanished to be replaced, amongst much of the rank and file, by a radically different collective syndrome: a psychology of mistrust, defiance, even of betrayal.[169]

Lacking legitimacy in the eyes of many activists, the authorities within the Party experienced acute difficulty in securing compliance. On key managerial issues, the NEC encountered stubborn resistance. Bermondsey CLP refused to accept the official rejection of Peter Tatchell as the parliamentary candidate. Hornsey brazenly defied the Executive's instruction not to allow Tariq Ali into membership.[170] And the three constituency parties in which Militant's editorial board resided stubbornly refused to deprive them of membership.[171]

The scale and the intensity of the clash between left and right had another consequence: the effective disintegration of any sense of political community, that is of a feeling of belonging to a community with shared aims and ideals, linked together by a common authority structure. 'Left, right and centre'. *Tribune* Editor, Richard Clements, lamented 'the Labour Party seems to be gripped by a collective hysteria . . . [it] is fast beginning to look like the worst example of a sectarian organisation tearing itself to pieces in doctrinal and unfraternal argument'.[172]

The sense of political community was increasingly displaced by what may be called 'wing solidarity'. Wing solidarity needs to be distinguished from the more visible growth of pluralistic politics in the Labour Party – the rise in importance of organised groups like CLPD, the LCC and Labour Solidarity. Such groups played a key role in opinion-formation and membership – moblisation within the Party. But whilst only a minority of activists joined, or even associated themselves with pressure groups, the great majority did identify, in some unstructured way, with the left or right. Such broad ideological alignments have always been a feature of Labour's internal life; what was novel, from the late 1970s was the intensity of rank and file attachments to left and right, and the perception of them as antagonistic rather than competitive wings.

Wing solidarity was hardened in the period 1979–82 by the experience of many activists (primarily on the left) of involvement in 'common' causes, firstly the campaign for constitutional reform and then the Benn deputy-leadership bid. This not only fostered a polarised image of the Party but directly affected attitudes to Militant. Whilst nationally the Tendency was notoriously reluctant to combine with other left groups, at the grass roots Trotskyists and non-Trotskyists worked closely together and with a sense of cameraderie, to defeat the right.

The polarised image of the Party, engendered by severe factional discord, formed a prism through which most activists viewed intra-party politics. Hence the deep resonance of Militant's claims that the attack upon it prefigured a broader onslaught on the left as a whole, and was actuated primarily by the right's determination to regain its lost hegemony. Most left-wingers in the CLPs willingly sank their differences with Militant in the common cause of repelling the right.[173] The unwillingness of the wider left to accept repeated assurances from Foot and Mortimer – both men with a left-wing past – that the assault on the Tendency would not envelop it too was itself testimony to the crisis of authority within the Party.

The deligimation of authority, by paralysing the centre's ability to exert normative control, seriously damaged its capacity to elicit obedience from Labour's rank and file. In calculating the costs, risks and benefits of more drastic and effective measures against Militant, Labour's leaders had to take account of the uproar and resistance within the constituencies, and the electorally grievous effects of yet more evidence of disunity within the Party. The game didn't seem worth the candle.

11.8 The aftermath

'Militant has won – game, set and match' groaned one right-winger.[171] In so far as the intention – as set down in the Haywood–Hughes Report – had been to eliminate the Trotskyist 'party within a party' it had not been fulfilled. The Tendency's major concern throughout had been to protect its organisation and its PPCs – and this had been realised. The 'inner-core' had survived. In the short term, at least, the Trotskyist group had positively benefited: the sales of the paper rose, its ranks swelled, and its prestige on the left burgeoned as it wore its martyr's crown with pride. The outcome of months of demoralising publicity had confirmed rather than dispelled the popular image of Labour as a strife-torn party rife with 'extremists', and Militant had emerged stronger than ever.

But the outcome was not one of unalloyed success for the Tendency. Its foes could claim some significant advances; the principle that the Trotskyist organisation was in contravention of the Constitution had been established. It had been proscribed and a workable definition of Militant membership had been agreed. Further these steps had been endorsed by very large majorities at Conference. It is easy to disparage this – Conference had long ceased to be the formidable force of earlier years. Nevertheless, Conference decisions *did* still weigh heavily with rank and file activists and trade unionists. As the cannier realised, the moral force of a Conference decision (amongst those least disposed to accept expulsions) paved the way for fresh action against Militant, when circumstances were more favourable. Game, set, perhaps, but not yet match.

Chapter Twelve

Militant and the revival of central authority

12.1 Transition 1983–1985

Labour's massacre at the polls in the 1983 general elections traumatised opinion throughout the Party. It contributed to a significant shift, both in the balance of forces within the Party and in the pattern of internal alignments. These effects, however, only gradually manifested themselves.

As was expected, Michael Foot's leadership did not survive the Party's defeat. The elimination of Tony Benn from the running (he lost his parliamentary seat) and the new method of electing the leader (the electoral college) gave Foot's protegé and close ally, Neil Kinnock, a head start over his only serious rival, Roy Hattersley. Strategically placed in the centre-left, Kinnock swept to an easy triumph.[1]

At the same Conference, the right lost its overall majority in the NEC, returning the balance, as in 1981–2, to the centre-left leadership loyalists whom Kinnock inherited from Foot. On Kinnock's prompting, this grouping generally aligned itself, on managerial issues, with the right. The consolidated centre-right bloc narrowly outnumbered the left and, via its possession of the key chairmanships, largely directed the Executive's handling of its managerial function.

In the aftermath of the 1983 general election there was one significant institutional change. In order to allow the Organisation Committee more time for organisational work, it was decided to set up an Appeals and Mediation Committee to take over from the Organisation Committee its responsibilities for hearing appeals and mediating disputes. It was composed of five members chosen from and elected by the Organisation Committee but was to report directly to the NEC. The first committee was dominated by the right: it comprised four right-wing trade unionists (Ken Cure, the Chairman, Neville Hough, Roy Evans and Alan Hadden) and one left-winger who had gravitated into the

Kinnock camp (Alex Kitson of the TGWU).[2] The following year a some-what more balanced committee was elected with sitting members Cure, Hadden and Hough – joined by left-wingers Eddie Haigh from the TGWU and Dennis Skinner[3], but with right retaining both the chair (Cure) and its majority.

In these years a tightening of Labour's managerial regime occurred. But the process was a slow, halting and uneven one. In the area of adjudication, there was a definite retreat from the left's approach earlier in the decade. Thus the Executive intimated its approval for stricter Group discipline. For example, in February 1985, it upheld the withdra-wal of the whip from five Coventry Councillors for abstaining on a motion to support the closure of a primary school.[4] And in a related dispute in Coventry North East CLP, the Executive interceded on behalf of the right in a deeply polarised constituency party.[5] In both cases, the Appeals and Mediation Committee's decision was only narrowly ratified by the NEC.[6] On another appeals case, the Committee recom-mendation was actually rejected. In Sunderland, five Councillors were deprived of the whip for voting against a Council plan to merge two primary schools. In this case the rebels also had the support of the District Labour Party which claimed that the Council was acting con-trary to election policy. Nevertheless, their appeals were dismissed.[7] This proved too much for the NEC to swallow and the Appeals and Mediation Committee minute was referred back.[8]

The right's efforts to restore an older adjudicatory approach were, then, only partially successful. This was not only because of the absence of a dependable majority. Circumstances at local level had also changed. The historical weakness of the left on Council Groups had been largely remedied, with left-wing administrations running several major authorities, including the GLC, Liverpool, Manchester, Sheffield, Edin-burgh and the majority of Labour-held London boroughs. Maintaining the authority of Group-based establishments ceased to be synonymous with perpetuating the right's local hegemony.

In two ways the NEC became somewhat more active in the field of parliamentary selection. Kinnock and the majority on the Executive wished to curtail the role of General Committees by introducing an (optional) system of one member one vote; but the issue was poorly handled and they were rebuffed by the 1984 Conference. Secondly, although the NEC's ability to intervene in selection contests was now limited by the rules to cases of procedural irregularities, this did leave some leeway and, in a number of instances, the Executive ordered re-runs or lesser changes, usually in constituencies about to select left-wing candidates. But in all cases, once the infringments had been rectified, the left candidates triumphed.[9]

Awareness of the centre-right bloc's very slim majority – and the

willingness of one or two centre-leftists occasionally to break ranks –
undoubtedly constrained the drive, spearheaded by the right-wing
chairmen of the Organisation and Appeals and Mediation Committees
(Charlie Turnock and Ken Cure) to revive a more stringent managerial
regime. At least as important, however, was the desire to conserve
energies for what was seen, both by the right and the new party leadership, as the key managerial issue, the continuing struggle against the
Militant Tendency.

12.2   Militant and the constituencies

The NEC, in 1983, had confined expulsions to the five members of
Militant's editorial board. But it had also proscribed the Militant Tendency, which meant that any person, proven to be a member of the
Tendency, was not eligible to remain within the Labour Party. The NEC
majority was content, for the moment, to bide its time. But any constituency party was free – or, taking a more legalistic view, required – to
expel any amongst its number whose membership of Militant could be
established. Shortly after the general election, a trickle of expulsions
began, commencing in Blackburn. A member of the constituency party,
Michael Gregory had involved himself in the local branch of the Tendency, taking copious notes of all the meetings he had attended. He then
presented these to the constituency as evidence of the existence of a
Militant branch. The party decided to expel six people identified by
Gregory as Militant members.

Gregory subsequently embarrassed the Blackburn party by defecting
to the Liberals. Though denounced as right-wing witch-hunters, the
party in fact had left-wing sympathies;[10] this was an important straw in
the wind. The six appealed but their expulsions were confirmed, though
by a narrow majority.[11] This started the ball rolling. Two members of
Militant's central committee, Bill Hopwood and Bill Mullins, were
expelled by Newcastle East and Warley West CLP's.[12] Further casualties followed in Rhondda, Sheffield Attercliffe, Mansfield and New-
castle-Under-Lyme; and by the autumn of 1985 expulsions were in the
pipeline in several other constituency parties.[13]

But although the anti-Militant bloc on the NEC commanded a majority, it was only a narrow and somewhat shaky one; the left voted solidly
against expulsions and were occasionally joined by one or two
centrists.[14]

Militant itself appeared not to be making as much progress as
expected. It held high hopes of boosting its contingent of two MPs at the
next election. But in a series of sometimes closely fought contests, its
candidates were spurned. These included the one-time Militant preserve of Brighton Kemptown; and Derbyshire North East where for the

first time since the war the NUM's sponsored candidate – who sported a Militant label – was rejected.[15] Nevertheless, the Tendency remained entrenched in its major stronghold, Liverpool.

12.3 Kinnock strikes

Kinnock had for years been bitterly hostile to Militant. In 1982–3, he had voted for the expulsion of the editorial board and, during the leadership election contest, hinted that further action might be necessary.[16] However, for the first two years of his leadership, he had avoided a frontal attack. Other matters were far more pressing – revamping the Party's organisation, working for a successful outcome in the ballots trade unions were obliged by Tory legislation to hold to retain their political funds, responding to the miners' strike and securing agreement on controversial policy issues like defence and the economy.

Nevertheless, the question of Militant was not ignored. During this period, Kinnock and the NEC pursued a strategy of graduated pressure. This consisted of four key elements. Firstly, a determined effort was made to prevent the adoption of Militant parliamentary candidates, outside its Merseyside heartland. The string of defeats inflicted upon the Trotskyist organisation reflected not only rising anti-Militant sentiment; it was also a product of organised lobbying from the centre. In such places as Gateshead East and two Glasgow constituencies, contacts were made with trade union officials and other local notables urging them to mobilise their forces (by taking up union delegations to the full, ensuring that all delegates attended the Selection Conference etc.) and concert their tactics (e.g. by tactical voting, agreeing to back the best-placed non-Militant) to block the adoption of Tendency candidates.

Secondly, the NEC took steps to deny official facilities to Militant front organisations (e.g. Further Education Labour Students) which had been set up to penetrate the Party further. Thirdly, although the Tendency was too deeply implanted in Labour's youth organisation for it to be uprooted, attempts were made to curb its influence by cutting the LPYS's budget and subjecting it to somewhat closer scrutiny. Finally, Militant's jewel in the crown, Liverpool, was not entirely neglected. The leadership recognised that, politically and ideologically, the city was dominated by the Tendency; its primary aim, therefore, was not to supplant it but to encourage and sustain the morale of elements (like the local branches of NUPE and the Black Caucus) opposed to it.

The Party enjoyed some success in halting Militant's advance on the parliamentary selection front; otherwise the strategy of graduated pressure made no notable impression upon its power, particularly in Liverpool. Then, in the autumn of 1985, Kinnock changed tack and decided to use his speech at the Party Conference to invest Militant's Merseyside citadel. This was primarily in response to the Militant-run City Council's own clumsy tactics. Firstly, its decision to levy a 9% rate, far less than was required to fund its expenditure programme, indicated that it was set upon a course of confrontation with the Government which the leadership felt Liverpool could not win and would damage the Party nationally. Secondly, and more importantly, in September the Council committed a serious error. It decided, as a tactical ploy, to issue redundancy notices to all Council employees; this was designed to pile up the pressure on the Government. Nobody, Liverpool's leaders insisted, would actually lose their jobs. But the bulk of employees were not convinced and, indeed, whatever happened to their jobs, many stood to lose legal safeguards with the break in employment. The once-solid front of union support for the Council splintered and the municipal employees' Joint Shop Stewards Committee disintegrated. Many union leaders were furious with Militant whose tactics seemed to be imperilling the very jobs they were designed to save. Kinnock grasped his opportunity.

For much of his Conference speech, the leader sounded a radical note and was warmly applauded by delegates. He then, suddenly, turned on Militant and its 'implausible promises'. 'I'll tell you', he declaimed 'what happens with impossible promises. You start with far-fetched resolutions. They are then pickled into a rigid dogma, a code, and you go through the years sticking to that, outdated, misplaced, irrelevant to the real needs and you end' – this to a rising crescendo of cheers and abuse in the auditorium – 'in the grotesque chaos of a Labour Council hiring taxis to scuttle round a city handing out redundancy notices to its own workers'.[17]

It was one of the most dramatic moments of any Labour Party Conference. Eric Heffer ostentatiously stalked off the platform. David Blunkett 'stood up to try and calm the ruinous bedlam. Hundreds of people were on their feet, shouting . . .'[18]

Kinnock's speech was a watershed. He had thrown down his gauntlet. Why? His long-range objective had always been to emasculate Militant as a significant political force. Its own errors, especially alienating the local unions by issuing the redundancy notices, had rendered it vulnerable. Kinnock was determined to press his advantage home. But, secondly, the attack on Militant had a more general purpose – to allay the fears (which opinion surveys suggested had cost the Party dear in 1983) that Labour was too left-wing. Kinnock wanted to demonstrate that the Party would have no truck with 'extremists'. His assault was part of a broader strategy – to reassure frightened electors by refurbishing Labour's image as a responsible and pragmatic party; this entailed, in Hugo Young's words, erasing 'as far as he possibly can all hard left tendencies from the visible profile of the Labour Party'.[19]

Labour's electoral problems were compounded by a widespread perception of a weak and ineffectual leadership incapable of bringing order and discipline to a strife-torn Party. Here Kinnock employed the method used from time to time by his predecessors to demonstrate leadership prowess: a willingness to stand up, without flinching, to 'the left'. In other words, he used the issue of Militant to impress his authority upon the Party and to project to the electorate the image of a tough, but responsible leader. 'At last', one veteran Labour MP was reported as enthusing, 'we have a leader who leads from the front'.[20] Kinnock's speech was enthusiastically acclaimed by the media and the Party's ratings in the polls promptly rose (though – this was less noticed – they soon subsided again).

Enthusiastic coverage from the media was predictable. What was less so and, hence, more impressive, was the response of Conference itself. Kinnock won an 'ecstatic ovation'.[21] It was estimated that half to two-thirds of the (predominantly left-wing) constituency delegates applauded.[22] Whilst the hard left was shocked and angered, there was no doubt Kinnock's polemic struck a chord amongst the delegates, particularly but not solely from the unions. 'You could feel', one trade union leader declared, 'the emotional release across the hall'.[23] To understand why, we must turn to the major shifts occurring in Labour's internal pattern of alignments.

12.4 The re-alignment of the left

The period of the late 1970s and early 1980s was one of unusual and extreme polarisation within the Party.[24] But, after 1983, the broad Bennite coalition began to fragment. There had always been tensions within that coalition.[25] By late 1984 they had become both more public and more pronounced; for example, a widely publicised front page article by *Tribune's* new editor (and former close Benn aide) Nigel Williamson, pleaded for maximum unity, behind the existing leader, in the Party and condemned as 'irresponsible' the proposal mooted by Benn for a general strike over the coal dispute.[26]

All this provoked much speculation about 'the re-alignment of the left' and by 1985 a distinct new 'soft left' current had emerged clustered around the LCC, the more left-wing Tribunite MPs, the weekly *Tribune*, and prominent local government radicals, like David Blunkett, leader of Sheffield City Council. It included several former leading Bennites, including close advisers and lieutenants like Michael Meacher, Frances Morell (head of ILEA) and Ken Coates.[27]

A complex of issues separated the soft and hard left (grouped around the new Campaign Group of MPs, the Benn–Heffer–Skinner nexus on the NEC, CLPD and Militant's smaller Trotskyist rivals like Socialist Organiser and Socialist Action). Underlying the growing strains between the two were significant differences in social and political analysis,[28] but the most conspicious (and, for our purposes relevant) disagreements were over strategy and tactics. The soft left was profoundly shaken by the electoral trauma of 1983. They drew the lesson that the Party 'needs unity and cannot afford another period of extreme polarisation'.[29] Labour, the argument ran, could only survive as a credible electoral force if it remained a broad coalition encompassing right as well as left. This implied reaching a modus vivendi with the right, a willingness to debate and settle differences in a sober and restrained manner.

A second, though interlinked, point of disagreement between the two left's was over attitudes to the Kinnock leadership. Though often critical of Kinnock, for example over his handling of the miners' strike, his lack of sympathy for left-wing Councils in their struggle with the Government and his tendency to slide away from more radical policies, the soft left nevertheless were convinced that outright opposition was both tactically misplaced and electorally suicidal. 'We can't win', Ken Livingstone told the traditional *Tribune* rally at the 1985 Conference 'by denouncing Neil Kinnock'.[30] Thus, unlike the hard left, the soft left were keen to engage in a constructive dialogue with the leadership, to promote more radical policies by participation rather than opposition. Finally, many former Bennites were increasingly disenchanted by the negative and unrealistic stance taken by their one-time allies on the hard left: the Benn–Skinner call for a general strike to help the miners in late 1984 was an important catalyst in that it confirmed the feeling that the hard left were losing their grip on political realities. This growing rift between the two sections of the left spelt the end of the extreme polarisation – with its corresponding 'wing solidarity' – which had characterised internal party alignments in the early 1980s.

The soft left's approach had considerable resonance in the constituencies. Though many, especially in London, remained strongholds of the hard left, the deep yearning for unity, the desperate desire to avoid any repetition of the fratricidal and electorally debilitating conflicts of the past few years encouraged a perceptible mood towards a soft left perspective. Two other factors operated in the same direction. Firstly, activists became increasingly aware that the chasm of entrenched hostility and mistrust that had separated the rank and file and the leadership in recent years impaired Labour's capacity for collective action and harmed it in the public eye. Secondly, the new system of electing the leader and deputy leader strengthened authority within the Party by contributing to its relegitimation. Unlike his predecessors, Kinnock could demand loyalty from the Party as a whole because all sections –

not just the PLP – had voted for him. A system designed to extend democracy by widening the franchise also created the conditions for the rehabilitation of authority by vesting the leader with a stronger democratic mandate. In a way foreseen by few the constitutional reforms of the 1980s assisted the building of a new procedural consensus.

These shifts in constituency opinion both reflected and reinforced deeper changes in membership outlook. The purposive-minded activists, who had seen Labour solely as a *vehicle* for the attainment of certain goals or ideals – and had usually found it wanting – and not as a value in itself, now came to realise that its broader electoral appeal was a precondition for the realisation of their hopes. And, at the same time, as their years of Party membership lengthened, many became socialised into its norms and conventions, and imbued with a greater feel for its traditions. These two processes engendered within a widening circle of activists a sense of attachment and loyalty to the Party as an institution, a value in its own right. In short, these years witnessed a rebirth, amongst a new generation of activists, of the 'party patriotism' of earlier decades.[31]

Constituency activists became less opposition-minded, but they were by no means transformed into uncritical admirers. The hard left retained large pools of support, but for growing numbers the soft-left stance of constructive dialogue struck the right note. This shift of opinion was manifested and symbolised by the catapulting of David Blunkett into top slot on the constituency section of the NEC in 1985, displacing Tony Benn from a position he held for more than a decade.

A notable feature of the soft left outlook was a mounting antagonism towards Militant. But this did not automatically translate into support for expulsions. Attitudes in the soft left were divided and ambivalent. Many acclaimed Kinnock's lashing of Militant's revolutionary posturing and arid dogma but were unsettled by his failure to acknowledge the desperate financial predicament of poverty-stricken Liverpool. No-one felt this more deeply than the new hero of the constituencies, David Blunkett.

Blunkett's olive branch
Blunkett was dismayed by the Leader's onslaught on Militant 'shaking with sadness', according to one witness.[32] Kinnock, in his view, had displayed scant understanding of Liverpool's plight and failed to appreciate the genuine popularity which the Council's combative stance towards an implacable Government aroused within the city party. Fearing also that Kinnock's bellicose words prefigured a new wave of expulsions, he seized the initiative and offered Liverpool's leaders an olive branch. He urged them to accept a proposal, already mooted, for the General Secretaries of the eight unions representing the city's

municipal workforce to undertake an independent inquiry into Liverpool's finances and seek an acceptable solution.[33] The Liverpool leadership readily accepted the offer, disarming many of their critics. Kinnock was angry that Blunkett had let Liverpool's Militants off the hook; but the outcome of the Sheffield leader's attempt at conciliation was to be very different from that anticipated.

Arising out of this initiative, a team of four local government financial experts, led by a former top GLC official, Maurice Stonefrost, was invited by the Party and the eight General Secretaries to submit proposals to alleviate Liverpool's budgetary crisis. The report was completed by the end of October. It recommended a series of measures, including some rent and rate increases, a freeze on recruitment, the use of creative accounting techniques and a partial use of capital funds for housing repairs (capitalisation) which would reduce Government grant penalties. As part of a broader package, the Labour controlled Association of Municipal Authorities (AMA) pledged financial assistance if Liverpool balanced its books.

Intensive negotiations then took place between the Liverpool Council and both the General Secretaries group and the AMA. In a series of meetings, the trade union team, which included John Edmonds, the General Secretary-elect of GMBATU, Ron Todd, of the TGWU, and Rodney Bickerstaffe of NUPE, urged Liverpool to accept a settlement on the basis of the Stonefrost proposals. However, the Liverpool representatives, headed by Militant deputy leader Derek Hatton, Tony Byrne, Chairman of the Finance Committee, and a close ally of Militant, and Tony Mulhearn, Militant Chairman of the district party, were in an uncompromising mood. The proposals were 'absolute nonsense' Byrne declared.[34] It soon became evident that Liverpool's Militant leadership was not interested in a negotiated outcome, preferring a strategy of confrontation which, they argued, would squeeze further concessions from the Government.[35] The trade union barons were further alienated by the Liverpool team's abrasive and, at times, abusive manner. Eventually, talks with both the trade unionists and the AMA broke down in bitterness and recrimination; John Edmonds, who had maintained a cool demeanour throughout the stormy talks, exclaimed afterwards that he wanted 'Hatton's head on a platter'.[36]

A collapse in Liverpool's finances, a confrontation with the Government and mass redundancies all seemed inevitable. Then the Council suddenly backed down. It was now clear that Liverpool's leadership could no longer rely upon the continued allegience of the local branches of the two unions which had most firmly supported it in the past, the GMBATU and the TGWU. There seemed no option but to retreat. The City's Militant leaders castigated both trade union and Party leaders for their betrayal and then, out of its bag, the Council suddenly plucked the Swiss deal.

The deal, which temporarily resolved the crisis, was in fact not dissimilar to the Stonefrost offer.[37] Two facts incensed the unions: firstly, Liverpool was prepared to accept from Swiss bankers proposals which it contemptuously rejected when offered by the Labour Movement. Secondly, as soon became apparent, the deal had largely been negotiated months before, and held in reserve, yet no mention was ever made of it in the Stonefrost talks.

The furious trade union leaders felt they had been conned,[38] as, too, did Blunkett, who now gave up the role of peace-maker. After consulting Kinnock, the General Secretaries of the TGWU and GMBATU, Ron Todd and David Basnett, wrote to the NEC requesting an enquiry into Liverpool Labour Party.

12.5 The Liverpool investigation

Perhaps carried away by bravado and their own rhetoric, or overestimating their strength, Liverpool's Militant leaders had played into the hands of their enemies. Kinnock's rousing attacks on the Tendency had remained on the verbal level; now the opportunity arose to act. At the November NEC, in response to the General Secretaries' request, two prominent soft-leftists, Tom Sawyer and David Blunkett, proposed an investigation into 'the procedures and practices' of the Liverpool Labour Party. This was agreed by the surprisingly wide margin of twenty-one votes to five.[39]

An eight-person Committee of enquiry was set up. This was neatly balanced with four right-wingers (Charlie Turnock, who chaired it, Betty Boothroyd, Tony Clarke and Neville Hough) and four left-wingers (Margaret Beckett, Eddie Haigh, Tom Sawyer and Audrey Wise). It was to be serviced by the recently appointed General Secretary, Larry Whitty.

The Report took much longer than intended to compile. Large numbers of Party members were interviewed and a considerable body of evidence, of varying quality, submitted. The Report was presented to the NEC at the end of February, signed by six members; the remaining two, Margaret Beckett and Audrey Wise, prepared their own Minority Report.

The Majority Report claimed to have unearthed 'very serious and deep-seated problems about the functioning and practices of the District Labour Party and the Party generally in Liverpool'.[40] Breaches and abuses of the rules, it asserted, had 'severely damaged' the Party's reputation.[41] In line with its terms of reference, the Report devoted most of its attention to the working of the DLP. It identified a whole series of irregularities in the system of affiliation, the composition and

voting procedures of the district party. It criticised the DLP for inter-
fering in, indeed effectively directing, the day-to-day management of the
Council, including industrial relations and personnel issues, hence
encroaching upon the proper sphere of the Group.

The Minority Report largely concurred in identifying these irregularities, but pointed out that they were not particularly exceptional and
certainly did not justify disciplinary measures. The Majority Report,
however, diagnosed something far more serious: not haphazard abuses
of the rules, but a classic case of entryism, where an outside body, with
its own command structure and internal disciplinary system, had
secured effective control of the Liverpool Party, which it sustained by a
combination of rigorous organisation, patronage and intimidation.[42]

Thus the investigation uncovered a process of (to use a term coined by
Trotsky in his pre-Bolshevik days) 'substitutionism' – the progressive
displacement of democracy by oligarchical forms of party organisation.
The DLP arrogated to itself functions which properly belonged to the
Group; but, although formally sovereign, the DLP itself was effectively
subordinated to the district party Executive. Executive control was
sustained by a variety of techniques. Firstly the use of 'aggregate' meetings to which all Party members were invited but where, in practice,
those on the grapevine were given privileged access; these meetings
effectively supplanted normal, properly constituted, meetings of the
DLP and made, or endorsed, key decisions during the budget dispute.
Further, district meetings were 'totally dominated by the Executive
Report'.[43] The DLP itself was provided with inadequate information,
and its agenda and proceedings were shaped by the Executive. The
Executive, in contrast, met frequently and was well-briefed; its capacity
to control the unwieldy poorly informed district party, combined with
the latter's status as the key policy-making body, enabled it to accumulate 'immense power'.[44] Finally, the supremacy of the ruling group was
strengthened yet further by a 'general air of intimidation' including, in
its more extreme manifestations, the threat and, occasionally, actually
resort to physical violence.[45]

The power of the Executive was not confined to the DLP but extended
far more broadly: its senior members occupied key positions in the
unions and in the Council. But the Executive itself was not the ultimate
source of power; it, in turn, was the Report concluded, 'largely dominated by the organisation of the Militant Tendency' which 'although it
is secret, is widespread and determined a line to be taken on the agendas
of all Party bodies in Liverpool.'[46]

The Report's recommendations fell into two categories. Firstly it
suggested reforms in the rules, standing orders and operation of the
Liverpool party and the appointment of two full-time organisers for at
least two to three years to aid this process. Secondly, it proposed that the

General Secretary should, in light of the evidence, prefer charges against persons alleged to be responsible for abuses and breaches of the Party Constitution and Rules, and against those alleged to be involved in Militant and, hence, ineligible for Party membership. The signatories to the Report differed over how many should be charged. Ten names were agreed: Tony Mulhearn (chair of the DLP), Terry Harrison (Vice Chair, DLP), Felicity Dowling (Secretary, DLP), Josie and Tony Aitman, Derek Hatton, Richard Knights, Ian Lowes, Cheryl Varley and Richard Venton. The four right-wing members of the investigating team added the following six: Paul Astbury, Roger Bannister, Carol Darby, Pauline Dunlop, Sylvia Sharpey-Schafer and Harry Smith.[47]

There is no doubt that the experience of the investigation had a profound effect upon those members of the team (Sawyer and Haigh) who, although critical of Militant had previously opposed expulsions. They (and others on the Executive, like Blunkett) were perturbed not only by what the Report described but also by matters merely alluded to (because they lay outside the investigation's remit). Foremost amongst these – and constituting the hidden agenda of the Enquiry – were the emerging details of Militant's municipal machine.

As the enquiry team dug deeper, it became evident that grafted upon the Tendency's democratic centralist organisation was a Tammany Hall or Cook County system of municipal patronage. At the centre lay Derek Hatton, formally deputy leader of the Council but, in practice, far more powerful than the popular but ineffectual official leader, John Hamilton. Hatton was also Chairman of the Council's Personnel Committee responsible for hiring and promotion within the Town hall (the Committee had a majority of Militant supporters).[48] Hatton worked closely with Tony Byrne, Chairman of the Finance Committee. Byrne, a non-Militant, had enjoyed a rapid rise to prominence within the Liverpool Labour Party, due to his energy and his unrivalled grasp of complex financial matters. He was a man with a single passion in life – the implementation of an ambitious programme of Council house construction (known as the Urban Regeneration Strategy). Militant was willing to make this programme the centre-piece of its policy for Liverpool, so Byrne became an eager ally. Partly because of the city's financial crisis, Byrne ensured that he personally must approve all expenditure decisions. As a result, he became a key figure in the patronage network: whilst Hatton controlled the personnel function, Byrne held the purse-strings.

The patronage system operated via two main channels. The first was the creation and staffing, largely with Militant supporters, of new functional campaign units (the Campaign or Central Support Unit and the more shadowy so-called 'A-Team').

The second major patronage channel lay through control over access to Town Hall manual employment – extremely important in a city where most other sources of work were fast disappearing. In January 1985, GMBATU, the largest local authority manual union, was granted 100% 'nomination rights' (i.e. the right to nominate applicants for Council jobs). This was extremely useful since the two largest GMBATU branches were under Militant control. (The Convenor of the biggest branch, number five, was Ian Lowes, a key figure in Militant's Liverpool hierarchy.)[49]

GMBATU was a keystone in the Tendency's Mersey machine. It supplied the largest single contingent of delegates to the DLP (combined with the TGWU, where Militant influence was also strong, it outnumbered the total of all CLP and branch delegates) and, through its 100% nomination rights, was crucial to Militant's patronage network in the Town Hall. It was here that the resemblance with American style city machines was most striking. GMBATU rapidly obtained the status of a 'Sweetheart' union, and was awarded preferential treatment in both personnel and industrial relations matters. It soon became apparent that membership of Militant gave anyone seeking jobs an edge in a work-starved city.[50] This was a deliberate policy – to give an ever-widening circle of municipal employees a vested interest in Militant's continued supremacy.

But the single most controversial feature of Militant's Liverpool machine lay outside these two channels: the Council's Static Security Force (SSF). Its original role was innocuous enough, to provide security for municipal buildings. This altered under Hatton's guidance. The force both grew in size and diversified in roles. Uniformed members attended meetings of the DLP, usually sitting near known opponents of Militant and, in at least one case, helping to eject a DLP member from the meeting.[51] Reports about the use of the SSF to police Party meetings, and evidence that this was part of a wider pattern of intimidation contributed, more than any other single factor, to the estrangement of the soft left and large numbers of constituency activists throughout the country from Militant.

12.6   The anti-Militant offensive

In February 1986, after a long and heated debate, the NEC approved the Report by 19 votes to 10. It was agreed to suspend Liverpool DLP, which was replaced by a Temporary Co-ordinating Committee; and the General Secretary was instructed to consider evidence and then formulate charges against the sixteen named individuals.[52]

The new drive against Militant and the stern action taken against Liverpool DLP delighted the right. They had long hankered after a restoration of the sterner managerial regime of the 1950s. 'Those of us',

Hattersley declared, 'who believe that socialism actually stands for something that can be defined naturally insist that it must be defended against both external aggression and internal subversion'.[53] The stance of the hard left was equally unequivocal. Led, on the NEC, by the Benn–Heffer–Skinner triumvirate, and outside by a variety of ginger groups, including the Campaign Group of MPs and CLPD,[54] the hard left were immovably opposed to any expulsions. They were often depicted in the media as sympathisers, even fellow-travellers of Militant. This (with one or two exceptions) was unfair. Few on the hard left (including smaller Trotskyists groups like Socialist Organiser and Socialist Action) felt much sympathy with the Tendency; indeed it was fashionable to condemn its 'reactionary' views on race and gender.[55] The non-Trotskyist hard left opposed disciplinary action on principle; but they also interpreted the revival of the campaign against Militant as one prong of the leadership's drive to wrench Labour to the right. The Party's radical policies on nationalisation, planning and the EEC were already being cast overboard. The proposed purge of Militant was, the hard left alleged, designed to placate a hostile press and to isolate and discredit the left; furthermore, its effect was to distract attention from the real struggle against the Tories and the Alliance.[56]

The hard left also deeply resented the attacks on Liverpool's leadership. It was, they claimed, the one Council with the guts to stand up to the Government. This was the theme of Liverpool MP Eric Heffer's repeated and vehement volleys against the leadership. 'Attacks were being made', the MP for Walton complained, 'on good Labour people who believe in socialist priorities . . . and whose only crime is to want to fight the Labour Party's political enemies.'[57] Of all the arguments against 'the Liverpool witch-hunt' this was the one that made the deepest impression on constituency opinion. Placed in the context of the appalling difficulties the new Labour Council had inherited – massive unemployment, some of the worst housing conditions in Western Europe, urban blight and totally inadequate financial resources – coupled with an intransigent Government unwilling to listen to the reasoned and convincing arguments of city officials,[58] its obdurate stance was at least intelligible. Heffer's argument was particularly poignant for, throughout 1986, 47 Liverpool Councillors (Militant and non-Militant) were threatened with almost certain surcharge, disqualification and bankruptcy, for voting for an illegal budget.

Finally, the hard left (and, indeed, others) feared that expulsions of Liverpool's Militant leaders presaged a wider purge. Already significant numbers of Militant adherents were being expelled by constituency parties. It was, Eric Heffer charged, 'reminiscent of the days of Gaitskell and Sara Barker'.[59]

Between the right and the hard left stood two main currents of opinion: the Kinnock loyalists and the soft left. Kinnock's antipathy towards Militant was considerably stronger than his predecessor's; indeed it verged on the obsessional 'living, eating, sleeping Militant'.[60] Even before succeeding to the leadership he had stated forcefully that 'a democratic socialist party wishing to safeguard its organisational integrity and ideological distinctiveness will have to take organisational steps'. He added that 'if we are a political party and not a skittles club, then we eventually have to draw a perimeter of membership and of our ideology'.[61] However, he was conscious (as the right often were not) of the danger of posing the issue in starkly ideological terms – it merely confirmed Militant's claims that it was being persecuted for its views. Further he was well aware (unlike his deputy) that 'there is formally nothing in the Party Constitution or in the conventions of the Party which actually denies membership to people simply because they hold particular opinions'.[62]

It is important here to distinguish between the *motives* of Militant's enemies, and the *grounds* upon which its members could be expelled. There is little doubt that many of those who favoured disciplinary action did so for ideological and political reasons, but, for constitutional reasons, the offensive against Militant could only be framed in more limited, organisational terms. Ideally, Kinnock would have liked to completely eradicate Militant 'a maggot in the body of the Labour Party'. But, for the time being at least, he was prepared to settle for lesser measures: the expulsion of Hatton, Mulhearn and other senior Liverpool Militants, and the disbanding of Liverpool DLP, whilst backing action taken elsewhere by constituency parties.

The soft left

The combination of the right and Kinnock loyalists was sufficiently powerful to furnish a majority for fresh disciplinary action in both the NEC and Conference. But the majority within the NEC would be tissue-thin, and whilst the trade union bloc votes could – as it had in the past – bulldozer the constituencies, stiff rank and file resistance could plunge the Party into another bout of electorally debilitating strife. The right might have been willing to take the risk, but Kinnock was not.

In the early 1980s, the Party's procedures for resolving conflicts and reaching authoritative and binding decisions had broken down, and the Party slipped into near-chaos. Kinnock was determined to avoid a repetition. A prime consideration in any decision on a controversial matter was that it must be made to stick. Decisions taken in the teeth of stiff opposition from important sections of the Party would be an invitation to perpetual strife. The safest way to avoid this was to ensure that they were approved by substantial margins on the NEC and overwhelming ones at Conference. This meant that the backing of the soft left was indispensable.

Although there were, in early 1986, only four soft leftists on the Executive (Blunkett, Meacher, Tom Sawyer of NUPE, Eddie Haigh of the TGWU), this current of opinion was highly influential amongst the trade unions (including two of the four largest unions, the TGWU and NUPE); and Blunkett's recent triumph suggested strong support amongst the constituencies (although this was less certain). With the soft left firmly placed in the anti-Militant coalition, resistance would be enfeebled. And this is precisely what happened. In 1983, one and a half million had opposed expulsions; by 1986 this had shrunk to less than 400,000. The sheer size of the majority made it much more difficult to dispute the expulsions. The soft left had been converted to disciplinary action against Militant. Why?

One can identify three main factors. The first was the belief that the Liverpool investigation had revealed such gross abuses that disciplinary action was the only appropriate remedy. These abuses took two forms. The first was breaches of the rules. The soft left accepted that the enquiry team had unearthed compelling evidence of systematic and orchestrated manipulation of the rules, inspired by Liverpool's Militant leadership. To reject disciplinary action *on principle*, as did the hard left on the NEC, struck their soft left colleagues as a complete abdication of their duty to safeguard the rules.[63] But it was not so much abuses of the rules but abuses of the basic morality of the Party which really offended the soft left. If socialism was about fellowship, abjuring violence, respect for other human beings and democratic decision-making, then it seemed reasonable to expect that such norms should govern relations amongst socialists. The methods employed by Militant in Liverpool – intimidation of opponents, the use of the SSF to police Party meetings, actual physical violence, 'unacceptable and obscene employment practices'[64] were, in David Blunkett's words, 'outside the acceptable parameters of behaviour for democratic socialists'.[65] It was this sense of revulsion which provoked Tom Sawyer's furious attack at NUPE's 1986 Conference. 'In an atmosphere of intimidation fuelled by parading Council security guards and hundreds of non-delegates, NUPE representatives were threatened and intimidated because they would not toe the Militant line. Some of the things I saw as a member of the Liverpool inquiry have more in common with the extreme right in European politics than with the left.'[66]

The second factor primarily concerned NUPE, a key element within the soft left and the only major union to have opposed the establishment of the Register and the expulsion of Militant's editorial board – in fact, it had provided about a third of the votes cast against these decisions. A reversal of NUPE's position would be a powerful boost for the anti-Militant camp. In 1983, its Deputy General Secretary, Tom Sawyer, in an article calling for a reinstatement of the editorial board, had declared 'We cannot stand back and watch a purge; it has to be stopped.'[67] He correctly predicted future expulsions – but did not anticipate that he would support them. Sawyer's *volte face* reflected that of his union. The first shift in its position had in fact occurred at its 1985 Conference (in May). The delegates approved a motion, proposed by Jane Kennedy, Secretary of NUPE's largest branch in Liverpool which declared that, as Militant was in contravention of Clause II of Labour's constitution, its adherents were ineligible to be members of the Party and, for good measure, denounced the Tendency's 'disgraceful and divisive methods'. Sawyer, on behalf of the union's executive committee, supported the motion but with the notable proviso that the executive committee considered the appropriate way to handle Militant was by 'debate and argument' and not by 'witch-hunts and expulsions'.[68] By the end of the year the proviso had been dropped and the 1986 NUPE Conference, by an overwhelming majority, supported disciplinary action against Militant[69] (a position taken by other soft left unions like the Transport Workers and the NUR).

NUPE was influenced by the range of motives common to the soft left as a whole. But a crucial additional factor was the treatment of its own members in Liverpool. This was a direct consequence of Militant's patronage system and, in particular, the privileged status accorded to GMBATU. NUPE's Head Office received a stream of reports from its Liverpool branches complaining about discrimination over both individual employment prospects and collective bargaining rights.[70] Top NUPE officials like Bickerstaffe and Sawyer had been gravely disturbed by Liverpool's redundancy tactic and by its obduracy during the Stonefrost talks. Mounting evidence that the union's industrial role, its ability to defend the rights of its members, was being undermined by Militant's tactics, convinced them that action was essential.[71]

The third factor was a shift in the managerial perspective of the soft left unions as a whole. As we have seen, a major cause of the loss of managerial control in the 1970s was the emergence of a strong block of left-wing unions unwilling to allow the NEC to be used as a protective shield of the Parliamentary leadership. After 1981, Foot had succeeded in reconstituting a loyalist majority on the Executive, which Kinnock inherited on his assumption to the leadership. By 1986 the restoration of a strong managerial centre had proceeded so far that Tony Benn rather acidly commented that 'the composition of the present NEC reminds one strongly of the late fifties, when Hugh Gaitskell enjoyed the protection and support of the praetorian guard of right-wing trade union leaders who used their block votes, at conference, to isolate and defeat the left'.[72] In one sense, this claim was correct. By 1986, the work, begun several years earlier by John Golding, of constructing a solid bloc of leadership loyalists encompassing virtually all trade union members of the Executive had been completed.[73] However, Benn's observation is misleading in a number of respects.

Firstly, the loyalistic bloc was not politically monolithic; it included centrists like Alex Kitson and soft-leftists like Haigh and Sawyer as well as right-wingers. Secondly, unlike the Praetorian Guard in the Bevanite period, its prime inspiration was not factional – to crush the left – but electoral; the carnage at the polls in 1983 had shaken the unions no less than the constituencies. Furthermore, they were in the front line of Thatcherism's counter-revolution; the public sector unions (including NUPE) had been particularly badly mauled and were desperate for the return of a Labour Government.

The priority given to Labour's electoral recovery predisposed the left wing unions to look more sympathetically upon Kinnock's efforts to reassert his authority. The image of a weak, vacillating leader, lacking a firm grip on his party – so the experience of Michael Foot suggested – was electorally damaging. This predisposition was reinforced by the introduction of the electoral college. The widening of the franchise to embrace the unions (who cast 40% of the votes) and the constituencies strengthened the legitimacy of the leader and rendered the unions – particularly those on the soft left who had voted for him – more attentive to his views than they might otherwise have been.[74]

Kinnock, in turn, devoted considerable attention to wooing senior left-wing trade unionists. But he could have had few illusions about a 'Praetorian Guard'. The failure of his efforts to alter the procedure for parliamentary selection demonstrated that the soft left's loyalism had its limits.[75] The leader had to work hard to construct a majority. Nevertheless, left-wing union leaders *were* increasingly loath to act in ways that might publicly injure the standing and authority of the leader and, hence, the Party. Kinnock had committed his prestige to a renewed campaign against Militant; the trade union left, with almost complete unanimity, were prepared to see him through.

The soft left were agreed that Liverpool Militants found guilty of malpractices and breaches of the rules should be punished. There were, however, differences over the second charge, membership of a proscribed organisation, which carried the automatic penalty of expulsion. Some soft leftists, like Blunkett, were reluctant to back disciplinary action on these grounds. If sanctions were confined to the first charge, then clear boundaries could be laid; if they encompassed Militant membership it would be more difficult to contain the spread of disciplinary action. Blunkett feared that, unless the right's disciplinary instincts were curbed, they would 'suck a broad swathe of the Party into a very authoritarian and rigid mould'.[76]

Others on the soft left, however, did not share these doubts. Because of the experience of social-democratic centralism the left had, in the past, been reluctant to confront the question of entryism as pursued by democratic centralist organisations (pre-eminently, of course, by Militant). By 1986, many on the soft left were prepared to address themselves to it. Sawyer, for example, as a result of his experience on the inquiry team became convinced that the root of the problem in Liverpool was entryism 'the existence of a separate party, Militant, organising deeply and extensively within the Labour Party'.[77] Militant, the NUR's soft-left leader, Jimmy Knapp, declared, was 'a parasite' driven by its very nature to 'the systematic abuse and manipulation of . . . the Labour Party's rules and constitution'.[78] The real objection to Militant was not its separate programme or network of branches – features which it shared with a range of Party pressure groups – but its concealed democratic centralist and entryist character. The ultimate loyalty of members of pressure groups (like CLPD, the LCC or Labour Solidarity) was to the Party itself; that of Militant's adherents, bound by its own, rigid organisational discipline was to Militant. Could any party, however tolerant, sensibly continue to harbour within its ranks a body committed to its own destruction?

The traditional left-wing response to Trotskyism was to assert that its influence could best be combatted by discussion: good ideas would drive out bad. The hard left continued to take this position. The majority of soft leftists, including its trade union adherents, the LCC and *Tribune*, dissented. The roots of Militant's strength in Liverpool lay not in its ideas but in its organisation – its secretive, tightly-disciplined machine staffed, in Merseyside alone, by more full-timers than the Party could muster in the whole of Northern England, now fortified by its web of Town Hall patronage. 'It operated', Sawyer declared 'at every level of the party, through a very strong, independent organisation, and there's no way that argument and debate is going to deal with an organisation of that strength in Liverpool'.[79]

12.8 Discipline and natural justice – again

In March 1986, the sixteen Liverpool Militants were formally charged with offences against Party rules. They immediately responded – as Militant had previously done in 1982 – by recourse to the courts. They applied to the High Court for an injunction restraining the NEC from proceeding with the hearing unless it met four conditions: that they be given copies of all evidence; that members of the Enquiry Team be excluded on the grounds of bias from participating in the hearings; that the accused be given the right to call their own witnesses and cross-examine those who had provided evidence against them, and, finally, that they be allowed legal representation. The Party was back with the problem of natural justice.

At the High Court hearing, the Vice-Chancellor, Sir Nicholas Browne-Wilkinson agreed that a 'domestic tribunal', like the NEC could and should not be bound by the same precepts as a law court. Nevertheless – and not for the first time – the Court delivered a severe blow to the Party. On two key counts, Brown-Wilkinson found in favour of the plaintiffs (the twelve accused). On the first count, that of confidential evidence, the NEC's position was badly damaged when Larry Whitty Labour's new General Secretary acknowledged that such evidence would not only be withheld from the accused: it would not be available to anyone. Instead, Whitty would simply allude to confidential evidence being the basis of a charge.

This was, in the Vice-Chancellor's highly quotable (and, afterwards, frequently quoted) words 'a manifestly dangerous procedure' and one 'without precedent' even in domestic tribunals. The accused were denied any right to test the evidence upon the basis of which they were being charged. This went well beyond the understandable desire to protect the anonymity of witnesses and was contrary to the rules of natural justice.

Browne-Wilkinson's judgment was even more embarrassing on the question of bias. Even accepting the NEC's status as a domestic tribunal, and not a court of law, it was a 'minimum requirement' that the persons charged should have reasonable confidence in its impartiality. A reading of the Majority Report clearly indicated that its authors did not possess an 'open mind' as to the guilt or innocence of those charged with breaches of the rules, or membership of Militant.

There was some consolation for the NEC in the rest of the judgment. The Vice-Chancellor denied that defendants before a domestic tribunal possessed an absolute right to call or cross-examine witnesses. This was only appropriate in certain circumstances, e.g. where there was a dispute over the facts. Similarly, there was no absolute right to legal representation, except where the evidence was of so technical a character as to be beyond the competence of the average layman. Thus, on both counts, the NEC was awarded some discretion[80]

The judgment was a double setback for the NEC. It propelled the issue of Militant back into the headlines, and in such a way as to present the Party in an unfavourable light – incompetent, heavy-handed and guilty of 'manifestly dangerous' procedures. All this was grist to the mill of its opponents – the hard left, Militant itself and the right-wing media. Secondly – and in a repetition of the Party's experience three years previously – it guaranteed that the trial of Militant would be a difficult, drawn-out process.

The NEC had, in fact, been advised by its solicitors that it was vulnerable on the issue of bias but had a reasonable chance of winning on all other counts, though much would depend on which judge took the hearing.[81] Nevertheless, given the element of doubt, relying so heavily on confidential evidence and allowing the members of the enquiry team to vote on the issue at the NEC was clearly a risky course. Why then did the Executive follow it?

On the question of bias, there were strong political reasons for staffing the enquiry with (an unusually large number of) NEC members: it was important to give it authority, and it was anticipated – accurately – that a direct encounter with Militant's methods might well make a powerful impression on the minds of the investigators. Nevertheless, it would have been wise to pre-empt an unfavourable legal judgment by excluding the eight investigators from the voting. Two considerations appeared to have weighed with the NEC. Firstly the problem of mustering a quorum without the eight, which we shall discuss in a moment. Secondly, and rather more fundamentally, there was an ingrained reluctance, particularly amongst right-wing Executive members, to acknowledge that the NEC must now operate within legally defined limits.

Similarly, there were apparently persuasive reasons for the reliance on confidential information. The investigating team had experienced some difficulty in amassing reliable evidence. Many of the most valuable details about the organisation and operations of Militant, and the identities of its senior personnel, had been furnished by people who wished to remain anonymous.[82] But it was a risky step, for in December 1982 the Courts had refused Militant's plea for an injunction on a very similar point purely on a technicality – indeed the judge had conceded the principle that the accused should have access to evidence upon which charges were based. The NEC should have known better. At the special NEC called to conduct the hearings against the Liverpool twelve, the disciplinary procedure was amended in light of the Court's ruling. None of the eight members of the Committee of Investigation was to participate in the disciplinary proceedings; confidential evidence would not be considered and any charges which relied upon it would be dropped. At this point events descended into melodrama: seven of the remaining Executive members rose and solemnly (and in the full glare of television and press cameras) quit the meeting. The meeting, rendered inquorate, was then abandoned.[83]

Once more, in the lengthening saga of the combat with Militant, the NEC was made to appear clumsy and foolish – and on the eve of a crucial by-election (Fulham). The Party's opponents were gleeful: according to David Steel, the walk-out demonstrated that Labour was 'riddled with extremists'. Kinnock's attempts to portray himself as a strong leader presiding over a respectable party looked distinctly less convincing; this, at least, was evidently his fear as in a procession of TV and radio interviews he proclaimed his unflinching determination 'to clear this matter up once and for all'.

If, in the short-term, Kinnock and the NEC found themselves with egg on their faces, the longer-term effects of the walk-out strengthened their hand. A meeting of the Executive was hurriedly called to reduce its quorum, enabling the expulsions to proceed. The real losers were the seven who walked out. Kinnock's tart response – 'infantile and stupid' – was widely shared in the Party, especially in the unions, and the growing isolation of the hard left deepened. Blunkett berated the seven for 'a tragic and saddening misuse of the trust placed in them'[84] and such stalwarts of the trade union left as Mick McGahey (Vice-President of the NUM) and Ken Gill (General Secretary of TASS) – champions of rival wings of the Communist Party – privately angrily condemned what they saw as irresponsible behaviour.[85] It was a maladroit political move.

12.9   The soft left's dilemma

Unlike the enthusiasts for a tougher disciplinary regime, the soft left perpetually had to grapple with a dilemma. In Blunkett's words: how could one tackle an 'organisation within an organisation' and 'prevent Militant from destroying us from within' without succumbing to the 'purge mentality'.[86] As a direct result of the Browne-Wilkinson Judgment, their response – to focus on malpractices and breaches of the rules rather than Militant membership – began to come apart at the seams. This judgment not only dashed hopes of a speedy conclusion of the operations against Liverpool's Militant; it also compelled the General Secretary to revise the NEC's case. The charges concerning misconduct and manipulation of the rules had to be reframed – to avoid further legal challenges – to meet two criteria: the alleged offences had to take the form of itemised violations of specific rules and to be backed up by evidence of a kind that would be acceptable to the Courts. This entailed discarding the charges that most perturbed the soft left – patronage, intimidation etc. – either because they did not involve overt breaches of the rules or because they had relied upon confidential verbal evidence.

This weakened the NEC's case. Most of the breaches which could be identified and substantiated by adequate documentary evidence were often committed elsewhere (and, indeed in Liverpool prior to the Militant take-over) and often rested on a rather narrow interpretation of the rules.[87] Above all, none seemed of sufficient gravity to justify stern disciplinary measures: the punishment seemed disproportionate to the crime. All of this appeared to support Militant (and the hard left's) claim that the NEC was manipulating the Party's rule-book solely to place Militant in the dock, and that the actual charges were no more than flimsy pretexts for politically-inspired expulsions – the case skilfully argued by Tony Mulhearn's written submission[88] and in his verbal defence.

The Party was, in fact, advised by its solicitors, after the March High Court judgment, to concentrate on the charge of Militant membership. This was more straightforward and, since the automatic penalty, if proven, was expulsion, it rendered the others redundant. The advice was accepted, confronting the soft left with an unpalatable choice. They could either rest their case for discipline on rules offences: but these – even if they could be proven – would not seem to warrant the drastic step of expulsion. The alternative was to vote for expulsion on grounds of Militant membership. This would for many involve reversing their previous opposition and expose them to the hard left's charge that they were abandoning the fight to arrest the drift to harsher discipline.

The soft left were, in fact, disturbed by a number of NEC decisions which appeared to signal a desire to restore a tougher managerial regime. Most of the decisions concerned the expulsion of individual Militant members. David Blunkett was especially disquieted by the NEC's confirmation – by a majority of one – of the expulsion of a member of his own Labour Group, Paul Green, despite the Group's unanimous opposition.[89] But the most controversial and high-handed decision was the expulsion of two non-Militant left-wingers, Amir Khan and Kevin Scally, from Birmingham Sparkbrook CLP.

Scally was expelled for appearing on a Channel Four programme, the Bandung File (one of whose producers was Tariq Ali) to complain about his CLP's failure to investigate charges of serious membership irregularities; the thrust of his case was that members had been improperly recruited for political reasons – to protect the political base of Sparkbrook's MP, Labour's deputy leader, Roy Hattersley. The same fate befell Councillor Amir Khan (a member of Birmingham Labour Group). His offence was to organise a public meeting promoting the case for Black Sections – deemed to be highly provocative since Hattersley was an outspoken opponent. The constitutional grounds for the expulsions were in fact very thin – engaging in 'conduct which ran the risk of bringing the Party into disrepute' (a non-existent offence) and breaching a CLP rule barring communication with the media on internal party matters. Nevertheless, their appeals, heard in April 1986 by Ken Cure and David Hughes, the Party's Senior National officer, were dismissed.[90]

The report's recommendations represented a clear regression to the mentality of the social-democratic centralist era. No serious abuse of Party rules was involved and the motivation for the expulsions was patently political. Not surprisingly, a heated discussion took place in the NEC. Hardline right-wingers, like Turnock and Cure, strongly urged endorsement of the report. The soft left joined forces with their estranged hard left colleagues demanding rejection. Blunkett, in particular, was outraged; and the soft left, as a group, complained bitterly to Kinnock about the 'intolerable' behaviour of Turnock and Cure. Opinion was evenly balanced and the expulsions were ratified by a single vote. Two men whose impartiality was questionable – Hattersley and Cure – participated in the final vote.[91]

The Khan/Scally affair became a cause celebre. A campaign for their reinstatement drew support from across the whole left-wing spectrum. The hard left taunted those on the soft left who had believed 'that the witch-hunt could be limited once it was begun. Comrades like Khan and Scally would not be outside the Party today were it not for the precedent established by the witch-hunt against the Liverpool party'.[92] In fact the expulsions were primarily the outcome of the internal politics of the Sparkbrook party. Nevertheless, the NEC's decision (by the narrowest margin) to confirm them suggest that the soft left's anxieties about an incipient authoritarianism on the hard right (represented by people like Cure and Turnock) were not misguided, though as yet they only represented a minority.[93]

The expulsions also occurred at – for the soft left NEC members – a particularly inauspicious moment, for it was at this point (April and May 1986) that they were forced to choose between backing expulsions on grounds of Militant membership or effectively (since other grounds had ceased to be legally and politically feasible) rejecting the disciplinary option. They chose the former option and voted for expulsions in those cases (the majority) where they felt the evidence sufficed.[94]

This exposed the soft left to the charge of inconsistency. Why expel Militants in Liverpool but not, say, in Sheffield? After some hesitation, most soft leftists came to accept Sawyer's definition of the problem as primarily one of entryism by a democratic centralist organisation. Sanctions, became necessary when, but only when, local organisations of Militant gathered such strength as to impair the operation of Party democracy.

12.10 The expulsions and the breakdown of Labour's disciplinary system

The disciplinary hearings were themselves astonishing spectacles, as the NEC was forced to engage in the most lengthy and contorted procedures to protect itself against legal challenge. Demonstrating Militant membership was, in itself, no easy task. How do you prove that individuals are members of an organisation which they consistently deny exists in the absence of membership cards or other irrefutable documentary evidence?

As we have seen, in January 1983 the National Executive had adopted a three-fold set of criteria for establishing membership of Militant: 'involvement in financial support for and/or the organisation of and/or the activities of the Militant Tendency'.[95] The accused acknowledged donating funds to the *Militant* paper, and speaking at its meetings but denied membership. Finding adequate evidence was no easy task and of the sixteen on the original list, six – who almost certainly were Militant members – were acquitted.[96]

In the end, after the longest, most numerous and doubtless most exhausting series of meetings ever held by the NEC on a single issue in a short space of time,[97] nine of the accused were expelled (in the case of Hatton in his absence as he contrived never to be available for his hearings), Tony Mulhearn, Ian Lowes, Tony Aitman, Derek Hatton, Richard Venton, Roger Bannister, Terry Harrison and Cheryl Varney.[98]

Endless hours of procedural wrangles and pouring over the minutiae of evidence sufficed to convince the NEC that the Party's existing disciplinary code required a complete overhaul. Any doubts were removed by the collapse of the efforts of a sizeable number of constituency parties to evict Militant members.

By the beginning of 1986 constituency action was claiming a growing number of victims; 42 Militant adherents had been expelled and twenty more cases were in the pipeline. Then the drive stalled; as with the Party nationally, local parties found themselves foiled by a series of legal challenges. Militant's lawyers obtained injunctions blocking proposed expulsions (and, in some cases, forcing reinstatement of ejected members) in Stevenage, Cannock, Exeter, Mansfield, Ipswich and Eddisbury Labour parties.[99] In the process a number of CLPs found themselves landed with heavy legal costs (threatened Militant members were generally able to obtain legal aid). In each case, constituency parties were forced to back down on the grounds that they had not properly observed the rules of natural justice. The NEC reacted to this barrage of adverse judgments by urging local parties to defer any further disciplinary action until steps were taken to bring the Party's disciplinary rules and procedures into line with the requirements of natural justice.

It may be useful at this point to rehearse these requirements. As Browne-Wilkinson had observed in his judgment, the rules of natural justice 'though a convenient portmanteau expression' were not 'fixed and immutable'.[100] Nevertheless, there appeared to be three irreducible elements: the right to receive specific charges, to be heard in answer to those charges and to be judged by an unbiased tribunal.[101]

For most of the Party's history, it had been taken for granted that the character and extent of the NEC's disciplinary powers were set by the Constitution: its only obligation, in discharging its managerial tasks, was to ensure that its actions complied with the rules. Because it was entrusted with the right to determine the 'meaning and effect' of any rule it had considerable discretion in deciding the limits of its own powers.

Developments since the Pembroke judgment of 1969 had progressively narrowed that discretion. The Courts had so developed the concept of natural justice that it was now the standard against which the Party's own constitution and procedures had to be measured. These had now been weighed and found wanting. In a statement submitted to the 1986 Conference, the NEC was forced to acknowledge that now 'if challenged, our basic rules and long-standing procedures may well be deemed by the courts to be incompatible with natural justice in certain respects'. 'As the judgment in the Liverpool case and the injunctions granted against CLPs indicate', the NEC continued 'our current rules and procedures themselves fail to meet even [the] basic requirements of natural justice.' The conclusion was irresistible: 'revisions to the rules and procedures relating to disciplinary matters should be adopted which are comprehensive and radically alter the structure of decisions on disciplinary actions within the party'.[102]

The legal imperative for change was compelling enough, but there were others too. It is rare for any institution to want to relinquish any of its powers; but after undergoing over forty hours of procedural wrangles and Militant rhetoric, the inhibitions of the NEC on that score were swiftly relieved. Similarly, Larry Whitty, the man who, as General Secretary, was primarily responsible for conducting the case against the Liverpool Militants was dismayed at the debilitating drain on his time and energies.[103]

By the spring of 1986, Labour's offensive against Militant had become mired into the political equivalent of Flanders trench warfare with a huge expenditure of effort securing minimal gains. There was intense frustration that the demands of the Courts were paralysing the Party's capacity to manage its own affairs as it saw fit. 'It can't possibly be the intention of the courts of this country', complained one official 'to make it impossible for parties to uphold their own constitution and to expel people when there has been a clear breach of the rules'.[104] Not the least worrying aspect of the Party's vulnerability to legal challenge was the growing burden of litigation expenses which it could ill-afford.

The contrast with the social-democratic centralist era was striking. Then the NEC had felt itself endowed by the Constitution, with expansive power to regulate the internal life of the Party. Individuals, organisations, even newspapers were charged and disciplined for offences which did not explicitly figure in the rule book and on the basis of procedures which paid little respect to the precepts of natural justice.[105] As Larry Whitty observed: 'Where there was near total deference to the authority of the Party and the bureaucracy of the Party, it was probably useful to the authorities to have a loosely-written rule-book. Now it is no use to those authorities to have one that can be challenged in the Courts.'[106]

There was, then, virtual unanimous support for a rewriting of Labour's disciplinary code; the only question was what shape it would take.

12.11 The National Constitutional Committee

In the summer of 1986, the NEC and its Organisation Committee discussed proposals for a new disciplinary system submitted by the General Secretary. The hard left wanted to maintain the NEC's disciplinary function intact, but to make its judgments subject to appeal to an independent Appeals Tribunal whose decisions would be final (though required to be reported to Conference).[107] This option was rejected. The majority was convinced that – given the need to observe natural justice and minimise the danger of legal challenge – a viable disciplinary capability could only be retained by separating the two functions of 'prosecution' and 'judge and jury'.

The Vice-Chancellor's judgment had been the final blow to Labour's tottering disciplinary edifice. The Liverpool Militants' injunction was granted, it will be recalled, primarily on the grounds that they could not be guaranteed a fair hearing by an unbiased 'tribunal', since eight members of the NEC had participated in the Committee of Investigation. This decision, as the Executive acknowledged, had 'profound implications for other aspects of the Party's disciplinary procedure where a preliminary assessment – usually with a quite explicit recommendation – has hitherto not excluded those involved in that preliminary assessment from participating and voting at the next stage'.[108]

An ever greater danger lurked. Unlike its continental sister parties (e.g. the SPD and the French Socialists)[109] Labour combined political and disciplinary functions in one body, the NEC. But, with a judiciary increasingly insistent that the precepts of natural justice be upheld in voluntary organisations, the feasibility of maintaining such an arrangement was now highly questionable. As a standard text on administrative law argues, to avoid the charge of bias an adjudicator 'must not be reasonably suspected, or show a real likelihood of bias'. Grounds, it continues, for such a suspicion might be provided in 'partisanship expressed in extra-judicial pronouncements'.[110] Given the loathing for Militant frequently articulated by many NEC members, it surely was but a short step before the Courts questioned the Executive's ability – as a political body – *ever* to offer Militant's supporters reasonable prospects of a fair trial. To compound the problem in disciplinary cases it itself instigated, the NEC acted as prosecutor, judge and jury.

The only safe course was to completely redraft the Party's disciplinary code, devolving the Executive's judicial function to another body. This step was taken and a new unit of Party organisation, the National Constitutional Committee (NCC) was established.[111] Under the revised disciplinary rules, the NCC inherits many of the NEC's duties as judge and jury, but the Executive retains its 'prosecuting' function. It is empowered to instruct the General Secretary to investigate and report back to it any alleged breach of the Constitution, Standing Orders and Rules of the Party. Upon receipt of his report it can then instruct him to to formulate charges and present them to the NCC.[112]

The NCC is charged with three main responsibilities: to hear and determine disciplinary matters referred to it, firstly, by 'the General Secretary or National Officers of the Party on the instructions of the NEC', and, secondly, by constituency parties.[113] Thirdly, it operates as an appeals court to hear and determine appeals against withdrawals of the whip by Labour Groups and exclusions from the panel by local parties.[114] In performing these duties it is authorised to take 'such disciplinary measures as it sees fit, whether by way of reprimand or suspension from holding office in the Party, or being a delegate to any party body, or withholding or withdrawing endorsement as a candidate of the party or expulsion from membership of the party or otherwise'. Its decisions on these matters are to be final.[115]

However, the NEC has not, by any means, relinquished all its disciplinary and managerial powers. Firstly, it is still empowered to discipline any Party *organisation* which, in its view, has not complied with the constitution and rules.[116] Why this distinction between individuals and organisations? Aside from the fact that natural justice does not impinge upon organisations in quite the same way as individuals, the ability to control all local Party organisations was seen as an essential part of the Executive's general responsibility for administering and managing the Party. To have surrendered this right would have substantially weakened the NEC's managerial powers and, for this reason, was rejected out of hand by the bulk of Executive members.

Secondly, the NEC retained its full control over parliamentary selections, including the rights to withhold endorsement, invalidate a selection or (as was shortly to be seen) impose a candidate, without any right of appeal. This power is (as we have seen in earlier chapters) so crucial that it is difficult to imagine any Executive ever foregoing it by conceding a right of appeal.

Thirdly, and despite the title bestowed upon the new body, the NEC remains responsible for determining 'the meaning, interpretation or general application of the Constitution, Standing Orders and Rules', its decision to be 'final and conclusive for all purposes'.[117] It could be objected that, as a *constitutional* committee, the NCC was the natural repository for such a power; indeed in the SPD, the federal arbitration commission rather than the Executive exercises it.[118] However, as the NEC was under no (legal) pressure to abandon this power it saw no reason to do so, particularly at a time when the centre-right bloc was keen to tighten managerial control. Finally, and for a similar reason, the Executive retains the right to refuse applications for membership, presumably because the legal status of an individual denied membership was different from that of a member punished by being deprived of his membership.

There were two particularly contentious items in the new disciplinary code. The first was the introduction of a new disciplinary offence: involvement 'in a sustained course of conduct prejudicial to the Party'. The Party leader had been pressing for some months for the addition of this new offence. The rationale was spelt out in the NEC's document on Disciplinary Procedures: 'In many cases', it suggested, 'damage done to the Party by individuals does not relate primarily to specific breaches of rule'.[119] But what constituted 'conduct prejudicial to the Party'? Here opinions differed. An elastic definition of disreputable conduct could, potentially at least, encompass a broad range of actions, including policy decisions taken by Party organisations to which the NEC might object on political grounds.

The right may well have been sympathetic to such a definition but others (including the Party's General Secretary) were not. The NEC's document on Disciplinary Procedures (in a section originally written by Whitty) pointed out that 'the nature of political parties makes the definition of "disrepute" a difficult and subjective task: this could lead to a dangerous escalation of the use of disciplinary action for factional or malicious purposes'.[120]

The outcome was a compromise: it was left to the NCC to determine whether a member was guilty of conduct prejudicial to the Party. However, certain parameters were laid down. Firstly, prejudicial conduct had to be 'sustained'. This qualification, inserted after pressure from Whitty and the soft left, was designed to prevent a Khan/Scally type scenerio, where a single 'misdemeanour' could be used as a basis for disciplinary action. Secondly, two illustrative criteria for defining prejudicial conduct were inserted: 'Where appropriate, the NCC shall have regard to involvement in financial support for and/or the organisation of and/or the activities of any organisation declared ineligible for affiliation to the party under Clause II (3) and II (4) of the Constitution; or to the candidature of the member in opposition to an officially-endorsed Labour Party candidate or the support for such candidature'.[121] The effect of the first criterion was to incorporate into the constitution the guidelines, adopted by the NEC in January 1983, for determining whether a person's association with Militant (and, presumably, any other proscribed organisation) amounted to de-facto membership. The second criterion merely repeated an existing ground for expulsion. One could conclude, then, that this new offence did not significantly extend the range of sanctionable conduct – were it not for the qualification 'where appropriate'. This implied that other, unspecified, acts could be deemed 'prejudicial'; much, then, depends upon how strictly the NCC chooses to construe the term, a point to which we shall return. There was, however, one important category explicitly defined as non-sanctionable. The NCC, the new rules stated, 'should not have regard to the mere holding or expression of beliefs and opinions'.[122] Those, on the right and centre, who wished to throw a perimeter of belief around the Party were rebuffed – an obvious concession to soft leftists who feared the onset of a 'purge mentality'.

The second contentious issue was the right of appeal. Under the existing rules, any member disciplined by a constituency party or a Labour Group had the right of appeal to the NEC. An individual or organisation disciplined by the NEC could appeal to Conference through referral back of the appropriate section of the NEC report. The effect of the new rules was actually to narrow the right of appeal. The NCC only hears appeals from those expelled from a Labour Group or excluded from the local government panel. For all others the right to appeal is abolished; the decisions of both the NEC and NCC are final. The NCC is required to submit a report to Conference, but Conference cannot refer back individual items, only the whole report. This, of course, would be extremely unlikely, though no consideration was given to what happens if the unlikely occurs.

The role of the NCC

There was a broad measure of agreement for the new disciplinary package that finally emerged. It was approved by twenty votes to five on the NEC[123] and by a vastly greater margin (6,014,000 votes to 436,000) at Conference.[124] There was some disagreement over the composition of the NCC. This centred over the precise balance between CLP and trade union representation, with the left seeking to enhance the former, and the centre and right the latter. The eventual compromise was, inevitably, weighted more to the preferences of the centre-right majority. There were to be eleven members: five were to be elected by the unions, three by the CLPs, two (the women's section) by Conference as a whole and one by the Socialist Societies.[125] This means that the unions controlled the election of seven of the eleven members – a balance denounced by the hard left as unfair, but roughly consistent with the spread on the NEC itself.

Discord over the composition of the new body was, of course, prompted less by abstract considerations of fair representation than calculations as to its likely political complexion. As was anticipated the centre-right bloc did secure a majority on the new Committee, winning four of the trade union seats, both seats in the women's section and the seat assigned to the socialist societies. All three constituency representatives were left-wingers, as was the fifth member of the trade union section. This gave the centre-right a seven to four majority, producing a committee more slanted to the right than the NEC itself.[126]

The result reinforced widespread anxieties about the role of the NCC, particularly pronounced on the hard left.[127] Thus, CLPD, whilst conceding that the new disciplinary system remedied 'the most obvious injustices' of the old, felt it to be seriously flawed. Both the NCC and the NEC, it predicted, would act in an intolerant manner and the flail of Party discipline would bear down harshly on left-wing dissidents.[128]

The NCC's first judgments, reached by majority decisions along left-right lines, certainly indicate a willingness to expel further Militant adherents where evidence of Militant membership is deemed to be sufficient. But CLPD's view exaggerates the ease with which a stiffer disciplinary regime can be imposed.

Firstly, it is by no means inevitable that the members of the NCC will conceive their role in a narrowly political way. Evidence from similar trade union bodies suggests that whilst it is bound to be, to an extent, an arena for factional conflict, its members may also be influenced by more objective judicial norms. Indeed, precisely because it is a new body, its members would have institutional interest in seeking to rise above the political fray. Too overt a factional bias would inevitably damage the NCC's authority. On the other hand, it may well be that an ascendant right is prepared to pay the price. A constant tension between rival political and judicial role conceptions is inevitable.

There are, however, other factors likely to restrain an over-zealous, intolerant majority. Some doubt must attach to the operational effectiveness of the new body. Not only will a weight of disciplinary and adjudicatory responsibilities borne by no other institution in the Party's history be heaped upon its shoulders, but it will also have to follow a set of procedures which – in comparison to Labour's past practices – are of positively labyrinthine intricacy. Given Labour's perennial problem of inadequate resources, it is difficult to envisage it receiving generous administrative assistance. The sheer workload of the NCC's members – all of whom are likely to have full-time jobs – is bound to operate as a disincentive to those who would like (in Larry Whitty's phrase) to chase every eighteen-year-old Militant seller in sight.[129] For this practical reason it will probably echo the NEC's injunction to constituency parties to use discipline only as a last resort.[130] This consideration will not restrain a new national offensive against Militant but it will most likely ensure that the NCC will be keener to temper rather than stoke the disciplinary ardour of local parties.[131]

Finally, the threat of legal challenge has been reduced, but not removed. The new disciplinary code includes detailed procedural guidelines, designed to ensure observance of natural justice. If these are not properly followed, an aggrieved member can appeal to the Courts. Hence the length and complexity of the procedures will operate as a double guard against hasty and arbitrary action.

In the course of time, the NCC will doubtless evolve its own disciplinary canons. Much will depend upon the priorities it establishes — and the preferences of those who will order its workload and fix its agenda.[132] But for the reasons cited above, fear of a relapse into the stringent managerial regime of the past are unlikely to be fully realised.

12.12   The continuing struggle over Liverpool

The completion of the NEC's protracted efforts to expel the Liverpool Militants was by no means the end of the story. It had to ensure that the expulsions were actually put into effect by the constituency parties of which the Militants were members and (in the case of Councillors Hatton, Mulhearn and, later, Felicity Dowling) by the Labour Group.

The expelled members belonged to four constituencies: Broadgreen, Garston, Mossley Hill and Riverside. In the last — where anti-Militant forces were well-entrenched — the expulsions of Terry Harrison and Richard Venton were accepted without too much difficulty. The independent-minded Mossley Hill constituency (of which Ian Lowes was a member) also complied. The two harder nuts to crack were Broadgreen and Garston, both Militant bastions; Hatton was a member of the former, Mulhearn of the latter.

Garston, initially, was defiant but when it realised it was courting suspension, it backed down.[133] Far better to submit, let the storm blow itself out, and then resume normal political activities — with Militant bloodied but unbowed. These considerations applied equally to Broadgreen — indeed they were more pertinent, since the constituency boasted one of Militant's two MPs, Terry Fields. But Broadgreen (which included on its membership rolls, besides Hatton, its Chairman, two other expellees) proved to be the least co-operative of the Liverpool parties. Joyce Gould, Labour's Director of Organisation[134] was despatched to help sort out its affairs. But the patience of Labour's officials was sorely tested by Broadgreen's (mainly Militant) officers whose attitude oscillated between foot-dragging and outright disobedience and in September 1986 the party was suspended. The Executive's troubles were by no means at an end. It had to complete the process of reconstituting the district party and to ensure that the Group complied with the expulsions of Hatton, Mulhearn and (later) Felicity Dowling. But the Group was in anything but a co-operative mood. Party officials were

snubbed by being refused entry to Group meetings, and the majority of
Labour Councillors insisted on the right of their three expelled colleagues to remain within its fold and retain their Council position. After
the NEC threatened disciplinary action, all group members finally, after
much prevarication, signed a pledge to abide by party rules. But they also
(in November) voted to replace Hamilton, who was keen to cooperate
with the National Executive, by the more obdurate Byrne.[135] The new
leader promptly cast doubt on his willingness to toe the line by offering
his support for Hatton's continuation as deputy leader of the Council.[136]
An exasperated NEC responded by instituting an enquiry into Byrne's
conduct, but this was soon overtaken by events.[137]

12.13   Labour's assault in Militant Liverpool: the balance sheet

What was the NEC seeking to achieve in Liverpool?[138] It is doubtful
whether it ever developed a coherent and agreed strategy, tending to
respond in an *ad hoc* fashion to developments. Nevertheless, one can
distinguish between two main approaches to the problem of Militant
Liverpool: a minimalist and a maximalist. The minimalist approach
would to be limit NEC intervention to the enforcement of the expulsions and the rectification of the various rule-infringements uncovered
by the NEC investigation. The maximalist would be to attempt to break
Militant's hold on Liverpool Labour Party. For a variety of political and
organisational reasons, the NEC may initially have been content with
the former. In practice, however, the choice never really availed itself.
Force of circumstance – obstruction and outright defiance in
Broadgreen and the Labour Group – impelled the NEC, simply in the
pursuit of the minimalist strategy, to take harsher measures, the
suspension of Broadgreen CLP and the Group. Whatever its own
intentions, the Executive found the question of Militant's power in
Liverpool thrust on its agenda and, by the autumn of 1986, it had veered
towards the maximalist approach.

This provoked hard-left denunciation of a revival of the implacable
discipline of the 1950s; but, in practice, the NEC's struggle with Militant in Liverpool illustrates the degree to which central power was now
trammelled. The Party encountered three main constraints. The first (by
now familiar) was legal: the NEC could only take such steps as were
specially authorised by Party rules; and it had to be careful to observe
the principles of natural justice. Anxiety about incurring the high costs
of litigation, which the Party could ill-afford, in itself operated as a
significant restraint.

The second constraint was organisational. Decisions were only
effective to the extent that they were fully implemented. A new
Liverpool organiser (Peter Kilfoyle) was appointed in April 1986 and one

of the small band of North West regional officials was assigned full-time to Merseyside. But ranged against them were the many more full-timers Militant could muster, either on its own or the Town Hall's pay-roll.[139] Further, unlike Militant's staff, Labour Party regional officials were primarily administrators rather than political organisers. Far from 'policing' the Party – as the hard-left often alleged – regional officials now shied away from involvement in contentious political matters, preferring to confine themselves to their administrative responsibilities.[140] Further, Labour's centralised system of decision-making meant that a certain bureaucratic sluggishness and remoteness from events on the ground inhibited the Party's capacity to react in a swift and effective manner.

The third constraint stemmed from Labour's confederal structure. The source of Militant's strength in Liverpool lay less in the constituencies than in unions, particularly GMBATU and the TGWU; their branches furnished the Tendency solid blocks of delegates at all levels of Party organisation and, especially in the case of the former union, indispensable components of its patronage machine. Some of the techniques used by Militant to maximise its support from trade unions were certainly dubious, such as inflating the delegate entitlement of branches by exaggerating the number of political levy-paying members it had in the various constituencies, or by appointing as delegates people who were not strictly eligible.[141] But there was also genuine support for the Tendency amongst union activists.

The affiliated unions in Liverpool were clearly a crucial terrain in the battle against Militant. At a minimum, the NEC had to curb the abuses of the rules which enabled the Tendency to artificially boost its influence. But its ability to intervene effectively was sharply limited by the Party's confederal structure; as one senior official commented, union autonomy 'is a real problem for us'. The NEC could plead, cajole and persuade, but it could not direct. Even where Labour did possess powers – as in the size of delegate entitlements – it was very wary about treading on trade union toes; as one senior trade union leader (and a member of the NEC) commented, the matter was a 'sensitive one' for the unions and Party interference was not welcome.[142]

By the summer of 1986, the national leadership of both GMBATU and the TGWU were as eager as the Party to tackle Militant in Liverpool. But the unions were far from the monoliths sometimes depicted in the media. In both the general unions, the authority of the centre was checked by a baronial system which devolved considerable powers to the regions. So even with the backing of John Edmonds and Ron Todd, there were limits to which could be achieved by central direction.

Whilst Militant members and sympathisers only constituted a minority of activists and officials in the Liverpool branches of the two general unions, the majority, still inclined to equate Militant with 'the left', were unwilling to co-operate in any drive against the Trotskyist organisation and, at the close of 1986, it remained well-entrenched. GMBATU did launch an investigation into the running of the all-important Number 5 branch, and a series of rule-infringements were uncovered. But progress was slow; as a well-informed observer noted 'When Peter Taaffe, *Militant's* editor, pulls strings in London, thousands respond. By comparison, if Larry Whitty or Joyce Gould is allowed to pull a string, the other end gets lost in union structures and the labyrinthine complexities of Labour's federal structure'.[143]

The NEC's position, then was a far cry from the 1950s. It does not follow, however, that it was helpless – indeed, as 1986 wore on its hand visibly improved – for it still retained valuable power resources.

Firstly, it was custodian of the rule book and, hence, supervised the way subordinate Party units operated. Its capacity to intervene in Liverpool's affairs was enlarged by the suspension of the DLP, most of whose power and duties it (the National Executive) inherited. In the hands of a tough and resourceful Party official, like Peter Kilfoyle, responsibility for applying the rules was a potent source of power. Thus in the compilation of the panel of candidates for the 1987 local elections (normally a district party function) he interpreted and enforced the rules in such a way as to weed out a number of Militant adherents.

Secondly, although Labour had far fewer organisers than Militant, they did have the advantage of acting in the name and with the delegated authority of the NEC. They were able to operate more openly than Militant's full-timers, and, as official agents of the Party, had less need to establish their personal credentials. They enjoyed a more or less automatic access to trade union officials and were able to capitalise on loyalty to the Party.

Thirdly, whilst discipline, on a scale sufficient to break Militant's hold on Liverpool politics, was never a feasible option, sanctions were a useful adjunct to other methods. By the beginning of 1987 both Liverpool DLP and Broadgreen CLP were suspended. The NEC is no longer in a position to employ the traditional technique of reorganisation – using the process of reconstitution to remove undesirable elements from the Party.[144] Suspension does however provide a breathing space for the Executive to bring its influence to bear by other methods. Furthermore, as we have seen, it retains its powers, under the new disciplinary code, to disband any party organisation and fresh disciplinary measures have by no means been ruled out.

As in 1982–3, a key factor in the campaign against Militant was rank and file sentiment. In 1986, senior Party officials feared a substantial backlash against its anti-Militant drive. But – in contrast to the first offensive – this never materialised. There were several reasons for this.

As Militant grew in strength, more people were exposed to its style and methods – its hectoring tone, its intolerance and its sloganising. Further, many in the constituencies who had previously opposed expulsions were dismayed by the revelations of the Liverpool investigation – in particular, the 'policing' of Party meetings by the SSF, the intimidation and patronage. And with the publication of Crick's studies on Militant awareness of its democratic centralist and entryist character spread, disabusing those who had believed that it was just another current of opinion organised around a paper 'like *Tribune'*. Finally, the so-called re-alignment of the left had broken up the 'wing solidarity' of the early 1980s. Rather than rallying to the defence of 'comrades on the left' many constituency activists were much more likely to look askance at anyone seen to disrupt the unity or tarnish the image of the Party.

The shift of opinion in the constituencies was dramatically illustrated by the vote on the expulsion of the Liverpool Militants at the 1986 Conference. In 1982 an estimated 90% of constituencies opposed the Register; the following year two-thirds voted against the expulsion of Militant's editorial board. Three years later, this percentage was reversed, with 450,000 votes cast in favour of the expulsions and 263,000 against.[145] The NEC elections provided another significant indicator. David Blunkett, the NEC constitutency member most closely identified with the campaign against Militant was targetted by the hard left umbrella group, Labour Left Liaison, for ejection from the Executive. Instead – in a vote which reflected the growth of soft left sentiment – he retained his position as top of the constituency section; the point was underlined by the defeat of the Liverpool MP, Eric Heffer, one of militant's most outspoken defenders.

These two votes undermined the hard left's argument that the attack on Militant was instigated in defiance of constituency opinion. It was now clear that there would be no repetition of the mass hostility to expulsions of 1982–3, with its public display of strife and venom. Further, Conference's overwhelming endorsement of the expulsions – by 6,146,000 votes to 325,000 – greatly enhanced the moral authority of the NEC's actions; conversely it gravely embarrassed the hard-left opponents of expulsion most of whom had campaigned for years on the platform of Conference sovereignty. Even the consolation of 1982–1983 – that the expulsion had been rammed through by the bloc vote – was no longer available. By the end of 1986 Militant's stock amongst activists had so far fallen that Kevin Scally – stressing the importance of left-wing unity in securing his reinstatement – could write of its adherents that 'they have now become so deeply unpopular within the Party that association with them becomes hazardous'.[146]

Militant was, of course, more deeply implanted in Liverpool than elsewhere. It also benefitted from a fierce local patriotism. The surcharge and disqualification of 47 Labour Councillors evoked considerable admiration for their courage and tenacity in defending the city against the Tory Government's depradations. All this compounded strong local resentment against interference from national party headquarters. Yet the backing of a significant proportion of Party members in Liverpool was essential to the NEC's project. Even in the social-democratic centralist period, the Party, in its struggle with a much less for formidable Trotskyist opponent, relied heavily upon the co-operation of local activists.[147] In 1985 that co-operation would not have been forthcoming. Even the anti-Militant left (represented by Merseyside LCC and Liverpool Labour Left) had opposed disciplinary action. But, by the second half of 1986, they had swung solidly behind the expulsions – and many wanted tougher measures still.

Anti-Militant sentiment was chrystalised by the deposition of Hamilton from the leadership of the Labour Group (though this almost certainly was not the outcome of a Militant-inspired coup, as it was depicted in the press).[148] Hamilton, if ineffectual, was a much revered and well-liked left-winger of a traditional stamp. Many activists felt outraged by this unfraternal treatment of a man who had been so loath in the past to publicly criticise Militant and who could not be charged with disloyalty to the Liverpool Party.[149] Hamilton himself began, for the first time, to publicly criticise the Council's largely Militant leadership's 'ruthless and autocratic attitudes'.[150]

By the second half of 1987, Militant was clearly on the defensive. The marginalisation of key cadres by a combination of expulsion from the Party and surcharge and disqualification of Councillors proved damaging. The temporary Liberal administration placed in office by the removal of the 47 disqualified Labour Councillors did not survive the 1987 local elections, when Labour returned to power with a small majority but the political balance of the Labour Group had altered. A new anti-Militant leader, Ken Rimmer, was elected with the backing of about two-thirds of the Group. Militants and their allies comprised the remaining third but – this was the crucial point – the Tendency had lost its grip on the Council and, hence, it patronage network. As activist opinion continued to swing against it, the Tendency lost ground in the Liverpool constituencies. Similarly, whilst its position remained intact in the GMBATU (now GMB), it forfeited the support of the TGWU, where Regional Secretary, Bobby Owens, now adopted a tough anti-Militant posture.[151]

Ousted from control of Liverpool Council, Militant had lost the jewel in its crown. But it was still strongly implanted in all levels of Party organisation in the city and had islands of support elsewhere. It would be a sanguine observer who was prepared to discount the Trotskyist group. Militant was down but not out.

Chapter Thirteen

Conclusion

13.1 Social-democratic centralism

The fundamental managerial dilemma with which Labour has had to grapple has been posed by a man who was at different stages of his career, both dissident and leader: 'How to encourage freedom without which political parties will become moribund, whilst not destroying their cohesion without which they will cease to be effective instruments of government and opposition.'[1] The social-democratic centralist response had been forthright: in Attlee's words 'in politics, as in other forms of warfare, the leader must be able to rely on his troops when he is fighting his opponents. The more that discipline is self-imposed the better, but discipline there must be unless one is prepared to lose the battle.'[2]

However, the problem here is that discipline may be as easily used to suppress dissent as to promote effective management. Years ago Michels commented on leaders' 'notable fondness for arguments drawn from the military sphere' where 'the general interest' could be invoked to stifle 'embarrassing opposition'.[3] Aneurin Bevan recognised the importance of cohesion but rejected the social-democratic centralist approach. There were, he suggested, two ways of reconciling unity and diversity. The first was the method of discipline – of proscriptions, expulsions and Standing Orders. The second was 'to lay most emphasis on the common factor which binds us together . . . By this we achieve unity of action and distinctiveness of purpose. This factor is socialism'.[4] 'Discipline', he opined 'is only necessary if the policy followed does not command the enthusiasm of its members . . . an enthusiastic movement disciplines itself.'[5] These two approaches represent polarities between which Labour's party management has oscillated since 1951.

From the opening of our period in 1951 and for the next decade and a half, the Party was managed according to the precepts of social-democratic centralism. Its origins lay in the inter-war period as Labour's managerial regime stiffened in response to systematic Communist attempts at penetration and to the problems of dealing with a confederal and highly factionalised party.

These experiences were absorbed into a frame of reference inherited primarily from the trade unions. The unions, as internally democratic organisations locked in a continuous struggle with employers, had developed a distinct organisational ethos which stressed the virtues of unity, solidarity and loyalty to majority decisions. Labour's interwar experiences blended with this ethos to fashion its own social-democratic centralist doctrine, with its three key precepts, majority rule, maintenance of Party cohesion, and the protection of organisational and ideological integrity.[6]

Social-democratic centralism survived for a generation. We have suggested that the corner-stone holding it in place was not the power of the Party machine but normative control.[7] Normative control was rooted in two prominent characteristics of Labour's political culture until the late 1960s. The first was the prevalence amongst much of the membership of a solidaristic mode of involvement. Solidarism was essentially the transposition of class loyalties to the Labour Party: the sense amongst many working-class members that Labour was their party and that loyalty and solidarity were essential if it was to prevail in the struggle against its opponents. In this, as in so many other ways, the Party's organic connection with the industrial wing of the movement permeated its internal life. As within the unions at the time loyalty towards the institution was often transmuted into loyalism, a respect for and fealty towards leadership. Loyalism was, in turn, reinforced by widespread sentiments of deference towards authority; in this Labour was a microcosm of the wider political culture.

Not all Party members, even in this period, were drawn to political activity by solidaristic impulses; a significant number were always inspired by idealistic motives, exhibiting the purposive mode of involvement.[8] But they too shared much of this respect for authority which, in their case, took the form of a willingness to accord it legitimacy. This, in turn, was rooted in a large measure of consensus within the Party – over values and purposes but, above all, over procedural norms. It is here that social-democratic centralism doctrine functioned as an essential ingredient of the tough managerial regime. The accent on unity and, even more, the faith in majority rule operated as a legitimating ideology, justifying the distribution and exercise of power in the centralist era.

Managerial control in the social-democratic centralist era was fortified by two other features of the Party. The first was the prestige and influence of (at least the more capable members of) the regional staff – the key intermediaries between Head Office and the constituencies. The superior political expertise and experience of such officials, their skill in constructing extensive networks of contacts and, again, deference towards authority all fostered their capacity to intervene at strategic points, particularly in the crucial field of candidate selection.

The second feature was the highly concentrated character of Labour's power structure in this period. The pluralist potential of the Party's constitutional framework (arising from its confederalism and separation of powers between Parliamentary and extra-Parliamentary organs) was countervailed by the ascendancy of the right in all major institutions – the PLP, the NEC, Conference and the bulk of the unions. The ideological affinity between the industrial and political leadership, coupled with an agreed division of labour between the unions and Party engendered a high degree of elite consensus. Hence the system of integrated organisational control: an NEC prepared to define its managerial role in a way that met the needs of the Parliamentary leadership, and confident that the disciplinary zeal of the predominantly right-wing unions would furnish both moral support and bloc votes at Conference.

We have considered at length the features and operation of the social-democratic centralist regime from 1951 to the mid-1960s. We can summarise it in terms of its two principal characteristics, centralisation and discipline.

Centralisation
Social-democratic centralists were convinced that order and harmony could only be maintained, and hence the energies of the Party harnessed to the full, by strict observance of the rules. Like many such texts, Labour's Constitution and rules were loosely-worded and ambiguous. In the 1950s and early 1960s they were consistently interpreted, by the NEC, in a centralist manner, which provided a constitutional underpinning for the forcible exercise of its powers.

Though social-democratic centralists genuinely believed that vigorous central direction was in the interests of the Party as a whole, there is little doubt that throughout this period the NEC used its powers to promote the factional cause of the dominant right, both locally and nationally. The outstretched arm of the Party centre was felt over the whole range of internal Party activities. Local Party organisations (and individual members) were discouraged from engaging in activities (like holding conferences) unless they were expressly authorised. The Proscribed List was employed to limit the rights of members to associate with Communists or work alongside them in organisations with aims (like friendship with the Soviet bloc) which the NEC found objectionable.[9] Further, where politically charged disputes occurred at local level, the Executive almost invariably interceded on behalf of the right.[10] Finally, in the crucial field of parliamentary selection, the NEC exerted a significant measure of control through two main types of devices: negative controls, like screening candidates for the B List and endorsement, and influence mechanisms, like utilising the prestige of regional officials and deploying their contact networks to effect selection outcomes.[11]

Discipline

The second main component of the social-democratic centralist regime was its reliance upon discipline as a managerial instrument. Labour's democratic system would only function smoothly, it was held, if major-ity decisions (whether promulgated by the Party's sovereign body, Annual Conference or – in the case of political activity in the House of Commons – by the PLP) were obeyed by all. What did this actually entail? Social-democratic centralism fell considerably short of demo-cratic centralism in that it did not curtail criticism of the leadership. But it did look askance at sustained and organised efforts by dissidents to challenge a whole range of official policies. However, no rigid lines were drawn. A decision whether or not to ban organisations, prohibit activi-ties or punish individuals held to be defying the majority view was very much influenced by political circumstances at the time. Thus the Bevanite group was banned but, although menacing noises were made, the Brains Trust and Victory for Socialism were not.[12]

Majority rule was not only an end but a means: it provided a method for the resolution of conflicting views and, hence, for the preservation of Party unity. Whereas the left was prone to claim that vigorous debate was a sign of democratic vitality, social-democratic centralists were fearful lest continuous dissension would divert the Party's energies and tarnish its electoral appeal. Hence the rights of minorities were squeezed in the name of both majority rule and cohesion, for example during the NEC's war of attrition against the Bevanites between 1951 and 1955.[13]

As a political formation wedded to the Parliamentary road to socialism, social-democratic centralists insisted upon Labour's right to set down clearly defined perimeters of belief; those who proferred a revolutionary ideology lay outside and should be rigorously excluded from the Party; entryist activities, in particular, were regarded as intolerable intrusions into the Party's inner life to be combatted by disciplinary measures. Thus, during this period, the NEC utilised a range of techniques, notably proscriptions, constituency reorgani-sations, expulsions and ideological screening to eradicate Trotskyist entryist groups and defend Labour's borders.

The myth

Was the social-democratic centralist era 'the Golden Age of Witch-hunting, when a Sara Barker and a Ray Gunter could go up and down the country expelling people';[14] a time when the leadership 'seemed determined to crush the rights of the rank and file' and 'the central machinery of the party was used to extinguish dissent'.[15] Defined in these terms the 'age of witch-hunting' is mythology. Bans, proscriptions and expulsions never reached a scale remotely resembling the rigid discipline of old-style Communist Parties. The Party did not suppress all dissent; even avowed Trotskyists like Ted Grant survived as Party members during these years. Further, the centre was never omnipotent. For example, the NEC's ability to control the parliamentary selection process was bounded by a series of constraints: the scarcity of organisational resources, the jealous defence of trade union prerogatives, the reliance upon voluntary electoral labour in single-member constituencies and the strength of particularistic sentiments in the provinces.[16]

But if the rigours of social-democratic centralism can be exaggerated, they were real enough. The banning of the Bevanite group and the attempted expulsions of Bevan and Bertrand Russell *did* reflect a deep-seated authoritarianism within the dominant right; and the procedures used by the Party *did* often display scant regard for the rights of members and for natural justice. Further, there is little doubt that organisations like Victory for Socialism were inhibited by the fear of precipitating the fate to which the Bevanites and, earlier, the Socialist League, had succumbed. Not surprisingly, the sudden fervour with which disciplinarians from this period, like Denis Healey (who had favoured Bevan's expulsion) embraced 'tolerance', 'the rights of minorities' and 'the right of dissent'[17] when *they* found themselves in the minority[18] were treated with cold scepticism by left-wing veterans of the Bevanite wars.

13.2 Liberalisation and the erosion of central control

From the second half of the 1960s a series of developments combined to undermine the social-democratic centralist regime.[19] The survival of the regime was always likely to be put at risk if its opponents assumed positions of power. This is what happened from the mid 1960s, in two stages. The first, which affected mainly the PLP occurred with the rise to prominence of former Bevanites who, whilst no longer aligned with the left, retained their distaste for past managerial practices. Richard Crossman had been, in the 1950s, one of the sharpest critics of the traditional regime. He had assailed the rigid imposition of majority rule and the trampling of minority rights as 'one of the most important causes of [Labour's] internecine conflict'.[20] A decade later he was appointed Leader of the House by another erstwhile Bevanite and convinced opponent of the older regime, the Prime Minister, Harold Wilson, with a mandate to liberalise discipline in the PLP. This task, with the assistance of the Chief Whip, John Silkin, and Wilson's support, he successively accomplished and the changes introduced in this period (the late 1960s) proved permanent.

The second stage was the steady expansion of the left on the NEC evident from the late 1960s onwards (though the left fell short of an outright majority till the middle of the next decade). Several left-wing NEC members (most notably Ian Mikardo) had themselves had bruising encounters with the social-democratic centralist regime; all were united in a determination to dismantle it. They were joined in this by Ron Hayward, appointed National Agent in 1969 and General Secretary three years later. He was the first person not identified with the right to hold these positions and made a significant contribution to the adoption of a more lenient managerial regime.

The swing of the NEC to the left was, in turn, mainly the result of the rise of left-wing trade unionism. The social-democratic centralist regime had been sustained by a trade union mentality which both emphasised the indispensibility of discipline and was strongly right-wing in complexion. By the late 1960s a new breed of capable left-wing Labour union leaders had emerged. Initially the effect on the composition of the NEC was limited (this registered somewhat later) but left-wing unionism had an immediate and major impact on the political atmosphere. The trade union ethos of solidarity and majority rule could no longer be readily invoked to uphold a tough managerial regime of the traditional stamp.

By the mid 1970s left ascendancy on the NEC (coupled with the more even balance of alignments amongst the affiliated unions) had an even more far-reaching consequence: the breakdown of the system of integrated organisational control. The Executive was no longer prepared to fulfil the role enacted by its predecessors in the social-democratic centralist era – policing the wider Party on behalf of the Parliamentary leadership. MPs facing deselection looked in vain for help from the NEC. More crucially, the Parliamentary leadership was deprived of access to a range of procedural mechanisms – available only to the Executive – which could have been used to stifle the campaign for mandatory reselection.[21]

Under left-wing control a new liberal regime emerged with characteristics which contrasted sharply with those of social-democratic centralism. Centralisation and discipline gave way to decentralisation and leniency.

Decentralisation
The period witnessed a retraction of central control in favour of greater autonomy for constituency parties. This was most evident in the sphere of candidate selection. The NEC abandoned its selection controls, such as the use of its powers over admission to the B List and endorsement to filter the flow of parliamentary candidates. Further, Regional Organisers were discouraged from intervening for political purposes in the selection process. Most importantly of all, the NEC enunciated the Mikardo doctrine which confined its right to review the deselection of sitting MPs to cases of procedural irregularities. More generally, the NEC discarded all associational controls which had been employed to regulate the political activities of the rank and file.

Leniency
During the liberal era, the NEC was markedly reluctant to utilise its disciplinary powers. Left Executive members (and sympathetic senior officials like Hayward) favoured conciliation as a method of settling internal differences. They regarded as counterproductive the older approach of rigidly applying the rules, backed by sanctions. This, they contended, merely inflamed and hardened divisions. As we have seen, after 1979 local conflicts became so severe that the left NEC's emmolient adjudicatory style was rarely able to bridge the gulf. But it did have one major consequence; bereft of the national support their predecessors could rely on, local right-wing establishments were less capable of resisting the advance of the left.[22]

The most controversial aspect of the left managerial regime was the NEC's open toleration of the Militant Tendency. To many observers the crucial decision which opened the sluice gates to Trotskyism was the abolition of the Proscribed List in 1973. Thus Philip Williams has argued that the left, on securing a majority 'promptly changed the rules to eliminate the barriers against infiltration by the far left', who were seen as 'potential allies in the factional struggle within the Party'.[23] We have shown that this view is, in fact, mistaken[24]; that the scrapping of the List was neither a crucial nor a contentious decision (though the motives and expectations of those who backed the move differed) — indeed none of the four Executive members later to defect to the SDP lodged any serious objections. In any case, the List as a managerial weapon had fallen into desuetude after the Russell Affair in 1962. The real significance of abolition lay not in its affect but in the manner it came to symbolise the whole liberalisation process.[26]

The left NEC's refusal to use disciplinary measures against Militant was influenced by a range of factors: a recollection of the intolerance of the social-democratic centralist era and a determination not to rescuscitate it; a belief in the virtues of ideological and organisational pluralism;

and a conviction that – at a time of intensifying polarisation between left and right – there were 'no enemies on the left'.[27]

13.3 The crisis of managerial control

The shift of the NEC to the right with the detachment from the left of a grouping which rallied behind the new leader, Michael Foot, eventually brought the left's managerial regime to a close. These developments made possible a (partial) renewal of the partnership between the parliamentary leadership and a centre-right NEC and, hence, the reconstitution of a managerial centre.

It was this that rendered feasible an organisational assault on the Militant Tendency.[28] The right had been keen for years to tighten discipline, for both ideological and factional reasons. To this was added another powerful consideration: many in the Party were extremely disturbed by a widespread public perception – fostered by the media and, indeed, by senior right-wing Labour politicians – of rampant 'extremism' within Labour ranks. A display of determination to stand up to 'extremists', it was felt, was essential for electoral reasons.

But it was at this point (1982) that the NEC discovered that the conditions which had sustained social-democratic centralism in the past no longer obtained.

Three major factors now constrained the reassertion of managerial control. The first stemmed from a profound alteration in the composition and outlook of the Party's (active) membership. Activists were, by the early 1980s, predominantly young, middle class and radical in temper. They lacked the reverence for established authority and the instinctive Party loyalism which had typified earlier generations of solidaristic members. One effect of this was to weaken the power and influence of Regional Organisers, who now lost advantages they had formerly enjoyed as they increasingly had to deal with an educated, articulate and politically more sophisticated membership.

Nevertheless, this transformation of the membership need not, of itself, have precluded effective central control; rather it rendered the rank and file's willingness to accede to authority conditional upon the extent that it was deemed to be legitimate, that is fairly and properly constituted. But it was precisely at this moment that Labour was afflicted by a prolonged crisis over the nature of democracy and the legitimate structure of power within the Party – a crisis which drastically reduced rank and file respect for established authority.

The second constraint arose from a development no less important in its effects upon managerial control though, unlike the first, it was overlooked both by commentators and by those who lamented the lack of discipline: the growth of intervention by the Courts in the internal affairs of the Party. As we have seen, social-democratic centralism was underpinned by the doctrine of constitutional centralism. As I have argued, the Pembroke judgment exposed the doctrine's fragile legal foundations.[29] Neither the Pembroke nor the later (Newham North East) Appeals Court Judgment of 1977 were necessarily binding on later cases. But they gave unambiguous testimony to the drift in judicial thinking. The thrust of the two judgments was to establish two parameters for the exercise of NEC powers: firstly it could only act in such ways as it was clearly empowered to do by the Party's rules; secondly, it was under an obligation in any disciplinary measures it took to conform to the precepts of natural justice. This new judicial activism seriously diminished the NEC's discretion in the use of its disciplinary powers – as it learnt to its cost in 1982 when it was forced, in humiliating circumstances, to abandon its plans to ban Militant via the ill-conceived device of the 'Register'.

The third constraint was the vigorous and almost universal opposition of the left – at all levels from the NEC down to the predominantly left-wing constituency activists – to the disciplining of Militant. The left's traditional objection to the use of discipline as a managerial instrument was reinforced by a widespread belief that the Militant issue was being exploited by the right to discredit the left as a whole and stage a political come-back – a belief that had some basis in fact.

13.4   The revival of managerial control

The scale of the loss of managerial control only became apparent when the centre-right bloc ousted the left in 1982 and sought to re-assert the authority of the NEC. The campaign against Militant faded away with few tangible results after months of strenuous effort. Social Democratic defectors loudly proclaimed that the Party was incapable of re-asserting its authority against left-wing 'extremism'. Events were to prove them wrong. The years since 1983 witnessed a re-imposition of a significant measure of managerial control exemplified by the greater success of the NEC's second assault on Militant.[30]

Three main factors were responsible for this turn of the tide. Firstly, the impact of electoral catastrophe in June 1983. There were, of course, several factors which contributed to the debacle, but many Party members agreed that Labour had paid dearly for the debilitating strife which had consumed so much energy and presented such a poor image to the public since 1979. As a result, appeals for unity fell upon much more receptive ears than they had done in the past. Unity inevitably entailed unity behind the existing leadership and, indeed, many members in all sections of the Party came to feel that the authority of the leadership must be upheld if Labour was to win the next election.

This was coupled with the second factor: thanks to the institution of the electoral college, Kinnock could claim a stronger democratic mandate than any of his predecessors.

The third, and perhaps most important, factor was the reorientation of the attitude of a substantial section of the left (the soft left) to party management in general, and to the threat posed by Militant in particular. In 1982, the line between supporters and opponents of disciplinary action against Militant more or less coincided with the ideological cleavage between the left and the centre and right. By 1986 it cut through the left, a development more than any other responsible for the different outcomes of the two campaigns against the Trotskyist organisation. The shift in the soft left's perspective in part arose from a different political context. In 1986, unlike in the earlier year, the attack on Militant was not part of a general offensive against the left despite the attempts of much of the hard left to depict it in these terms. A more important influence, however, was the mounting evidence of widespread misconduct on Militant's part – its use of intimidation to cower opponents, its willingness to violate rules to promote its objectives – disclosed in the Liverpool investigation. After some hesitation, the soft left concluded that the malpractices were not accidental but were rooted in the existence of Militant itself, a democratic centralist organisation pursuing an entryist tactic willing, in Jimmy Knapp's words, 'to use the most unscrupulous means to further its ends'.[31]

To the hard left, the soft left's support for expulsions represented a betrayal: they had become accomplices in – indeed helped to foment – a witch-hunt against 'good socialist comrades'. In fact the soft left's position did not represent as sharp a rupture with the left's traditional managerial approach as was so often portrayed. The left, in the past, had consistently denounced the use of arbitrary and needlessly repressive methods. But influential left-wing voices had always been willing to accept that, in the *New Statesman's* words, the Party 'must have rules of discipline and, in the last resort, when persuasion has failed, must be prepared to enforce them against disruptive elements'.[32] In his oft-quoted attack on the proscription of *Socialist Outlook* in 1954, Michael Foot also acknowledged that 'there *is* a case for proscribing certain organisations . . . such action may be justified as an unavoidable measure for dealing with Communist methods of infiltration'.[33] And one of the most devastating critiques of entryist and democratic centralist practices employed then by the Communist Party and subsequently pursued by Militant was written in 1946 (in an official Labour Party pamphlet) by the influential socialist thinker and left-wing NEC member, Harold Laski.[34]

The relative success of Labour's second drive against Militant was bought at a considerable cost in scarce time, energy, and organisational and financial resources. The main stumbling block was, again, a legal one with the NEC once more falling at the bar of natural justice. Its failure fully to anticipate this highlighted a significant defect – an inability to develop an organisational memory which could have avoided a repetition of past mistakes.

To conform to the courts' rulings, the Executive was compelled to undergo the most protracted and exhausting procedural contortions. The experience convinced even the most hardened right-wingers that the Party's disciplinary system required radical surgery. The upshot was the establishment, by the 1986 Conference, of a National Constitutional Committee which inherited many of the NEC's disciplinary powers.[35] This effected the most fundamental alteration in Labour's disciplinary rules since the 1918 constitutional settlement.

With the new disciplinary code approved, the expulsions of prominent Liverpool Militants confirmed by a huge majority and with the NEC elections further weakening the hard left – all within the setting of the most efficiently stage-managed Conference Labour had seen for years – the crisis of party authority appeared to be over. With a little hyperbole the *Guardian's* columnist Hugo Young commented: 'We witness the menacing spectacle of a leadership which carries all before it'.[36] During the following months, though action by the NEC in blocking one aspiring parliamentary candidate (Les Huckfield in Knowsley North) and removing an endorsed one (Sharon Atkin in Nottingham East) offered impressive demonstrations of the revival of central control[37] To the hard left this was yet further evidence that the harsh and exacting discipline of the social-democratic centralist era is being reintroduced. This charge is overstated. The principles and practices of the liberal regime of the 1970s have not all been reversed. On the one hand the NEC is seeking to assert firmer control and evinces a greater propensity to use disciplinary means to resolve managerial problems; and with the closure of the gap between the Parliamentary and wider parties a viable centre has re-emerged. But on the other, a series of obstacles stand in the way of the restoration of the older centralised regime. Local parties still retain a considerable discretion in the way they conduct their activities,[38] and mandatory reselection has enhanced their role. Similarly, a galaxy of Party pressure groups continue to operate with a degree of freedom far greater than that conceivable under social-democratic centralism. Further, though loyalist feelings have been re-awakened, they fall far short of the deference of the past. Loyalty, for many activists, is still contingent upon the leadership's willingness and ability to realise the Party's ideals.

Finally, and most important of all, the constellation of political forces within the Party is now quite different. The trade unions are politically much more evenly balanced; as long as organisations as powerful as the

TGWU and NUPE remain on the left, the Praetorian Guard of the past cannot be resurrected. Similarly, whilst the hard left has been effectively marginalised the very effort of constructing a broad political base for the leadership has placed the soft left in a position of some influence, at least on managerial issues. This influence will be used to temper the zeal of the disciplinarians.

None of this is to deny a steady drift towards tighter discipline and firmer central control. The outcome of the 1987 general election is likely to accelerate this drift. Though the Party suffered another severe defeat, the authority of the leadership was enhanced by the efficient manner in which Labour's election campaign was conducted. Both Kinnock and the NEC are clearly keen to strengthen their grip in the Party machine; and elements on the right take over the reimposition of a strict disciplinary regime. If the balance of forces within Labour's ranks were to alter – if, for example, the TGWU shifted to the right – this latter might become a feasible option. There is as yet no evidence that the leadership favours such a course. And even if it were to do so, the combination of a much more assertive membership than a generation ago plus the continuing danger of intervention by the courts would exact a high political price in a party more than ever desperate for unity.

Notes

Notes to Introduction

1 The major works have been: R. T. McKenzie, *British Political Parties*; Ralph Miliband, *Parliamentary Socialism*; S. H. Beer, *Modern British Politics*; Lewis Minkin, *The Labour Party Conference*.

2 The two polar types are represented by the highly regimented or 'democratic centralist' Communist Party and the highly permissive American party.

3 Sara Barker, as National Agent, was the Party official primarily responsible for disciplinary questions.

4 *The Observer*, 24th November 1985.

5 Reported in *The Financial Times*, 16th June 1981.

6 Campaign for Labour Party Democracy *Newsletter*, May 1986.

7 Labour's National Executive Committee is the body primarily charged with the task of managing the Party.

Notes to Chapter One

1 Ross McKibbin, *The Evolution of the Labour Party*, pp. 5–11.

2 *Ibid.*, p. 94.

3 The Parliamentary Labour Party (PLP) was largely autonomous in this sphere.

4 LP Constitution, Clause 6(b), *LPCR 1919*, pp. 176–9.

5 *Ibid.*, Clause 7.

6 *Ibid.*, Clause 2.

7 D. J. Wilson, *Party Bureaucracy in Britain*, pp. 32–4.

8 LP Constitution, Clause 7(a), *LPCR 1919*, p. 178.

9 McKibbon *op. cit.*, pp. 131, 162.

10 Thesis, 3rd Congress of the Comintern, quoted in S. Graubard, *British Labour and the Russian Revolution*, p. 144. In September 1920 the CPGB urged the NEC to treat its application favourably on the grounds that Labour was 'so catholic in its composition and constitution that it could admit to its ranks all sections of the working class movement that accept the broad principles of working class action'. *LPCR 1921*, p. 20.

11 T. A. Jackson.

12 In 1921, on a procedural vote, by 4,115,000 to 224,000, *LPCR 1921*, p. 167; the following year by 3,086000 votes to 261,000, *LPCR 1922*, p. 199; in 1923

(again on a procedural vote) by 2,880,000 to 366,000 *LPCR 1923*, p. 189. And, in the last of this series, in 1924 by 3,185,000 to 193,000, *LPCR 1924*, p. 131.

13 'Thesis of the Communist International', quoted in NEC Report *LPCR 1922*, p. 81. The official weekly *The Communist* promised, in January 1922, that 'the Communists will continue their campaign of merciless exposure of every non-Communist leader and policy'. Graubard *op. cit.* p. 153. Two years later the CP Congress agreed to continue the campaign for affiliation 'to unmask the treacherous elements in the Labour Party'. L. J. MacFarlane *The British Communist Party*, p. 105.

14 *LPCR 1922*, p. 199.

15 For the questionnaire and the CP's response, see *ibid.*, pp. 77–80.

16 *Ibid.*, p. 81.

17 Lansbury and other Labour Councillors were gaoled because they insisted – unlawfully according to the Courts – on using rate income to increase the wages of Council employees.

18 Thus, in 1923, Frank Hodges of the Miners' Federation, could proclaim that all constituent units in the Party 'had a belief in the fundamental principles of political democracy, a belief in Parliamentary institutions and in Parliamentary action'. *LPCR 1923*, p. 187.

19 *LPCR 1922*, p. 177.

20 *LPCR 1924*, pp. 30–40.

21 R. Michels, *Political Parties*.

22 R. Hunt *German Social Democracy* 1918–1933, pp. 48–9.

23 *LPCR 1924* NEC Statement to Conference, pp. 39–40.

24 *LPCR 1922*, p. 114–5.

25 *LPCR 1923*, p. 188. The next year, he added with bravado, there would be 100.

26 Macfarlane, *op. cit.*, pp. 101, 103.

27 Ibid., p. 108

28 According to MacDonald, Communists were capable of securing the passage of their resolutions in about 30 CLPs. *LPCR 1925*, p. 187.

29 *LPCR 1922*, p. 74. This was carried by 342 votes to 161. *Ibid.*, p. 179.

30 G. D. H. Cole, *History of the Labour Party from 1914*, p. 145–6.

31 Quoted in B. Donoughue and G. Jones, *Herbert Morrison, Portrait of a Politician*, p. 100.

32 Constituency delegate speaking at Conference, *LPCR 1923*, p. 186.

33 *LPCR 1926*, p. 183.

34 Thus Lansbury described Communist 'philosophy' (as against 'method') as 'sound'; *ibid.*

35 Hunt, *op. cit.*, pp. 77–80.

36 NEC Statement 'The Labour Party and the Communist Party', *LPCR 1924*, p. 38.

37 *Ibid.*, p. 40.

38 *Ibid.*

39 *Ibid.*, pp. 123–4.

40 Ibid., p. 131. The major speakers against the motion were three prominent Communists; Harry Pollitt, Saklatvala (an MP) and William Paul, an endorsed parliamentary candidate.

41 *Ibid.*, p. 123.

42 Ibid., p. 131.

43 *Ibid.*, p. 131.

44 It would also restrict their choice of delegates to local, borough and regional Party bodies.

45 Quoted in Donoughue and Jones, *op. cit.*, p. 101.

46 NEC Statement 'The Communist Party', *LPCR 1925*, p. 38. Emphasis added. The differential approach emerged also in the rider attached to the two resolutions, which warned that they 'must be consistently administered by Constituency and local Labour parties in the appointment of their officials'; *ibid.*

47 *Ibid.*, p. 188.

48 *Ibid.*, The reference back was defeated by large majorities on both motions, *ibid.*, pp. 187, 188.

49 *LPCR 1926*, pp. 18–191 *LPCR 1927*, p. 15.

50 *LPCR 1925*, p. 188.

51 The NMM was designed to appeal to all militant trade unionists, but was controlled by the CP. See R. Martin, *Communism and the British Trade Unions 1925–1933*.

52 Cole, *op. cit.*, p. 147. Union leaders were especially indignant at the work of Communist 'factions' or cells, which they regarded as subversive and disloyal. MacFarlane, *op. cit.*, p. 185–9.

53 *LPCR 1928*, p. 23. The recommendations were carried by large majorities.

54 MacFarlane, *op. cit.*, pp. 149–150.

55 *Ibid.*, pp. 189–90.

56 *Ibid.*, p. 193.

57 *Ibid.*, p. 150.

58 Donoughue and Jones, *op. cit.* pp. 101–2.

59 *LPCR 1926*, p. 19.

60 *LPCR 1926*, p. 19; *LPCR 1927*, p. 15; *LPCR 1928*, p. 19; *LPCR 1929*, p. 12.

61 *LPCR 1929*, p. 12.

62 Thus Labour's show of force did not itself overpower the Left-Wing Movement, or eliminate its influence on the Party. By the Autumn of 1928, there were 75–80 Left-Wing Groups inside local Labour Parties, and in South Wales they were becoming an important political force. Twenty-one Labour Party organisations were represented at the third Annual Conference of the NLWM. The Communist Party was now to achieve what the Labour Party alone could not accomplish – the disintegration of the Left-Wing Movement. Under direction from Moscow, now following the ultra-left 'New Line', the CP withdrew all support from the NLWM – which accordingly collapsed. 'The Communist Party had itself removed the main thorn from the Labour Party and put an end to one of the most interesting and successful experiments in Communist penetration'. MacFarlane, *op. cit.*, p. 229.

63 The Constitution of the Labour Party, LPCR 1936, pp. 267–72, Clause VIII 2(b, 3).

64 Clauses VIII 2(a) III 1(c) 2.

65 Clause VIII 2(b).

66 The crucial character of these revisions (slightly amended in the 1950s) was disclosed in a more litigatious era. The powers of the NEC were tested in two major Court actions (one High Court, the other Court of Appeal), the Pembrokeshire CLP and Newham North East CLP cases in 1969 and 1978. Without the 1929 constitutional additions, the whole structure of central authority would, when put to the test, probably have been dismantled. See below, p. 168.

67 Clause III 1(a) (b) 3(a). The same applied to delegates to Conference. Members of the delegations of affiliated organisations were required 'individually' to conform to the Constitution and '3 P's'. Clause VIII 1.

68 Clause II 3. This also applied to delegates to Conference (from whatever organisation); in addition 'persons acting as candidates or supporting candidates in opposition to duly endorsed Labour candidates' were also ineligible to act as delegates. Clause VII 6(a) (b).

69 LPCR 1930, p. 29.

70 See Chapter 11 below.

71 *LPCR 1930*, pp. 29–37.

72 *Ibid.*, 1930, p. 29.

73 See below, Chapter 3.

74 Clause VIII, 4.

75 See below, Chapter 4.

76 Clause 7(a) LPCR 1919, p. 178.

77 Clause X, 2, 3, 7.

78 Also co-operative societies, but this is not germane to the discussion.

79 For most of the 140 Labour MPs who wore it, the ILP label was only notional.

80 Clause 4(c) 7(b) *LPCR 1919*, pp. 177, 178.

81 R. K. Alderman 'The Conscience Clause of the PLP' *Parliamentary Affairs* Vol. 19 1966, p. 227.

82 Quoted in R. T. MacKenzie, *British Political Parties*, p. 437.

83 The NAC had organised into a 'compact group', with regular meetings, an executive and unofficial whips, the 17 ILP MPs who had elected to accept the authority of the ILP Conference. MacKenzie *op. cit.*, p. 434.

84 LPCR 1931, p.94.

85 *Ibid.*, p. 33. The second amendment replaced the earlier commitment 'to discharge the responsibilities established by Parliamentary practice'.

86 Cole, *op. cit.*, pp. 274–7.

87 N. Greene, *Crisis and Decline: The French Socialist Party in the Popular Front Era*, passin.

88 e.g. 'The Relief Committee for the victims of Hitler Fascism' of which Labour's Chief Whip in the House of Lord (Lord Marley) was chairman.

89 LPCR 1934, p. 141.

90 *Ibid.*, p. 142.

91 *Ibid.*, p. 13.

92 *Ibid.*, p. 139.

93 *Ibid.*, p. 140. He had (as he made abundantly clear) his near-namesake Bevan particularly in mind.

94 The Socialist League was formed in 1932. It consisted largely of ex-members of the ILP who had opposed disaffiliation. Stafford Cripps soon emerged as its leading figure, with Aneurin Bevan also playing a prominent part.

95   *LPCR 1937*, p. 27.

96   Ben Pimlott, *Labour and the Left in the 1930s*, pp. 48–58.

97   Morrison, LPCR 1937, p. 163.

98   NEC circular, 26th May 1937, *ibid.*, p. 27.

99   *LPCR 1939*, p. 43.

100   Pimlott, *op. cit.*, pp. 170–81.

101   *LPCR 1939*, p. 228.

102   *Ibid.*, pp. 231–2.

103   Letter from the National Agent to A. Bevan and others in *ibid.*, p. 51.

104   *Ibid.*

105   For Cripps's expulsion see Donaghue and Jones, *op. cit.*, p. 231.

106   Minkin, *op. cit.*, p. 21

107   *LPCR 1939*, p. 228.

108   *Ibid.*, p. 231. Dalton was speaking on behalf of the NEC.

109   In Herbert Morrison's words 'This Executive is the servant of Conference, but it has a duty to lead the Conference . . . and I hope that every Executive that has responsibility will never hesitate to give Conference firm advice as to what it ought to do.' *LPCR 1937*, p. 163.

110   Cohesion has been usefully defined as 'the extent to which, in a given situation, group members can be observed to work together for the group goals in one and the same way'. E. Osbudon *Party Cohesion in Western Democracies*, p. 305.

111   *LPCR 1937*, p. 136.

112   *LPCR 1939*, p. 46.

113   This body campaigned successfully for a constitutional change transferring the right to select the Constituency section of the NEC from Conference to the CLPs themselves. See Pimlott *op. cit.*, pp. 118–24.

Notes to Chapter Two

1   Ian Mikardo, 'The Hateful, Fateful Fifties', *New Socialist* March–April 1982.

2   R. K. Alderman, 'Discipline in the PLP, 1945–51', *Parliamentary Affairs* Vol. 18, 1965.

3   *New Statesman*, 15th March 1952.

4   L. Hunter, *The Road to Brighton Pier*, p. 47.

5   P. Williams, ed. *The Diary of Hugh Gaitskell*, p. 313. According to Hunter about 100 Labour MPs and several top trade union barons, including Arthur Deakin of the TGWU supported the expulsion of Bevan and his closest associates, including Michael Foot, J. P. W. Mallallieu, Tom Driberg, John Freeman and Harold Wilson. *op. cit.*, pp. 47–8.

6   Hunter, *op. cit.*, p. 47.

7   *The Times*, 12th March 1952.

8   PLP Standing Orders, *LPCR 1952*, P. 201.

9   *Ibid.*, p. 80.

10   A tactic favoured by the platform to rally uncommitted opinion. See Minkin *op. cit.*, pp. 219–20.

11   Michael Foot, *Aneurin Bevan, 1945–1960*, p. 377. 'The most ferocious conference I have ever attended' recalled Jo Richardson, MP, then Secretary of the Bevanite group. Interview.

12   *New Statesman*, 4th October 1952.

13   *Ibid.* According to *The Times*, abrasive speeches by Arthur Deakin, Will Lawther and Tom Williamson, leaders of three of the biggest unions, the TGWU, NUM and GMWU barely conveyed their actual feelings. *The Times*, 4th October 1952. According to Douglas Jay, a Labour right-winger close to Hugh Gaitskell, the majority of Labour MPs regarded the eviction of Morrison and Dalton in favour of 'what looked like an organised Bevanite ticket' as 'a mortal blow at the Party'. D. Jay, *Change and Fortune*, p. 225.

14   Quoted in P. Williams *Hugh Gaitskell*, p. 304.

15   *The Times* 6th October 1952.

16   Leslie Hunter (the well-informed political correspondent of the *Daily Herald* and a confidant of Morrison) recalled: 'In speeches all over the country, in articles and at private meetings the [right's] campaign was carried on with a fury which reflected the depth and seriousness of the reaction to the Bevanites' success at Morecambe'. *op. cit.*, p. 62.

17   *The Times*, 4th October 1952, referring mainly to the views of Deakin, Lawther and Williamson.

18   In a speech punctuated by noisy protests, he insisted that the Bevanites get rid of their whips; dismiss their business managers and conform to the constitution'; and demanded that they cease their 'vicious attacks' on the leadership. *LPCR 1952*, p. 127.

19   *New Statesman*, 11th October 1952.

20   *The Times*, 13th October 1952.

21   *The Times*, 17th October 1952.

22   R. H. S. Crossman, *Backbench Diaries*, p. 157.

23   *The Times*, 24th October 1952.

24   Quoted in R. K. Alderman, 'Parliamentary Discipline in Opposition: the PLP 1951–64', *Parliamentary Affairs* Vol. 21 1967–8, p. 127.

25   Crossman *op. cit.*, p. 374. Another incident illustrates the same point. In October 1954, at their regular lunches, the senior Bevanites discussed proposals for the establishment of a 'Friends of Tribune' group (this was at the time when the NEC was contemplating the expulsion of the paper's editorial board). Bevan and Jenny Lee advised against 'such reckless action' on the grounds that it might precipitate the wrath of the NEC. Crossman, *op. cit.*, pp. 355–6.

26   *The Times*, 6th October 1952.

27   See Chapter 5 below, p. 122.

28   *Tribune*, 16th January, 1953.

29   Crossman, op. cit., p. 196.

30   *NEC Minutes*, 28th January 1953.

31   Crossman, *op. cit.*, p. 196.

32   *NEC Minutes*, 28th January 1953.

33   Peggy Duff, *Left, Left, Left*, pp. 43, 44.

34   The report struggled hard to find fault with the Brains Trusts. One criticism is that they were held without reference to the Party's official machinery. *Org. Sub.*, 18th February 1953.

35 Crossman, *op. cit.*, p. 203.

36 *Ibid.*

37 *Org Sub Minutes*, 18th February 1953. Precisely how the Trusts contradicted the 'spirit' of PLP decisions was never spelled out.

38 Quoted in Foot *op. cit.*, p. 391.

39 *NEC Minutes*, 25th February 1953, Crossman, *op. cit.*, p. 205.

40 The Bevanites did, however, agree – to propitiate the NEC – that the Executive members should refrain, for a decent interval, from participating in the Trusts. Crossman, *ibid.*

41 Foot, *op. cit.*, p. 391.

42 Crossman, *op. cit.*, p. 205.

43 *Tribune*, 13th November 1953.

44 Crossman *op. cit.*, p. 279. Shortly after, Ian Mikardo was formally censured by the NEC for writing a *Tribune* article criticising TUC policy in British Guiana. *NEC Minutes*, 16th December 1953.

45 Crossman, *ibid.*, p. 330.

46 'A Slander on the Dockers', Tribune, 22nd October 1954.

47 Earlier he described *Tribune* as 'a medium of publicity for a dissident element who constantly seek to challenge decisions which have been reached in a democratic manner within the Movement'. *Tribune*, 21st March 1952.

48 *NEC Minutes*, 27th October 1954. Crossman, *op. cit.*, pp. 359–60.

49 Hunter, *op. cit.*, p. 48. Percy Cudlipp, in the *News Chronicle*, quoted in *Tribune*, 29th October 1954.

50 Foot, *op. cit.*, p. 451.

51 Crossman, *op. cit.*, p. 361–2.

52 'The Case for Freedom' (reprinted as a pamphlet), *Tribune*, 12th November 1954.

53 *NEC Minutes*, 24th November 1954.

54 Though – perhaps as a face saver – Morgan Phillips warned that 'similar conduct in the future will compel the executive to take action', *ibid.*

55 In 1960, at the height of the unilateralist controversy, Tom Williamson unsuccessfully urged the NEC to take action against the weekly. *The Times*, 15th June 1960; *Tribune*, 22nd July 1960.

56 Hunter, *op. cit.*, p. 86.

57 See, in particular, Crossman, *op. cit.*, pp. 386–412, Foot, *op. cit.*, pp. 453–78 and *Gaitskell Diaries*, pp. 364–401.

58 See Foot, *op. cit.*, p. 473, Hunter, *op. cit.*, p. 93. This view was shared by many others, including a rising young star of the right, Denis Healey, who called for 'prompt and effective action to shut him [Bevan] up'. In *New Republic*, quoted *Tribune*, 14th May 1954.

59 Kenneth Harris, *Attlee*, p. 529.

60 Reproduced in *Gaitskell Diaries*, pp. 375–82.

61 *Ibid.* and Foot, *op. cit.*, p. 427.

62 Foot comments that some of his closest friends regarded his resignation as 'an act of impulsive folly which could ruin the whole Bevanite cause', *ibid.*

63 *Gaitskell Diaries*, p. 365.

64 By 132 votes to 72, the PLP passed a resolution stating 'That for members of the Party to take action in direct contradiction to a decision of the

Parliamentary Party taken four sitting days previously makes a farce of Party Meetings, and brings the Party into disrepute.' *Ibid.*, p. 380.

65 Foot claims that Bevan was misinterpreted, *op. cit.*, p. 460.

66 *Gaitskell Diaries*, pp. 380–81; Foot, *op. cit.*, pp. 460–62.

67 *Ibid.*, p. 462.

68 *Gaitskell Diaries*, pp. 368–70.

69 Most Bevanites believed he had behaved badly and urged him to be conciliatory. Foot, *op. cit.*, p. 466.

70 *Gaitskell Diaries*, pp. 383, 388.

71 Harris, *op. cit.*, pp. 530. 1.

72 *NEC Minutes*, 23rd March 1955.

73 *NEC* 30th March 1955 (minutes of the Special Sub-Committee held on 29th March 1955); all charges referred to infringements of PLP discipline. The specific constitutional grounds for expulsion from *the Party* were left somewhat hazy.

74 *NEC Minutes*, 30th March 1955.

75 Mikardo recalled: 'Edith Summerskill was so ravingly angry with me for denying her a casting vote that she couldn't bring herself to pronounce my name, and when, later, she called me to speak, she called me as "that man over there in the brown suit". From then on' Mikardo adds, 'and for as long as Edith remained on the executive, I always wore a brown suit at every NEC meeting'. I. Mikardo 'The Fateful, Hateful Fifties', *New Socialist*, March/April 1982.

76 That is, of the 28 members of the executive, 16 (taking account of Haworth's change of mind) favoured expulsion, but could never be mustered to vote together.

77 *Ibid.* Two CLP's backed the PLP.

78 *The Times*, 21st March 1955.

79 Hunter, *op. cit.*, p. 104.

80 *Gaitskell Diaries*, p. 400.

81 *The Times*, 11th March 1955. The Bevanites were 'thought to be active' promoting left-wing candidates. Deakin complained of 'strong-arm methods' being used by the left in some constituencies. *The Times*, 14th March 1955.

82 *Gaitskell Diaries*, p. 388. Another piece of luck helped Bevan. George Brinham, under great pressure from his union, the ASW, reluctantly voted against expulsion. The union leadership evidently felt that having succoured the platform at the 1954 Conference on German rearmament (the ASW vote was crucial) at the expense of breaking a clear conference mandate, they could not carry an anti-Bevan line as well. *Ibid.*, p. 400.

83 Harris, *op. cit.*, pp. 499, 542–3.

84 Williams, *op. cit.* A widespread feeling that Bevan's opponents had gone too far also contributed to a relaxation of the disciplinary regime. Interview, Ian Mikardo.

85 The Treasurer is elected by the Conference as a whole.

86 'The End of Bevanism', *New Statesman*, 12th October 1957.

87 MacKenzie, *op. cit.*, p. 643.

88 *LPCR 1952*, pp. 126–7. In 1954 the NEC passed a resolution making its decisions binding on all its members. The following year Barbara Castle – who had made a speech charging (with some truth) that only 'dirty dealings' had

secured a majority for German rearmament at the 1954 Conference – was censured for violating the resolution. *NEC Minutes*, 18th May 1954, 26th January 1955.

89 Earl Attlee, 'Party Discipline is Paramount', *English and National Review*, January 1957, p. 16. For a similar view, see Gaitskell's letter to 'Cassandra' (26th May 1954) reprinted in *Gaitskell Diaries*, pp. 352–6.

90 See Joint Meeting of the NEC and TUC General Council, *NEC Minutes*, 28th January 1953 and David Howell, *British Social Democracy*, pp. 190–99.

91 Crossman, *op. cit.*, p. 280 (entry 3rd December 1953).

92 *Ibid.*, p. 410 (entry 24th March 1955).

93 *Gaitskell Diaries*, p. 33. Nothing came of the move.

94 Crossman, *op. cit.*, p. 410 (entry 24th March 1955). Earlier, Crossman described at one PLP meeting a 'barrage of attacks on the [Bevanite] journalists who have a monopoly of the left-wing press'. *Ibid*, p. 330 (entry 19th May 1954).

95 S. Neumann (ed), *Political Parties*, p. 408. Similarly Lipset has argued that where the leadership exercises monopoly control over communications opposition is 'atomized, privatized or restricted to politically irrelevant groups'. S. M. Lipset *et al.*, *Union Democracy*, pp. 260–61.

96 The three members of *Tribune's* editorial board, Michael Foot, Jenny Lee and J. P. W. Mallallieu were all part of the Bevanite inner circle. Crossman was deputy editor of the *New Statesman*. Tom Driberg, a Bevanite NEC member, had a regular column in the left-wing Sunday paper, *Reynolds News*.

97 Gaitskell's 'only factional activity' according to his biographer 'was to try and counteract the Bevanite propaganda machine'. To this end, he aired proposals to buy Forward (Labour's Glasgow weekly) or the Spectator and persuaded sympathetic trade union leaders to purchase the right-wing monthly Socialist Commentary (to keep it afloat). He responded to the possibility that the Daily Herald might shift to the left under its new editor by energetically lobbying trade union members of its board. All these activities were conducted in the closest secrecy. Williams, *op cit.*, pp. 320, 855.

98 This was designed to complement the work of the inner Parliamentary Circle. As the heat upon this – the First Eleven – increased, the Second Eleven was upgraded and, by 1954, adopted a formal (though limited) organisational structure. Its main objective was to encourage CLPs to adopt left wing candidates. It also engaged in the framing and dissemination of radical policies and the establishing of a network of contacts in the Constituencies. It brought together senior Bevanite MPs, journalists and trade union and Party activists. Duff, *op. cit.*, pp. 46–8. Mark Jenkins, *Bevanism*, pp. 168–71.

99 Letter to *New Statesman*, 16th August 1952.

100 Duff, *op. cit.*, p. 49. Peggy Duff was *Tribune's* business manager. The practice of compiling 'slates' for the NEC is now commonplace but in the 1950s it aroused much resentment and was, as Duff notes, more surreptitiously undertaken.

101 Crossman, *op. cit.*, p. 125 (entry 23rd July 1952). The exchange was perhaps more informal and candid than usual as Morrison was visiting Crossman to offer condolences for the death of his wife.

102 *Ibid.*, p. 410 (entry 24th March 1955). Gaitskell also claimed to discern 'extraordinary parallels between Nye and Adolf Hitler. They are demagogues of exactly the same sort', *ibid.* This was at the height of the crisis over the attempted expulsion of Bevan which might account for Gaitskell's fervour.

103 Crossman, *op. cit.,* p. 125. The *New Statesman* (in an anonymous article, in fact written by Crossman, its deputy editor) acknowledged that the 'mere existence' of Bevanite group 'did arouse suspicion and hostility' in a Party which by tradition 'fiercely opposed organised minorities' and 'sniffed at the danger of sectionalism'. *New Statesman,* 18th October 1952 and Crossman, *op. cit.,* p. 158.

104 Arguing in favour of complying with the PLP instruction to disband the Bevanite Group, Bevan warned that failure to do so would 'alienate the people we are trying to win in the Parliamentary Party and we shall lose the support of nearly half the constituencies within twelve months because they will be able to pillory us as a sectarian conspiracy'. Crossman, *op. cit.,* p. 157.

105 *The Times* 31st March 1952. Similarly, his biographer wrote of Deakin that 'with his fundamental trade union belief in rule by the majority, he objected strenuously to factional activities'. This lay at the root of his acute antipathy to Bevanism. V. L. Allen, *Trade Union Leadership,* pp. 126–7.

106 R. H. S. Crossman, *Socialism and the New Despotism,* p. 9.

107 Uttered at a special meeting of the NEC on Party Unity. Crossman, *op. cit.,* p. 329 (entry 18th May 1954). At the same meeting Edith Summerskill, another member of the trade union-dominated women's section, raged at 'that man Mikardo . . . the real organiser of subversion in the Party', *ibid.* Earlier, Will Lawther had denounced Bevan as 'a man with his feet in Moscow and his eyes on No. 10 Downing Street', *Tribune* 17th October 1952. Bevan had, in fact, suggested the use of arms to break the Berlin blockade a couple of years previously, Foot, *op. cit.,* p. 228.

108 Lawther (President of the NUM) described Bevanite activities as 'a deliberate attempt to undermine the leadership in the same way as Hitler and the Communists did. There is no difference whatever between them. Their goal is the same, the glorification of power.' *Daily Telegraph,* 29th January 1953, reproduced in *NEC Minutes* 25th February 1953.

109 Howell, *op. cit.,* p. 186.

110 Interview, Ian Mikardo.

Notes to Chapter Three

1 This was clearly evident during the lifetime of the Attlee Government when, with the approval of the NEC, Party Secretary, Morgan Phillips used the resources of Head Office 'to bolster up the position of the leadership at every turn'. K. O. Morgan, *Labour in Power 1945–51,* p. 70.

2 For a few months earlier in the year responsibility was given to the Elections Sub-Committee.

3 *NEC Minutes,* 26th October 1955. This followed the Wilson Report which graphically described the poor state of Party organisation. It was felt that the Organisation Committee should have more time to devote itself to the matter and relieved of (increasingly) onerous disciplinary responsibilities.

4 *Chairmen's Sub Minutes,* 21st October 1958. Wilson, Chairman of Organisation Sub, objected but was over-ruled. *Organisation Sub Minutes,* 17th

February 1959.

5 *Organisation Sub Minutes*, 12th December 1962. According to its terms of reference, its conclusions would be reported to the Organisation Committee but would not normally be debated.

6 Memo on NAD. *NEC*, 16th December 1959.

7 Interview, Lord Underhill.

8 The term 'local party' will be used to refer to all lower-level party units, including central (borough), constituency and ward organisations.

9 Letter from N. Coghill, J. Mendelsam and F. M. Slee. *New Statesman*, 21st June 1952. The letter concluded: 'if this ruling remains unchallenged it means that any constituency party holding independent views is effectively isolated'. The previous year (during the lifetime of the Labour Government), two left-wing MPs (Sidney Silverman and Fred Messer) had been instructed by the NEC to abandon preparations for a conference on 'Socialism and Peace' on the grounds that it challenged official Party policy, usurped the authority of the NEC and Conference and threatened Party unity (the organisers reluctantly acceded) *NEC Minutes*, 21st March 1951; 25th April 1951.

10 *Organisation Sub Minutes*, 16th January 1962; 18th September 1963. The Oxford party gave way; there is no reference to Aberdare's response but since the item did not reappear in the Committee's agenda, it presumably acquiesced.

11 *Elections Sub Minutes* 21st March 1955; *The Times* 21st March 1955. The conference was probably overtaken by events.

12 Minkin, *op. cit.*, passim.

13 In 1956 Croydon South CLP circulated all constituencies requesting support for a constitutional amendment. The same year *Victory for Socialism* convened a conference to discuss its proposals for constitutional reforms. In 1961 Coventry borough Labour Party called for an eve of Conference meeting of CLPs to draw up a joint emergency resolution on the international situation. In each case the organisers were reprimanded for acting unconstitutionally. *NEC Minutes*, 25th July 1956. *Chairmen's Sub Minutes*, 15th March 1956; *NEC Minutes*, 19th September 1961. The outcome of the first and third cases is not known but lack of any further reference to them suggests they complied with the Executive's rulings. As in the Ealing South case, regional officials may have succeeded in stopping other conferences before the matter reached the NEC.

14 *The Times*, 9th April 1956.

15 It almost certainly would have suffered the same fate if it had.

16 Stephen Swingler, *Tribune*, 21st February 1958; *The Times*, 13th February 1958.

17 Crossman, *op. cit.*, p. 669 (entry 28th February 1958).

18 *Chairmen's Sub Minutes*, 25th February 1958; *NEC Minutes*, 26th February 1958.

19 LP Constitution, Clause 11(3). See below, pp. 57–8.

20 Morgan Phillips to Stephen Swingler, MP 26th February 1958. Morgan Phillips Correspondence Box 11 GS/VS/78. *LP Archives*.

21 *Chairmen's Sub Minutes*, 11th March 1958; *NEC Minutes*, 26th March 1958.

22 *The Times*, 7th March 1958.

23 Williams, *op. cit.*, p. 477. In fact, local branches were formed; presumably what was at issue was the degree of central direction.

24 Interview, Jo Richardson MP.

25 See Minkin, *op. cit.*, p. 35.

26 Crossman, *op. cit.*, p. 669.

27 Morgan Phillips wrote to Sir Frank Soskice, QC, MP, asking his advice on this matter. Soskice's reply does not appear in the archives but the NEC's subsequent more reticent attitude suggests it was not encouraging. Letter to Sir F. Soskice, Box 11, Phillips Correspondence GS/VS/76. *LP Archives.*

28 'Activities of Organisations Formed to Influence Labour Party Policy', *Organisation Sub*, September 1961.

29 Williams, *op. cit.*, p. 477. In the meeting with the VFS, Gaitskell was at pains to distinguish between 'legitimate' and 'illegitimate' dissent. 'A national organisation', he stated 'composed of like-minded people, with an Executive annual conference and branches, existing not only to discuss policy but also to propagate views, seemed to go beyond the limits of what was permissible.' *Chairmen's Sub Minutes*, 4th March 1958.

30 *The Times*, 1st March, 3rd March 1958.

31 See above, Chapter 2, pp. 48–9.

32 Clause VIII, 2(a) (b) 3. See above, Chapter 1, p. 16.

33 According to the National Agent, Len Williams, the above rule gave the NEC 'all the power it requires to meet any situation which may arise'. Memo to Morgan Phillips. Morgan Phillips Correspondence Box 28 GS/CMR/20. *LP Archives.*

34 See, e.g., resolution reprimanding VFS *NEC Minutes* 21st March 1956.

35 See, e.g., letter from Morgan Phillips to Sir Fred Messer, MP, then VFS Chairman, 7th March 1956. M. Phillips Correspondence Box 11 GS/VS/19. *L P Archives.*

36 See, e.g., Chris Mullin, 'The Party Machine', *Tribune*, 18th May 1979.

37 See above, Chapter 1, pp. 17–18.

38 *LPCR 1946*, p. 14. The recommendation was approved by 2,413,000 votes to 667,000, *ibid.*, p. 174, and was incorporated as Clause II(3) of the constitution.

39 'List of Proscribed Organisations', *Chairmen's Sub*, 22nd January 1957. Organisations were placed on the list in three ways; firstly when they had been declared ineligible for affiliation to the Labour Party; secondly when membership had been declared incompatible with membership of the Party; thirdly, when they had been declared ancillary or subsidiary organisations of the Communist Party. In each case, the NEC was required to report a proscription to Conference and obtain its endorsement; *ibid.*

40 See below, Chapter 6, pp. 121–9.

41 This section draws heavily upon an interview with a former Transport House official.

42 *LPCR 1952*, p. 17. The Union Movement was also added to the List, as the successor of the British Union of Fascists; *ibid.*

43 *LPCR 1953*, p. 12.

44 At least one NAD official was approached by a member of the Special Branch (and brother of a future International Secretary) offering 'assistance'. Interview, former NAD official.

45 According to Sam Watson (speaking on behalf of the NEC) 'peace' and 'friendship' societies were agents for 'the destruction of social democracy and the propagation of international Communism'. *LPCR 1953*, p. 190. Two other factors reinforced Labour's anti-Communism: the ruthless manner in which the new Communist regimes in Eastern Europe suppressed socialist parties, and the continuing bitter struggles between the right-wing establishments and Communist-led left-wing groups in a number of unions, like the NUM and AEU.

46 *LPCR 1953*, p. 12.

47 One such person was Jim Mortimer, Vice-Chairman of the British–Chinese Friendship Association (and subsequently Labour's General Secretary from 1982 to 1985), who refused to relinquish his post after the Association's proscription and was removed from the Party. (Interview, Jim Mortimer.) In another case three members of North Hendon CLP were expelled for their association with a banned peace organisation but never appealed. J. Cattermole. Organiser's Report. 3rd March 1952. *Cattermole Papers* MSS/9/3/14/42. Warwick University MRC. The cases that did go to appeal may have been atypical since (presumably) the more aggrieved or unjustly treated an individual felt, the more likely he or she was to complain.

48 Letters from Smithson to *Tribune*, 15th January 1954, 30th August 1957 and a report in *Tribune*, 9th August 1957.

49 *Tribune*, 9th August 1957.

50 *LPCR 1953*, p. 12.

51 *Organisation Sub Minutes*, 18th February 1953.

52 Report of an enquiry into an appeal (henceforth REA) against expulsion by Councillor Redfern, *Organisation Sub*, 17th February 1954. The appeal was dismissed. In the same year three members of North Kensington CLP were expelled by the local party on grounds of their involvement with the North Kensington Tenants Association – alleged to be 'ancillary or subsidiary' to the Communist Party but not actually proscribed. The enquiry, conducted by Sara Barker complained of the 'embarassment' caused to the Labour Party by the activities of the appellants and upheld their expulsion. REA against expulsions, *Organisation Sub*, 15th June 1955.

53 *Organisation Sub Minutes*, 21st January 1953; *NEC Minutes*, 28th January 1953.

54 A. L. Williams 'Enquiry into the State of Party Organisation in Hull', *Organisation Sub*, 19th March 1953.

55 Party members (including a number of MPs and future MPs) were also banned, on pain of expulsion, from participating in conferences organised by the CP's organ, the *Daily Worker*. *Organisation Sub Minutes*, 17th November 1959; 13th December 1960; 17th January 1961.

56 It is also worth noting the strength of the personal links between Transport House and Yorkshire – both Len Williams and Sara Barker had been Party officials in the area.

57 Thus Jim Mortimer rejoined the Labour Party in 1956, after changing constituencies. He was never asked about his continued membership of proscribed organisations. Interview.

58 *New Statesman*, 17th November 1961.

59 *New Statesman*, 23rd March 1962. Senior party figures were also prepared to use less orthodox measures to embarrass their opponents. In 1960, the height of the unilateralist controversy, George Brown with the approval of Gaitskell, apparently sought the help of MI5 to unmask alleged 'crypto-Communists' within the PLP. The Prime Minister, Harold Macmillan, was not co-operative, and help was not forthcoming. Chapman Pincher, *Inside Story*, p. 22.

60 Sara Barker succeeded Len Williams (promoted to the General Secretaryship) during the course of the year. According to her Assistant National Agent, Reg Underhill, she 'got too involved' in an 'unfortunate episode'. Interview, Lord Underhill.

61 *Organisation Sub Minutes*, 15th May 1962.

62 Collins was unable to reply at once.

63 *NEC Minutes*, 23rd May 1962. He added: 'I presume that you have sent similar letters to Mr. Gaitskell and Mr. Brown, pointing out that they are flouting the policy of the Labour Party on Polaris and the Tests as laid down at the last . . . Conference.'

64 *The Times*, 24th May 1962.

65 *NEC Minutes*, 23rd May 1962.

66 *Organisation Sub*, 19th June 1962; *The Times*, 20th June 1962.

67 *Organisation Sub*, 19th June 1962. At a party held in the House of Commons to delebrate his 90th birthday, the impenitent philosopher declared: 'I cannot submit my judgment to anybody, so I shall go on doing what I think fit, and if that means the Labour Party doesn't want me I don't very much mind.' *The Times*, 26th May 1962.

68 *Organisation Sub Minutes*, 19th June 1962. Russell's reply remained one of studied indifference. According to his Secretary, Ralph Schoenman, he was 'paid up, though he doesn't care one way or another.' *The Times* 20th June 1962.

69 This was, coincidentally, acknowledged in a paper on membership submitted to the Organisation Committee the previous month. The reason was 'faulty collecting machinery in most parties'. *Organisation Sub*, 15th May 1962. This rendered the Committee's resolution of the Russell problem even more absurd.

70 *NEC Minutes*, 27th June 1962.

71 *Organisation Sub Minutes*, 19th June 1962.

72 *NEC Minutes*, 27th June 1962.

73 More correctly, ratifying expulsions.

74 The amendment was approved by the NEC by 17 votes to 8. *NEC Minutes*, 25th July 1962.

75 *Tribune*, 3rd August 1962.

76 *Ibid*.

77 *The Times* 3rd October 1962. *Tribune* 5th October 1962 (Reports of private session of Conference).

78 *Tribune*, 5th October 1962 for a general account and quotations. Also *The Times*, 3rd October 1962. *LPCR 1962*, p. 152.

79 *Tribune*, 5th October 1962. It estimated that over 95% of the CLP vote was cast against the amendment.

80 Interview, Ian Mikardo.

81 See below Chapter 8, pp. 172–177.
82 Sec, e.g. P. Williams 'The Labour Party: The Rise of the Left', *West European Politics*, Vol. 6, 1983.
83 Within the SPD 'anti-Communism was increasingly used to threaten dissident members with expulsion and to ensure the loyalty of those who remained'. W. Graf, *The German Left Since 1945*, p. 145. For examples of expulsions and bannings see *ibid.*, pp. 164, 239.
84 Interview, Ian Mikardo.
85 In May 1962 – the same month when the moves against Russell *et al.* were mooted – the 'Independent Nuclear Disarmament Electoral Committee' (INDEC) – an off-shoot of CND aiming to promote candidates at elections – was proscribed. *Organisation Sub Minutes*, 15th May 1962.
86 See below Chapter 8, p. 176.

Notes to Chapter Four

1 Clause VIII 4, *LP Constitution* 1960.
2 Set A Model Rules for CLPs, Clause XIV 3.
3 Clause 9, Standing Orders for Labour Groups. The NEC also, of course, had final responsibility for interpreting and enforcing the Party constitution and rules.
4 Wilson *op. cit.*, pp. 68–70.
5 A. L. Williams, 'Procedure for Dealing with Disputes and Disciplinary Cases', *Chairman's Sub*, 12th December 1955. Regional Executive Committees, the executive organs of Labour's Regional Councils, were bodies with few powers and limited influence.
6 Interview, Lord Underhill.
7 Williams *op. cit.*
8 Interview, Harold Sims.
9 As far as can be ascertained. It is possible that, in some cases, for political or other reasons, certain facets of a dispute were not spelt out or given their due importance.
10 An example taken at random illustrates this. In January 1955 the Organisation Committee considered four enquiry reports. All consisted of appeals by individuals against disciplinary action taken by Labour groups or local parties; in every case the disputes precipitating such action revolved around either personality clashes or differences over parish-pump issues. *Organisation Sub*, 19th January 1955.
11 Donaghue and Jones *op. cit.*, p. 136.
12 *LPCR 1930*, pp. 12, 165.
13 *LPCR 1936*, pp. 305–7. The memorandum was altered slightly in 1939.
14 The relevant party unit might be the central, borough or local party, the trades council and Labour party or (in the case of London) the Local Government Committee with representatives from CLPs within the borough. For simplicity's sake we shall refer to all as the 'local party'.
15 Clauses 5(a) (b) (d), Standing Orders for Labour Groups. *LPCR 1939*, Appendix XIII.
16 Memorandum, *LPCR 1939*, Appendix XIII.

17   See, e.g., J. G. Bulpitt, *Party Politics in English Local Government*, *passim*; G. Jones, *Borough Politics*, pp. 173–4; H. V. Wiseman 'The Working of Local Government in Leeds', Part I, *Public Administration*, Vol. 41 (1963), p. 54. The two notable exceptions were in Liverpool and Nottingham. These are discussed below.

18   Memorandum, *op. cit.*

19   Report of an enquiry into a dispute between Eton and Slough CLP and Slough Labour Group, *Chairmen's Sub*, 27th November 1956.

20   Report on an Enquiry into the Appeals (henceforth REA) against the withdrawal of the whip from eight councillors by Birmingham Labour Group. *Organisation Sub*, 15th January 1964.

21   Nottingham City L.P. Constitution and Rules, Clause 12, 1956. See also S. A. Barker, 'Selecting Local Government Candidates', *Labour Organiser*, November 1968.

22   However Janey Buchan MEP recounts one incident during this period where she displaced a sitting councillor at a selection conference (in Glasgow) whom the NEC then insisted must be reinstated. *Tribune*, 8th August 1975.

23   Eton and Slough dispute, op. cit. *Chairmen's Sub*, 27th November 1956.

24   *Organisation Sub Minutes*, 9th July 1957.

25   Report of an enquiry into complaints of seven members of Deptford Labour Group against Deptford CLP. *Organisation Sub*, 15th May 1962.

26   *LPCR 1939*, pp. 222–3.

27   See REA against exclusion from the Panel by Salford LP *Organisation Sub*, 9th December 1958. Enquiry into Reading LP, *Organisation Sub*, 17th January 1961; *Organisation Sub Minutes*, 14th February 1961. Report of an Enquiry into a dispute between Derby LP and Group, *Organisation Sub*, 16th July 1968.

28   Note, *Organisation Sub*, 9th July 1957.

29   Circular to local parties, September 1957, quoted in Enquiry into the affairs of Derby LP *Organisation Sub*, 16th July 1968.

30   The paucity of research into local Labour politics means that the above observations are based on only limited evidence. Jones, *op. cit.*, pp. 170–73; Wiseman, *op. cit.*, p. 54; R. Butterworth, 'Islington Borough Council: Some Characteristics of Single-Party Rule', *Politics*, Vol. 1, May 1966; J. Gyford, *Local Politics in Britain*, pp. 72–3. See also the discussion of Liverpool and Nottingham below. The general picture is confirmed by internal Party enquiry reports and interviews with former Party officials.

31   See, e.g., REA by twelve Councillors against their expulsion by Peckham and Dulwich CLPs, *Chairman's Sub*, 12th April 1956. (According to *Tribune* the expelled included the President, Vice-President and Treasurer of the Peckham Party; *Tribune*, 10th February 1956. Later, it reported that in one ward 85 Party members resigned in protest; *Tribune* 2nd March 1956.) Enquiry into charges made by Peckham CLP, *Chairman's Sub*, 18th September 1956, *Chairman's Sub Minutes*, 5th December 1956.

32   It also enjoyed extraordinary longevity. Most of the senior figures in the 1950s were still in place in the early 1980s – when they decamped *en masse* to the SDP. See Chapter 10 below.

33   Butterworth, *op. cit.*, pp. 22–6; A. Howard, 'Islington's Last Hurrah', *New*

Statesman, 17th August 1962. In 1962 every member of the Executive of the East Islington party was a councillor; *Tribune*, 16th November 1962.

34 Butterworth, *op. cit.*, p. 27.

35 See Chapter 6 below, p. 130.

36 Report of a meeting with a deputation from Islington E CLP, *Organisation Sub*, 17th March 1959.

37 One was a former Communist who had quit the Party over Hungary. As an NEC report explained 'it will be some time before he can accustom himself to the more liberal way of thinking that we require in the Labour Party'. East Islington, report by Jim Raison, London District Organiser. *Organisation Sub*, 20th January 1959.

38 Letter, G. Palmer to J. Raison, London District Organiser. *London LP Archives*, Box 'Disputes Within Parties'. (Palmer was one of the pacifists.)

39 A. L. Williams, 'East Islington', *Organisation Sub*, 14th July 1959.

40 Palmer was asked by Len Sims, London Regional Organiser, whether, as a condition of entering the Labour Party he was prepared to terminate his association with CND. He declined. L. Sims, Organisers' Report, 16th February 1959. London LP Archives *op. cit.* A little later another applicant barred from East Islington found his appeal dismissed because he refused to put loyalty to the Labour Party before that of CND's 'Committee of 100' (a direct-action splinter group). REA against the decision of Islington East to refuse membership, *Organisation Sub*, 15th May 1962.

41 Letter from National Agent to Mr and Mrs Maddison, 25th May 1959; *London LP Archive, op. cit.*

42 *New Statesman*, 13th June 1959. As it happened, the weekly found itself at the centre of the next controversy over membership in East Islington. In 1962 the Party blocked the admission of two people, both of whom were simply trying to transfer their membership. One – a member for thirteen years – was the *New Statesman's* office manager. He was summoned before the full E C of the party and cross-examined about his beliefs – whether he was a member of CND, read *Tribune* or approved of Michael Foot. His application was rejected. The wide publicity his case attracted clearly embarrassed the NEC which used his move to another constituency to drop appeal proceedings. *New Statesman*, 13th July, 3rd August 1962. *Tribune*, 8th March 1963.

43 *Standing Orders for Labour Groups*, 7(c), *LPCR 1939* p. 381–3. Emphasis added.

44 *Ibid.*

45 *Ibid.*, 7(a). Similarly, if a question at a council meeting was 'in conflict with the policy' of the group, prior consultation with a group officer was required, *ibid.*, 7(b).

46 *Ibid.*, 9.

47 'Memorandum', *op cit.* It added that 'too great a rigidity would be unwise'.

48 Bulpitt, *op. cit.*, pp. 41–2 (Salford), 61–3 (Manchester), 81 (Rochdale), 100 (Sale). E. Dell, 'Why Whip the Council?', *Socialist Commentary*, February 1960 pp. 7–9 (Manchester). H. Heçlo, 'The councillor's Job', *Public Administration*, Vol. 47, 1969, p. 195 (Manchester).

49 Bulpitt, *op. cit.*, pp. 24–5 (Middleton), 100 (Macclesfield); Butterfield, *op. cit.,* p. 29 (Islington); Jones, *op. cit.,* pp. 183–4 (Wolverhampton).

50 See Chapter 10 below.

51 Two of a handful of exceptions, in Liverpool and Nottingham, are discussed below.

52 These observations are based upon a reading of all enquiry reports (well into the three figures) which figured on the NEC's agenda in the 1950s and 1960s.

53 S. Barker, 'A Model Labour Group', *Labour Organiser,* June 1952, p. 106.

54 *Ibid.*

55 In one case the NEC dismissed the appeal (though it commuted the sentence) of a councillor disciplined for defying a group decision on the funding of sports facilities. The councillor, however, had a record of previous 'offences'. REA against withdrawal of the whip by Dagenham Labour Group, *Organisation Sub,* 15th May 1963.

56 One Party official commented: 'it would scarcely be too much to say that, in so far as these [i.e. group] Standing Orders are specific, the principle of leadership, as the indispensible element in the functioning of a Labour Group, is clearly indicated'. J. W. Raisin, 'How to Keep Group – Party Relations Sweet', *Labour Organiser,* July 1953.

57 REA's against withdrawals of the whip by Chislehurst and Sidcup, and Nuneaton Labour Groups, *Organisation Sub,* 17th November 1959; *Chairmen's Sub,* 26th November 1957.

58 In both the cases referred to in the preceding footnote, appeals were dismissed but the sentences reduced. A common NEC judgment was to accompany a rejection of an appeal against the loss of the whip with a rider that it be restored once an appellent agreed to abide by Standing Orders in the future. See, e.g., REA's against withdrawals of the whip by Billingham and Aberdeen Labour Groups, *Organisation Sub,* 21st June 1960; 20th November 1962.

59 See, e.g., REA against expulsion from Bridgewater CLP, *Chairman's Sub,* 26th February 1957. REA against withdrawal of the whip by West Bromwich Labour Group, *Organisation Sub,* 19th February 1964.

60 For example in Islington where the council was, at the time, 100 per cent Labour. See REA against withdrawal of the whip by Islington Labour Group and Expulsion by Islington N CLP, *Chairmen's Sub,* 24th June 1958. Altogether five councillors were expelled (although only one bothered to appeal) for voting against a differential rent scheme (a very emotive issue at the time). Butterworth, *op. cit.,* p. 29.

61 The Birmingham Labour Group, led by the redoubtable Alderman Harry Walton, maintained a strict disciplinary regime. See A. Howard, 'The Chamberlain Legacy', *New Statesman,* 7th August 1964.

62 REA against the withdrawal of the whip by Birmingham Labour Group. *Organisation Sub,* 15th January 1964. K. Newton *Second City Politics,* pp. 269–72. Newton's conclusion that the episode dispelled the 'myth' of group discipline in Birmingham is unconvincing. The rebels were, indeed, readmitted but not only failed to have the least impression on council policy, but would undoubtedly have been severely punished if they had broken their undertaking 'to observe the Labour Group whip in future'. In rather similar circumstances more than 15 years later, rebel Manchester councillors received more favourable treatment from the NEC and went on to wrest control from the existing group leadership.

63 In Sara Barker's words 'differences should be settled within the Group, and not carried to the floor of the Council Chamber or into the public press', *op. cit.*, p. 106.

64 The Councillor had – on the initiative of the group's chief whip – been expelled, not from the group but from his CLP – an irregular procedure, as the enquiry acknowledged. REA against expulsion by Islington S W CLP, *Organisation Sub*, 17th July 1966.

65 S. Barker, 'A Model Labour Group', *Labour Organiser*, June 1952, p. 106.

66 Arthur Latham, 'Whipless in Romford' *Tribune*, 24th May 1963.

67 Bulpitt, *op. cit.*, pp. 39, 56, 64–5, 73–4, 93–4.

68 *Ibid.*, p. 103.

69 Butterworth, *op. cit.*, pp. 29–31.

70 See, e.g., Reports into Reading L P, *Organisation Sub*, 17th January 1961; *Organisation Sub Minutes*, 14th February 1961; and Islington North CLP; *Organisation Sub*, 20th November 1962.

71 Quoted in *Tribune*, 1st January 1960.

72 'Labour in the Sixties' quoted in *Tribune* 12th August 1960.

73 This was the case in Birmingham. Newton, *op. cit.*, pp. 98–101.

74 A study of the NEC's handling of dissension in Liverpool Labour Party in this period is also valuable because it supplies a useful background for our later, more detailed, analysis of the national Party's response to Trotskyist ascendency in the city. See below, Chapter 12.

75 R. Baxter, *Liverpool Labour Party*, 1918–1963, passim. Unpublished doctoral thesis. See also R. Baxter, 'The Working Class and Labour Politics', *Political Studies*, Vol. 20, 1972 pp. 100–104.

76 Interview, Lord Sefton. The TCLP acted as both trades council and as central Labour Party, and was the most powerful local Party unit in the city.

77 Baxter, *op. cit.*, pp. 205–6.

78 Interim Report into Liverpool TCLP, *Organisation Sub*, 15th July 1953; Final Report, *Organisation Sub*, 16th September 1953; *Organisation Sub Minutes*, 20th January 1954.

79 Baxter, *op. cit.*, p. 311–12.

80 *Ibid.*, pp. 315–17.

81 This asserted that the whip should be imposed on all matters coming before council and not simply major items of policy. REA of Councillor Walker against withdrawal of whip by Liverpool Labour Group, *Chairmen's Sub*, 25th February 1958.

82 The five councillors included Dick Crawshaw, a right-winger and subsequently an MP, and Bill Sefton. His close ally Brian Crookes disagreed with him on this issue. Interview, Lord Sefton.

83 REA against withdrawal of the whip by Liverpool Labour Group, *Organisation Sub*, 20th January 1959.

84 *NEC Minutes*, 28th January 1959.

85 *Organisation Sub Minutes*, 17th March 1959.

86 *NEC Minutes*, 25th March 1959.

87 These included exerting pressure on councillors coming up for

re-election (presumably threatening to exclude from the panel).

88 Report of a meeting between Alderman Braddock, Simon Fraser, Secretary of the Labour Group and the TCLP and Reg Wallis, North West Regional Organiser, *Organisation Sub*, 15th March 1960.

89 *Ibid.*

90 In a policy statement, 'Labour and the Sixties'. See above p. 77.

91 *Organisation Sub Minutes*, 15th March 1960.

92 Baxter, *Political Studies*, *op. cit.*, p. 103.

93 *Organisation Sub Minutes*, 17th January 1961.

94 Report of meeting between Braddock, Fraser and Wallis, *op. cit.*

95 The following rule changes were applied to Liverpool TCLP: a reduction in the frequency of meetings, a redistribution of funds in favour of the CLPs and (a later addition) separate meetings of the political and industrial sections; *LPCR 1957*, p. 15.

96 *Organisation Sub Minutes*, 9th July 1957.

97 Report of an inquiry into Liverpool TCLP. *Organisation Sub*, 16th January 1962. The delay was due to a decision to postpone the enquiry until after the local elections.

98 Interview, Eric Heffer.

99 Interview, Lord Sefton.

100 One exception was Walter Aldritt, a GMWU official and later MP, who expressed apprehension of a likely Trotskyist take-over of a separate Liverpool Labour Party. Reg Wallis also opposed the division of the TCLP.

101 Baxter 'Liverpool Labour Party', *op. cit.*, p. 226.

102 Wilson, *op. cit.*, p. 111. Although he pushed for the demotion of the TCLP he never favoured its dissolution.

103 Reports on Liverpool TCLP, *Organisation Sub*, 27th September 1968, 27th November 1968. *NEC Minutes*, 18th December 1968. *Organisation Sub Minutes*, 14th January 1969.

104 'Separation of the Liverpool TCLP', *Organisation Sub*, 27th September 1968.

105 Michels *op. cit.*, passim. See below, Chapter 7.

106 *Nottingham Evening Post*, 5th October, 1965; (Nottingham) *Guardian Journal*, 6th October, 7th October, 1965.

107 *Nottingham Evening Post*, 10th November 1965, 12th November 1965; *Guardian Journal*, 11th November 1965. J. Cattermole, 'Organiser's Report', 9th November 1965; *Cattermole Papers*, MSS/9/3/20/292 Modern Records Centre. (MRC), Warwick University.

108 *Organisation Sub Minutes*, 8th December 1965.

109 K. Coates, *The Crisis of British Socialism*, p. 94.

110 REA of Ken Coates against expulsion by Nottingham West CLP, *Organisation Sub*, 17th May 1966.

111 Report into Nottingham City Labour Party, *Organisation Sub*, 17th May 1966.

112 John Callaghan, *British Trotskyism*, pp. 127–8.

113 Two other members were future Labour MPs, Harry Selby and Martin Flannery.

114 Interview Ken Coates. Coates attributed his success in winning the

Presidency of the city party mainly to his efforts to commit the Labour Group to more progressive policies on comprehensive education and council house building and not to alleged Trotskyist 'hegemony'.

115 *Ibid.*
116 *Guardian Journal*, 11th November 1965.
117 Report into Nottingham L P, *op. cit.*
118 *Ibid.* In addition, the NEC issued a number of directives designed to curb the influence and status of the Nottingham party. It was instructed to meet less frequently (in line with decisions of the 1957 Party Conference) and warned that if the situation failed to improve within a year the city party would be dissolved and replaced by a less prestigious local government committee. *Ibid.*
119 Possibly Cattermole. According to Coates he 'played the press very systematically to indict myself and people who were presumed to be close to me'. Letter to author, 31st October 1984.
120 *Guardian Journal*, 11th November 1965.
121 Interview, Jim Cattermole.
122 *Ibid.*
123 J. Cattermole, Organiser's Report, 22nd October 1965; *Cattermole Papers*. MSS 9/3/20/276 MRC Warwick University.
124 *Tribune*, 10th June 1965.
125 *L P Archives.*
126 See below, Chapter 6, pp. 119–21.
127 J. Higgins, 'Spotlight on Labour's Citadels: Nottingham', *New Statesman*, 30th August 1974. The report added – confirming Coates' attacks upon the Labour group the previous decade – that the council's housing record was 'uniformly abysmal'.
128 *NEC Minutes*, 30th September 1966.
129 *NEC*, 25th January 1967.
130 *Organisation Sub Minutes*, 17th January 1967.
131 *Tribune*, 14th April 1967.
132 *Organisation Sub*, 14th March 1967.
133 *Ibid.*
134 *Ibid.*
135 See below, Chapter 8, pp. 168–71.
136 *Tribune*, 19th April 1967.
137 See below, Chapter 8, pp. 168–71.
138 *Organisation Sub*, 19th November 1968.
139 Interview David Robertson. At one meeting, in a bid to dissuade the NEC from consenting to Coates's reinstatement, she read out a long document spelling out Coates's many criticisms of the Prime Minister Harold Wilson (who was present at the meeting and visibly embarrassed). Interview Ken Coates. Coates suggests that the episode gave irate trade unionists, angered by the 'In Place of Strife' White Paper, an opportunity to snub Wilson. *Ibid.*
140 Interview, Ron Hayward.
141 Report on Ken Coates, *Organisation Sub*, 16th September 1969.

Notes to Chapter Five

1   A. Ranney, *Pathways to Parliament*, p. 10.

2   CLPs can vary these rules, but only with the NEC's permission.

3   *Model Rules for CLPs* (henceforth, CLP Rules), Clause XII.

4   M. Rush, *The Selection of Parliamentary Candidates*, pp. 132–3.

5   CLP Rules, Clause XII 3(d).

6   At one point a proposal to alter this was mooted. See below p. 96. Rush has suggested that on one occasion invalidation may have been used to exclude a candidate, but this was an exceptional case. Rush, *op. cit.*, pp. 133–4.

7   *LP Constitution 1957*, Clause IX 3.

8   *CLP Rules*, Clause XII 5.

9   *Ibid.*, Clause XII 4.

10   *LPCR 1948*, p. 209.

11   All candidate selection matters were dealt with by the appropriate Sub-Committee; in this period three were, at different times, charged with the responsibility: Elections, Chairmen's and Organisation.

12   'Shall List B be Changed?', *Labour Organiser*, May 1960, p. 94.

13   Ranney, *op. cit.*, p. 139.

14   'The Selection of Parliamentary Candidates', *Elections Sub*, 28th September 1955.

15   *Elections Sub Minutes*, 23rd November 1953. Zilliacus had been expelled in 1949: he had been one of the fiercest and most unremitting critics of Bevin's foreign policy in the PLP and was suspected of Communist associations. The Elections Sub was disturbed by the 'tone of his speeches and writings since his re-admission into Party membership'.

16   *Chairmen's Sub*, 23rd June 1955; 26th November 1957; 21st January 1958.

17   *Chairmen's Sub*, 25th February 1958. Hobden had briefly left the Party to join the C.P. After his return he had served as Secretary of a borough and constituency party and as a councillor in Brighton.

18   *Chairmen's Sub*, 15th December 1958.

19   *Chairmen's Sub*, 15th March 1956; 12th April 1956; 24th July 1956. *Tribune*, 9th May 1956. Chamberlain claimed that both the National Agent and the Chief Whip opposed his inclusion on the list. Later he fell victim to the stricter regime introduced in 1960 and was again removed from the list; *Organisation Sub*, 20th June 1961. Lesley Solley, a former MP expelled for his Communist associations in 1949 was readmitted to the Party in 1958 but barred from the B List; *Chairman's Sub*, 21st October 1958.

20   Though the minutes sometimes state that a decision was deferred to permit further enquiries into the 'party activities' of nominees. See, e.g., *Chairmen's Sub*, 25th February 1958; 15th December 1958.

21   From time to time acceptance on to the A List – usually an automatic procedure – was deferred or rejected. The former happened in the case of four nominees – all members of the Communist led Electrical Trades Union – in 1959. One was later admitted after having offered 'emphatic' support for Party policy. *Chairmen's Sub*, 23rd March 1959; 2nd June 1959.

22   *LP Constitution 1957*, Clause IX 7.

23 Rush, *op. cit.*, p. 137.

24 In some cases, it is not clear whether the difficulty was entirely political in character.

25 *NEC Minutes*, 26th September 1952; *Elections Sub Minutes*, 20th November 1952. In 1964 Floud was elected MP for Acton. Nigel West claims that he was recruited as a Soviet agent whilst at Oxford. He was investigated by MI5 in 1967, but committed suicide that year 'for reasons completely unconnected with his interrogations'. N. West, *A Matter of Trust: MI5 1945–72*, pp. 167–8.

26 See below, Chapter 6, p. 122.

27 *Elections Sub Minutes*, 10th June 1953; See also *Tribune*, 9th October 1953.

28 M. Jenkins, *op. cit.*, pp. 94–100

29 *NEC Minutes*, 30th April 1952; *Elections Sub Minutes*, 21st March 1955. Wimbledon dug its heels in, earning itself a warning that it would be disbanded if it failed to select another candidate. *Elections Sub Minutes*, 25th April 1955.

30 *Chairmen's Sub*, 21st January 1958.

31 NAD papers on Braddock, *Chairmen's Sub*, 21st October 1958; 26th January 1959. *Chairmen's Sub Minutes*, 23rd February 1959.

32 A group of Trotskyists, led by John Lawrence, veered close to the Communists in the mid-1950s.

33 *Chairmen's Sub Minutes*, 27th November 1956; 20th May 1958; *NEC Minutes*, 17th December 1958. 'S. Goldberg', Note by National Agent, *Chairmen's Sub.*, 20th May 1958; Ranney, *op. cit.*, p. 163.

34 Mikardo *New Socialist, op. cit., Elections Sub Minutes*, 3rd May 1955.

35 They were William Warbey, a former and future MP and staunch left-winger, J. Holland, E. Fletcher, J. Foord and G. McCartney. *Elections Sub Minutes*, 25th April 1955; *Chairmen's Sub Minutes*, 12th April 1956; *NEC Minutes*, 25th April 1956; *Chairmen's Sub Minutes*, 14th June 1956; 20th April 1959.

36 It is also worth noting that Labour's selection procedure is organised in such a way as to afford few opportunities, either to selectors or to Party officials, to gain much insight into candidates' political beliefs.

37 According to one study, regional officials report to Transport House 'any significant policy differences between the views expressed by a candidate and those of the Labour Party'. E. C. Janosik, *Constituency Labour Parties in Britain*, p. 127. Janosik describes one case where a candidate expressed unilateralist views, which were conveyed to Head Office in a Regional Organiser's report. Initially the NEC refused to endorse the candidate but, after the CLP protested, agreed to do so on the understanding that he explained official Party policy in the campaign, *op. cit.*, pp. 128–9.

38 *CLP Rules*, Clause XII 7(b).

39 Brian Crookes, a leading member of the anti-establishment camp, was Secretary of the local Party.

40 *Elections Sub Minutes*, 21st June 1954. Ranney *op. cit.*, p. 189. Jack and Bessie Braddock, *The Braddocks*, pp. 90–91.

41 *Elections Sub Minutes*, 21st June 1954.

42 Report of an Enquiry into Liverpool Exchange CLP. *Elections Sub*, 20th

October 1954. The report also called upon the CLP to remove the Trotskyist element it claimed existed in Exchange. It was approved by the NEC.

43   *Elections Sub Minutes*, 4th April 1955.

44   'Report of an Enquiry into the Parliamentary Selection Conference of Liverpool Exchange CLP', *Elections Sub*, 25th April 1955.

45   Braddocks, *op. cit.*, p. 92; Ranney, *op. cit.*, p. 190. Later the CLP was disbanded 'and reformed without the Communist and Trotskyist elements'. Braddocks, *op. cit.*, p. 92.

46   Ranney, *op. cit.*, p. 190.

47   *Elections Sub Minutes*, 21st March, 3rd April 1955; Ranney *op. cit.*, p. 191. Miss Burton now sits as an SDP peer in the House or Lords.

48   *Elections Sub Minutes*, 25th April 1955.

49   R. Jackson *Rebels and Whips*, p. 266.

50   *NEC Minutes*, 30th March 1955.

51   See below, Chapter 8, pp. 168–171.

52   It suggested that nominations could be invalidated 'if information is brought to [the Sub Committee's] notice that might result in the NEC refusing endorsement'. *Chairmen's Sub Minutes*, 24th June 1957.

53   *NEC Minutes*, 24th July 1957. The prime mover in blocking the recommendation appeared to be Aneurin Bevan.

54   'The Selection of Parliamentary Candidates', *Elections Sub*, 28th September 1955.

55   See 'Parliamentary Panel Game', *New Statesman*, 3rd August 1957.

56   'The Selection and Financing of Parliamentary Candidates', *Chairmen's Sub*, 7th May 1957.

57   *Chairmen's Sub Minutes*, 25th February 1958.

58   Len Williams to Morgan Phillips, 12 Jan 1960; M. Phillips Correspondence, Box 28 'Constitution', *L P Archives*.

59   A. L. Williams, 'Improving the Method of Compiling List B', *Organisation Sub*, 11th April 1960. According to Barbara Castle Gaitskell was the prime mover behind the drive for more central control. Castle, *op. cit.*, p. 134.

60   *Organisation Sub Minutes*, 17th May 1960.

61   *LPCR 1960*, p. 243.

62   In the year September 1960 to September 1961, 114 nominees were interviewed. *LPCR 1961*, p. 10. Many, the National Agent (Sara Barker) later commented, 'were given the benefit of the doubt'. 'Procedure for the Compilation of List B', *Organisation Sub*, 20th January 1965.

63   *Organisation Sub Minutes*, 14th March 1961 (the tenacious Braddock was by now 74 – the reason given for excluding him; 20th June 1961.

64   *Organisation Sub Minutes*, 20th September 1960 (Sefton); 19th June 1963 (Crookes). In 1963 the Organisation Committee reversed its decision on Sefton; *Minutes*, 18th September 1963.

65   *Organisation Sub Minutes*, 20th June 1961.

66   *Organisation Sub Minutes*, 18th July 1961. She was included two years later when she agreed to provide the undertaking: by then Gaitskell had been replaced by Wilson. *Organisation Sub Minutes*, 17th July 1963.

67   *Op. cit.*, *Organisation Sub*, 20th January 1960.

68   *Organisation Sub Minutes*, 10th May 1961.

69 *Organisation Sub Minutes*, 18th May 1965. Harrington was by then a GLC Councillor. The decision was so obviously inconsistent that it was reversed a couple of months later – though not without stiff resistance. 'We were soon in the middle of one of those good, old-fashioned NEC rows', Crossman recorded in his diary; 'I voted for the left, in the traditional way', *Diaries of a Cabinet Minister*, Volume One, p. 229 (entry 26th May 1965); *Organisation Sub Minutes*, 20th July 1965.

70 *Tribune*, 5th January 1962.

71 *The Times*, 6th October 1961.

72 A. Howard, 'Labour's New Electoral Army', *New Statesman*, 11th May 1962.

73 See above, Chapter 3, pp. 62–5.

74 *Organisation Sub Minutes*, 12th December 1961.

75 Three names are unfamiliar to the author: A. C. Brownjohn, R. Spurway, I. S. Davidson, the candidates for Richmond, Harrow Central and Aberdeen East. The others were Eric Varley, Stan Newens, James Kerr, Bill Molloy, Ernie Roberts, Iltyd Harrington, Stan Thorne, John Palmer, W. Dow, Hugh Jenkins, Dennis Hobden, Carol Lever, and S. E. Spicer.

76 Including Stan Newens, Stan Thorne, Bill Molloy, Hugh Jenkins and Dennis Hobden.

77 *Organisation Sub Minutes*, 14th November; 12th December 1961.

78 *NEC Minutes*, 23rd May 1962; *Organisation Sub Minutes*, 19th June 1962.

79 *Organisation Sub Minutes*, 11th April; 15th May 1962. A. Howard, 'The Dover Road', *New Statesman*, 1st June 1962.

80 *Organisation Sub Minutes*, 14th November; 12th December 1961; *Tribune*, 29th December 1961; 9th February 1961. The NEC rubbed salt in the wounds by then removing him from the A List. *Organisation Sub Minutes*, 20th February 1962.

81 *Organisation Sub Minutes*, 12th December 1962.

82 *Organisation Sub Minutes*, 20th July 1965.

83 *Organisation Sub Minutes*, 20th July; 16th November 1965; letters by Palmer to *Tribune*, 11th March 1966 and *The Guardian*, 9th December 1981 (Palmer was then the paper's European Editor).

84 *Organisation Sub Minutes*, 14th September 1965; 16th November 1965.

85 *Organisation Sub Minutes*, 10th April 1963. According to an NEC Member, Harrington was 'marginal, not clearly unacceptable like Sam Goldberg or Ernie Roberts'; Quoted in Ranney, *op. cit.*, p. 164.

86 Clause IX 7(c), LP Constitution, 1957.

87 Palmer was a leading figure in the Trotskyist International Socialism Group in the 1960s.

88 *NEC Minutes*, 23rd May 1962; *Organisation Sub Minutes*, 17th July 1962; *Tribune*, 8th June; 24th August 1962.

89 *Organisation Sub Minutes*, 15th May 1962; article by Jenkins in *Tribune*, 7th April 1967; Interview Lord Jenkins. Protests from other 60 CLPs were not enough, however, to save Ernie Roberts, who did not fit into the borderline category.

90 See above, Chapter 1, p. 2.

91 'The Selection of Prospective Parliamentary Candidates', *Chairmen's Sub*, 24th June 1958.

92 Two involved the steel workers' union, BISKTA, in Pontypool and Middlesborough East; *NEC Minutes*, 25th September 1958; Ranney *op. cit.*, pp. 146–7. The third involved the NUM in Caerphilly; *Organisation Sub Minutes*, 11th June 1968.

93 *Organisation Sub Minutes*, 17th July 1963; *New Statesman*, 16th August 1963, 20th September 1963.

94 An obviously embarrassed Driberg told the NEC that, in the circumstances, he didn't wish it to exercise its right to insist that he be placed on the short-list. *Chairmen's Sub Minutes*, 15th April 1958; *NEC Minutes*, 23rd April 1958; *Tribune*, 2nd May 1958.

95 *Chairmen's Sub Minutes*, 24th June 1958.

96 Ranney, *op. cit.*, pp. 145–6.

97 'The Selection of Parliamentary Candidates', *Elections Sub*, 26th September 1955.

98 Thus, in the 1986 Spanish general election, the numbers of left-wingers in the Socialist Party's list of candidates were reduced because of their opposition to NATO membership. They were warned that there was no room for those who publicly questioned official Party policy, as established by the Prime Minister, Felipe Gonzalez. *The Guardian*, 17th June 1986.

99 Interview, Harold Sims.

100 Ranney, *op. cit.*, p. 177.

101 See below, Chapter 7, pp. 148–9.

102 A vivid illustration of this is Tom Driberg's failure to secure a place on the short-list for the St Helens seat, to which we have already referred. A whole range of local interests, which included a Catholic faction as well as NUM lodges protested at the attempt to draft the very cosmopolitan (and metropolitan) figure of Tom Driberg. *Times*, 1st May 1958; *New Statesman*, 3rd May; 10th May 1958.

103 A complaint was lodged by Margaret Herbison, a right-wing member of the NEC. *Organisation Sub Minutes*, 12th December, 1962.

104 S. A. Barker, 'Procedure for the Complilation of List B', *Organisation Sub*, 20th January 1965.

105 *Organisation Sub Minutes*, 14th June 1966.

106 Interview Lord Underhill (at the time, Assistant National Agent and given the responsibility of conducting the interviews).

107 However, rather oddly, Geoffrey Bing, a former Bevanite MP, was kept off the A List, a decision strongly contested by the left on the NEC. No reason was given. *Organisation Sub Minutes*, 14th May 1968; 18th March 1969; *NEC Minutes*, 22nd May 1968; 26th March 1969.

108 M. Downing, candidate for the very safe Tory seat of Esher.

109 See above, pp. 90–100.

110 *CLP Rules*, Clause XII 4, 5.

111 Rush, *op. cit.*, p. 143.

112 Interview, Harold Sims.

113 *Ibid.* He claimed to have helped three members of the Shadow Cabinet at the time of interview (July 1984).

114 Interview, Jim Cattermole.

115 Interview, Harold Sims.

116 In 1958 the NEC accepted a NAD recommendation that CLPs should be encouraged to seek the help of Regional Organisers in contacting potential nominees. *Chairmen's Sub Minutes*, 24th June 1958.

117 The procedure, Janosik has noted, 'in some ways seems designed to conceal rather than reveal the basic political attitudes of nominees', *op. cit.*, p. 154.

118 *Organisation Sub Minutes*, 15th March 1960. This was a delegation of the NEC's own power to authorise the commencement of the procedure.

119 Interview, Harold Sims.

120 Regional Organiser's Report 6th January 1965. *Cattermole Papers*, MRC. MSS/9/3/20/S.

121 Interview with a journalist covering the area at the time. The candidate in question was selected and subsequently elected MP.

122 *Ibid.*

123 The short-list was drawn up by the CLP Executive, subject to ratification by a specially convened meeting of the GC. It was compiled from those individuals who had succeeded in obtaining at least one nomination. All ward parties and affiliated trade union branches or socialist societies were empowered to nominate.

124 Interviews, Harold Sims, Ian Mikardo.

125 Ranney, *op. cit.*, pp. 159–60.

126 P. Seyd, *Factionalism Within the Labour Party – A Case Study of the Campaign for Democratic Socialism*, Unpublished M. Phil dissertation, p. 202.

127 Interviews, Reg Wallis, Jim Cattermole; these were the two most successful placers of parliamentary candidates.

128 This was changed in 1965. Henceforth only individual members of the Party were eligible to stand as delegates for the GC. *LPCR 1965*, p. 174. The alteration was much resented by the NUM which wrote to Len Williams 'expressing its dismay at the effects the change would have on the miners local influence' Andrew Taylor, 'The Modern Boroughmongers', the Yorkshire Area (NUM) and Grassroots Politics, *Political Studies*, Vol. 32 1984 p. 891.

129 This was altered in 1979. Henceforth a delegate, to be eligible to vote at a selection conference, had to have attended at least one GC meeting within the twelve months prior to the selection conference.

130 In Birmingham, the senior city organiser presided over a 'totally centralised' electoral machine and made sure that the person he wanted secured any vacant candidature. A. Howard, 'The Chamberlain Legacy', *New Statesman*, 7th August 1964. In the early 1960s a number of able young Gaitskellites were selected in the city: Roy Hattersley, Brian Walden and Dennis Howell.

131 This was to change in the 1970s with the spread of left-wing pressure group activity to the constituencies. Those groups which boasted their own full-timers – pre-eminently the Militant Tendency – were particularly well placed to promote their chosen candidates.

132 'Affiliations to CLPs', *NEC*, 28th September 1955. According to a former Yorkshire Regional Organiser, union delegates generally comprised the majority of total delegates on GC's in his area. Interview, Harold Sims. To this weight of numbers, unions – which sponsored candidates – added the allure of ready cash. CLPs were perenially starved of funds, not least in Labour strongholds where membership (and hence subscription income) tended to be lower than average. The appeal of a sponsored candidate – with the promise that the sponsoring union would pick up the election tabs – was not always easy to resist. See T. E. M. McKitterick., 'The Selection of Parliamentary Candidates: The Labour Party', *Political Quarterly*, Volume 30, 1959, p. 223; Rush *op. cit.*, p. 232–3.

133 Interview, Harold Sims. Unlike Cattermole, Sims was not influenced by political or factional considerations. Prescott, for example, was a left-winger.

134 Interview, Jim Cattermole.

135 Interview, Bill Jones. In 1965–6, for example, Jim Cattermole urged senior officials of Notts NUM to encourage more participation by NUM lodges in two constituencies were vacancies were likely to occur. Regional Organiser's Reports 28th October 1965; 21st January 1966; *Cattermole Papers*, MRC MSS 9/3/20/282, 9/3/21/24. A study of a selection in the mining constituency of Ince in Lancashire noted 'a dramatic increase in affiliation amounts [most probably] caused by the desire on the part of the NUM branches to ensure that the union maximised its delegate entitlement Eric McPherson "The Trade Union as a local pressure group" Unpublished MA thesis, Liverpool University pp. 77–8.

136 Janosik, *op. cit.*, p. 152. The 1965 rule-change (requiring all GC delegates to be Party members) made this more difficult, but by no means impossible. Party membership subscriptions during this period, it is worth noting, were very low (and could be defrayed by an affiliated organisation).

137 This is akin to April Carter's concept of 'pure authority': 'To recognise authority [in this sense] is to be persuaded . . . that whatever is advocated will be worthy of respect and compliance'; A. Carter, *Authority and Democracy*, p. 13.

138 Interviews, former Regional Organisers.

139 This paragraph is drawn from an interview with David Robertson.

140 Throughout the 1950s and early 1960s there were between 200 and 250 agents. By the late 1970s, there were less than eighty.

141 This changed later when a number of agents were recruited into the National Agency Service.

142 D. J. Wilson, *Power and Party Bureaucracy in Britain*, p. 57.

143 Cattermole claimed to have assisted a series of 'good right-wingers' – Tony Crosland, Dick Taverne, Geoffrey de Freitas, Phillip Whitehead. Interview.

144 Interview, Bill Jones.

145 A view that most former Regional Organisers interviewed by the author held. This influence was not necessarily used to promote candidates of a particularly political stripe.

146 Interview, Harold Sims.

147 Quoted in Ranney, *op. cit.*, p. 143. The organiser was Jim Cattermole, 'a career politician', one of his former colleagues commented 'who happened to be an organiser'. Interview.

148 Ranney, *op. cit.*, p. 159.

149 Seyd, *op. cit.*, p. 197. Others involved were Arthur Hayday, of the GMWU, Patrick Gordon-Walker, MP, and Lord Peddie, Chairman of the

Co-operative Party. A report in the *New Statesman* suggested that these meetings were organised on the initiative of George Brown, Chairman of the Organisation Committee, and saw them as part of a process of 'building up the power of the central machine'. *New Statesman*, 28th September 1962.

150 He names Donald Alger, John Anson, Jim Cattermole, Ron Hayward, Jim Raisin, Len Sims and Reg Wallis, *op. cit.*, p. 197. Anson, Cattermole, Raisin and Wallis were definitely dedicated right-wingers; Hayward's inclusion (as Southern Regional Organiser) is more surprising and he denies it. He recalls he was approached by two CDS members who asked for access to his files. 'I sent them away with a flea in their ears.' He intimated that the CDS received a more favourable reception from some of his colleagues. Interview. According to Lord Underhill, Seyd exaggerated the number of CDS sympathisers within the regional staff. Letter to author.

151 Seyd, *op. cit.*, p. 209. Relations became particularly strained over a selection conference at Colne Valley in 1962, when the NAD and CDS were pushing rival candidates; as a result neither won. *Ibid.*

Notes to Chapter Six

1 M. Crick, *Militant*, p. 31–5.

2 Transport House kept a wary eye on the RCP but after an investigation the Organisation Sub-Committee concluded that its size and influence was too slight for it to warrant proscription. *Organisation Sub Minutes* 10th December 1947. At this time the NEC was far more concerned with the activities of Communist Front organisations and fellow travelling MPs.

3 It was formally launched by the Labour Publishing Society whose officers included Jack Stanley, General Secretary of the Constructional Engineering Union and Ernie Roberts, subsequently Assistant General Secretary of the AEU and then an MP. M. Jenkins, *op. cit.*, p. 91–2.

4 J. Callaghan, *op. cit.*, p. 68–9.

5 *Organisation Sub Minutes*, 19th July 1950.

6 *Jenkins, op. cit.*, p. 93–5.

7 Interview, Lord Sefton, a member of Liverpool S.F.

8 *Jenkins, op. cit.*, p. 98–9.

9 *NEC Minutes* 23rd April 1951.

10 'Trotskyism in Britain', Report to the *Chairman's Sub-Committee*, 24 June 1958.

11 *Organisation Sub Minutes*, 21st July 1954. For a more detailed discussion, see below, p. 122.

12 A. L. Williams, 'Trotskyism – recent development', *Organisation Sub*, 17th March 1959.

13 See above Chapter 1.

14 Interview, Lord Underhill.

15 See, e.g., *Chairmen's Sub Minutes*, 24th June 1958.

16 Also, interviews, Reg Wallis, Lord Underhill.

17 Anson to Sims 16th February 1961. *London LP Archive*, Box 'Infiltration and Expulsion'.

18 Jones to Sims 17th February 1961, *Ibid.*

19 Sims to Johnson 29th February 1960, *ibid.*

20 Johnson to Sims, 3rd February 1960 *ibid.* This 'Mr. Knight' was later identified as Ted Knight, expelled from Norwood Labour Party in 1954 and later leader of the Council in Lambeth. He was said to 'hang around Manchester's left-wing Coffee House a lot'. Johnson to Sims, 10 May 1960, *ibid.*

21 A letter from Sims to a London party agent indicates the type of material which was gathered. Noting a high level of Trotskyist activity in London he asked for a 'private and confidential' report about 'personal political affiliations and political activists' of leftists in Hackney; Sims to R. W. Masters, *ibid.*

22 Sims to Williams 8th November 1960. Sims noted the difficulty in obtaining precise information about their effectiveness as a group, but concluded that they were 'more of a grouping of marxists than a group with a set purpose, such as the SLL', *ibid.*

23 Loftus to Williams 13th May 1959 London LP *op. cit.*

24 See below, Chapter 11.

25 See above chapters 1 and 3.

26 LP Constitution 1957.

27 *Ibid.* Clause II, Sections 3, 4.

28 *Organisation Sub Minutes*, 10th December 1947.

29 NEC report, *LPCR 1954* p. 12. The relevant Organisation Sub resolution also referred to SF's 'disturbing effect' on Labour's League of Youth. *Organisation Sub Minutes*, 18th April 1954.

30 *Organisation Sub Minutes*, 21st July 1954.

31 Circular from Morgan Phillips, *ibid.*

32 M. Foot 'I call this an outrage' *Tribune* 13th August 1954.

33 *New Statesman*, 14th August 1954; *Organisation Sub*, 21st September 1954 (for resolutions). Bevan and Crossman attempted to refer back the decision: they mustered nine votes (as against 14 against) – an unusually high figure which implies that some centre-rightists must have had their doubts too. *NEC*, 28th July 1954.

34 *Tribune*, 5th October 1954, in an editorial entitled 'Witch-hunt'. This particular witch returned to haunt Michael Foot years later when his denunciation of the banning of *Socialist Outlook* was contrasted by a successor as editor of *Tribune* with his support for the expulsion of five Militant supporters in his period as leader.

35 It is worth noting that, at this stage, *Tribune* did *not* call for the abolition of the Proscribed List. Foot's attitude, at least, was more nuanced. 'There *is* a care for proscribing certain organisations . . . such actions may be justified as an unavoidable measure for dealing with Communist methods of infiltration. But it is a long and dangerous step from this to the action which the NEC has now approved to try and kill a newspaper'. *Tribune*, 13th August 1954, *op. cit.* For a similar view, see *New Statesman*, 6th November 1954.

36 According to Len Williams, the Healyites possessed 'considerable influence' in parties in Leeds, Salford, Liverpool, Birmingham, Streatham and Norwood. 'Trotskyism – Recent Developments', *Organisation Sub*, 17th March 1959.

37 *LPCR 1959*, p. 103.

38 *NEC Report, ibid.*, p. 21.

39 *Ibid.*, p. 103.

40 See above, Chapter 2, pp. 28–9.

41 Interview, Lord Underhill: Nicholas, *op. cit.*, p. 103; Alice Bacon, on behalf of the NEC, *LPCR 1954*, p. 165.

42 Report of the Enquiry into Young Guard, *Organisation Sub*, 17th July 1962. Three of the members of the editorial board were in fact enthusiastic Trotskyists – Gus Macdonald (later of Granada), John Palmer (later of *The Guardian*) and Keith Dickenson (later of *Militant*).

43 *NEC Minutes*, 23rd May 1962.

44 *NEC Report, LPCR 1965*, pp. 13–14.

45 Interview, Lord Underhill.

46 Letter, A. L. Williams to W. Preston, Secretary, Leeds LP, 30th April 1955; *LP Archive*, Box 'R. H. Sedler'. (Emphasis added.)

47 Title of article by John Marullus (Michael Foot), *Tribune*, 7th August 1959.

48 *Yorkshire Post*, 11th April 1959; *Tribune*, 17th April 1959.

49 *Tribune*, 22nd May 1959.

50 See, e.g., REA A Stanley against expulsion by NW Lancaster CLP, *Organisation Sub*, 16th February 1960 and letter from Stanley, *Tribune*, 29th May 1960.

51 Report of the enquiry into R. H. Sedler, *Organisation Sub*, July 1959.

52 Interview with Ron Sedler (including quote); *Yorkshire Post*, 21st May 1959.

53 'Summary of charges against R. H. Sedley', *LP Archive*, Box 'R. H. Sedler'.

54 Report of the enquiry into R. H. Sedler *Organisation Sub* July 1959.

55 According to Sedler, his expulsion helped demoralise the left. Interview.

56 Circular from Morgan Phillips, 3rd April 1959.

57 'Members and others v Sedler', Opinion, L. Ungoed-Thomas 12th May 1959, *LP Archive* 'R. H. Sedler'. (Emphasis added.)

58 A. L. Williams, 'Expelled for Opinions', *Labour Organiser*, January 1955, p. 12.

59 Williams, *op. cit.*, p. 12.

60 NEC Report, *LPCR 1959*, p. 21.

61 Report of Inquiry into the affairs of East Islington CLP conducted by Alice Bacon, George Brinham and Sara Barker, *Organisation Sub*, 17th November 1954.

62 Report of Inquiry into the appeals of Mr and Mrs Shaw, Nottingham East CLP conducted by A. Skeffington and Sara Barker, *Organisation Sub*, 17th November 1954. In both this and the above case expulsion was confirmed on the grounds (amongst others) of subscribing to principles incompatible with membership of the Labour Party.

63 Emphasis added. Report of an inquiry into the Appeal of P. Cadogan against expulsions by Cambridge CLP conducted by Sara Barker, *Organisation Sub*, 4th January 1960.

64 *LP Constitution*, 1957, Clause 3(a).

65 M. Phillips, 'Constitution and Standing Orders Development 1900–1951', *LP Archive*, M. Phillips Correspondence, Box 28 'Constitution'.

66 See W. Graf, *The German Left since 1945, passim*.

67   M. Phillips, 'Constitution and Standing Orders Development', p. 19, *op. cit.* See also *NEC Minutes*, 27th January 1960; 17th May 1960.

68   See special NEC to discuss Gaitskell's proposals to amend the constitution, *NEC Minutes*, 16th March, 1960.

69   In 1959 Ray Gunter and Len Williams interviewed the historians E. P. and Dorothy Thompson. The Thompsons, who had quit the Communist Party in 1956 over the invasion of Hungary, had been prevented, by the Yorkshire REC, from joining the Labour Party. Their constituency party, Halifax, appealed on their behalf and Gunter and Williams had been selected to conduct the inquiry. Much of the interview was spent in efforts to gauge the Thompsons' political beliefs. The inquiry report concluded that the two historians remained unclear in their own minds 'about where they stand in relation to the basic issues which have divided constitutional and democratic socialists from supporters of revolutionary and authoritarian forms of socialism'. The Report added that 'Mr. Thompson is sure to exercise a powerful influence', which might not be 'helpful' and recommended that his (and Mrs Thompson's) application for admission be deferred for a year. Report, *Organisation Sub*, 14th April 1959. A decade later, Gunter quit the Labour Party.

70   *Organisation Sub Minutes*, 21st September 1954.

71   The document is reproduced in a pamphlet by T. Mercer, D. Finch and E. R. Knight entitled *'Expelled for Socialist Opinions'*.

72   Inquiry into the affairs of Norwood CLP conducted by Alice Bacon, George Brinham and Sara Barker, *Organisation Sub*, 17th November 1954.

73   Inquiry into the affairs of Islington East CLP, *Organisation Sub*, 17th November 1954.

74   Interview, Bill Jones.

75   Inquiry into the affairs of Islington East CLP, *op. cit.* The enquiry conducted by Alice Bacon, George Brinham (NEC Members) and the Assistant National Agent, Sara Barker was denounced by *Tribune* as a 'travelling tribunal' and Alice Bacon was accused of launching a 'general inquisition' into the opinions of the Hunters. The weekly pointed out that the expulsions were engineered by a minority in Islington East led by the Agent (Bill Jones); *Tribune*, 3rd December 1954.

76   S. A. Barker Report on the Reorganisation of Islington East CLP *Organisation Sub* 16th March 1955.

77   See P. Duff, *Left, Left, Left*, pp. 83–5.

78   *Chairman's Sub*, 20th May 1958.

79   Reports on the reorganisation of Holborn and St. Pancras South CLP, *Chairman's Sub*, 24th June, 22nd July 1958.

80   Regional Organiser's Report, 9th April 1959, *London LP Archives.*

81   W. A. Jones, Organising Assistant's Report, 14th April 1959; L. Sims Regional Organiser's Report, 12th May 1959 *London LP Archives, Organisation Sub Minutes*, 26th May 1959.

82   L. Sims, Regional Organiser's Reports 9th April, 15th April, 20th April 1959, *London LP Archives.*

83   *Chairman's Sub Minutes*, 26th May 1959.

84   Report by J. Keys on Paddington South CLP, 9th December 1964, *London LP archives; Organisation Sub Minutes*, 20th January 1965.

85 The tactics and practices the Healyites used included abuse, intimidation and actual physical violence. Interviews John Crouch (in 1959 a non-Trotskyist left-winger in Streatham initially opposed to expulsions), Lord Underhill. Rumours about the SLL's unsavoury methods had for long abounded in left-wing circles.

86 See below, p. 140.

87 See, e.g. *Organisation Sub Minutes*, 26th May 1959. On occasion a Party official might be instructed by the NEC to attend all EC or GC meetings of a CLP or even to take control of a party for a period. Letter from Lord Underhill to the author.

88 Standard letter, copies in *London LP archives*.

89 See, e.g. Tulse Hill ward Minutes, 16th June 1959; *London LP archives*.

90 Not all the expelled were Trotskyists; some were merely associates or sympathisers who were opposed in principle to expulsions and for this reason defied the authority of the NEC. Interview, Bill Jones.

91 Standard letter, copies in *London LP archives*.

92 Interview, Lord Underhill.

93 Any reply which failed to provide the specific undertakings required was regarded as unsatisfactory.

94 E.g. Vivien Mendelson and Bill Boakes, both active Healyites, categorically denied any association with the SLL. L. Sims Regional Organiser's Report, 12th May 1959, *London LP archives*.

95 See, e.g., *Tribune*, 29th May, 12th June, 4th December 1959. At one point, at the height of the drive against the SLL in 1959, it condemned the 'near-totalitarian procedures governing expulsions', *Tribune*, 31st July 1959. It persistently urged the Party to establish an independent appeals tribunal that could ensure that the rights of members were safeguarded and the violations of natural justice avoided. See, e.g., *Tribune*, 29th May 1959, 14th September 1962.

96 But see below, Chapter 8 for a discussion of the High Court judgment on the reorganisation of Pembrokeshire CLP in 1969.

97 Occasionally the NEC did uphold an appeal if it was felt a CLP was unduly harsh.

98 Letter, Scottish Labour Party secretary to London Regional Organiser, 25th May 1962, *London LP Archives*.

99 See above, Chapter 4, pp. 72–3.

100 REA Angus Macdonald, *Organisation Sub* 16th January 1963.

101 In 1967 several members of the Trotskyist International Socialism (IS) group sought admission into Islington East, but were spurned. The NEC endorsed the constituency party's decision on the grounds of the applicants' views and affiliations (though IS was never proscribed). See REA's R. Cox, C. Chapman and T. P. O'Brien, *Organisation Sub*, 20th June 1967, 14th February 1968.

102 See, e.g., reports to *Chairman's Sub*, 18th September 1956; *Organisation Sub* 20th September 1966.

103 E.g. in 1964 Leeds E and Birmingham Sparkbrook were prepared to readmit excluded members but the NEC refused; *Organisation Sub Minutes*, 19th February 1964, 15th April 1964. The same fate befell Peter Cadogan: the support of his CLP did not prevent successive NEC vetoes. See *Organisation*

Sub, 15th November 1960; *Organisation Sub Minutes,* 20th February 1962.

104 See, e.g., the case of the Bretts, expelled from Norwood CLP in 1959 *Organisation Sub,* 16th July 1968.

105 Report of Enquiry Committee, *Organisation Sub,* 14th May 1968.

106 When the NEC revised its posture in the 1970s and allowed Trotskyists to enter/re-enter sharp disputes sometimes occurred with CLPs who wished to keep them out. See below, Chapter 11, p. 223.

107 Regional Organiser's Report 4th June 1959. *London LP archive.*

108 This was particularly so in Paddington South. Interview, John Keys.

109 See, e.g. Regional Organiser's Report 8th June 1959 (Norwood) *London LP Archives* and A. L. Williams 'Preliminary Report on the Reorganisation of Holborn and St. Pancras South CLP' *Chairman's Sub* 24th June 1958.

110 S. Barker, 'Report on Reorganisation of Streatham CLP', *Organisation Sub,* 17th November 1959; S. Barker 'Report on Reorganisation of Paddington South CLP,' *Organisation Sub,* 13th April 1965.

111 Developments in Streatham CLP offer an illustration of this. Within a year or two of its reorganisation most of its leading posts were occupied by a group of non-Trotskyist left-wingers who had originally opposed the NEC's action, but came to take a more supportive view. Indeed, by 1962, they were instigating disciplinary action against SLL members themselves. Interview, John Crouch, and documents in Streatham file, *London LP archives.*

112 E.g. Sims ruled, at a crucial GC meeting in Norwood, that three alleged Trotskyists had no right to vote. See *Lambeth Labour News,* undated, *London LP archives.* Jones tried the same tactic, less successfully at an earlier meeting. Organising Assistant's report 14th April 1959, *op. cit.*

113 When the Streatham GC rejected Sims' ruling that Healy had no right to attend its meeting he declared the meeting unconstitutional and he and a number of loyalists walked out. Regional Organiser's Report, 20th April 1959, *London LP archive.*

114 When Trotkyist problems resurfaced in Streatham, Sims informed Len Williams that 'in view of all that has happened in Streatham and the capacity of those in control to bungle things, I thought it best to have Mr. Jones at meetings in order to keep behind the loyalists all the time'. Regional Organiser's Report, 10th November 1961, *ibid.*

115 *Organisation Sub,* 26th May 1959; *Organising Assistant's Reports* (Jones to Sims) 13th May 1959, 25th May 1959, *London LP archive.* Jim Cattermole, East Midlands Regional Organiser, outlined the tactic in a discussion with the Secretary of Leicester South-East CLP, a constituency in which the SLL-backed YS had gained a strong grip and where the GC could not be relied upon to approve a resolution expelling the leading Trotskyist. 'I suggested she [the CLP Secretary] ought to get a dozen or so reliable members to sign a letter asking Transport House to hold an investigation into the activities of some people in the constituency, which I'm sure they will be only too willing to do'. Regional Organiser's Report, 9th April 1965. *Cattermole Papers Warwick University MRC* MSS 9/3/20/110. This was the sequence of events that had occurred in Holborn and St Pancras South, and Paddington South (though not, as it happened, in the Leicester constituency) as well as in Norwood.

116 There was also a fear that, in the absence of surgical strikes, the disease would spread. Urging a rapid halt to 'Trotskyist infiltration' in Norwood and Streatham, Bill Jones (later to be Deputy Secretary of London LP) warned that 'if any of the canker is left behind we may find a further operation necessary in a few years time'. Organising Assistant's Report, 14th April 1959, *London LP archive*. Sims, the London Regional Organiser, concurred. Regional Organiser's Report 16th April 1959, *ibid.*

Notes to Chapter Seven

1 John Rex, 'The Labour Bureaucracy', *New Reasoner*, Autumn 1958, p. 49.

2 R. H. S. Crossman, *Socialism and the New Despotism*, p. 21.

3 Michels, *op. cit.*, p. 72.

4 W. L. Guttsman, *The German Social Democratic Party 1875–1933*, pp. 219–67.

5 McKibbin, *op. cit.*, pp. 170–71.

6 The paragraph draws heavily upon the NEC's 'Interim Report on Party Organisation' (The Wilson Report), *LPCR 1955*, pp. 63–92 and 'Our Penny Farthing Machine', Supplement to *Socialist Commentary*, 1965.

7 Wilson Report, p. 75.

8 Relations between agents and Transport House, *Socialist Commentary* reported, were 'dismal', with very weak central direction *op. cit.*, p. XI.

9 *ibid* p. XXI They were also hampered, according to the Wilson Report by excessive routine paperwork *op. cit.*, p. 68.

10 See above, Chapter 5, p. 105.

11 *New Statesman*, 17th November 1961. The appointment of George Brown, deputy leader of the Party, shortly after to the chairmanship of the Organisation Sub was designed to convert the Party machine into a more effective instrument of leadership control. *New Statesman*, 23rd March 1962.

12 If this sounds too hypothetical, it is worth noting that in many social-democratic parties (e.g. in Spain, France, Israel) the centre has a considerable say in the selection of Parliamentary candidates.

13 *New Statesman* 1st October 1955. The Wilson Report itself acknowledged the possibility when it postulated, as an essential condition of a national agency service that it should be used neither by the NEC nor Head Office 'for the purpose of furthering particular policies which may be the subject of controversy within the movement', *op. cit.*, p. 77.

14 S. Neumann, *Political Parties*, p. 357.

15 The Swedish Social-Democratic Party (SAP) remains the most impressive example of a 'party of democratic integration', although its major function is now an electoral one. See M. Linton, *The Swedish Road to Socialism*.

16 Michels, *op. cit.*, p. 334.

17 M. Duverger, *Political Parties*, p. 63.

18 For an excellent discussion of this in the early years of the SPD, see C. Schorske, *German Social Democracy 1905–1917*, passim.

19 A. de Crespigny, 'Power and its Forms', in A. de Crespigny and A. Wertheimer (eds.), *Contemporary Political Theory*, p. 53.

20 K. Dyson, 'Party Book Administration', *Public Administration Bulletin*,

No. 25, December 1975, pp. 10–11.

21 These modes are intended as ideal types, rather than as descriptive categories; thus an individual member could be influenced by all three modes. Our point is that one tends to be predominent.

22 Bulpitt, *op. cit.*, p. 103. Similarly, Taylor observes that activists in the Labour heartland of the Yorkshire coalfield were 'concerned primarily with the allocation of the spoils of office', *op. cit.*, p. 387.

23 Baxter, *op. cit.*, p. 292.

24 A. H. Birch, D. V. Donnison and G. Jahoda, 'Put Policy on the Agenda', *Fabian Journal*, February 1952.

25 This mode is generally corellated with manual worker status and residence in inner cities – hence in Labour areas; it was much rarer in Conservative and more middle class areas, and in marginals where political activity was higher.

26 Interview, former regional officials.

27 Michels, *op. cit.*, p. 93.

28 D. H. Wrong, *Power*, p. 53. Wrong sees competent authority as divorced from a formal position in a hierarchy of authority; this account sees it as an extension of the formal authority which inheres in such a position.

29 Interview, Harold Sims.

30 Interview, Ian Mikardo. C. F. Michels's observation: 'Just as the patient obeys the doctor, because the doctor knows better than the patient, having made a special study of the human body in health and disease, so must the political patient submit to the guidance of his party leaders, who possess a political competence impossible of attainment by the rank and file'; *op. cit.*, p. 114.

31 It should be stressed as noted above that these modes represent ideal types. In reality, many ideologically minded members (of whatever social background), become socialised into the norms and traditions of the Party and develop a powerful moral and affective attachment to it: the sense of being cross-pressured, between disappointment and estrangement from the leadership and loyalty to the Party was an essential part of the experience of the Labour left.

32 A. L. Williams, 'Procedure for Dealing with Disputes and Disciplinary Cases' (emphasis added), *Chairmen's Sub*, 12th December 1955. This is illustrated by the experience of Peter Cadogan, expelled for membership of the proscribed SLL in 1959. Many members, Cadogan observed, voted for his expulsion, although they objected to proscriptions and, indeed, at the same meeting proceded to send to Conference a motion against proscriptions. They did so on the grounds that the NEC 'is empowered to act between conferences and must be supported at least until the next conference. In face of an impending election, delegates', Cadogan complained, 'allow themselves to be moved to maintain apparent unity by sticking to the letter of the constitution.' Letter to *Tribune*, 19th July 1959. The contrast with CLP responses to expulsions of members of the proscribed Militant Tendency a quarter of a century later could not be starker.

33 D. Easton, *A Systems Analysis of Political Life*, p. 292.

34 Howell identifies, as a major characteristic of Bevanite policy preoccupations, a concentration 'on international and defence issues to the virtual exclusion of almost everything else'. And even this, Howell pointed out, took place within a restricted framework which included support for NATO membership, *op. cit.*, p. 187. The controversy in 1960–61 similarly focussed on the area of foreign and defence policy.

35 In interviews, former Party officials frequently bewailed the passing of the comradeship and sense of kinship which, they claimed, characterised Party life in earlier years.

36 There is a clear parallel with the French Socialist Party (SFIO) in the same period. 'Time and again', one of its students observed, party leader Guy Mollet 'used the "patriotisme du parti" and the feeling of community that seemed to suffuse many militants [i.e. activists] to reinforce party discipline', H. G. Simmonds, *The French Socialists in Search of a Rule 1956–1967*, p. 209.

37 Minkin, *op. cit.*, passim.

Notes to Chapter Eight

1 For full accounts see R. Jackson, *Rebels and Whips*, especially pp. 138–58, 182–82, and R. K. Alderman, 'Parliamentary Party Discipline in Opposition: The PLP 1951–1964', in *Parliamentary Affairs*, Vol. 21, 1967–8.

2 Alderman, *op. cit.*, p. 132.

3 *The Times*, 4th March 1960. Gaitskell attacked this display of 'organised conscience'.

4 Alderman, *op. cit.*, p. 133.

5 *The Times*, 17th March 1961; 28th July 1961. It was only with difficulty that Harold Wilson, the new leader, persuaded the Shadow Cabinet in 1963 to re-admit Foot and the other four rebels. Crossman, *op. cit.*, p. 987.

6 *Ibid.*, pp. 825–6.

7 Alderman, op. cit., p. 134.

8 *The Times*, 13th December 1961.

9 Respectively Edward Short, Herbert Bowden (a former Chief Whip) and Manny Shinwell.

10 *The Times*, 9th July 12th July (quote) 1966.

11 *The Times*, 5th August, 10th August, 11th August 1966.

12 *The Times*, 10th August 1966.

13 *The Times* 28th October, 3rd November 1966. According to Crossman, the first two ground rules were introduced to placate right-wing traditionalists and reconcile them to the liberal regime. Richard Crossman *Diaries of a Cabinet Minister* Vol. 2 p. 103.

14 *The Times* 1st March 1967.

15 *The Times* 3rd March 1967.

16 Crossman, *op. cit.*, pp. 262–4, 266–7, 276–7,

17 *The Times* 11th May, 12th May, 3rd June 1967.

18 Crossman, *op. cit.*, p. 95.

19 Richard Crossman, 'Reflections on Party Loyalty', *New Statesman*, 2nd April 1955. See also 'The Price of Conformity', *New Statesman*, 25th October 1952.

20 Crossman, *Diaries*, op. cit., p. 96.

21 *The Times*, 15th June 1967. See also D. Wood, *The Times*, 6th March

1967.

22 R. K. Alderman, 'The Conscience Clause of the PLP', *Parliamentary Affairs*, Vol. 19, 1966, p. 224–5.

23 Earl Attlee, 'Party Discipline is Paramount', *English and National Review*, p. 148; January 1957, p. 15. Alderman argues that, in practice, this interpretation was not rigorously adhered to, *op. cit.*, p. 230. This may be so, but it represented a flexible application (to meet political realities) of a highly restrictive definition of 'conscience'.

24 Crossman, *op. cit.*, p. 95. Emphasis added.

25 Ibid., pp. 103–4. *The Times*, 3rd November 1966.

26 *LPCR 1955*, p. 201.

27 Crossman, *op. cit.*, p. 96.

28 *The Times*, 28th October, 3rd November 1966. This grant of discretion to the Chief Whip to determine whether an 'alliance' was organised or not provoked a riposte from veteran rebel Konni Zilliacus. 'Some Russian rabbits escaped across the frontier into Poland. When asked why, they told Polish rabbits that the Soviets had banned camels. "But you" said the Polish rabbits "are not camels". And the Russian rabbits answered "You tell that to the OGPU" ' (predecessor of the KGB). *The Times*, 3rd November 1966.

29 *Tribune*, 4th November 1966.

30 Interview, John Silkin.

31 Silkin laid down two, permissive, criteria: that the Chief Whip be informed of their membership and that he, or his deputy, were eligible to attend. Silken himself later joined the Tribune group.

32 A view held by Gaitskell. See *Gaitskell Diaries*, p. 356.

33 D. Wood, *The Times*, 12th May 1967.

34 For a defence of the liberal regime along these lines, see Crossman's speech reported in *The Times*, 9th March 1967.

35 Interview, John Silkin.

36 *Ibid.*

37 *The Times* 9th October 1967.

38 Wilson himself later described his canine metaphor as a 'throw-away reference'. H. Wilson, *The Labour Government*, 1964–70, p. 484.

39 *The Times*, 19th January 1968.

40 *The Times*, 22nd January, 23rd January 1968. Silkin was sharply rebuked by both Houghton and Willie Hamilton, Vice-Chairman of the PLP (and, ironically, simultaneously, a hardliner and one of the rebels) for arrogating to himself powers that properly belonged to the Liaison Committee. Wilson called the move both 'unwise and unconstitutional'. Wilson, *op. cit.*, p. 617.

41 In the interim, the chief whip was authorised (anticipating the new code), with the approval of the PLP, to suspend the rebels; this, it was hoped, would placate the loyalists clamouring for action; *The Times*, 24th January, 1st February 1968. Several other minor rebellions occurred (mainly over the phasing out of free school milk to secondary schools) but no-one was penalised. *The Times*, 21st February, 27th February, 1968.

42 *The Times* 29th February, 22nd March 1968.

43 Code of Conduct, Clause 3.

44 *Ibid.* Clause 4(b).

45 Interview, John Silkin. Some loyalists were demanding the summary expulsion of left-wing rebels as a warning to others. *Times* 28th February 1968.

46 *The Times*, 22nd May, 2nd July, 3rd July, 11th July, 18th December 1968.

47 Peter Jenkins, *The Battle of Downing St.*, pp. 72–4.

48 *The Times*, 24th April 1969. The Liaison Committee recommended that four MPs be suspended but this was overtaken by events (the replacement of Silkin and the crisis over *In Place of Strife*) and no action was taken. *The Times*, 26th April, 30th April 1969.

49 *The Times*, 30th April 1969.

50 At a joint NEC–Cabinet meeting in June 1967, Joe Gormley, the Lancashire Miners' leader and Chairman of the Organisation Sub Committee 'made a tremendous attack on lack of discipline among MPs. "It's MPs and their bloody conscience votes that are wrong" he shouted. He wasn't "going to try and discipline the unfortunate members of the constituency parties unless the MPs had some discipline too".' Tom Bradley of TSSA (and PPS to Roy Jenkins) also attacked the Crossman-Silkin regime. Crossman, *op. cit.*, pp. 375, 376.

51 C.A.R. Crosland, *Can Labour Win?*, pp. 20, 23.

52 *The Times*, 9th May 1968. Coincidentally or not, at this point the trade union group elected a left-winger and former Bevanite, Victor Yates, as its acting Chairman. *Ibid.*

53 'Mr. Wilson evidently concluded that Mr. Silkin would not prove tough enough to ensure the Government's survival through the dangers of summer, and chose the strongest whip-cracker in sight.' *The Times*, 30th April 1969. Similarly, Peter Jenkins wrote that Silkin's 'liberal regime had ended in tears', P. Jenkins, *op. cit.*, p. 96.

54 Howell, *op. cit.*, pp. 262–3.

55 *The Times*, 9th May 1969.

56 Conference voted overwhelmingly to reject the legislation in 1968. *The Times* 30th September, 1st October 1968.

57 D. Houghton, 'Making MPs Accountable', *Political Quarterly*, Vol. 43, 1972, p. 377.

58 See here the exchange between Anthony Arblaster and Michael Foot. In response to Arblaster's injunction that 'men of principle and integrity must fix limits to their allegiance to persons and parties', Foot made quite clear that in no conceivable circumstances would the Parliamentary left risk the ousting of the Labour government. A. Arblaster, 'The Limits of Loyalty', *Tribune*, 6th December 1968. M. Foot, 'The Left and Parliament', *Tribune*, 13th December 1968.

59 Disapproval of the liberal regime was shared by a number of cabinet ministers including, according to Crossman, Callaghan, Healey and Crosland. Crossman, *op. cit.*, p. 259–60, 614. Silkin adds Jenkins to their ranks, interview.

60 Crossman *op. cit.* p. 95. (He was referring in particular to statutory wage controls). In practice, as Crossman knew, this entailed extending the right to vote against the Government.

61 Jenkins, *op. cit.*, p. 67. Orme was the left-wing MP for Salford West.

62 Two hardline right-wingers (George Jeger and Carol Johnson) abstained on a confidence motion (along with 22 left-wingers) for this reason. *The Times*, 19th January 1968.

64 *The Times*, 9th May 1968.

65 Alan Watkins, 'The John Silkin Story', *New Statesman*, 2nd May 1969. At the end of the year there were sizeable revolts over Vietnam, Biafra and pay policy; Mellish responded very much in the spirit of the Crossman-Silkin regime. Minkin, *op. cit.*, p. 310. *The Times*, 18th December 1969.

66 Attlee, *op. cit.*, p. 15. Emphasis added.

67 LPCR 1955, p. 52. In the Conference debate on the expulsions Bob Mellish had declared himself 'nauseated and sickened to death' by those who refused to accept 'the majority decision', *ibid.*, p. 206.

68 *The Times* 29th October, 30th October 1971. More important than the actual vote on the principle of entry, under the Government's terms, was the consistent support provided by a smaller, but still significant, number of Labour MPs to ensure passage of the consequential legislation. A. Watkins, *New Statesman*, 23rd June 1972.

69 See, e.g. M. Foot *Parliament in Danger*.

70 However, unlike the ascendent right in earlier years, the left showed little enthusiasm for disciplining those who defied the majority view.

71 Watkins, *ibid.* Similarly, Carol Johnson, who had flouted the whip in a division in 1968 to register his indignation at the failure of Silkin to impose firmer discipline abstained on 38 votes. *Ibid.*

72 E.g. Willie Hamilton *The Times* 20th October 1971.

73 In 1961, attacking those MPs who claimed 'complete independence of decision and action', George Brown argued that 'there is not one of us who puts up for Parliament otherwise than as a Labour member or whose return is not wholly dependent on the loyalty and hard work and sacrifice of the Party and trade union stalwarts'. *The Times* 20th March 1961.

74 George Brown in *The Times* 28th October 1971.

75 Not all pro-marketeers, however, were of this lineage.

76 Interview, Alan Haworth.

77 *NEC Minutes*, 27th March 1968.

78 *Organisation Sub Minutes*, 8th April 1968. Justice Megarry's summing-up in the subsequent High Court Case gives us something of the flavour of the meeting. 'The Plaintiff (party chairman) perhaps prodded Mr. Donnelly in the back with his gavel. Mr. Donnelly pushed the plaintiff, perhaps mightily so that he fell against the wall . . . Mr. Donnelly pulled out a chair for Mr. Moores to stand on and address the meeting: but he fell off it'. *All England Law Reports*, 1969 Vol. 2 p. 289 (henceforth Megarry).

79 *NEC Minutes*, 24th April 1968. The NEC was particularly concerned since the CLP possessed properties worth £48,000.

80 See above Chapter 6, pp. 133–6.

81 R. Underhill, 'Report on the Reorganisation of the Pembroke CLP', *Organisation Sub* June 1968.

82 H. Rajak, 'Thrown out by Judges', *The Guardian* 2nd May 1983.

83 Interview with a lawyer specialising in administrative law.

84 Megarry, *op. cit.*, p. 275.

85 Megarry, *op. cit.*, p. 303. Megarry continued 'It might be, [Labour's counsel] added, that they ceased to be members when they inwardly harboured disloyal notions in their bosoms, a concept which seems to me to give rise to many interesting speculations'.

86 *Ibid.*, pp. 307, 308.

87 Report into the affairs of Pembroke CLP conducted by J. Gormley, A. Kitson, T. Lane and the National Agent. *Organisation Sub*, 18th February 1969.

88 *Organisation Sub Minutes*, 13th May 1969 *LPCR 1969* p. 9.

89 Letter from Goodman, Derick and Co. *NEC*, 23rd October 1968.

90 This certainly applied to the procedure of reorganisation. Its value as an instrument of control was significantly reduced by the Megarry judgment, since the specific mechanism utilised by Transport House to ensure its success – the barring from participation in the re-establishment of parties those deemed to be disloyal – was judged to be wrong, as it deprived members of the benefits of membership in a manner contrary to natural justice. For a general discussion of the impact of this shift in judicial thinking see below chap 11, pp. 238–9.

91 Interviews Lord Underhill, Walter Brown. The steps the NEC felt it had to take immediately pursuant to Megarry's judgment illustrate this. An immense amount of time and effort was clearly expended on the second enquiry (the final report was one of the longest ever submitted). This was a major distraction at a time when electorally the party was in a very poor shape.

92 The Appeals Court had, as yet, to pronounce on the matter. See below chapter 11, p. 238; and the full political implications had to be absorbed.

93 Ron Hayward recalled that it was welcomed by senior figures in the Party. Interview.

94 A view shared by Hayward himself who was astonished that he had won.

95 Sara Barker was visibly pained and anguished when it was announced that Hayward had been elected. Interview with a Party official.

96 At the first ballot, Hayward gained eleven votes, Underhill nine, and Jim Cattermole, a committed right-winger, two; both of Cattermole's votes – almost definitely cast by right-wingers – went to Hayward in the run off. *NEC Minutes*, 22nd January 1969.

97 Interview, Ron Hayward.

98 He explicitly eschewed the bureaucratic role conception of his predecessors. At one meeting, shortly after his appointment, he told surprised (and slightly disturbed) Regional Organisers that they were 'politicians not civil servants'; they had to exercise a political judgment both in interpreting NEC decisions and in resolving disputes through conciliation rather than discipline. Interview, Ron Hayward.

99 The trend slightly pre-dated Hayward's appointment; he accelerated it.

100 Knight was expelled in 1955. He was finally re-admitted in 1970 (after many attempts) after convincing his listeners in an interview that he had finally severed his ties with the SLL and rejected revolutionary views. Report of Inquiry Committee. *Organisation Sub*, 9 November 1970.

101 See, e.g. *Tribune*, 17th October 1969, 30th January 1970.

102 See above Chapter 3, pp. 57–66 and Chapter 6, pp. 117–124.

103 See above Chapter 3, pp. 62–65.

104 *Organisation Sub Minutes*, 18th July 1967.

105 The RAM was basically a Liberal 'front organisation' led by David Steele. The idiosyncratic Labour MP, Peter Jackson, was also involved. See S. Barker, 'Radical Action Movement', *Organisation Sub* 18th February 1969.

106 *Organisation Sub Minutes*, 20th June 1967.

107 NAD document 'Labour Research Department', *Organisation Sub* 6th December 1971.

108 *Organisation Sub Minutes*, 15th September 1970.

109 Although at one point (presumably as a sop) it was agreed to circularise affiliated unions reminding them of the 'regulations which govern the relationship between individual members of the Labour Party and [proscribed] organisations'. *Organisation Sub Minutes*, 15th April 1969.

110 Interview, Ron Hayward.

111 *Organisation Sub Minutes*, 7th February 1972.

112 *NEC Minutes*, 25th October 1972.

113 *NEC Minutes*, 22nd November 1972.

114 In fact MACV was never formally proscribed.

115 R. Short. Note on MACV *Organisation Sub*, 15th January 1973.

116 'Friendship Societies', *Organisation Sub*, 15th April 1973; 7th May 1973; 'Proscribed organisations', *Organisation Sub* 7th May 1973.

117 *Organisation Sub Minutes*, 15th April 1973.

118 *Organisation Sub Minutes*, 7th May 1973.

119 R. Underhill 'List of Proscribed Organisations', *Organisation Sub*, 11th June 1973.

120 *Organisation Sub Minutes*, 11th June 1973.

121 NEC Circular, 'Discontinuation of the Proscribed List', July 1973.

122 P. McCormick, 'The Labour Party: Three Unnoticed Changes', *British Journal of Political Science*, vol. X, p. 382.

123 P. Williams 'The Labour Party: the Rise of the Left', *West European Politics*, Vol. 6, 1983 p. 33.

124 *Organisation Sub Minutes*, 11th June 1973.

125 The procedure used to alert the NEC to the more important decisions. Out of 29 NEC members (all minuted as attending) 15 were right-wingers. *NEC Minutes* 26th June 1973. None of the four members who subsequently joined the SDP raised an objection.

126 Underhill *op. cit.* (emphasis added)

127 *Ibid.*

128 Interview with a former Regional Organiser (widely regarded as a right-winger) who supported abolition. Another former Party official, who had a general responsibility for upkeep of the list, believed it was no longer enforced. He suggested that the initiative for its abolition came from within the NAD. Interview.

129 Jack Jones' predecessor, Frank Cousins, was, of course, also a left-winger. But Jones worked much more closely with the political left (he had served on the NEC) than Cousins. Interview, Ian Mikardo. He was also a much less isolated voice than his precurser. Another senior TGWU official and NEC member, Alex Kitson, played an active part in urging the termination of the List.

130 Bill Jones, a senior officer of the TGWU was President of the proscribed British Peace Committee.

131 See Williams, *op. cit.*, p. 33.

132 See above, p. 174.

133 The effect of the 1946 amendment was to block organisations from affiliating to the Labour Party, not to prevent their members, as individuals, from joining it. The purpose of the amendment was to end repeated Communist bids to secure affiliation. See above Chapter 3, pp. 57–8.

134 This was not the intention.
135 NAD paper, 'Clapham CLP and Mrs. Margaret McKay, MP.', *Organisation Sub*, 10th February 1970.
136 See above Chapter 5, pp. 133–4.
137 *Organisation Sub Minutes*, 10th February 1970.
138 T. Driberg, *New Statesman*, 14th November 1975.
139 *Organisation Sub Minutes*, 10th February 1970.
140 *LPCR 1970*, pp. 16, 158.
141 See report (of the private session) in *Tribune*, 2nd October 1970.
142 The McKay case never reached this stage as the MP resigned just prior to the 1970 elections.
143 See above Chapter 5, p. 108.
144 Dick Taverne, *The Future of the Left* p. 28.
145 *Ibid.*, p. 30.
146 *Ibid.*, p. 47.
147 A. Watkins in *New Statesman*, 23rd June 1972.
148 Taverne, *op. cit.*, p. 67.
149 *Ibid.*, p. 69.
150 A. Watkins, 'The Case of Dick Taverne', *New Statesman*, 4th August 1972.
151 A. Watkins, *op. cit.*
152 See 'Appeal by Dick Taverne'. *Labour Party Archives* (unclassified) and 'Report of the Inquiry into the Appeal of R. Taverne, MP', *Organisation Sub*, 25th July 1972.
153 This (factually incorrect) statement prompted some tart reflections from Dick Crossman who (as we have seen) was instrumental in introducing this 'long established' right six years earlier. Pondering a comment by Roy Jenkins (defending Taverne) that the Party should 'preserve its tradition of tolerance', he recalled 'the experience of the tyranny of the majority under which some of us suffered for so long. From 1945 . . . I lived under what I felt to be an utterly illiberal and stupid system of Party discipline'. He argued that Taverne exploited the 'newly won rights' instituted by the liberal regime by participating in a small inner group which sustained the Government in a series of crucial divisions over EEC entry. R. Crossman, 'The Strange Case of Mr. Taverne', *The Times* 2nd August 1972. According to Silkin, Jenkins himself had been critical of the liberal regime. Interview, John Silkin.
154 See above p. 170 for Justice Megarry's definition of the term.
155 Watkins, *op. cit.*
156 *Organisation Sub Minutes*, 25th July 1972; *NEC Minutes*, 26th July 1972. Of the twelve, ten were left-wingers – hence the votes of the two others (Lady White and George Chambers of the NUM) were decisive. *The Times* 28th July 1972.
157 See above, Chapter 5, pp. 93–6.
158 Taverne Appeal, *op. cit.*, p. 7.
159 Interview, Bill Jones.

160 Hayward had, with the agreement on the two sides, been despatched to Lincoln to try and reconcile them. The Constituency officers agreed to meet Taverne on condition that the media would not be present. Hayward urged the MP to accept the condition as media coverage would not help the Party. But, Taverne resisted, 'it will help Dick Taverne'. The meeting was never held and Hayward refused to participate in any further attempt at conciliation. Interview, Ron Hayward.

161 *LPCR 1974*, pp. 180–1. Crossman reached a similar conclusion via a slight different route. Accepting that MPs were elected 'to sustain the Party line' he argued that the liberalising of PLP discipline meant that 'the only check on our behaviour is that which our constituency parties can exert'. If convinced that their MP had failed them, 'their right to remove them was as essential to democracy as the MPs's freedom to vote according to his conscience'. *The Times*, 2nd August 1972.

162 *LPCR 1974*, p. 181. For a discussion of the Mikardo doctrine see below, Chapter 9, pp. 191–3.

163 See above, Chapter 7, pp. 152–3.

164 K. O. Morgan, *Labour in Power*, p. 70.

165 See above, Chapter 2, p. 49.

166 Minkin, *op. cit.*, p. 342.

167 Minkin, *op. cit.*, p. 329.

168 Letter from Jim Mortimer to the writer.

169 Minkin, *op. cit.*, pp. 248–256.

170 Of the twelve votes cast in favour of the motion, nine came from trade unionists. *The Times*, 30th September 1968.

171 *NEC Minutes*, 26th March 1969.

172 *NEC Minutes*, 25th February 1970.

173 Minkin, *op. cit.*, p. 300.

174 Wilson, *op. cit.*, pp. 692–3.

175 Interview, Ian Mikardo. In 1972, in response to a letter urging him to support Dick Taverne, he referred to the 'strict rule' he had made in 1963 not to intervene in such matters, which properly lay in the province of Transport House and the NEC. Letter, Harold Wilson Taverne File *LP Archives*.

176 Simpson Report, *LPCR 1967*, p. 341. The idea originated with Dick Crossman.

177 By the casting vote of the NEC chairman, Tony Benn. *NEC Minutes*, 29th March 1972.

178 Minkin, *op. cit.*, p. 329.

Notes to Chapter Nine

1 Ranney, *op. cit.*, p. 10.

2 *The Times* 20th July 1974. The complaint, eagerly exploited by the press, was tendentious. He was removed for a whole series of reasons, including his poor record as a constituency MP, his unwillingness to consult with his local Party as well as political differences between a right-wing MP and a CLP shifting to the left. Interview, Harold Sims (Yorkshire Regional Organiser at the time) and (for a detailed account) A. Young, *The Reselection of MPs*, pp. 84–102.

3   Interview, Ian Mikardo.

4   *Ibid.*

5   As he truthfully boasted to Conference: 'in my twenty-odd years in the Executive I have been fighting like a tiger cat for the right of the Constituency Labour Party, without interference from anybody, unconditionally to select who shall be their Labour candidate'. *LPCR 1974*, p. 180.

6   *Ibid.*, p. 181.

7   At one point, he had topped the poll in the elections to the Shadow Cabinet.

8   He called upon moderates to 'stand up and be counted' *The Times*, 29th November 1973.

9   *The Times*, 20th March 1975.

10   'Report of an Inquiry into the Appeal of R. Prentice MP', *Organisation Sub*, 14th November 1975.

11   See, e.g., David Wood in *The Times*, 23rd February 1976.

12   *The Times*, 17th, 18th, 19th July 1975.

13   *The Times*, 22nd July 1975.

14   Prentice appeal, *op. cit.*

15   Prentice's invocation of natural justice reflects the impact of the Pembroke judgment; but (as in the Taverne case) the meaning he gave to the term extended well beyond the legally accepted definition. In effect he complained about the inadequacy of the procedure and not whether it complied with natural justice.

16   Three of the following right-wingers must have voted against the Williams amendment: John Chalmers, Tom Bradley (both members of the inquiry panel), Harold Hickling and T. Jones. The amendment was seconded by Bill John. The six left-wingers were: Tony Benn, Nick Bradley (YS representative) Judith Hart, Eric Heffer, Alex Kitson and Ian Mikardo. *Organisation Sub Minutes*, 10th November 1975.

17   In a letter to Neville Sandelson MP, an ardent Prentice supporter. *The Times*, 22nd July 1975.

18   *The Times*, 27th November 1975.

18   *NEC Minutes*, 26th November 1975.

20   Interview, Ron Hayward; *Organisation Sub Minutes* 8th March 1976.

21   See, e.g., David Wood in *The Times*, 23rd February 1976.

22   Interviews, former Party officials. One commented: 'Some of his policies would have gone down well in the National Front'.

23   On one occasion, his sponsoring union, the GMWU had 'whipped in' its Hammersmith party members to foil a deselection bid. *The Times* 28th October 1974.

24   'Report of an Inquiry into the Appeal of F. Tomney MP', *Organisation Sub*, 12th July 1976.

25   *The Times*, 9th May, 21st May 1977.

26   *The Times*, 5th July 1976.

27   *NEC Minutes*, 12th April 1976. The motion was seconded by Brian Stanley, the right-wing General Secretary of the Post Office Engineering Union.

28   McCormick, *op. cit.*, pp. 384–5. McCormick (along with Julian Lewis) had played an active part in the Newham North East dispute, firstly, as a

champion of Prentice and then, later, as the organiser of a right-wing counter-offensive against the dominant left in the constituency. He was responsible for numerous legal actions against the NEC which culminated in the Appeals Court. See below Chap 11 p. 238.

29 'Report of an Enquiry into the Appeal of Mrs M. Colquhoun, MP', *Organisation Sub*, 9th January 1978.

30 *NEC Minutes*, 25th January 1978.

31 In addition a later, considerably better attended, meeting of the branch in question did reconsider the matter several months later and overwhelmingly backed the original decision. See letter from CLP press officer. *New Statesman* 5th September 1977.

32 McCormick, *op. cit.*, p. 385.

33 The NEC resolved to hold an enquiry only 'if evidence can be produced that there had been constitutional irregularities in connection with the meeting held [to ask Baird to retire] on 5th February 1963', *Organisation Sub Minutes*, 20th February 1963. No such evidence was found and Baird was removed without any right of appeal; *NEC Minutes*, 27th February 1963. Baird was unseated for his poor performance as an MP rather than his views (Interview, Ian Mikardo). To compound the irony, he was on friendly terms with a number of future leaders of Militant. Crick, *op. cit.*, p. 45.

34 McCormick, *op. cit.*, p. 384.

35 M. Colquhoun, 'The Northampton Storm', *New Statesman*, 21st October 1977.

36 Labour Party, *The Regoranisation of Party Structure*.

37 *Ibid.*, para 50.

38 *Ibid.*, Proposal 26.

39 *LPCR 1974*, pp. 179, 180. He added 'We all resent the business of bodies being brought in just to hold up their hands for the one single vote of selection ... There is lobbying going on and people being drummed up just for that purpose.' *Ibid.*, p. 179.

40 LP Constitution 1979 clause XIV 7(c).

41 *LPCR 1974*, p. 179.

42 This observation does not refer to the behaviour of all regional officials.

43 Interview, former Regional Organiser.

44 *Ibid.*

45 Interview, Bill Jones.

46 Tomney appeal, *op. cit.*

47 Interview. Bill Jones. The incident was not an isolated one. The same Regional Organiser assisted efforts to unseat e.g. Perry, MP for Battersea South, who was persuaded to retire, and Neville Sandelson, MP for Hayes and Harlington, who narrowly survived a deselection bid in 1977 but pre-empted a less favourable outcome later when he defected to the SDP. *Ibid.*

48 R. H. S. Crossman, Introduction to Bagehot's *The British Constitution*, p. 42.

49 Ranney, *op. cit.*, pp. 11, 142.

50 See D. and M. Kogan *The Battle for the Labour Party*. CLPD was ably led by its Secretary, Vladmir Derer, Victor Schonfield and Pete Willsman.

51 Draft Report on *Reorganisation of Party Structure* para 72.

Organisation Sub 16th January 1974. The report was open-minded about introducing a form of mandatory reselection. The NEC was against and the above paragraph was deleted in the final Report.

52 Interview with Ian Mikardo, *Labour Weekly*, 4th November 1977.

53 *NEC Minutes*, 26th November 1975.

54 *NEC Minutes*, 24th March 1976.

55 R. Underhill, 'Selection of Prospective Parliamentary Candidates', *Organisation Sub*, 26th January 1976.

56 C. Hughes, 'Note on Selection of Parliamentary Candidates', *NEC*, 24th March 1976.

57 *The Times*, 10th February 1976.

58 *The Times*, 25th March 1976.

59 A call to overturn this decision managed to muster over 2¼ million votes at Conference, an indication of the growing appeal of mandatory reselection. *The Times*, 28th September 1976.

60 *NEC Minutes*, 30th September 1977.

61 *LPCR 1977*, p. 324. *Labour Weekly*, 7th October, 14th October 1977. The resolution was remitted.

62 Minkin, *op. cit.*, Chapter 3. If Mikardo had been outvoted on the NEC, the agenda item on reselection either would not have been reached or the composite would have been defeated, foreclosing debate until 1980.

63 *Labour Weekly*, 4th November 1977; *The Times*, 6th December 1977; R. Underhill 'Reselection of MPs'; and minutes *Organisation Sub*, 5th December 1977.

64 *NEC Minutes*, 14th December 1977; *The Times* 15th December 1977. After the vote the PM 'jokingly but with undisguised relief said "I could have left earlier" ', *ibid.*

65 NAD 'Working Party on the Reselection of MPs', *Organisation Sub*, 6th February 1978.

66 *Organisation Sub Minutes*, 6th February 1978.

67 *The Times*, 2nd March 1978.

68 Report of the Working Party on the Reselection of MPs', Appendix to *LPCR 1978*.

69 *Tribune*, 2nd June 1978.

70 *The Times*, 25th May 1978. The vote was 15 to 4.

71 *LPCR 1978*, p. 281.

72 *Organisation Sub Minutes*, 12th February 1979; NEC Minutes 28th February 1979 (the vote was 10 to 11).

73 *Organisation Sub Minutes*, 12th March 1979.

74 *NEC Minutes*, 4th July 1979; *Organisation Sub Minutes*, 10th September 1979. The vote in favour was 17 to 9. The original motion, at the Organisation Sub, was moved by a new member, Neil Kinnock. *Organisation Sub Minutes*, 11th June 1979.

75 Initially the CAC dug its heals in. *CAC minutes*, 29th August 1979. The NEC insisted on its rights, under Standing Order 2(6) to require an issue, considered to be of 'immediate importance' to be debated; Derek Gladwin (Chairman CAC); *LPCR 1979*, p. 175.

76 It was carried by a majority of a million in 1979 and by just under half that

in the decisive vote the following year. *LPCR 1979*, p. 271; *LPCR 1980*, p. 142.

77 This widened the franchise for electing the leader. Thirty per cent of the total vote was given to both the PLP and the CLPs, the remaining 40% to the unions.

78 90 MPs signed a letter of protest against the NEC's decision to push the three constitutional reforms, charging that they would reduce the PLP to 'the role of a poodle of Party Conference' and turn MPs into 'mere cyphers' of their parties. Callaghan was said to be 'furious'. *The Guardian*, 26th July 1979. The NEC's determination to press for constitutional changes designed to prune the power of the PLP and Parliamentary leadership was strengthened by its own experience of impotence in the policy sphere during the recently expired Government. In the words of the Research Secretary, Geoff Bish, it was reduced to the status of 'a mere pressure group, just one among many' with minimal influence over 'the direction of Government policy'. Extract from Research Paper 'Working Relations between Government and Party', reprinted in K. Coates (ed) *What Went Wrong* p. 164. Despite their much vaunted 'power', trade unions also became increasingly disenchanted with the rightward shift of Government economic policies after 1975. Thus TUC General Council delegates in the Government – NEC – TUC Liaison Committee tended more and more to vote with the NEC rather than the Government. As a result, the left wing unions (in particular) were in no mood to succour the Parliamentary leadership after 1974.

Notes to Chapter Ten

1 In one case an NEC inquiry confirmed the withdrawal of the whip from a Councillor who voted against a Group decision on a peripheral matter (the eviction of a Council tenant). (REA, Councillor Taylor against withdrawal of the whip by Wallsend Labour Group, *Organisation Sub*, 11th January 1971.)

2 See, e.g. the enquiry into the exclusion from the panel of Alderman Carnie by the Wandsworth Local Government Committee; *Organisation Sub*, 7th December 1970.

3 See, e.g., *Tribune* 14th July 1972, 12th January 1973.

4 Traditionally a preserve of right-wing trade unionists.

5 REA, Newham councillors against disciplinary action by the Labour Group, *Organisation Sub*, 11th September 1972.

6 See above, Chapter 4, pp. 70–1.

7 REA against exclusion from the panel of seven councillors by N.E. Derbyshire CLP, *Organisation Sub*, 12th February 1973; REA against exclusion from the panel of three councillors by Stafford and Stone CLP, *Organisation Sub*, 18th April 1973. It could be argued that natural justice was of paramount concern where councillors ran the risk of law-breaking. More likely, it was a rationale, ready to hand, to justify the NEC overturning local decisions which it regarded as unreasonable.

8 J. Gyford and R. Baker, *Labour and Local Politics*, p. 7.

9 *Ibid.*

10 *Organisation Sub Minutes*, 7th July 1973.

11 Circular to Labour Groups, August 1973.

12 Report of Special Committee on Conduct of the Party in Local Government, *Organisation Sub*, 6 July 1975. The recommendations were incorporated into the Memorandum on Standing Orders for Labour Groups.

13 REA, four members of Newham Labour Group, *Organisation Sub*, 7th February 1977.

14 REA, two members of Newham Labour Group, *Organisation Sub*, June 1979. The report significantly added a rider suggesting that this interpretation of conscience was anomalous and ought to be widened.

15 Interview, Walter Brown.

16 Newham Report, *op. cit.*

17 J. Gyford, *The Politics of Local Socialism*, pp. 25–6.

18 *Ibid.*, p. 27.

19 Interview, former Regional Organiser who attended Organisation Sub meeting as a staff representative.

20 REA, Councillor Evans, *Organisation Sub*, 9th September 1974.

21 REA, Councillor Evans against expulsion by Nottingham East CLP, *Organisation Sub*, 21st July 1975 and Supplementary Report. *Organisation Sub*, 10th November 1975. Other grounds were his rebellious record and his refusal to accept CLP decisions.

22 *Ibid.*

23 *Organisation Sub Minutes*, 10th November 1975; 8th December 1975.

24 See, e.g., G. Bell, 'Islington: Labour's Rotting Borough', *New Statesman*, 29th November 1974. C. Hitchens, 'Islington's Last Hurrah', *New Statesman*, 21st May 1976; *The Times*, 29th May 1976.

25 See above, Chapter 4, pp. 72–3.

26 Report of an inquiry into the appeal of K. Veness, *Organisation Sub*, 12th April 1976.

27 *Organisation Sub Minutes*, 7th June 1976; former Party official.

28 Report of an enquiry into Islington North CLP, *Organisation Sub*, 4th April 1977. *Organisation Sub Minutes*, 4th April 1977; 2nd December 1977; 12th June 1978. The first lengthy report was supplemented by a number of others.

29 *Organisation Sub Minutes*, 10th July 1978; 12th February 1979; 12th March 1979.

30 See, e.g., article by Bruce Page, *New Statesman*, 27th March 1981; *Tribune*, 26th March 1982.

31 See Gyford, pp. 16–18.

32 Resolution on 'Tolerance within the Party', *Organisation Sub Minutes*, 7th July 1980. See also circular to Secretaries of Labour Groups on Group Discipline, *Organisation Sub*, 9th June 1980.

33 D. Hughes, 'Appeals Against Disciplinary Action', *Organisation Sub*, 9th February 1981.

34 Speech to Labour's Local Government Conference in 1976, quoted by D. Hughes, 'Labour Group Discipline', *Organisation Sub*, May 1980.

35 REA, two members of Scunthorpe Labour Group, *Organisation Sub* and Minutes, 9th February 1981.

36 REA ten members of Coventry Labour Group, *Organisation Sub* and *Minutes*, 10th November 1980. The inquiry reports had in both cases dismissed the appeals but recommended more lenient penalties.

37   REA, eight members of Bristol Labour Group, *Organisation Sub* and *Minutes* 9th June 1980. REA, thirteen members of Manchester Labour Group, *Organisation Sub* and *Minutes*, 9th June 1980.

38   *The Guardian*, 16th June 1980; interviews Walter Brown and former Regional Organiser. For similar cases see two reports of inquiries into appeals by members of the mid Glamorgan Labour Group, *Organisation Sub*, 9th March 1981; 7th July 1982.

39   Interview, Tony Benn.

40   Gyford, *op. cit.*, pp. 8–10. D. Green, *Power and Party in an English City*, pp. 69–74.

41   For example, in the series of inquiries into Liverpool Labour Party in the 1950s and early 1960s, Braddock's oligarchial system of decision-making was never mentioned.

42   It is worth noting that the years 1979–81 saw the culmination of the drive to introduce a wider measure of accountability into Labour's internal processes at the national level. The NEC was in the forefront of the campaign and there was inevitably a spill-over into the sphere of adjudication.

43   REA, ten members of Southwark Labour Group, *Organisation Sub* 11th June 1979. See also the appeal inquiries into Conventry and Bradford Labour Groups, *Organisation Sub*, 10th November 1980, 12th July 1982 and the Manchester report cited in footnote 37.

44   The 1975 NEC report on 'The Conduct of the Party in Local Government' had expressed concern at the practice of councillors holding office in both the Group and local party organisations which promoted 'particularly in some traditionally strong Labour areas' the excessive concentration of power in a few hands. *Organisation Sub*, July 1975.

45   E.g. in Newcastle, Green, *op. cit.*, pp. 39–46 and in Birmingham G. W. Jones and A. Norton, *Political Leadership in Local Authorities*, p. 177.

46   Gyford, op. cit., pp. 16, 39.

47   See, e.g., speech by David Blunkett on behalf of the NEC, *LPCR 1984*, pp. 181–3.

48   T. Benn, 'Standing Orders for Labour Groups', *Organisation Sub*, 7th July 1980.

49   *The Guardian*, 9th July 1980.

50   See, e.g., letters from the leaders of Birmingham and Mid-Glamorgan Labour Groups and from Jack Smart, Labour Leader of the Association of Metropolitan Authorities, *NEC*, 23rd July 1980. Virulent attacks on the Benn proposals were also made by Roy Hattersley and Peter Shore, *The Guardian* 12th July 1980; 3rd March 1981.

51   *NEC Minutes*, 23rd July 1980.

52   *Organisation Sub Minutes*, 9th September 1980.

53   In fact the proposals adopted by Conference in 1984 had been largely agreed by July 1981. See 'Recommended Amendments to Model Standing Orders for Labour Groups', *Organisation Sub*, July 1981.

54   *LPCR 1984*, p. 181.

55   In a number of cases, this was a prime consideration leading the NEC to overturn inquiry recommendations. See, e.g., reports of inquiries into appeals of members of Scunthorpe, Hounslow and mid-Glamorgan Labour Groups, *Organisation Sub* 11th February 1980; 14th September 1981; 7th July 1982; the Bristol case cited above and the report by David Hughes into the Manchester DLP and Group, Organisation Sub, 14 September 1981. Interview, Tony Benn.

56 See above, Chapter 4, pp. 74–7.

57 See above, Chapter 8, p. 172.

58 *LPCR 1984*, p. 267 (quote). Interview, Walter Brown.

59 The best example of this is the 'Heffer Agreement' designed to resolve the conflict in Coventry. See Report into the Coventry Dispute, *Organisation Sub*, 9th November 1981. As elsewhere, however, this effort at compromise failed.

60 P. Wintour, 'Whose Party is it Anyway?', *New Statesman*, 11th December 1981; interview John Keys; *The Guardian*, 10th December 1981.

61 See below, Chapter 11, pp. 226–8.

62 REA, eleven members of Southwark Labour Group, *Organisation Sub*, 9th November 1981. *Organisation Sub Minutes*, 9th December 1981. Both decisions were overwhelmingly approved.

63 In London, LGCs performed the functions of district parties elsewhere.

64 Quoted in P. Tatchell, *The Battle for Bermondsey*, p. 87. According to the Secretary of Southwark Local Government Committee 'All we were presented with [from Heffer] was a barrage of comments about Party Unity.', D. Fryer, 'NEC Challenge to Southwark', *London Labour Briefing*, March 1982.

65 NAD paper, 'Southwark Local Government Committee', *NEC*, 27th January 1982. Tatchell *op. cit.*, pp. 87–8. At one point, an irate Heffer exclaimed 'This is not the 1950s and I'm not Ray Gunter'. Tatchell comments tartly that 'some of us felt, however, he gave a very good imitation of Gunter', *ibid.*

66 *NEC Minutes*, 27th January 1982.

67 *Organisation Sub Minutes*, 8th February 1982. *The Guardian*, 10th February 1982.

68 Where the left split, with the majority narrowly accepting the authority of NEC. Tatchell, *op. cit.*, pp. 88–90.

69 This section draws upon interviews with Ron Hayward, Walter Brown and a number of former and current Regional Organisers.

70 'Organising for a Labour Victory', unpublished report from the Regional Staff, *NEC*, February 1984.

71 According to the left-wing Labour Co-ordinating Committee, the conduct of regional officials was 'sometimes unduly influenced by styles and attitudes prevalent in an earlier period', LCC, *Party Organisation: An Enquiry*, p. 16. The tone of other left-wing comment was often less measured. See Chris Mullen, 'The Party Machine', *Tribune*, 18th May 1979.

72 Interview, Graham Stringer. An earlier example of this occurred over a dispute in Brigg and Scunthorpe CLP where left-wingers lobbied sympathetic members of the NEC and secured a reversal of an enquiry recommendation to uphold the appeal of the former right-wing Council leader against expulsion. REA of councillor Nottingham, *Organisation Sub*, 7th February 1977; *Organisation Sub Minutes*, 7th March 1977; interview David Robertson. This provoked an angry letter from Les Bridges, East Midlands Regional Organiser and a member of the inquiry team, *NEC*, 23rd March 1977.

Notes to Chapter Eleven

1   'Entryism in the Labour Party', 1964, *Jimmy Deane Collection*, Manchester Polytechnic.

2   RSL E. C. Minutes 7th July 1964. RSL statement on agreement between RSL and the International Group (forerunner of the IMG) 13th September 1964 (quote) both in *ibid.*

3   'Entryism in the Labour Party', *op. cit.*

4   After a while, the appelation RSL ceased to be used and the organisation adopted the title of its paper, Militant, or the Militant Tendency.

5   In 1972, the LPYS was given a place on the NEC. This (with one brief interval) has always been held by a Militant member.

6   In fact, the anti-Prentice element in Newham North East was abroad coalition of left-wingers.

7   Interview, Lord Underhill.

8   Underhill, *op. cit.*

9   Crick, *op. cit.*, p. 85.

10   *Organisation Sub Minutes*, 12th November 1975.

11   Crick, *op. cit.*, p. 86.

12   *Organisation Sub Minutes*, 12th November 1975.

13   *NEC Minutes*, 26th November 1975. This was the meeting which also discussed the Prentice case and mandatory reselection.

14   Harold Sims, North East Regional Organiser, speaking on behalf of a number of colleagues, publicly berated the NEC for its inaction – a most unusual move for traditionally discreet officials. *The Times* 2nd December 1976.

15   The General Secretary and one right-wing trade unionist (Harold Hickling) – who was apparently unaware of Militant's existence – voted for Bevan. Webster's argument that the Bevan appointment was 'the most notorious example' of the NEC left's policy of 'encouraging the movement of insurrectionary Socialists into the Labour Party' (D. Webster *The Labour Party and the New Left* p. 20) is, thus, way off the mark. The left did oppose right-wing attempts to reverse the decision – but this was motivated by what they considered to be discrimination upon an individual on account of his left wing beliefs.

16   *The Times* 6th December 1976.

17   *Ibid.*

18   *NEC Minutes*, 15th December 1976.

19   *NEC Minutes*, 26th January 1977; *Labour Weekly* 28th January 1977; *The Times*, 27th January 1977.

20   Interview, Ron Hayward.

21   'Report of Special Committee to Examine Documents on Entryism', *LPCR 1977*, pp. 383–5.

22   *NEC Minutes*, 25th May 1977. A proposal that the Underhill documents be more widely circulated was defeated on the grounds they might be misrepresented by the press. *The Times*, 26th May 1977.

23   Crick, *op. cit.*, p. 163.

24   *Organisation Sub Minutes*, 11th February 1980.

25   *Organisation Sub*, 14th April 1980.
26   D. Hughes, 'Underhill Report on Entryism', *Organisation Sub*, 14th April 1980.
27   *Organisation Sub Minutes*, 14th April 1980.
28   *Tribune*, 18th February 1977.
29   In this period (i.e. 1978–80) the whole of the left on the NEC, including those who, like Michael Foot, Neil Kinnock, Joan Lestor and Alex Kitson, later backed disciplinary action against Militant, was united on this point.
30   R. Underhill, 'Entryist Activities', *op. cit.*
31   This was the clause which stated that organisations with their own 'Programme, Principles and Policy for distinctive and separate propaganda' and with 'branches in the Constituencies' were ineligible for affiliation to the Party and the membership of such organisations was incompatible with Party membership. *LP Constitution*, Clause II, 3, 4(b).
32   *Organisation Sub Minutes*, 7th July 1980.
33   The most controversial case was that of Ted Heslin. Heslin, a leading member of a Trotskyist sect, the Workers Socialist League, was expelled by Oxford CLP. His appeal was dismissed by an NEC inquiry panel but upheld by the Executive itself, despite the most vigorous resistance from the Oxford Party. REA the expulsion of Ted Heslin, *Organisation Sub* 7th January 1980; *NEC Minutes* 23rd January 1980. D. Hughes 'Oxford CLP – Mr. E. Heslin' *Organisation Sub* 10th November 1980.
34   *The Times*, 11th December 1976.
35   See, e.g. speech by Shirley Williams, *The Times*, 22nd January 1977.
36   See, e.g. speech by Tony Benn, *The Times* 11th December 1976.
37   One Foot loyalist was quoted as saying that their aim was 'to push Benn as far along the branch as possible – and then saw it off'. *Sunday Times*, 4th October 1981.
38   In November 1981 there was a highly publicised row between Foot and Benn over compensation for the re-nationalisation of industries privatised by the Tories. This led to a final break between the two men and the latter's departure from the shadow cabinet.
39   *The Guardian*, 26th March 1981.
40   *Organisation Sub Minutes*, 9th December 1981.
41   Interview, David Hughes.
42   Interview with Foot in *Tribune*, 12th February 1982.
43   *Daily Telegraph*, 11th December 1981.
44   NEC Minutes 16th December 1981. Aside from Foot himself, Judith Hart, Doug Hoyle, Neil Kinnock and Alex Kitson joined the right in backing the motion. The ten dissentients were Frank Allaun, Tony Benn, Eric Clarke, Lawrence Coates, Eric Heffer, Les Huckfield, Joan Lestor, Joan Maynard, Jo Richardson and Dennis Skinner.
45   Mellish had been appointed to the London Dockland Development Corporation. He could not accept his salary whilst he remained an MP.
46   *The Guardian* 4th December 1981. The basis for Foot's claim was an article by Tatchell in the left-wing 'London Labour Briefing'. This had criticised the Party's 'obsessive legalism and parliamentarism' and called for a 'more militant form of extraparliamentary opposition which involves mass popular

participation and challenges the government's right to rule'. The last phrase, in particular, was siezed upon as evidence of Tatchell's anti-parliamentary views. In fact, it was carelessly used and it is doubtful whether Tatchell grasped the gloss which could be placed upon it. The article as a whole, and Tatchell's subsequent statements, indicates that, rhetorical flourishes aside, his views were in accord with the extra (not anti) parliamentary approaches favoured by large segments of the left (e.g. the Labour Co-ordinating Committee). See P. Tatchell *The Battle for Bermondsey*, pp. 53–4, 67–71.

47 *Organisation Sub Minutes*, 7th December 1981.

48 *Tribune*, 11th December 1981.

49 *Labour Weekly*, editorial 11th December 1981.

50 Duncan Campbell, 'The Real Mafia Man', *New Statesman*, 6th August 1982.

51 Tatchell, *op. cit.*, p. 66.

52 *The Guardian*, 8th December 1981.

53 For Tariq Ali, see below, pp. 232–3.

54 *The Guardian*, 2nd December 1981. *The Observer*, 13th December 1981.

55 A. Mitchell, *Four Years in the Death of the Labour Party*, p. 96.

56 The following voted to refer back the Organisation Sub's decision. Frank Allaun, Tony Benn, Eric Clarke, Lawrence Coates (LPYS), Judith Hart, Eric Heffer, Doug Hoyle, Les Huckfield, Alex Kitson, Joan Lestor, Joan Maynard, Sam McCluskie, Jo Richardson, Dennis Skinner. The following voted against: Betty Boothroyd, Gwyneth Dunwoody, Roy Evans, Foot, John Golding, Alan Hadden, Denis Healey, Neville Hough, Neil Kinnock, Gerry Russell, Shirley Summerskill, Syd Tierney, Russel Tuck, Eric Varley, David Williams. *NEC Minutes*, 10th December 1981.

57 *Organisation Sub*, 8th February 1982. A further 66 poured in to following month. *Labour Weekly*, 12th March 1982.

56 Interview, Ian Mikardo.

59 He publicly supported a non Labour candidate in a Council by-election. Pre-empting moves to expel him, he then quit the Labour Party claiming, with unintentional irony, that 'the tolerance of yesterday has gone'. *The Guardian* 3rd August 1982.

60 *Organisation Sub Minutes*, 12th July 1982.

61 *The Guardian*, 10th January 1983.

62 Letter to *The Guardian*, 8th March 1983. A Bermondsey Conservative who canvassed against Labour in the by-election, wrote to Tatchell 'I absolutely deplore the shameful and sick campaign against you. Most of all I deplore the fabricated lies . . . I was embarrassed by the press'. (Much was made of Tatchell's homosexuality and alleged extremism.) Quoted in M. Hollingworth, *The Press and Political Dissent*, p. 164. Hollingworth commented 'when Michael Foot disowned Tatchell publicly, it was the green light for Fleet Street to attack', *ibid.*, p. 153.

63 Ford, the *New Statesman* reported, had 'chosen to consort with a variety of distasteful regimes', including South Africa and Salazar's Portugal, and acted as a consultant for Bristol Ship Repairers in their attempts to avoid nationalisation by the recent Labour Government. *New Statesman*, 20th November

1981. Wall was selected as much because of his personal popularity and long record of service in the Party as the Tendency's strength in the constituency. Crick, *op. cit.*, p. 171. Interview, Harold Sims (Yorkshire Regional Organiser at the time).

64 REA Ben Ford, MP, against the decision of Bradford North not to reselect him. *Organisation Sub*, 8th February 1982.

65 *Organisation Sub Minutes*, 8th February 1982.

66 *NEC Minutes*, 24th February 1982. All but one Foot loyalist (Judith Hart) voted in favour of Wall's endorsement.

67 'Labour Man's Shock Vision of "Bloodshed" ', *Sunday Times*, 7th March 1982.

68 *The Guardian*, 8th March 1982.

69 *Organisation Sub Minutes*, 8th March 1982. *The Guardian*, 9th March 1982.

70 *The Guardian*, 26th June 1982. Ford stood as an independent in the 1983 general election, handing over the seat to the Tories.

71 *NEC Minutes*, 28th July 1982. *Sunday Times*, 25th July 1982. The left united in voting against Foot on this question.

72 Ron Hayward and David Hughes, 'Inquiry into Militant Tendency', *NEC Report 1982*, p. 133.

73 I.e. the clause which deemed organisations with their own 'programme, principles and policy for distinctive and separate propaganda' to be ineligible to affiliate to the Party.

74 *The Guardian*, 19th June 1982. Hattersley in contrast, backed the Report. *The Guardian*, 21st June 1982.

75 *The Guardian*, 29th June 1982. The vote was 23 to 21.

76 *The Guardian*, 23rd June 1982. Even the broadly sympathetic *New Statesman* criticised its failure to furnish evidence or a reasoned justification for its conclusions, *New Statesman*, 25th June 1982.

77 *NEC Minutes*, 23rd June 1982.

78 Mortimer disagreed: 'most of the public' he later commented 'only became aware of Militant because the Party chose to make it a big issue. It was . . . a largely self-inflicted wound,' letter to the author.

79 *The Times*, 22nd June 1982.

80 Interview, Jim Mortimer. John Golding, an astute and highly capable political operater who was an influential right-wing member of the NEC approved of the Register – though ideally he would have preferred an all-out purge – because he reckoned that anything that allayed the fears of the wider left would also make it more difficult to mobilise mass left-wing opposition to measures against Militant. Interview, John Golding.

81 See Chapter 6 above, pp. 121–9.

82 *The Guardian*, 5th December 1981.

83 *The Guardian*, 17th June 1982.

84 *The Guardian*, 26th July 1982.

85 See Peter Kellner's interview with Tariq Ali; *New Statesman*, 11th December 1981.

86 D. Hughes, 'The Labour Party and Other Organisations', *Organisation Sub*, 9th December 1981.

87   *Organisation Sub Minutes*, 9th December 1981.

88   He was only finally excluded in October 1983; *The Guardian* 27th October 1983.

89   Interviews, David Hughes, Jim Mortimer.

90   Interview, Jim Mortimer; Foot in *LPCR 1982*, p. 51.

91   Mortimer, *LPCR 1982* p. 41.

92   See above Chapter 1, p. 6.

93   This sentiment was shared by Jim Mortimer. Interview.

94   As one Tribunite critic of Militant acknowledged in his evidence to the Hayward-Hughes inquiry, 'Because of the atmosphere and practice of the NEC in the 1950s there is an understandable anxiety within the Party – which we share – against 'witch-hunts' and 'inquisitions' '. Jack Straw, Evidence *LP Archives*.

95   Interview, Jim Mortimer.

96   Quoted in *The Guardian*, 24th April 1982.

97   *Tribune*, 4th June 1982.

98   CLPD, a leading champion of Conference sovereignty was to be badly divided over the issue of registration. The leadership (and a very narrow majority at its AGM) favoured it on the grounds that refusal to recognise the Register amounted to defiance of a Conference decision. *New Statesman*, 4th February 1983.

99   *The Guardian*, 27th September 1982.

100   *NEC Minutes*, 23rd June 1982.

101   J. E. Mortimer 'Circular to all non-affiliated groups of Labour Party Members', *NEC*, 28th July 1982.

102   Letter to Militant, *ibid.*

103   *LPCR 1982*, p. 42.

104   Robert Taylor, the Observer's Labour Editor commented that 'the old discredited politics of union power-broking and wheeling-dealing behind the scenes scored a victory over the new radical forces which have swept through the Party since 1979'. *The Observer*, 3rd October 1982. A key role in mobilising the right was played by the shadowy 'St Ermine's Group' of right-wing union leaders.

105   All major left-wing groups (including CLPD and the LCC) refused to apply immediately for registration. This reflected the almost unanimous hostility of the left outside Parliament towards expulsions. See *Labour Weekly*, 30th July 1982.

106   Somewhat oddly, as this had not been stipulated as a criteria of eligibility. J. E. Mortimer, 'The Registrar of Non-affiliated Groups', *Organisation Sub*, 3rd September 1982.

107   Mortimer, ibid; *NEC Minutes* 22nd September 1982; *Labour Weekly* 24th September 1982.

108   *LPCR 1982*, p. 42.

109   In fact, Mortimer considerably underestimated the number of Militant's full-time organisers. Crick, *op. cit.*, pp. 185–6.

110   *The Guardian*, 5th November 1982.

111   *The Guardian*, 2nd October 1982.

112   P. Taaffe to J. E. Mortimer 16th October 1982. His arguments were amplified by further correspondence from Militant's editorial board: 8th November 1982; 23rd November 1982. *NEC*, 24th November 1982.

113 Even some of Militant's staunchest defendants on the NEC, like Tony Benn, found this disingenuousness irritating. Interview, Tony Benn.

114 Under Clause II(4). Taaffe in fact contested the constitutionality of this too on the grounds that Militant was not an organisation merely a newspaper.

115 Crick, *op. cit.*, p. 191.

116 *Labour Weekly*, 12th November 1982.

117 See above Chapter 8, pp. 168–71.

118 *NEC Minutes*, 27th April 1977. By this time, thanks to McCormick and Lewis's efforts, the constituency was wrapped up in a cloud of writs and injunctions.

119 Lewis v. Heffer and others. Court of Appeal January 1978. *All England Law Reports*, Volume 3, 1918, pp. 354–369.

120 *Ibid.*, p. 365.

121 Interview John Golding.

122 J. E. Mortimer, 'The Register of Non-affiliated Groups', *NEC*, 24th November 1982.

123 The Party continued to go through the motion of deliberating on application (and non-applications) for the Register. But, from this point on, this became a separate exercise from the campaign against Militant.

124 By 16 votes to 8. As in virtually all votes on the issue, the majority was formed by a coalition of the right and centre-left Foot loyalists. The NEC did not, at this meeting, take any disciplinary decisions (on legal advice); rather it approved the various stages of the procedure to be followed in the next three months.

125 *The Times* Law Reports 16th December 1982.

126 In carefully chosen language, to meet legal requirements, the motion referred to the authorisation given by Conference (via its acceptance of the Hayward-Hughes Report and Composite 48) to the NEC to act against Militant; noted that the Tendency 'as a Trotskyist "entryist" group is a political organisation with its own programme, principles and policy for distinctive and separate propaganda'; and proceeded, on these grounds, to declare it ineligible for affiliation to the Party. The vote reflected a consistent pattern of alignments. In favour: Betty Boothroyd, Ken Cure, Anne Davis, Gwyneth Dunwoody, Roy Evans, John Golding, Alan Hadden, Denis Healey, Neville Hough, Denis Howell, Shirley Summerskill, Syd Tierney, Russel Tuck, Eric Varley (from the right) John Evans, Michael Foot, Neil Kinnock, Alex Kitson (centre-left). Against: Frank Allaun, Tony Benn, Laurence Coates, Judith Hart, Eric Heffer, Jo Richardson, Dennis Skinner, Tom Sawyer, Audrey Wise. *NEC Minutes*, 15th December 1982.

127 In fact – although nobody appeared to recall it – only a short while previously the NEC had proscribed an organisation, the Social Democratic Alliance. However – and this is a key point – it was proscribed primarily because of its decision to field candidates against official Labour candidates. NEC Report, *LPCR*, 1981, p. 8.

128 Interview, Jim Mortimer.

129 Thus the GMWU never participated actively in the St Ermine's Group of right-wing unions. In addition, personal relations between Basnett and Duffy, President of the AUEW, were badly soured over the bitter Isle of Grain dispute between the two unions.

130 Interviews, John Golding, Jim Mortimer, David Hughes.

131 Interview, John Golding.

132 In a paper to the NEC, he suggested a three-fold criteria: anyone found to be a member of a central directing body, or anyone shown to have a record of 'sustained organising activity' for at least a year on behalf of Militant, or any of Labour's 'public representatives' who consistently and publicly identified with the Trotskyist group. Quoted in *Sunday Times*, 9th January 1983.

133 'The Militant Tendency – Further Legal advice', *NEC*, 26th January 1983.

134 The definition was to have a major impact upon future NEC action against Militant. It read in full as follows: 'That the National Executive Committee resolved that, in considering whether individual members of the Party are, contrary to Rule II (4) (b) of the constitution, members of the Militant Tendency (which pursuant to the Conference decision, was declared by the National Executive Committee on 15 December, 1982, to be ineligible for affiliation to the Party) and therefore liable to expulsion from the Party, it shall have regard in particular, to their involvement in financial support for and/or the organisation of and/or the activities of the Militant Tendency, and further resolves that it shall give written particulars of any such involvement alleged against any individual member of the party and an opportunity to make written and oral representations thereon prior to considering his/her expulsion from the party.' *NEC Minutes*, 26th January 1983.

135 The NEC in fact experienced difficulty in finding out the names of Militant's full-time organisers and senior personnel (whose numbers it consistently under-rated) never mind procuring watertight evidence of their involvement in the Tendency.

136 *NEC Minutes*, 26th January 1983.

137 J. E. Mortimer to Militant editorial board 3rd February 1983. *NEC*, 23rd February 1983.

138 Militant editorial board to J. E. Mortimer 16th February 1983. *NEC*, 23rd February 1983. In a legal opinion, Irvine and Blair advised that the NEC was not legally obliged to divulge evidence, and urged it not to do so. 'Joint opinion' *ibid*. The reason seems that the NEC and its legal advisers feared that Militant would be able to further embarrass the Party and stretch out proceedings if given access to the evidence, which was of uneven calibre.

139 *NEC Minutes*, 23 February 1983.

140 *LPCR*, 1983 p. 66.

141 *The Guardian*, 29th November 1983; Interview, David Hughes.

142 Interview, Jim Mortimer.

143 As we have seen, the centre-left within the PLP backed the drive against Militant. But, outside the Tribune Group of MPs, their influence was slight.

144 This was certainly the view of the majority of the two largest left-wing ginger groups, CLPD and the LCC and also of prominent leftists like Ian Mikardo.

145 Nigel Williamson, *Tribune*, 22nd June 1984 (review of Michael Crick's study of Militant. Williamson had succeeded Chris Mullin as editor).

146 *Tribune*, 26th November 1982.

147 *Sunday Times*, 14th February 1982.

148 *The Guardian*, 6th June 1981.

149 David and Maurice Kogan *The Battle for the Labour Party*, p. 37. The RFMC was an umbrella body linking together most left-wing groups. Militant played a passive role within it.

150 CLPD, the LCC and the umbrella RFMC were all accused of intimidation, intolerance and gross abuse of their opponents. See, e.g., *The Guardian*, 5th November 1980, 6th June 1982, 27th August 1981, 10th September 1981.

151 Daily Express 1st June 1981 quoted in M. Hollingsworth, *op. cit.*, p. 60. John Golding charged the 'bully boys of the left who support Benn' with 'acting like the Hitler youth'. BBC Radio Four, quoted in *ibid*.

152 *The Guardian*, 8th December 1981.

153 Hollingsworth *op. cit, passim*.

154 *Ibid*, p. 61. *Tribune* noted that, whilst Labour's opponents had for years been denouncing extremism within its ranks, 'what is new is that the leaders of the Labour Party are pumping out exactly the same message', *Tribune*, 25th June 1982.

155 Labour's defeated (Bennite) candidate at the Mitcham and Morden by-election, David Nicholas observed 'as anyone who has recently canvassed knows, [Benn] is extremely unpopular on the doorstep'. *Tribune* 11th June 1982. Hollingworth concluded that 'Labour's radical left is now perceived as unrepresentative and politically illegitimate, largely the product of a few Militant activists . . . Labour's left-wing is now effectively isolated and powerless' *op. cit.*, p. 75. One survey reported that 73% of respondents felt that Benn had 'dictatorial ambitions', *ibid*, pp. 65–6.

156 Interview, John Golding.

157 In one month alone, the NEC received 37 resolutions on the issue all condemning disciplinary action against the Tendency. *NEC* 15th December 1982.

158 Interviews, David Hughes, Jim Mortimer, John Golding.

159 J. E. Mortimer, 'The Register of Non-affiliated Groups', *NEC*, 24th November 1982.

160 See above Chapter 7, pp. 146–52.

161 P. Seyd and L. Minkin 'The Labour party and its members', *New Society* 20th September 1979. P. Whiteley 'Who are the Labour Activists?' *Political Quarterly*, Volume 52 1981. T. Forester, 'The Labour Activists', *New Society*, 13th October 1977. D. Hine 'Leaders and Followers', in W. E. Paterson and A. H. Thomas (eds) *The Future of Social Democracy*, p. 271. The typical activist increasingly became a teacher, social worker or local government official, caricatured by Peter Jenkins (then of *The Guardian*) as the 'lumpenpolytechnics'. The social transformation of Labour membership also greatly diminished the incidence of remunerative involvement within the Party hence undercutting instrumental control.

162 This paragraph is based on interviews with former and present Regional Officials.

163 Through meetings, bulletins and pamphlets, organisations like CLPD, the LCC and Militant played a significant role in disseminating information, mobilising opinion and inculcating a better awareness of Party rules and procedures. At the same time, the alterations in the physiognomy of Party membership considerably weakened, in many parts of the country Regional Organisers' once extensive networks of contacts, diminishing their influence and hence, indirectly that of the Party centre.

164   Peter Shore, *Guardian* 27th April 1981.

165   Denis Healey, *The Guardian*, 13th May, 9th June 1981.

166   *The Guardian*, 10th September 1981.

167   Patterson and Thomas, *op. cit.*, p. 279.

168   *New Statesman*, 1st January 1982.

169   This sense of betrayal was reinforced by a sense of outrage at the defection of former cabinet ministers and other MPs to form the SDP.

170   Tariq Ali finally settled the matter by withdrawing from the battle.

171   One reason why they eventually acquiesced was that Militant calculated that continued defiance would be counter-productive.

172   *Tribune*, 18th December 1981.

173   In a review of Crick's book. Tribune editor (and former prominent CLPD activist) Nigel Williamson recalled that many in the "democratic left", feared that action against Militant, although justified under the Party's rules, would be the signal for a more widespread purge of other legitimate groups which found themselves out of step with the Party leadership', *Tribune*, 22 June 1984.

174   Crick, *op. cit.*, p. 195.

Notes to Chapter Twelve

1   *LPCR 1983*, p. 15. Hattersley defeated Michael Meacher for the consolation prize, the deputy leadership, by a comparable margin.

2   *Organisation Sub Minutes*, 7th November 1983. For the duties of the new committee, see W. Brown (Assistant National Agent) 'Appeals and Disputes', *AMC*, 5th December 1983.

3   *AMC Minutes*, 5th November 1984.

4   REA, five members of Coventry Labour Group; *AMC*, 11th February 1985.

5   Report of an Inquiry into Coventry North East CLP, *AMC*, 11th February 1985. The Report recommended, *inter alia*, that a left-wing ginger group 'North East Left' should either 'cease to function' or apply to the Register for inclusion.

6   *NEC Minutes*, 27th February 1985 – in the second case, only on the casting vote of the Chairman.

7   REA, five members of Sunderland Labour Group, *AMC*, 11th February 1985.

8   *NEC Minutes*, 27th February 1985. The recommendation was then altered to a restoration of the whip after assurance had been obtained over future conduct. *AMC Minutes*, 11th March 1985.

9   For example in Bristol South (where the former chief whip, Michael Cocks, was deselected) and Stoke North. The one example of a more overt and politically charged intervention was in Hyndburn. An NEC enquiry held a left-wing caucus 'operating at an unacceptable level of discipline' to be 'incompatible with the proper operation of the CLP'. Although there had been no actual breaches of the rules, the NEC instructed Hyndburn to restart the selection process. None the less, a left-winger (Keva Coombes) was eventually selected. Report of an Inquiry into Hyndburn CLP Selection Procedure. *AMC*, 13th January 1986.

10 It voted a solid left-wing slate for the NEC elections, and backed Meacher for the deputy leadership in 1983. It had also opposed the register the previous year. *LPCR 1983; Tribune*, 1st April 1983.

11 The vote was 14 to 12. REA, 6 Blackburn CLP members, *AMC*, 9th April 1984; *NEC Minutes*, 25th April 1984.

12 M. Crick, *The March of Militant*, p. 306.

13 *New Statesman*, 11th October 1985.

14 For example, the Appeals and Mediation Committee minute approving the expulsion of Brychan Davies from Rhondda CLP was referred back by 14 votes to 13 with two Kinnock loyalists, John Evans and Alex Kitson in the majority. Evans later switched sides and the appeal was dismissed. *NEC Minutes*, 28th November 1984, 23rd January 1985.

15 *The Guardian*, 14th March 1985, 13th January 1986. Other notable setbacks were in Gateshead East, East Kilbride, Glasgow Provan and Glasgow Pollok; *The Guardian*, 26th February, 14th March, 22nd May, 17th June 1985. Frank Field beat off a strong challenge in Birkenhead. Its one gain was in Bermondsey where in Tatchell's days it had been weak; *The Guardian*, 21st February 1986.

16 Interview in *Tribune*, 15th July 1983. The rest of this paragraph and the following two are based on confidential interviews.

17 *LPCR 1985*, p. 128.

18 Beatrix Campbell, *City Limits*, 11th October 1985.

19 Young succinctly summed up Kinnock's strategy as 'the education of his party in realism rather than the instruction of the country in socialism'. *The Guardian*, 25th February 1986.

20 *The Observer*, 6th October 1985. The BBC2 Newsnight programme on 3rd October used 'He's a Hero' as its theme music for its coverage of Kinnock's handling of the Conference.

21 *The Guardian*, 2nd October 1985.

22 Interviews with people present at the Conference.

23 *The Observer*, 6th October 1985.

24 The emergence of a centre-left grouping of Foot (later Kinnock) loyalists effected alignments on the NEC and in the PLP but had little impact beyond.

25 Not all members of the 'Bennite' wing of the Party had been enthusiastic about Benn's campaign for the deputy leadership though, once began, all fell in behind it; an influential group of Bennites had, in 1982, privately but forcefully pressed Benn not to stand again when he appeared to be toying with the idea. Reflecting these strains, that same year the LCC withdrew from the umbrella Rank and File Mobilising Committee and a damaging split within CLPD was only narrowly averted.

26 *Tribune*, 4th January 1985.

27 See P. Seyd, 'Bennism Without Benn: Realignment on the Labour Left', *New Socialist*, 27th May 1985.

28 See the valuable discussion by Stuart Hall, 'Realignment' – for What?' in *Marxism Today*, December 1985.

29 'After the Landslide' special issue of *Labour Activist* (organ of the LCC) 1983.

30 *The Observer*, 6th October 1985.

31 See chap 7 above pp. 151–2.

32 Campbell, *op. cit.*

33 *LPCR 1985*, p. 177.

34 *The Guardian*, 22nd November 1985.

35 Mulhearn unveiled, to his sceptical trade union audience, his 'Brazil Scenario': a Liverpool default would either precipitate an international banking crisis (hence a crisis of capitalism) or, to avert this, the Government would step in to bale out the city. Interview, trade union official present at the talks.

36 *Ibid.*

37 *The Guardian*, 25th November 1985.

38 Interviews, trade union officials. Many suspected that, along with Kinnock, they had been fixed up in advance as scapegoats.

39 *NEC Minutes*, 27th November 1985. Aside from the soft left, three members normally associated with the hard left voted for the inquiry – Margaret Beckett, Jo Richardson and Audrey Wise. The five opponents were Benn, Heffer, Skinner, Joan Maynard and the LPYS representative. It could be that one consideration influencing the vote of their three allies was to assure places on the inquiry team. Audrey Wise and Margaret Beckett were in fact selected.

40 *Investigation into the Liverpool District Labour Party*, p. 4.

41 *Ibid.*, p. 38.

42 Militant's supremacy also rested – this point was not made by the Report – on genuine popular support.

43 *Ibid.*, p. 16.

44 *Ibid.*, p. 22.

45 *Ibid.*, p. 10.

46 *Ibid.*, pp. 35, 36. The impact of the Report was weakened firstly by the inclusion of the most minor technical irregularities (e.g. the DLP discussed international issues) and, secondly, by a drafting style that as often obscured as highlighted the key issues. These flaws were eagerly exploited by the NEC's critics.

47 *Ibid.*, pp. 43–4.

48 S. Kelly and I. Williams *The Rise and Fall of Mersey Militant* unpublished manuscript.

48 *Ibid.*

49 GMBATU No. 5 covered employment in parks and gardens and the Council's security force, No. 8 educational manual workers. In the course of 1986, the latter branch turned against Militant.

50 Kelly and Williams, *op. cit., Liverpool Echo*, 22nd January 1985. In an interview John Hamilton commented 'You can't get a job in here [the Town Hall] unless you're a Militant', D. Selbourne, 'On the Mersey Waterfront', *New Society*, 29th November 1985. Employment in private sector manufacturing and services had been so badly hit in Liverpool that around 25% of the workforce were employed by the Council.

51 *Ibid.*, Kelly and Williams, *op. cit.*

52 *NEC Minutes*, 26th February 1986.

53 *New Statesman*, 29th August 1986.

54 The various hard left groups, together with some small Trotskyist factions and ginger groups for blacks (the Black Sections) and women (Women's Action Committee) were shortly to assemble together under the umbrella of Labour Left Liaison. One of it major objectives was opposition to the 'witch-hunt'. From January 1986, the main hard left groups regularly published a joint newsletter called 'Witch Hunt News' which detailed all disciplinary measures taken by the NEC.

55 Militant was generally unsympathetic to the demands of the Black Sections (for separate black representation) and the women's movement.

56 *The Guardian*, 24th March 1986; T. Benn and E. Heffer, 'A Strategy for Labour', *New Left Review*, 158, 1986, pp. 63, 65; E. Heffer, *Labour's Future*, pp. 79–98.

57 *The Guardian*, 30th November 1985.

58 M. Parkinson, *Liverpool on the Brink*, pp. 85, 90, 95–6, 148–9.

59 *The Guardian*, 7th December 1985.

60 Interview, trade union official. See also R. Harris, *The Making of Neil Kinnock*, p. 175.

61 *Tribune*, 15th July 1983.

62 N. Kinnock, *The Future of Socialism*, p. 10.

63 D. Blunkett, *Labour Weekly*, 21st February 1986.

64 D. Blunkett, *Tribune*, 14th March 1986.

65 *Ibid.*

66 *The Guardian*, 20th May 1986. Sawyer's attack was quoted verbatim – and with equal strength of feeling – by Jimmy Knapp, the NUR's soft left leader, at its Conference; *NUR Journal*, 11th July 1986; interview NUR official.

67 'Labour Against the Witch-Hunt', *London Labour Briefing Supplement*, 1983.

68 *NUPE Annual Conference Report 1985*, pp. 150–53.

69 *The Guardian*, 20th May 1986.

70 These are detailed in a NUPE Head Office Circular 26th February 1986.

71 Interview, Tom Sawyer.

72 Introduction to 'Benn/Heffer documents', *New Left Review*, 158, 1986 p. 59.

73 This was separate from the right-wing caucus, to which a majority of trade union NEC members belonged. However, a significant minority of five (out of twelve) soft leftists and centrists did not. Interview, Tom Sawyer.

74 Interview, Tom Sawyer.

75 Leading soft-left trade unionists were also worried about Kinnock's propensity to align himself with the right on important questions of domestic policy; *ibid.*

76 *Tribune*, 3rd January 1986. He also resented Kinnock's tractic of using his toughness over Militant to stamp his authority as leader which, he felt, needlessly put the public spotlight on strife and 'extremism' in the Party; *ibid.*

77 'To Move Against Militant' Debate between Tom Sawyer and Audrey Wise. *New Socialist* April 1986.

78 Speech to NUR Conference, *NUR Journal,* 11th July 1986. *Tribune* concurred; see, e.g., editorial, *Tribune,* 28th February 1986.

79 Sawyer in *New Socialist,* op. cit.

80 High Court of Justice. Judgement by Sir Nicolas Browne – Wilkinson, official transcript.

81 Interview, LP official. This view was by no means universally shared. Indeed, according to Professor John Griffiths, an expert in this branch of the law, the High Court decision was quite predictable. *Labour Weekly,* 9th May 1986.

82 Crick, *op. cit.,* p. 281.

83 *NEC Minutes,* 26th March 1986. The seven who walked out where Benn, Heffer, Skinner, Frances Curran, Jo Richardson, Joan Maynard and Eric Clarke.

84 Letter to *The Guardian,* 2nd April 1986.

85 Interview, LP official.

86 *Tribune,* 3rd January 1986.

87 'Particulars of Charges', Report from the General Secretary, *NEC,* 18th April 1986.

88 *NEC Papers and Minutes,* 21st, 22nd May 1986.

89 REA by Councillor Green against expulsion by Sheffield Attercliffe CLP; *AMC,* 18th December 1985; *NEC Minutes,* 18th December 1985. Ironically, this split between the soft left and the centre-right bloc was overshadowed by an attack by Tony Benn on the Sheffield leader: 'David is too late – he should have thought of all this before he started the Liverpool witch-hunt'. Benn's former lieutenant, Michael Meacher, then weighed in on Blunkett's behalf, reprimanding his old chief; *The Guardian,* 19th December 1985.

90 REA by Amir Khan and Kevin Scally against expulsion by Birmingham Sparkbrook CLP, *AMC,* 9th June 1986.

91 *NEC Minutes,* 9th June 1986; *The Guardian,* 11th June 1986.

92 *Witch-Hunt News,* Conference edition 1986.

93 The Kinnock camp intimated that the leader only voted to uphold the expulsions so as not to publicise differences with his deputy. Interview. A call for immediate reinstatement was defeated at Conference by only a relatively small majority (3,443,000 to 2,715,000, *Tribune,* 3rd October 1986). But the NEC's position was legally very frail since Cure's participation in both the inquiry and the NEC vote was a clear breach of natural justice and it eventually (and overwhelmingly) reversed its stance and instructed Sparkbrook to re-admit Khan and Scally. *The Guardian,* 27th November 1986.

94 It should be noted that the soft left did not always vote in unison. Sawyer, for example, was slightly more likely to back expulsions than Meacher.

95 *NEC,* 10th January 1983.

96 The contract for the acquisition of Militant Headquarters in Lower Breck Road, in which Mulhearn, Harrison and Tony Aitman were named as guarantors, was used against those three individuals; other evidence was appearing as a signatory to leaflets supporting Militant, participating in meetings and rallies held under its aegis and the publication of articles in 'Mersey Militant'.

97 A series of special NEC meetings were held. *NEC Minutes,* 21st, 22nd May, 12th, 13th June, 24th July 1986; the issue also figured prominently at regular NEC meetings.

98 Felicity Dowling was expelled in October; *NEC Minutes,* 27th October

1986.

99 Martin Linton 'How Militan\ Got the Law on Its Side' *Guardian* 25th April 1986.

100 Browne-Wilkinson, *op. cit.*

101 These elements had first been laid down, in connection with the Labour Party, by Justice Megarry in his Pembroke judgment. See above, Chapter 8, p. 170.

102 *NEC Report 1986*; Appendix 'Disciplinary Procedures', pp. 66–7.

103 This was one reason for Whitty's lack of enthusiasm for expulsions. He was also uncomfortable with the role of disciplinarian and, initially at least, he felt there were other alternatives; later, he changed his mind on this point. Interviews with officials and observers of the Party.

104 *The Guardian*, 25th April 1986.

105 See, e.g., the Russell Case in 1962, above Chapter 3, pp. 62–5.

106 *The Guardian*, 9th June 1986.

107 Document on 'Disciplinary Procedures within the Labour Party', Annexe A, Constitutional Amendment by Joan Maynard. *Organisation Sub*, 14th July 1986. As we have seen, the left had pressed throughout the 1960s for an independent appeals tribunal, though interest had lapsed in the period of the left NEC in the 1970s.

108 'Appendix: Disciplinary Procedures. Proposal for a National Constitutional Committee', NEC Report 1986, p. 66. This document was the final version of a paper originally drafted by the General Secretary which underwent a number of redrafts.

109 See G. Braunthal *The German Social Democrats* p. 23 and D. S. Bell and B. Criddle *The French Socialist Party*, p. 209.

110 H. Street and R. Brazier (ed), *de Smith Constitutional and Administrative Law*, pp. 853, 854.

111 Appendix, NEC Report, 1986 'Disciplinary Procures' *op. cit.*

112 *Ibid.* New Clause IX 2(e)(ii) LP Constitution. The same principle of a division of judicial functions applies to constituency parties. They retain their responsibility to enforce the Party's Rules and safeguard its 'programme, principles and policy', but not their power to try and punish offenders. Instead they are empowered to investigate alleged breaches of the rules by appointing a 'panel of investigators', which submits a report to a constituency party's GC. If the GC finds that a prima facie case has been made out, it can instruct the investigators (after consultation with Regional office) to formulate and present charges to the NCC. New Clause XVI (3) CLP Rules, *ibid.* After prompting from the soft left, the NEC, in a later alteration, empowered a CLP to make a recommendation as to appropriate disciplinary action; *Organisation Sub Minutes*, 8th September 1986.

113 New Clause XVI 1(b) (i) and (ii) LP Constitution *ibid.*

114 New Clause XVI 1(b) (iii) *ibid.* The latter responsibility was inherited from Regional Executive Committees and not the NEC.

115 New Clause XVI 1(b)(iv) and (v) *ibid.*

116 New Clause IX 2(e)(i) *ibid.*

117 New Clause IX 2(e)(iii) *ibid.* This new formulation in fact added somewhat to the powers of the Executive in that hereto such decision was 'subject to any modification by the Party Conference'. *LP Constitution* 1984 Clause IX 3.

118 Braunthal, *op. cit.*, p. 23.

119 'Appendix: Disciplinary Procedures' *op. cit.*

120 'Appendix: Disciplinary Procedures' *op. cit.*

121 New Clause III 4 to the Constitution and New Clause IV 5 to CLP Model Rules *ibid.*

122 *Ibid.*, p. 71.

123 The two more peripheral members of the hard left did not reject the new rules outright. Jo Richardson backed them, whilst Audrey Wise abstained. *NEC Minutes*, 30th July 1986.

124 *Tribune*, 3rd October 1986.

125 *Organisation Sub Minutes*, 14th July 1986.

126 The five trade unionists were Fred Binks (UCW), Alan Hadden (GMBATU), John Weakley (AEU), David Brookman (ISTC). The sole left-winger was Alan Quinn (TGWU) – an odd choice for the T and G given his Militant links. The women's representatives were Rose Degiorgio and Dianne Hayter. The Socialist Society member was W. B. Dooley and the three CLP representatives were Mandy Moore, Ken Slater and John Burrows. *The Guardian*, 6th January 1987. Election of the NCC 1987/8, *NEC*, 28 January 1987.

127 Many in the constituencies were also unhappy at the failure of the NEC to consult them over what was, after all, the most drastic alteration in Labour's disciplinary system since 1918.

128 K. Cullen, 'Committee for Expulsions', *Campaign Group News*, November 1986.

129 *The Guardian*, 9th June 1986.

130 'Disciplinary Procedures', *op. cit.*, p. 66.

131 CLPs may also be inhibited by the fact that, whereas under the old system, expelled members might languish in the wilderness for many months before their appeals were heard, under the new system, no expulsions could take place until the case had reached the NCC. This might deter some members who might feel unhappy at rubbing shoulders at party meetings with people they are trying to expel.

132 The Secretary of the NCC is David Hughes, the Party's Senior National Officer.

133 Joyce Gould, 'Liverpool District Labour Party', *Organisation Sub* 14th July 1986; *The Guardian*, 28th May, 17th July 1986.

134 In Labour's Head Office reorganisation which occurred in 1985, Joyce Gould, formerly Assistant National Agent, was appointed to the new post of Director of Organisation, which inherited most of the National Agent's responsibilities. David Hughes, formerly National Agent had been appointed Senior National Officer retaining some advisory and disciplinary functions.

135 *NEC Minutes*, 22nd October 1986. *The Guardian*, 21st November 1986.

136 *The Guardian*, 24th November 1986.

137 *The Guardian*, 27th November 1986.

138 This section draws heavily on a series of confidential interviews.

139 It is extremely difficult to estimate with accuracy the number of Militant full-timers. One informed source suggested about forty.

140 In addition, even under the energetic Paul Carmody, the North West

Regional office had traditionally steered clear of the ever politically turbulent Liverpool parties.

141 Militant was by no means the only body which resorted to such methods; right-wingers, for example, deployed them to considerable effect in Dudley East to protect the sitting MP, Dr John Gilbert, from deselection. Thus the MP's wife, an Earls Court interior designer, was appointed as a representative of the quarrymen's branch of GMBATU and a fellow member on the delegation was the President of the local branch of the National Union of Teachers. *The Guardian*, 12th June 1985, 15th February 1986.

142 Interview, Tom Sawyer.

143 Ian Williams *New Statesman* 4th April 1986.

144 See above, Chapter 6, pp. 133–6.

145 The expellees did not help their cause by refusing at the last minute to utilise their right to appeal against their expulsions to Conference – refusals met by 'hoots of derision'. *Guardian*, 30th September 1986.

146 Letter to *Tribune* 5th December 1986. Demonstrations organised by Militant in protest against the expulsions were poorly attended, providing evidence for Scally's point.

147 See above, Chapter 6, p. 139.

148 Militant had merely intended to elect Byrne as Chairman of the meeting. His replacement of Hamilton was the result, as several sources have suggested, of a 'cock-up'.

149 Hamilton, as a surcharged Councillor, stood to forfeit his house as well as his political career if disqualified and bankrupted.

150 *The Guardian*, 22nd December 1986.

151 Interview, Party official.

Notes to Chapter Thirteen

1 Michael Foot, *Parliament in Danger*, p.

2 Clement Attlee, 'Party Discipline is Paramount', *op. cit.*, p. 16.

3 Michels, *op. cit.*, p. 218.

4 *Tribune*, 3rd December 1954.

5 *Tribune*, 10th October 1952.

6 See above, Chap. 1, pp. 26–30.

7 See above, Chap. 7, pp. 142–152.

8 As noted already members could be influenced by both considerations – we are, in effect, referring to the primary motivation, in aggregate terms.

9 See above, Chap 3.

10 See above, Chap 4.

11 See above, Chap 5.

12 See above, Chap 2 pp. 35–7 and Chap 4 pp. 53–5.

13 Robert MacKenzie noted in 1955 that Labour, in its striving to preserve unity, regarded 'all attempts to organise minority opinion as an intolerable threat to its survival', *op. cit.*, p. 643.

14 *CLPD Newsletter*, May 1986.

15 *Tribune*, 4th July 1975.

16 See above, Chap 5 pp. 100–5.

17 Speech by Denis Healey, reported in *The Guardian*, 11th September 1981.

18 Many prominent disciplinarians from this period, like Ray Gunter, George Brown (both former Chairmen of the Organisation Committee) and Herbert Bowden (former Chief Whip) defected when they felt themselves out of tune with the Party.

19 See above, Chap 8.

20 *New Statesman*, 2nd April 1955.

21 See above, Chap 9.

22 See above, Chap 10.

23 P. Williams, 'The Labour Party: The Rise of the Left', *op. cit.*, p. 33.

24 See above, Chap 8, p. 174.

25 The four included Shirley Williams and John Cartwright.

26 We also noted the confusion, on both left and right, between the right to proscribe (a power that was never removed) and the existence of the List, which was merely an application of that power.

27 See above, Chap 11, pp. 222–4.

28 See above, Chap 11.

29 See above, Chap 8, pp. 168–71.

30 See above, Chap 12.

31 *NUR Journal*, 11th July 1986.

32 *New Statesman*, 6th November 1954.

33 M. Foot, 'I call This an Outrage, *Tribune*, 13th August 1984. Bevan, too, was prepared to back expulsions, e.g. in the case of Konni Zilliacus in 1949. K. O. Morgan, *op. cit.*, p. 72.

34 'They act like a secret battalion of paratroopers within the brigade whose discipline they have accepted. They meet secretly to propose their own line of conduct; they have one set of rules to regulate their conduct to one another, and a different set of rules to be observed towards those who are not in the battalion ... The contradicition between the open profession and the secret purpose makes them willing to sacrifice all regard for truth and straight dealing . . . to the conquest of that vanguard they need for the future'. H. Laski, *The Secret Battalion*, p. 12. The pamphlet was written in defence of the NEC's opposition to the Communist Party's application for affiliation.

35 See above, Chap 12, pp. 281–3.

36 *The Guardian* 30th September 1986.

37 In the by-election in Knowsley North caused by Robert Kilroy-Silk's resignation, the NEC barred the front-runner, Les Huckfield MEP, from standing, out of fear that his friendly relations with Militant would be electorally highly damaging to Labour's prospects of holding the (formerly) rock-solid Merseyside seat. Further, the Executive imposed George Howarth upon an extremely reluctant constituency party. *NEC Minutes*, 24th September, 1986, 22nd October 1986. Howarth won, but on a much reduced Labour vote. In Nottingham East, in April 1987, Sharon Arkin was removed as Labour candidate by the NEC.

38 This statement rests on the judgment that the Knowsley North and Nottingham East interventions were prompted primarily by pressing electoral circumstances and were not harbingers of a more draconian system of control.

References

A note on sources

This study has relied heavily upon the minutes and papers of Labour's National Executive Committee and its relevant sub-committees (Organisation, Elections, Chairman's, Appeals and Mediation), which I have examined in detail in the period 1945 to the close of 1986. These have been supplemented by archival material from the following collections; the Labour Party Archives (Walworth Road); London Labour Party Documents; Cattermole Papers at the Modern Research Centre, Warwick University; Nottingham Records Office.

In addition, I have consulted the files of the *New Statesman, Tribune, The Times* (until 1980), *The Guardian* (after 1980), *Labour Weekly* and *Labour Organiser*.

Finally, I have interviewed between 1983 and 1987 over forty Labour Party politicians, officials and activists. Some preferred not to be personally named when comments have been attributed to them; this was especially so in the discussion (in Chapter 12) of recent events. With one or two exceptions (where complete anonymity was requested) those interviewed (in some cases on more than one occasion) are listed below in alphabetical order. In appropriate cases, the present or, in the case of the retired, most senior position achieved, is appended:

Tony Benn MP; Geoff Bish, Director of Policy; Allan Black, UCATT official; Walter Brown, former Assistant National Agent; Paul Carmody, former North West Regional Organiser; Jim Cattermole, former East Midlands Regional Organiser; Pat Cauvanagh, former NAD official; Ken Coates; Ernie Collect, former East Midlands and North West Regional Organiser; John Crouch; Roger Done, former Secretary, Manchester DLP; Bill Gilby, NUPE official; John Golding; Joyce Gould, Director of Organisation; Alan Haworth, PLP cfficial; Ron Hayward, former General Secretary; Eric Heffer MP; Peter Hildrew; Keith Hill, NUR official; Ellis Hillman; David Hughes, Senior National Officer (and former National Agent); Lord (Hugh) Jenkins; Bill Jones, former Deputy General Secretary, London Labour Party; John Keys, former General Secretary, London Labour Party; Peter Kilfoyle, Labour Party Organiser, Liverpool; Tony Mainwaring, Labour Party official; Dennis Merry, former North West Assistant Regional Organiser; Ian Mikardo MP; Jim Mortimer, former General Secretary; Jo Richardson MP; David Robertson, Yorkshire Regional Organiser; Tom Sawyer, Deputy General Secretary, NUPE; Ron Sedler; Lord (Bill) Sefton; Adam

Sharples, NUPE official; John Silkin MP; Harold Sims, former Yorkshire Regional Organiser; Graham Stringer, leader of Manchester City Council; Lord (Reg) Underhill, former National Agent; Reg Wallis, former North West Regional Organiser; Larry Whitty, General Secretary; Ian Williams.

Select bibliography

R K Alderman, Discipline in the PLP 1945–51, *Parliamentary Affairs*, Vol 18, 1965

R K Alderman, The Conscience Clause of the PLP, *Parliamentary Affairs*, Vol 19 1966

R K Alderman, Parliamentary Party Discipline in Opposition: The PLP 1951–64, *Parliamentary Affairs*, Vol 21 1968

V L Allen, *Trade Union Leadership*, London, Longman, 1957

Clement Attlee, *The Labour Party in Perspective*, London, Gollancz, 1937

Clement Attlee, Party Disicpline is Paramount, *English & National Review*, 148, 1957

S B Bacharach & E J Lawler, *Power & Politics in Organisations*, San Francisco, Jersey-Bass, 1980

R Baxter, Liverpool Labour Party 1918–1963, Oxford University, Unpublished D. Phil 1969

R Baxter, The Working Class & Labour Politics, *Political Studies*, Vol 20 1972

S Beackon, The Labour Party and the Working Class, *British Journal of Political Science*, Vol 6 1976

D S Bell & B Criddle, *The French Socialist Party*, Oxford, Clarendon Press, 1984

Jack & Bessie Braddock, *The Braddocks*, London, MacDonald, 1963

G Braunthal, *The German Social Democrats 1969–1982*, Bolder Colorado, Westview Press, 1983

G Brown, *In My Way*, London, Gollancz, 1971

J G Bulpitt, *Party Politics in English Local Government*, London, Longman, 1967

A H Brown, D V Donnison & G Jahuda, Put Policy on the Agenda, *Fabian Journal*, February 1952

R Butterworth, Islington Borough Council: Some Characteristics of Single Party Rule, *Politics*, 1 1966

John Callaghan, *British Trotskyism – Theory & Practice*, Oxford, Blackwell, 1984

A Carter, *Authority & Democracy*, London, RKP, 1979

John Carvel, *Citizen Ken*, London, Chatto & Windos, 1984

Barbara Castle, *The Castle Diaries 1964–70*, London, Weidenfeld & Nicolson, 1984

Ken Coates, *The Crisis of British Socialism*, Nottingham, Spokesman, 1971

Ken Coates (ed), *What Went Wrong*, Nottingham, Spokesman, 1979

GDH Cole, *History of the Labour Party from 1914*, London, RKP, 1948

A De Crespigny & A Wertheimer, *Contemporary Political Theory*, London, Nelson, 1971

Michael Crick, *Militant*, London, Faber, 1984

Michael Crick, *The March of Militant*, London, Faber, 1986

C A R Crosland, *Can Labour Win?*, London, Fabian Society, 1960

R H S Crossman, *Backbench Diaries*, London, Hamish Hamilton & Jonathan Cape, 1981

R H S Crossman, *Diaries of a Cabinet Minister Vol 2*, London, Hamish Hamilton & Jonathan Cape, 1976

R H S Crossman, *Socialism and the New Despotism*, London, Fabian Society, 1956

R H S Crossman, *Introduction to W Bagehot The English Constitution*, London, Fontana, 1963

E Dell, Why Whip the Council?, *Socialist Commentary*, February 1960

A D R Dickson, MPs Readoption Conflicts, *Political Studies*, Vol 23, 1975

B Donaghue & G W Jones, *Herbert Morrison: Portrait of a Politician*, London, Weidenfeld & Nicolson, 1973

D V Donnison & D E G Plowman, The Functions of Local Labour Parties, *Political Studies*, Vol 2, 1984

H Drucker, Leadership Selection in the Labour Party, *Parliamentary Affairs*, 29, 1976

H Drucker, Changes in the Labour Party Leadership, *Parliamentary Affairs*, 34, 1981

H Drucker, Intra-Party Democracy in Action *Parliamentary Affairs*, 37, 1984

H Drucker, *Doctrine & Ethos in the Labour Party*, London, Allen & Unwin, 1979

Peggy Duff, *Left, Left, Left*, London, Alison & Busby, 1971

M Duverger, *Political Parties*, London, Methuen, 1967

K Dyson, Party Book Administration, *Public Administration Bulletin*, 25, 1975

D Easton, *A Systems Analysis of Political Life*, London, John Wiley & Sons, 1965

H Eckstein & T Gurr, *Patterns of Authority*, London, John Wiley & Sons, 1975

H Elcock, Tradition and Change in Labour Party Politics, *Political Studies*, 29, 1981

A Etzioni, *The Comparative Analysis of Complex Organisations*, London, Free Press, 1975

L D Fairlie, Candidate Selection: Role Perceptions of Conservative & Labour Party Secretary/Agents *Political Studies*, 24, 1976

Michael Foot, *Aneurin Bevan Vol 1*, London, MacKibbon and Kee, 1962

Michael Foot, *Aneurin Bevan Vol 2*, London, Paladin, 1975

Michael Foot, *Parliament in Danger!* London, Pall Mall Press, 1959

T Forrester, The Labour Activists, *New Society*, 13 October 1977

R Frasure & A Kornberg, Constituency Agents in British Party Politics, *British Journal of Political Science*, 5, 1975

W Graf, *The German Left Since 1945*, Cambridge, Oleander Press, 1976

D G Green, *Power & Party in an English City*, London, Allen & Unwin, 1981

N Greene, *Crisis & Decline: The French Socialist Party in the Popular Front Era*, Cornell University Press, 1969

W L Guttsman, *The German Social Democratic Party 1875–1933*, London, Allen & Unwin, 1981

J Gyford, *Local Politics in Britain*, London, Croom Helm, 1978

J Gyford, *The Politics of Local Socialism*, London, Allen & Unwin, 1985

J Gyford & R Baker, *Labour & Local Politics*, London, Fabian Society, 1977

J Gyford & M James, *National Parties & Local Politics*, London, Allen & Unwin, 1983

W Hampton, *Democracy & Community*, Oxford, Oxford University Press, 1970

H J Hanham, The Local Organisation of the Labour Party, *Western Political Quarterly 9*, 1959

K Harris, *Attlee*, London, Wiedenfeld & Nicolson, 1982

R Harris, *The Making of Neil Kinnock*, London, Faber, 1984

M Harrison, *Trade Unions & the Labour Party*, London, Allen & Unwin, 1960

S Haseler, *The Gaitskellites*, London, MacMillan, 1969

D Hayter, *The Labour Party: Crisis & Prospects*, London, Fabian Society, 1977

H Heclo, The Councillor's Job *Public Administration*, 47, 1969

E Heffer, *Labour's Future*, London, Verso, 1986

D Howell, *British Social Democracy*, London, Croom Helm, 1980

D Howell, *The Rise and Fall of Bevanism*, Leeds, ILP N.D

Douglas Houghton, The Labour Back-Bencher, *Political Quarterly*, 40, 1969

Douglas Houghton, Making MPs Accountable, *Political Quarterly*, 43, 1972

Douglas Houghton, The Party We Love, *Political Quarterly*, 52, 1981

M Hollingworth, *The Press & Political Dissent*, London, Pluto, 1986.

R Hunt, *German Social Democracy 1918–1933*, London, Yale University Press, 1964

L Hunter, *The Road to Brighton Pier*, London, Arthur Barker, 1959

R J Jackson, *Rebels & Whips*, London, MacMillan, 1968

E G Janosik, *Constituency Labour Parties in Britain*, London, Pall Mall Press, 1968

D Jay, *Change and Fortune*, London, Hutchinson, 1980

M Jenkins, *Bevanism: Labour's High Tide*, Nottingham, Spokesman, 1979

P Jenkins, *The Battle of Downing Street*, London, Charles Knight, 1970

G W Jones, *Borough Politics*, London, MacMillan, 1969

G W Jones & A Norton (eds), *Political Leadership in Local Authorities*, Birmingham, INLOGOV, 1978

J JUPP, *The Radical Left in Britain 1931–41*, London, Frank Cass, 1982

D Kavanagh (ed) *The Politics of the Labour Party*, London, Allen & Unwin, 1982

D & M Kogan, *The Battle for the Labour Party*, Glasgow, Fontana, 1981

Labour Co-ordinating Committee, *Party Organisation: An Enquiry*, London, LCC, 1984

H Laski, *The Secret Battalion*, London, The Labour Party, 1946

Z Layton-Henry, Labour's Militant Youth, *Political Quarterly 45*, 1974

Z Layton-Henry, Labour's Lost Youth, *Journal of Contemporary History*, 11, 1976

Z Layton-Henry, Reforming the Labour Party, *Political Quarterly*, 50, 1979

M Linton, *The Swedish Road to Socialism*, London, Fabian Society, 1985

S M Lipset, M A Trow & J S Coleman, *Union Democracy*, London, Collier-MacMillan, 1956

P McCormick, The Labour Party: Three Unnoticed Changes, *British Journal of Political Science*, 10 1980

L J MacFarlane, *The British Communist Party*, London, MacKibbon & Kee, 1966

R T McKenzie, *British Political Parties*, London, Heineman, 1964

R T McKenzie, The Wilson Report & the Future of Labour Party Organisation, *Political Studies*, 4, 1956

R McKibbin, *The Evolution of the Labour Party*, Oxford, Oxford University Press, 1974

T E M McKiterick, The Selection of Parliamentary Candidates *Political Quarterly*, 30, 1959

E McPherson, The Trade Union as a Local Pressure Group, Liverpool University, Unpublished MA thesis 1972

C Martin & D Martin, Decline of Labour Party Membership, *Political Quarterly*, 48, 1977

R Martin, *Communism and the British Trade Unions 1924–33*, Oxford, Clarendon Press, 1969

R Michels, *Political Parties*, London, Free Press, 1962

L Minkin, *The Labour Party Conference*, London, Allen Lane, 1978

Ian Mikado, The Fateful, Hateful Fifties, *New Socialist*, March/April 1982

A Mitchell, *Four Years in the Death of the Labour Party*, London, Methuen, 1983

K O Morgan, *Labour in Power*, Oxford, Oxford University Press, 1984

S Neumann (ed), *Political Parties*, Chicago, University of Chicago Press, 1956

K Newton, *Second City Politics*, Oxford, Oxford University Press, 1976

M Parkinson, *Liverpool on the Brink*, Policy Journals, Hermitage, 1985

P Paterson, *The Selectorate*, London, McKibbin & Kee, 1967

W Paterson & A H. Thomas, *The Future of Social Democracy*, Oxford, Clarendon Press, 1986

B Pimlott, *Labour and the Left in the 1930s*, Cambridge, Cambridge University Press, 1977

B Pimlott, *Hugh Dalton*, London, Cape, 1985

C Pincher, *Inside Story*, Sidgwick and Jackson 1984

J R Piper, Back-Bench Rebellion, Party Government & Consensus Politics: Case of PLP 1966–70, *Parliamentary Affairs*, 27, 1974

A Ranney, *Pathways to Parliament*, London, MacMillan, 1965

J Rex, The Labour Bureaucracy, *New Reasoner*, 6, 1958

P G Richard, *The Backbenchers*, London, Faber, 1972

F Ridley, Liverpool is Different: Political Style in Context *Political Quarterly*, 57, 1986

R Rose, *The Problem of Party Government*, London, MacMillan, 1974

R Rose, Still the Era of Party Government *Political Studies*, 36, 1983

S Rose, Labour and German Rearmament *Political Studies*, 14, 1966

A Roth, *Harold Wilson, Yorkshire Walter Mitty*, London, Macdonald & Jones, 1977

M Rush, *The Selection of Parliamentary Candidates*, London, Nielson, 1969

M Rustin, Different Conceptions of Party: Labour's Constitutional Debate, *New Left Review*, 1981

P Seyd, Factionalism Within the Labour Party. A Case Study of the Campaign for Democratic Socialism, Unpublished M. Phil Thesis, Southampton University

P Seyd, The Tavernites, *Political Quarterly*, 1974

P Seyd & L Minkin, The Labour Party & its Members, *New Society*, 20 September 1979

H G Simmons, *French Socialists in Search of a Rule 1956–67*, London, Cornell UP, 1971

Socialist Commentary Supplement, Our Penny Farthing Machine, *Socialist Commentary*, October 1965

H J Steck, Grass-roots Militancy & Ideology; The Bevanite Revolt, *Polity* 2, 1970

H Street & R Brazier (eds), *De Smith. Constitutional & Administrative Law*, London, Pelican, 1985

P Tatchell, *The Battle for Bermondsey*, London, Heretic Books, 1983

D Taverne, *The Future of the Left*, London, Cape, 1974

A Taylor, The Modern Boroughmongers: Yorkshire Area (NUM) & Grassroots Politics, *Political Studies*, 32, 1984

A Taylor, *The Politics of the Yorkshire Miners*, London, Croom Helm, 1984

J E Turner, *Labour's Doorstep Politics*, London, Macmillan, 1978

H Valen, Factional Activities and Nominations in Political Parties, *Acta Sociologica*, 3, 1958

D Webster, *Labour and the New Left*, London, Fabian Society, 1981

N West, *A Matter of Trust, MI5 1945–1972*, London, Weidenfeld & Nicolson, 1982

P Whitely, *The Labour Party in Crisis*, London, Methuen, 1983

P Whitely, Who are the Labour Activists? *Political Quarterly*, 52, 1981

M Williams, *Inside Number 10*, London, Weidenfeld & Nicolson, 1972

P M Williams, *Hugh Gaitskell*, London, Cape, 1979

P M Williams, Foot-Faults in the Bevan-Gaitskell Match *Political Studies*, 27, 1979

P M Williams, The Labour Party: The Rise of the Left, *West European Politics*, 6, 1983

P M Williams (ed), *The Diaries of Hugh Gaitskell*, London, Cape, 1983

D J Wilson, *Power & Party Bureaucracy in Britain*, Farnborough, Saxon House, 1975

H Wilson, *The Labour Government 1964–1970*, London, Michael Joseph, 1971

H Wilson, *Final Term* Weidenfeld and Nicolson, and Michael Joseph 1979

J Q Wilson, *Political Organisations*, New York, Basic Books, 1973

H V Wiseman, The Working of Local Government in Leeds I & II, Public Administration, 41, 1963

M Woodhouse & B Pearce, *Essays on the History of Communism in Britain*, London, New Park Publications, 1975

D H Wrong, *Power*, Oxford, Blackwell, 1979

A Young, *The Reselection of MPs*, London, H.E.B., 1983

M Young, The Leadership, the Rank & File and Mr Bevan *Political Quarterly*, 24, 1953

Index